Teaching the Child Mathematics

second edition

C. W. SCHMINKE
University of Oregon

NORBERT MAERTENS
Kansas State University

WILLIAM ARNOLD
University of Northern Colorado

HOLT, RINEHART AND WINSTON

*New York   Chicago   San Francisco   Dallas
Montreal   Toronto   London   Sydney*

Senior Acquisitions Editor	*Richard Owen*
Senior Developmental Editor	*Louise Waller*
Managing Editor	*Jeanette Ninas Johnson*
Project Editor	*Robin Moses*
Production Manager	*Vic Calderon*
Art Director	*Robert Kopelman*

Cover photograph by Suzanne Szasz

Library of Congress Cataloging in Publication Data

Schminke, Clarence W.
    Teaching the child mathematics.

    Includes bibliographical references and index.
    1. Mathematics—study and teaching (elementary). I. Maertens, Norbert, joint author. II. Arnold, William Ramon, 1933– , joint author. III. Title.
QA135.5.S292   1978   372.7   77-18809

ISBN 0-03-020766-5

Preface

The authors of *Teaching the Child Mathematics* believe that children and teachers must be active partners in the process of learning mathematics. While this edition provides essential mathematics methodology for grades K through 6, the unique behavioral characteristics of children in regard to mathematics are also emphasized. Flow-charted lesson plans, activity or task cards, and discrete enrichment experiences are identified so that the basic activities and materials for teaching the major topics found in contemporary elementary school programs of major commercial publishers can be utilized by mathematics teachers. The second edition has not shifted considerably in orientation from the previous one. Still, the book has undergone extensive revision.

The authors continue to believe that those responsible for teaching must know the mathematics that children are to learn and must possess a knowledge of the diverse (though functional) instructional settings and strategies for developing and assessing mathematical growth in children.

Consider the idea of understanding the unique behavioral characteristics of children. In the revised edition, a good deal of attention is aimed at the human side of teaching mathematics. But we must do more than *understand* children; we must *teach* them. To do less is irresponsible and immoral. It is from this point of view that such recommendations as "exploration," "mathematics laboratory," "active learning," and "individualized instruction" have been postulated, and it is from this same point of view that they must be interpreted by the reader. What is required is systematic and direct planning for teaching that is executed in a human and sensible manner. In the final analysis, children's unique rates of learning mean little more than the rate at which they are taught.

Since 1972, several additional forces have exerted extensive, if not dramatic, pressure on elementary school mathematics programs. The influence of these forces—and the authors genuinely believe the influences to be positive—has resulted in two entirely new chapters for this book. One is Chapter 6, "Developing Measurement Concepts through Metric Measures"; the other is Chapter 12, "Teaching Special Children

Mathematics." Both chapters are self-contained and fully developed. Chapter 6 contains more than forty activities that may be used directly by teacher and children to gain confidence and competence with metric measures. The chapter builds in a manner that will avoid anxiety for the uninitiated. Chapter 12 reflects the attention now being focused on regular classroom teachers via the national movement toward "mainstreaming." The principal sections of this chapter provide models for diagnosing and assessing children in both cognitive and affective domains, as well as pinpointing specific classroom procedures for meeting the day-by-day challenges of the hard-to-teach and of the able child.

The advent of the hand-held calculator appears to be troublesome to some, and we believe that is unfortunate. We have given a rational treatment of the subject in Chapter 11, "Problem Solving Activities for Selected Topics in Elementary School Mathematics." There are recommendations of minicalculators most appropriate for use in elementary school classrooms, and more than twenty-five calculator explorations and activities.

Another totally new and important feature of this edition is in the section called "Activities, Projects, A Point of View," that follows each chapter. These exercises ought not be viewed as test items. Rather, they are an embodiment of the active learning/active teaching philosophy that encompasses the entire book. They are intended to actively engage the reader in investigations, inquiries, analyses, and discussions that will extend both insight and understanding of each chapter.

Finally, preparation of a manuscript, even though it be a revision, is a complex and arduous task. More importantly, it carries with it high moral responsibility. Without the considerable support of our families, our students, our institutions, selected reviewers, and the excellent staff at Holt, Rinehart and Winston, we would not have completed our task. We are grateful to all.

C.W.S.
N.M.
W.A.

Contents

CHAPTER 1

The Child and Mathematics

PERSPECTIVE The role of the teacher is to give each child the formal education in mathematics most suited to unique capabilities and environmental interests. To do this, it is essential that the teacher understand how the child grows in ability to encounter and understand mathematics, and how the educational and environmental climate affects mathematical growth. More explicitly, the teacher must decide what children are able to learn, what children should learn, and what techniques best bring about learning.

Consequently, in this chapter the reader will consider the cognitive quantitative growth of the child from a developmental point of view, along with selected psychological considerations which affect learning. The principal theoretical position of the Swiss psychologist Jean Piaget is presented with several other theories of learning and some important psychological considerations.

After study of Chapter 1 you should be able to:

1. Summarize Piaget's theory of intellectual development and state the characteristic behaviors for children at each level.
2. Describe the four levels of learning.
3. List three ways in which concepts and principles may be represented.
4. Identify the specific attributes of the affective domain which enhance a positive classroom climate.
5. Outline functional teacher behaviors which stimulate curiosity, promote independence, enhance self-concept, and maintain positive attitudes during the study of mathematics.
6. Write a personalized philosophy of teaching mathematics to children.

**PIAGET'S
LEVELS OF
INTELLECTUAL
DEVELOPMENT**

**Sensorimotor
Period (0–2 years)**

Much of a child's first two years is spent in sensing and manipulating. Such activities shape his perception of the environment. The child sees order and pattern in the world and is impressed by it.

A child's first perception of the world might be the ordered spacing of the bars on a crib, or the rectangular proportions of the perimeter of a crib. By the end of the first month of life, not only can children perceive relatively minor differences in the objects viewed, but they show a preference for complex patterns over simple, homogeneous stimuli.[1] For example, when presented with two rectangular frames of equivalent size, where one has a simple, cross-hatched design on its interior, the very young child will make definite movements toward the more complex rectangle.

Early relationships with others often involve forms of one-to-one correspondence—for example, between mouth and a baby bottle or mother's breast. This early experience with one-to-one correspondence is later strengthened when the mother places a rattle in a child's hand or a teddy bear in the crib.

Early in the first year of life, a child learns that certain acts will produce specific responses; as a result, they become intentional. A child knows that if the crib is shaken in a certain fashion a rattle or other object will move. The bars on a crib are defined in terms of the action taken toward them. The bars are to be shaken while a pacifier is to be sucked. The child is unaware of those things in which he is not involved. If an object is removed from sight, it ceases to exist for him.

Toward the end of the child's first year of life, an impressive change begins to take place. His ability to perceive the world gradually expands, so that he does not have to be involved in an act to be impressed by it. Objects develop permanence—they still exist whether or not they are in sight. When an object is removed, the child can form a mental image in his construction of space.

During these initial years, the child has learned that objects have permanence, that symbols may be used to represent real objects, and that actions may be imitated and internalized. The child uses these early perceptions and imitations throughout his entire education, for without them he is incapable of understanding the abstract qualities of mathematics. The cumulative growth of a child's initial years forms the transition to what Piaget calls the "concrete operations period."[2]

[1]Paul Mussen, John Conger, and Jerome Kagan, *Child Development and Personality* (New York: Harper & Row, Publishers, 1963, revised 1968), pp. 87–126.
[2]John A. Flavell, *The Developmental Psychology of Jean Piaget* (Princeton, N.J.: D. Van Nostrand Co., Inc., 1963).

Concrete Operations Period (2–11 years)

The child of about two years loves to imitate both human and nonhuman objects. Sometimes the imitation occurs immediately with the person she is copying; however, she also has the ability to defer imitation to other time periods. This is seen in the child's play. Whereas the younger child merely played games requiring simple motor skills, the child who is nearly two may imitate mother or father, and may use dolls or other concrete objects as representations for brothers and sisters. These early experiences enable the child to build a cognitive framework, which makes it possible to consider experiences, to assimilate them, and to make accommodations (reorganization of the mental structure) for later use. The child has internalized actions. She can now enter the world of make-believe. Without such a variety of experiences, the child can become educationally retarded and unable to move to more complex stages of learning. The concrete operations period is of particular concern to the teacher, for most elementary school age children are found here. The mental development of these years can best be understood by careful analysis of two easily discernible subperiods.

Preoperational Subperiod (about 2–7 years)

A child in the preoperational subperiod gains increasing facility with language, finally learning to discriminate between words and the physical objects they represent. Children organize behavior as it relates to a goal, trying alternate approaches to the goal rather than a single, rigid approach.

Whereas sensorimotor children are limited to very brief internalizations of events from the recent past, the preoperational child can include past, present, and future representations of reality. They do not need continuous access to direct experience. Past events can be signified through words; future events can be planned and described by using the same medium. Similarly, whereas the sensorimotor child is limited to the pursuit of concrete goals, the preoperational child is able to reflect on the most efficient behavior needed to attain the goal. He is capable of being taught about objects not directly present—elves, policemen, grandparents, and so on. Consider how these capabilities develop.

Assimilation and Accommodation The child of this age range gradually forms a vocabulary to express concepts of a particular object. At first, these ideas are bound to the actions. For example, the word *milk* may represent a two-year-old child's desire for a drink of milk or for a drink of juice or water. She does not recognize the need for a more discriminating vocabulary. Such beginning word concepts are typically broad, so that the word "milk" comes to represent anything which may be drunk. With growth, the child gradually refines her vocabulary to conform with the more precise definitions of the adult world. She understands that *milk* refers to a white liquid, and that it is independent of other liquids. A new vocabulary is developed to describe intended use of the liquid. The processes of assimilation and accommodation[3] are essential to learning mathematics. A child must be able to understand fiveness as a particular quantity, a quantity gained from experience and which exists independently of the operations that may be performed with it.

The thinking of preoperational children is still characterized by their need for concrete objects. Although children can perform mental manipulations at this stage, they only manipulate that for which they possess a mental image. The mental exercises merely represent what would actually be done with objects. Young children are not capable of analyzing or synthesizing without objects. For this reason, primary-grade teachers find it necessary to be very explicit in their teaching; they must use a variety of concrete objects to demonstrate desired actions precisely.

Reversibility The thinking of the preoperational child is also characterized by an inability to reverse actions mentally. For example, consider two plasticine balls of equal size. Determine with the child that the balls are identical in size. Roll one ball into a sausage shape.

When asked if the balls are still the same size, or if one has more plasticine than the other, the child usually responds that the sausage-shaped object has more plasticine than the round object. Sometimes he will select the round object, saying that *it* now has more plasticine. He is not capable of relating back to the point where the two balls were identical in size and shape. Although the child saw that only the shape was changed, he still makes his desicion on what is seen before him at the moment. Reasoning is perceptual rather than factually oriented.

Reversibility is an integral feature of mathematical operations and it is not automatic. For example:

(1.1)

$$4 + 3 = 7 \qquad 7 - 3 = 4$$

In this example the original quantity 4 was combined with 3 to produce the sum 7. To reverse this operation, 3 is subtracted from 7, yielding the original quantity 4. The size of a group was increased and then decreased, a demonstration of reversibility.

A further illustration of the importance of reversibility to mathematics is shown below:

[3]Irving E. Sigel and Rodney R. Cocking, *Adolescence: A Constructivist Perspective* (New York: Holt, Rinehart and Winston, 1977), p. 15.

4 + 3 = 7

This is a statement of equality. To maintain this equality for any changes made on one side of the equal sign equivalent changes must be made on the other side.

(4 + 3) + 1 = 7 + 1

The statement is changed by adding 1 to the addends 4 + 3. Having done this, the sum 7 must now be changed by also increasing it by 1.

What is apparent to an adult may be incomprehensible to a child. To understand that adding a quantity on one side of the equality symbol requires the addition of an equivalent quantity on the other side in order to maintain the equality, the child must be able to think back to the starting point where both quantities are equal. Then she must understand that adding 1 to one side of the equation destroys the equality, but only to the extent of the quantity added. In order to bring the statement into "balance" she must now add 1 to the other side.

The concept of reversibility is not normally attained by children until the end of the preoperational subperiod, or early concrete operations subperiod; therefore, teachers should be wary of rushing too quickly into mathematical operations which require children to reverse action and, thus, relate two operations.

The concept is easily demonstrated by having two equivalent piles of blocks and asking the child which pile has more. When the child responds that the piles are equal in number, one block is added to the first pile before asking if they are still equivalent. Relate this to the previous mathematical statement. When teaching the operation of addition, you must be aware of the child who does not seem to understand the relationships involved in joining and separating sets. For example, if a child cannot see that 4 + 3 = 7 and 7 − 3 = 4 are related in a unique way, then he cannot understand subtraction as the undoing of addition. For that child, mathematics is a series of disjoint operations with no common strands. It is better to delay such teaching with this child and spend additional time on learning experiences which are subordinate to the algorithm. For example, let him have the experience of physically joining different sets. Permit him the time to discover that joining a set of five objects with a set of two objects forms a set named by a new cardinal number. Let him describe the action by using the number sentence 5 + 2 = 7. In the same manner, encourage him to describe what happens when objects are removed. Continue such experiences until he can demonstrate awareness of the relationship of addition to subtraction.

Juxtaposition Preoperational children tend to focus attention on only one aspect of a total situation at a time. Whereas an adult might consider a

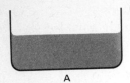

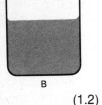

(1.2)

string of brightly colored beads as gaudy and out of place on a black evening gown, a child considers each independently. The adult considers the total situation—gown and beads. The child considers only the bright object, noting its color. He attends to spatial problems in much the same way.

Consider Figure 1.2. Equal quantities of water are added to container A and container B. The preoperational child is then asked if the containers have an equal quantity of water in them. Usually the child will say that container B has more water. However, occasionally the child will choose container A. When asked to explain the result, the child choosing container B will usually indicate that the water level in B is higher than in A. Those choosing A usually indicate that the container for A is larger than B. They have centered their attention on only one aspect of the total situation: either the apparent size of the container or the water level within a container.

To understand this water-pouring problem, the adult is able to construct mentally the sequence of events which occurred. Seeing the containers filled with water, she visually reconstructs the transformation from these containers into the containers of differing shapes. The preoperational child cannot do this. Attention is focused independently on each successive stage as it occurs. No relationship between stages is seen; she does not integrate the series of events into a logical whole.

When asked to explain the cause-and-effect relationship demonstrated by the addition of equal quantities of water to dissimilar containers, the preoperational child has a strong tendency to break up the whole sequence into a series of fragmentary and incoherent relationships. The order in which events occurred is often confused, as are logical or causal relationships. The child prefers factual descriptions to cause–effect explanations. These limitations render the child incapable of making a coherent whole out of the explanation. Such a phenomenon is called juxtaposition.

At approximately the age of seven or eight, a child begins to reflect and unify, as well as to avoid contradiction. It is only at this time that he becomes conscious of the logic of actions. Prior to this, a child could not think deductively. The implications of this finding for mathematics teaching are many. For example, again consider the addition sentence 4 + 3 = 7. The child must be able to reconstruct a sequence of events beginning with a pile of four blocks and ending with the physical joining of three blocks to form the sum of seven blocks; he must also be able to reverse the process mentally. The preoperational child cannot do this. Attention is likely to be focused on either the four blocks, the three blocks, or the joining act, without achieving synthesis. The teacher must proceed cautiously at this point in time, observing carefully when a child appears to appreciate temporal, cause–effect, and logical relationships. To push ahead prior to such understanding only invites associative (rote) learning.

In summary, during the preoperational period many subtle changes have occurred in the child's thinking. Rather than being rigidly tied to specific objects or situations, she has acquired the ability to think deductively. She has considerably developed the ability to perform mental operations and has gradually learned a vocabulary to describe actions. Despite these observable qualities of cognitive growth, a child's thinking remains immature. Conceptual understandings are still closely tied to concrete situations and are irreversible.

Subperiod B (7–11 years) In the initial subperiod, the child is unable to perform operations requiring a simple one-to-one relationship. For example, if several small cars are placed in a row and enough figures (see Figure 1.3) are piled nearby to provide a driver for each car, the early preoperational child is unable to arrange the figures so that they are in a one-to-one correspondence with the cars. Later on in the period he develops the ability to set up such a correspondence, but can be misled into believing that the correspondence no longer exists (see Figure 1.4) if someone increases the spacing between the objects of one of the sets.

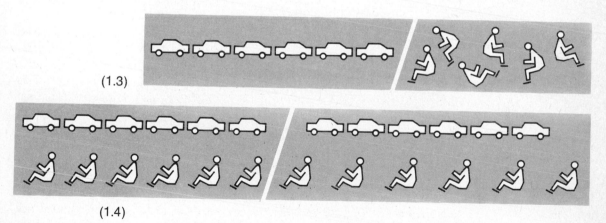

(1.3)

(1.4)

Once children have entered the concrete operations subperiod, they will no longer be fooled. They understand that changing the configuration of a set of objects does not affect their quantity. They no longer center on a particular aspect of an action, and are able to reverse the action mentally. They know that objects which were in a one-to-one correspondence, as in Figure 1.4, can again be placed into the same correspondence.

Conservation of Quantity, Length, Mass, and Volume Recall the experiment with the mass plasticine balls. The preoperational child could not reverse her thinking and thus center upon each state as an entity, comparing the transformed objects as they appeared at a given point in time. At about the age of seven, she acquires the ability to think back to a starting point. She understands that changing the form of a substance does not change its quantity. Thinking is no longer dominated by perception of the changed quantity.

The ability to conserve quantity is essential for a full understanding of mathematical processes. When children are able to conserve, they can understand examples such as the following:

> Seven bunnies are eating in Mr. Carter's field. After they finish eating, three lie down for a nap, while four play in another part of the field. How many bunnies are there in Mr. Carter's field now?

A correct answer of 7 indicates that the child realizes that 4 + 3 is merely a change in the arrangement, not a change of number. In this example we say that the child has internalized the invariance of number; he has learned to conserve.

Even though children may understand that changes in form do not change the quantity, they may still not understand that length, mass, and volume are also invariate. Conservation of length and mass occur at about the age of nine, while conservation of volume does not occur until about the age of eleven or twelve.

Numbering According to Piaget, numbering requires a synthesis of two operations: class inclusion, or cardination, and serial ordering. Children develop the ability to classify late in the preoperational stage. They understand that four balls are equal in number to four rectangles, and so on (see Figure 1.5). All classes of 4 are considered equivalent. They also develop the ability to order objects by size, from smallest to largest. They

(1.5)

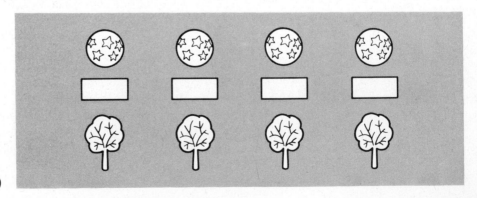

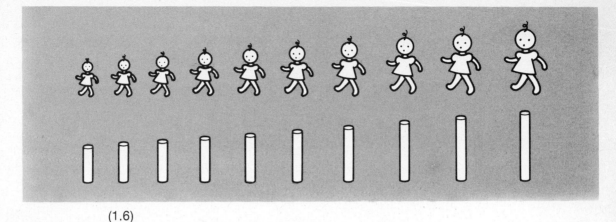

(1.6)

have not yet developed the competency to synthesize these two abilities into a single, reversible operation called numbering.

Piaget performed a series of experiments using dolls and sticks. A child was given ten dolls and ten sticks varying in size (see Figure 1.6). The child was told that the dolls were going for a walk and that they should be arranged so that each doll could find a stick of the same size. Piaget then asked the child to decide which stick each doll would take, while he pointed to the dolls one at a time.

Typically, beginning first-grade children can construct a series and can match the dolls and the sticks if they are arranged in the same order. However, if the order is reversed, as in Figure 1.7, many first-graders can no longer match the correct stick for a given doll. Their behavior for the reversed setting can be explained as follows: those dolls which are

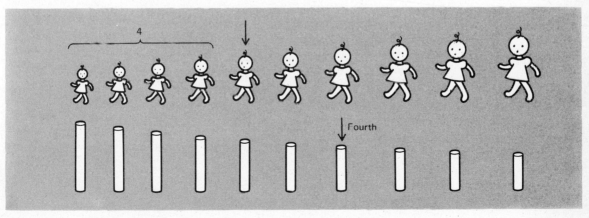

(1.7)

smaller than the selected doll are placed in a separate collection and the elements of the set are counted. Instead of eliminating the number of small sticks in the set, children often remember that there are four in the set and so select the fourth stick. They do not synthesize their classification of small dolls with a classification of small sticks, and so select an incorrect stick. By the time children enter the concrete operations stage, they simply eliminate the set of small sticks corresponding to the set of small dolls and choose the next higher of the remaining sticks. This indicates an attainment of the ability to number meaningfully.

The teacher's knowledge of a child's development of meaningful enumeration has direct application to teaching. The ability to label specific sets with certain numerical labels is essential to numeration, while the ability to arrange objects in some hierarchy is required to understand the ordinal property of numbers. A child who can synthesize the two can also solve such problems as those involving subtraction in the comparison situation:

> Sally has six dolls, while Mary has only four dolls. How many more dolls does Sally have than Mary?

The child classifies the set of Mary's dolls as 4 and removes that amount from Sally's dolls. The remaining dolls form the difference (see Figure 1.8).

$$6 - 4 = 2$$

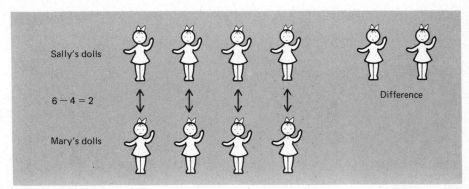

(1.8)

At about the age of seven, concrete operational children develop the capability to assimilate another's viewpoint on matters of interest. They develop a liking for playing games involving rules, and are capable of cooperative endeavor with others. Mathematical games become interesting.

During the concrete operations period, the child learns to perceive Euclidean space, time, movement, and velocity correctly. These perceptions are learned gradually throughout the period. Consider Figure 1.9.

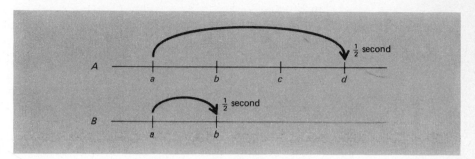

(1.9)

If an experimenter moves an object on line A from point a to point d, and simultaneously moves an object on line B from point a to b, the early concrete period child will probably say that it took longer for the object on line A because it is farther. Attention centers on the spatial aspect of the situation. A correct response to this problem requires a synthesis of concepts involving spatial movement and velocity. Studies of this type have broad implications for teaching elementary school mathematics.

It is common practice for teachers to use such aids as number lines and time lines. Some children in the early concrete operations period, grades one and two, may still be perceptually tied to spatial factors, centering on terminal position. Illustrations of 7 + 3 and 4 + 3 are shown in Figure 1.10. In both situations 3 is an addend. The placement of the addend 3 in line A is such that it might appear greater because it is positioned beyond the addend 3 in line B.

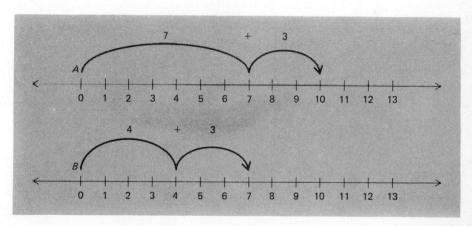

(1.10)

At the very least, Piaget's findings illustrate the need for careful drawing of the number line by the teacher so that equal distances between calibrations are maintained. The preoperational child tends to confuse spatial representations with concrete models, and it would seem wise to defer extensive use of the number line in teaching addition until he is well into the concrete operations period. Prior to that time, addition might better be shown exclusively as a joining of concrete sets of physical objects. Of course, a number line may be used earlier for counting and verifying.

To sum up, then, during the concrete operations period children have learned to conserve quantity, length, and mass. In addition, they have developed the ability to synthesize their concepts of classifying and ordering to form a concept of numbering. Their thinking has become less egocentric; they are able to respond to others' views on a variety of matters. While concrete operational children's thinking is still tied largely to concrete experiences, they can make limited extrapolations from data available either from the current situation or from past situations. It is here that the formal operations period begins.

Formal Operations Period (11 years and above) Whereas the concrete operational child has the ability to form hypotheses and test them through an experiment, the formal operational child now develops the ability to assemble, or synthesize, the results of several experiments to form logical relationships. In essence the operation is restructured. A cognitive pattern is formed which is used to solve problems. Consider the example $1/3 \div 1/7 = N$. To solve this example, the child must reorganize many abstract concepts involving fractions and operations with them. A possible solution might involve thinking such as the following:

$1/3 \div 1/7 = N$
I know that this is the same as $1/3 = N \times 1/7$ because I remember that $8 \div 2 = 4$ is related to $8 = 4 \times 2$.
I know that I can multiply the quantities on both sides of the equal sign by 7.
$7 \times 1/3 = N \times 1/7 \times 7$
Now I find $7/3 = N \times 7/7$ or $7/3 = N$

With experience, children's construction of reality becomes more extensive. They are able to fill in gaps between related events by forming and testing hypotheses, sometimes without actually needing to manipulate any concrete object.

The formal operational child is now capable of following a logical argument outside the context of the specific incident being cited. Phillips[4] uses the following syllogism to demonstrate this idea:

[4]John L. Phillips, Jr., *The Origins of Intellect, Piaget's Theory* (San Francisco, Calif.: W. H. Freeman and Co., 1969), p. 103.

All children like spinach;
Boys are children;
Therefore boys like spinach.

The young child will likely make a response such as, "But I'm a boy, and I don't like spinach." Formal operational children, however, follow the logic of the argument and are intrigued by it; they are impressed by its form. They solve mathematical problems because they enjoy finding a true pattern.

Thus, during the formal operations period, the child synthesizes operations into propositions which become a part of cognitive structure. Thinking, although originally evolving from past experience, is no longer tied to it but rather to the "reorganization" within the present mental framework. The content of a problem has now become subordinate to its form.

Cognitive Structure

A careful study of the work of Piaget reveals that each new experience must be accommodated by the child in the light of an existing structure before it can be internalized. At the same time, each new experience affects the child's existing cognitive structure by causing it to change in response to the new experience. Having progressed from the early sensorimotor period, when actions are almost always overt, the child now organizes representations of concrete objects into propositions which underlie logical thinking. Each new structure depends on and is made up of structures that were developed earlier.

SUPPORTING THEORIES OF LEARNING

Jean Piaget provides an excellent description of how children develop intellectually and of what they are able to do at certain stages. Yet learning is multidimensional, and there are supporting theories of learning that deserve the attention of prospective elementary teachers. Robert Gagné has identified levels at which children can learn.[5] Four levels that are important to mathematics may be identified as associative, concept, principle, and problem solving.

Associative Learning

Associative learning is establishing a memorized response to the presentation of a stimulus. It is the kind of learning emphasized in a traditional approach to teaching mathematics: the teacher demonstrates an algorithm while the children watch and then complete twenty to thirty exercises. Associative learning takes place when children focus on memorization and mastery. It is the lowest level of learning but is by no means useless.

[5]Robert M. Gagné, *The Conditions of Learning*, 3d ed. (New York: Holt, Rinehart and Winston, 1977), Chapter IV.

Concept Learning

Concept learning occurs when children attempt to identify characteristics that determine inclusion in or exclusion from a set or class. A common definition is that a concept is all the elements in a class that can be represented by one label. Thus, classes like "one," "ten," "addition," and "fraction" are concepts. Concept learning is emphasized when children focus on categorizing, classifying, ordering, and labeling.

Principle Learning

Principle learning results when children attempt to relate ideas. For example, children are learning principles when they study the sides and angles of triangles to determine the conditions under which triangles were similar or congruent. As another example, suppose some children were solving multiplication exercises such as t = 3 × 24. They would be learning a principle if they utilized number blocks as shown in Figure 1.11 to determine how the distributive property was employed in the algorithm. Principle learning is emphasized when children focus on relating, generalizing, analyzing, and synthesizing.

Problem Solving

Problem solving is, in Gagné's view of learning, the highest level at which people can function. In its broadest sense, problem solving occurs when children employ principles to achieve a goal. In actuality, problem solving arises in several contexts and at several levels. One necessary clarification here is that solving examples such as 6 − 4 = □, 46 × 6, 1/2 + 2/3 = □, and 14/$\overline{179}$ is not problem solving. To constitute problem solving, a task must require that children both select and apply certain principles in order to arrive at a solution. Problem solving is emphasized when children focus on applying, verifying, and proving (showing). Each of the previous levels of learning is explored in the recommendations found in Chapter 2 that retate to sequencing of instruction and the assessment of teaching.

Representation of Concepts and Principles

In much the same way as intellectual growth occurs—that is, informal to formal—concepts and principles can be represented at several levels. Jerome Bruner and others have investigated representation of concepts and principles. Their work has led to the belief that young children can learn concepts in some intellectually honest mode. Bruner's modes have been aptly named (1) enactive (concrete), (2) ikonic (illustrative), and (3) symbolic (abstract).[6]

In this hierarchy, the lowest level of representation is enactive or concrete configurations of objects. Suppose, for example, children are working with color rods. The children have made a series of configura-

[6]J. S. Bruner et al., *Studies in Cognitive Growth* (New York: John Wiley & Sons, Inc., 1966).

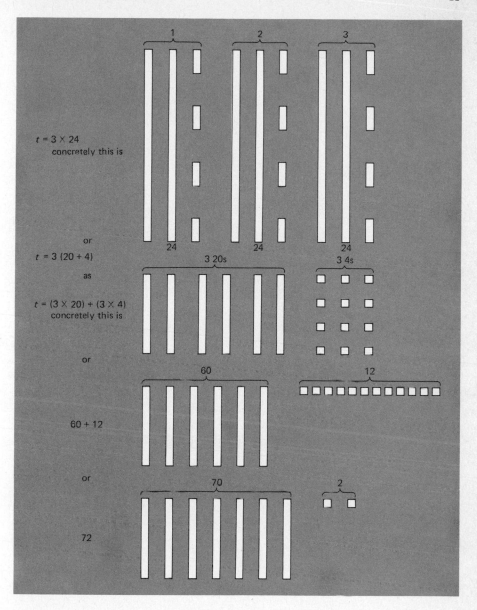

tions like that shown in Figure 1.12. The configurations of rods may be used as a concrete representation of the ordinal concept for number.

The next level of representation, ikonic, is illustrative or pictorial. Figure 1.13 is, by itself, an example of illustrative representations. Any picture or drawing of a mathematical idea or relationship is an illustrative representation. In this regard, many teachers mistakenly assume that

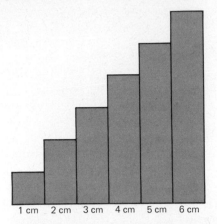

1 cm 2 cm 3 cm 4 cm 5 cm 6 cm

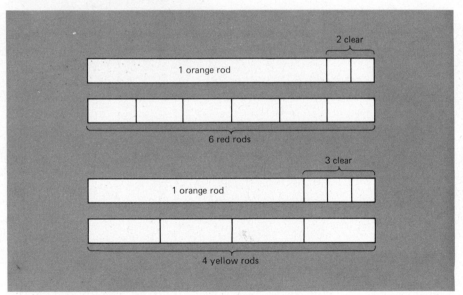

(1.13)

pictures represent concepts and principles as well as concrete objects. They may, but they are not the same thing. Children need many opportunities to work with concrete objects independent of pictorial representation.

The highest level of representation involves symbols. This need not necessarily be thought of as complex because symbols can be spoken or written. Again referring to Figure 1.13, the relationships shown could be represented verbally by saying, "Two multiplied by six equals twelve and three multiplied by four equals twelve." As well, the relationship could be written as:

$$2 \times 6 = 12 \text{ and } 3 \times 4 = 12$$

Symbols such as "1," "3/4," and "1,265" are literal representations of numbers while symbols such as "a/b," "$y = 2x + 6$," and "$d = r \cdot t$" are variable representations of numbers and the letters represent unknown quantities.

Since children grow intellectually from the preoperational through the concrete and formal operational stages, it is consistent that they should learn a particular concept or principle first through concrete representations and progress gradually to symbolic representations. Having children learn symbolic representations with only a vague background in concrete or illustrative representation forces them to learn at the associative level. Opportunities for learning at the concept, principle, and problem-solving levels occur when teachers have children work with objects, talk about what they observe, and then record the relationships they discover.

A PERSONAL THEORY OF INSTRUCTION

The discussion of learning, up to this point, has synthesized the work of Piaget, Gagné, and Bruner. To be useful, this information, together with selected important psychological dimensions of teaching, must be placed in a cohesive context that can become a personal theory of instruction. In order to do so, it is necessary to consider all dimensions of teaching that will help children learn.

Motivation and Interest

In behavioral studies, food deprivation and infliction of pain are employed to cause animals to respond. Children, however, respond in a relative absence of drives such as hunger, thirst, or pain. Observe children engaged in a game they "enjoy." Minor cuts are ignored, exertion is high, outside distractions are ignored. Clearly, children will learn more mathematics when it is made as enjoyable as possible. This occurs, generally, when children work with objects, play games, complete projects, and relate mathematics to real life situations.

Curiosity

For whatever reasons, children are curious about nearly everything. Two different theories are postulated as explanations of curiosity. One suggests that it is an innate characteristic given to each of us in varying measure. As such, it is considered by some to be a natural endowment, the same as physical size. Psychologists such as Brown[7] oppose this viewpoint. They believe that curiosity is a generalized response tendency which was acquired in former similar situations, a cumulative response to past experience. Despite their apparent divergence, for the purposes of teaching mathematics these theories may not be antagonistic.

---

[7] J. S. Brown, "Comments on Professor Harlow's Paper," *Current Theory and Research in Motivation* (Lincoln, Neb.: University of Nebraska Press, 1953), pp. 49–54.

It is essential that children's natural curiosity be encouraged, for curiosity is a potentially powerful motivator of elementary school children. If past experiences have been successful, and if the teacher structures mathematics learning experiences in a manner that capitalizes on their desire to explore, children will want to learn. Like adults, children want to find answers to unsolved problems, but only if the problem is relevant to them and only if their efforts may reasonably be expected to culminate in success.

Competition and Cooperation Numerous studies have shown that competition is beneficial and results in higher achievement when it occurs within proper limits. When work is structured so that friendly rivalries are allowed or so that every child makes a contribution to a group effort, increased performance results.

There is another element in competition—self-competition. In an important study,[8] students were told to compete against themselves to win a prize. They significantly outperformed students who were told that the group would be rewarded if everyone in the group had done well. This finding supports those previously discussed. The more personal competition becomes, the more effective it is.

During the planning session for the day, each child might predetermine reasonable goals for himself and establish appropriate rewards. Each student would be responsible to himself for gaining the reward, and the prerequisite requirements could be varied to take into account ability and background for learning. In most cases, successful completion of the self-imposed task is its own reward.

A final suggestion for positive competition involves a combination of self-rivalry and group cooperation. A classroom situation can be structured wherein each child is responsible for some aspect of a total group outcome. During the conduct of the unit, each person must improve his efforts at whatever his task is to be, and his improvement is noted as a part of the total. The size of the groups must be limited, and the objectives and tasks specific. In addition to being an effective method of improving achievement, there are many socially desirable side effects which accompany such cooperative endeavors.

Wisely used competitive games in a structured environment improve computational performance of individuals. The excitement and challenge that children experience has proven to be an aid to associative types of learning. Competition appears to be particularly effective in practice situations. However, when the teacher introduces new concepts or princi-

[8]C. Stendler et al., "Studies in Cooperation and Competition: I. The Effects of Working for Group and Individual Rewards on the Social Climate of Children's Games," *Pedagogical Seminary and Journal of Genetic Psychology*, Vol. 79 (1951), pp. 173–197.

ples, such stimulation could impede learning. At this point, children need time for reflective thought. The teacher must determine the proper balance to be maintained, judging technique in the light of objectives and the capabilities of the students.

Maintaining Positive Attitudes More than anything else that the teacher does, a failure on his part to maintain positive attitudes detracts from achievement. Many studies have shown that mathematics is a favorite subject of first-grade children and that by ninth grade it is a subject students hope never to encounter again. Clearly, something must happen during this period to cause this; too often, what occurs is that children experience conflict, frustration, and alienation. Such conditions destroy their commitment to learn.

In most instances conflict, frustration, and alienation grow out of the many thoughtless things people do. Some children who have eagerly awaited a chance to show their addition sentences on a flannelboard will be frustrated if the teacher ends the period because it is time for another subject. Children who do not express themselves well will become alienated from responding if they are consistently required to answer questions directed to a group or class. A severe conflict of purpose will arise between children who work slowly and accurately and a teacher who expects 90 percent accuracy on timed tests. The children will achieve nearly 100 percent on what they complete, but not on the whole test. Children will not feel free to learn and make mistakes if all their assignments are graded, with letter grades recorded in a grade book. This latter action becomes an end in itself. Children are much more likely to make progress when assignments are checked for errors, clarification is provided, and they are able to move to a higher order task. Subsequently, a test can be administered only after the children have had a reasonable opportunity to learn and to experience success.

Children who regularly experience the types of conflict and frustration cited above will soon "learn" that not responding and thereby avoiding mathematics is rewarding. In short, teachers must avoid utilizing procedures which make children feel inadequate. The cumulative effect of teacher enthusiasm and wise teacher behavior—based on awareness, from the child's point of view, of the subtle importance of motivation, curiosity, frustration and conflict, and desire for approval—will result in a classroom where appropriate human relationships are fostered. This atmosphere will provide the necessary environment for maintaining independence, self-direction, constructive self-concepts, and, equally important, positive attitudes toward the study of mathematics.

A Personal Philosophy of Teaching From the dominant features of child development, learning theory, and other psychological considerations, you must synthesize a personal philosophy for teaching mathematics. Current practice suggests that a personal philosophy which encompasses active learning is superior. The dominant features of a theory of instruction utilizing active learning are summarized in the following four points:

1. Maximum opportunity is provided for children to communicate with the teacher and with each other. Children have a natural proclivity for communication and this tendency provides a unique opportunity to foster language development while creating interest in the quantitative world. This must occur within the maintenance of appropriate respect for others.

2. The dominant aura of the mathematics period will be observation, exploration, inquiry, and problem solving. The classical arithmetic period leads children to grow weary of mathematics and a school day seemingly filled with the search for "right answers." An appropriate teaching philosophy is one which maintains in children a predisposition to learn.

3. There will be wise structuring of the mathematics period and constant modification of the immediate learning environment. Children respond positively when it is implicitly clear through classroom processes and procedures that the teacher has not abdicted responsibility for teaching. Teachers should discover that "open" and "structured" (or "planned") need not be antithetical. Teaching mathematics requires only that the subject be structured in some way that children can learn. This need not involve constant linear and sequential mastery of basic skills.

4. *Feelings of inadequacy, frustration, and fear in relation to mathematics are kept to a minimum.* The negative attitudes that some children and adults may hold about mathematics are learned. When learning tasks, processes, and activities are geared to appropriate developmental levels and types of reinforcement, all children will experience some success and feel secure with their teachers, their classmates, and with mathematics.

It must be recognized that these points cannot constitute an exclusive set of elements in a personal teaching philosophy for all persons. Constraints may include the physical setting in which one teaches—for instance, room size, number of children, and so forth. Other conceivable constraints include the commercially prescribed program mandated for use in a district, the prevailing philosophy of instruction in a school, and even the uniqueness of one's own personality. Still, none of these reasons should afford an excuse for failure to establish a personal theory of instruction for teaching children mathematics. The previous points provide a practical guide for you to follow.

SUMMARY   Children learn mathematical concepts according to Piaget's levels of intellectual development. The fact remains, however, that there are large, significant, and continuous differences among children as they progress through the mathematics curriculum in school. For this reason, these levels are a crucial reminder to teachers that children cannot absorb any information that they are unable to understand. Any tendency to ignore these ever-present differences during instruction can disrupt children's ability to learn more advanced material.

Although it is important to understand children's intellectual development, preparing them for subsequent mathematical experience involves other crucial factors. Our society places an increasingly high value on quantitative abilities. As a result, the levels at which children attain knowledge or concepts is of special importance in mathematics. There needs to be a constant and conscious effort to match materials and experience to the desired level of learning.

Knowing how and to what extent children can learn mathematics is very important. However, it is not quite enough. One must also know something of the psychological environment that surrounds the classroom. Recognizing, understanding, and responding to children's feelings, motivations, emotions, curiosities, and attitudes will help assure getting them off to a good start in mathematics. Experiencing failure in the early stages of mathematics instruction can severely limit future development.

ACTIVITIES, PROJECTS, A POINT OF VIEW

This section follows each chapter and is not intended primarily to test direct recall of the material presented. The considerations posed are intended to focus on ideas of importance when teaching children mathematics. The problems may serve as the basis for class discussion, or in some cases, individual and small group out-of-class activities.

1. In order to determine for yourself the validity of Piaget's theory, obtain some appropriate materials and try several "Piagetian-type" experiments. (See Figures 1.1, 1.2, 1.3, and 1.6) Interview at least two elementary school children, one in the age range of five to seven years, the other in the age range of eight to eleven years. Record what you asked the children to do as well as their responses. What did you find out?

2. Choose a mathematical concept with which you are familiar. Describe how teaching that concept might differ for a child at the concrete operations stage versus a child at the formal operations stage.

3. Review Burton's article, "Skinner, Piaget, Maslow, and The Teachers of Mathematics," which appeared in *The Arithmetic Teacher* for March 1977. What is the main message? Recall an illustrative example where your familiarity with concepts and applications of psychological theory benefited you in working with a child.

4. Criticize or support these statements:

a. Knowledge of intellectual and psychological factors will, in the final analysis, have little impact on practice because teachers are not able to use theory in the classroom.

b. Psychological considerations are more important in learning mathematics than in most of the remaining elementary school curricular areas.

c. The mathematics period offers the least desirable period of the school day for fulfilling the psychological needs of children.

5. What is the basis of your agreement or disagreement with the following statements?

a. Teaching children mathematics is the most neglected curriculum area in today's elementary schools.

b. All persons preparing to teach in elementary schools should have a liberal arts specialty—for example, mathematics, English, music, and so forth.

c. The abstract nature of mathematics is such that it will always be the least-liked subject for teachers and children in the elementary school.

d. Student teachers and beginning teachers (first year) should not employ an "active learning" philosophy when they engage children in mathematics.

SELECTED READINGS

Aiken, Lewis R., Jr. "Affective Facts in Mathematics Learning: Comments on a Paper by Neale and a Plan for Research." *Journal for Research in Mathematics Education,* Vol. I (November 1970), pp. 251–255.

Bauer, Gregory, and George, Linda. *Helping Children Learn Mathematics: A Competency-based Laboratory Approach.* Menlo Park, Calif.: Cummings Publishing Company, Inc., 1976, Chapters I and II.

Bruner, Jerome S. *On Knowing: Essays for the Left Hand.* New York: Atheneum Press, 1970.

Burton, Grace. "Skinner, Piaget, Maslow, and The Teachers of Mathematics— Strange Companions?" *Arithmetic Teacher,* Vol. 24, No. 3 (March 1977), pp. 246–250.

Fletcher, Robert F. "An Investigation of the Effect of an Operationally Defined Word on Conservation-of-Number Responses." *Arithmetic Teacher,* Vol. 17 (March 1970), pp. 255–261.

Gagné, Robert M. *The Conditions of Learning,* 3d ed. New York: Holt, Rinehart and Winston, 1977.

Green, George F. *Elementary School Mathematics: Activities and Materials.* Lexington, Mass.: D. C. Heath and Company, 1974, pp. 15–34.

Lipson, Joseph. "Hidden Strengths of Conventional Instruction." *Arithmetic Teacher,* Vol. 23, No. 1 (January 1976), pp. 11–15.

Lovell, Kenneth. *The Growth of Understanding in Mathematics: Kindergarten through Grade Three.* New York: Holt, Rinehart and Winston, 1971, Chapter 1.

Phillips, John L., Jr. *The Origins of Intellect, Piaget's Theory.* San Francisco, Calif.: W. H. Freeman and Co., 1969.

Picard, Anthony J. "Piaget's Theory of Development with Implications for Teaching Elementary School Mathematics, Vol. 69 (April 1969), pp. 275–280.

Skemp, Richard R. *The Psychology of Learning Mathematics.* Baltimore: Penguin Books, 1971, pp. 13–135.

Smedslund, Jan. "Development of Concrete Transitivity of Lengths in Children." *Child Development,* Vol. 34 (June 1963), pp. 389–403.

Verizzo, Quida. "Conceptions of Conservation and Reversibility in Children of Superior Intelligence." *School Science and Mathematics,* Vol. 17 (January 1970), pp. 13–36.

Sequencing the Curriculum Developmentally

PERSPECTIVE   In addition to the responsibilities for understanding the unique developmental stages of children and for deciding upon a personal philosophy of teaching, teachers have the responsibility for knowing (a) what mathematics children are to learn; (b) how to effectively sequence that mathematics; and (c) when children have learned that which has been taught. Fortunately, mathematical concepts appropriate to the elementary school may be sequenced in a hierarchical fashion compatible with developmental levels of children.

After study of Chapter 2 you should be able to:

1. Explain the principal result of the "new mathematics" movement on the curriculum.
2. List in a general outline the major topics included in current elementary school mathematics.
3. Identify the scope and sequence of mathematics for a single grade level.
4. Develop a learning hierarchy for a particular topic or concept.
5. Use a hierarchy to develop the specific objectives of instruction.
6. List the characteristics for each of the four levels of learning.
7. Develop a specific assessment activity appropriate to demonstrate mathematical knowledge at a given level of learning.

SCOPE AND SEQUENCE

The Contemporary Setting

The mathematics you will be asked to teach will probably not differ greatly in content from the mathematics you studied in the elementary school, especially if you were an elementary school student between the years 1960 to 1968. Just prior to 1960, however, certain forces and influences set in that year were to have considerable impact on the elementary school mathematics curriculum. Chief among these forces was a sweeping national concern that our nation's public schools were not producing young people sufficiently sophisticated in the sciences and mathematics. Consequently, the federal government, as well as private agencies, came forth with generous support for research and the development of curriculum projects that were to give elementary school mathematics a new look. The movement became known as "modern mathematics" or the "new math" and the ensuing controversy over whether or not it was the school's role to create minimathematicians actually generated more heat than light.

There was virtually no new mathematics in the "new math." There was, however, some reordering of the content of elementary school mathematics together with a new emphasis on the structure of mathematics. As a result, some topics now appeared in elementary programs that heretofore had received consideration in only highly selective secondary programs or in college. Thus, "new math" consisted chiefly of topics that were new to the elementary school curriculum.

Figure 2.1 portrays a hierarchy that represents the *general* order of development and presentation of concepts in contemporary elementary school mathematics programs. The extent to which topics appear and the specific level at which they appear varies considerably from program to program. Nonetheless, threads of continuity in the areas of structure and proof tie the different programs together, which include topics such as set theory, logic, functions, probability, coordinate systems, graphing, and number theory.

Examining Student Textbooks   Familiarity with the textbooks children use is the single best guide available to the current content of elementary school mathematics. That content has remained rather stable for the past decade. Table 2.1 portrays a typical model of a scope and sequence chart that might appear in the teacher's editions of texts which accompany a commercially prepared series. Because of space limitations, the chart displays a "typical" content for only grades two and five.

As part of your study of the content of elementary school mathematics, it would be exceedingly valuable for you to analyze in detail the teacher's edition of a pupil's text for the grade level of your choice. Your instructor can undoubtedly guide you to the location of a collection of pupil texts in current use.

In most teacher's editions, each page contains a facsimile of the pupil's page with the remainder of the page devoted to "prepared" suggestions for teaching. For your analysis, you may wish to utilize some of the illustrative criteria questions which follow. This activity need not be viewed as an evaluation, although admittedly some of the inquiries are value-laden. Still, they can guide you to further establishment of your personal teaching philosophy in the context of the content of elementary school mathematics.

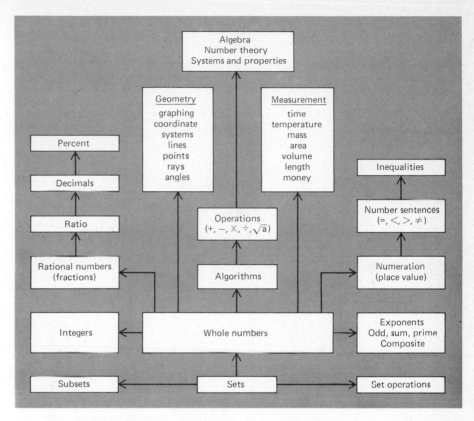

(2.1)

1. What is the essence of the content for the grade level you have chosen? Describe as specifically and economically as possible.

2. What specific or implied evidence is there that the authors recommend a "laboratory" approach to instruction in elementary school mathematics? An activity approach? Provide examples.

3. Do instructions provided *directly* to children (or indirectly through the teacher) contain any "pupil purposes" for the activities in which the children are to engage?

4. Are the desired outcomes of instruction stated behaviorally (i.e., in terms of what children ought to know or be able to do quantitatively)?

5. Can you make any general statement about the role of problem solving in the book you are analyzing?

6. What provisions are made for diagnosis and assessment (i.e., proposals for measuring pupil attainment of objectives of instruction?

7. In the planning helps to teachers, are suggestions given regarding individual- izations, small group instruction, classroom management, and so forth, that are specific and practical enough to be translated into teaching strategies? Provide some illustrative examples.

8. Make a summary statement about the implicit "role" ascribed to the teacher by the textbook you choose. (Imagine you would need to use the book as the adapted text in your first teaching position or while student teaching.)

TABLE 2.1   **An Illustrative Scope and Sequence: Grades Two and Five**

Content	Grade 2	Grade 5
Sets, numbers, numeration	Zero: as numeral for empty set Write numerals 0–19 Write numbers as tens and ones Write numerals to 100 in order Group into tens and ones Ordinal numbers: first through tenth Count by tens, fives Place value: 2-digit numerals Write numerals: hundreds and tens Write numerals to 200 Place value: 3-digit numerals Identify halves, fourths, and thirds Rename hundreds and tens as tens Count in order to 1000 Ordinal numbers: to twentieth Odd and even numbers Union of sets Different names for numbers Expanded notations	Write and read numerals: billions Value of a digit in a numeral Round numbers Write and read numerals: base five Write Roman numerals Fractional parts of regions and sets Fractional numbers greater than 1 Write equivalent fractions Write fractions in lowest terms Identify fractions as proper, improper Convert improper fractions Write and read decimals: thousandths Name equivalent decimals Ratios, rates Equivalent ratios, ratios as percents Divisibility by 2, 3, 5, 7, or 9 Find prime and composite numbers Whole number exponents Prime factors of a number Write and read integers
Operations, properties	Write addition sentences: sums to 5 Write inverse subtraction sentences Related number sentences Addition: sums of 6–10: numberline Subtraction: inverses: numberline Add and subtract tens: 2-digits Add with 3 addends Associative and commutative property Addition and subtraction facts: 11–18 Add and subtract tens and ones Multiplication with 2–6 as factors Multiplication: as repeated addition Relate multiplication and division	Add and subtract: 3-digit numerals Estimate sums, differences, products Multiply by 1, 2, and 3-digit factors Relate multiplication and division Use multiples to find quotients 1-digit divisors Divide by multiples of ten Divide by any 2-digit divisor, 3-digit Find averages Add and subtract: fractions; properties Add and subtract: mixed numerals Add and subtract decimals Multiply fractional numbers Multiply whole numbers by decimals Find percents—add integers
Problem solving	Read and solve number stories Solve number stories: facts, 11–18	Open and closed number sentences Solution sets, proportions

TABLE 2.1 **(cont.)**

Content	Grade 2	Grade 5
Geometry, measurement	Money: pennies, nickels, and dimes Time: hour and half hour, 5 minutes Measure, using nonstandard units Measure meter Liquid measure: liter Line segments Money: quarter, half dollar, and dollar Thermometer Measure, using the centimeter Symmetry, congruence Right angles, inside, outside	Identify points, lines, segments, rays Identify curves, polygons, angles Congruent segments, perimeter Identify quadrilaterals, triangles Measure in centimeters, millimeters Perimeter in metric units Areas of regions Determine a line of symmetry Transformations: line, point Convert linear measures Units of weight and liquid measure Area of a right-triangular region Constructions, arc Volume of a rectangular prism Identify cones, cylinders, pyramids Spheres Metric units of weight and capacity
Relations, functions	Compare numbers Compare 2-digit numerals Compare sums and differences Compare products, ordered pairs Cartesian product	Matrix addition Matrix multiplication Compare fractions, decimals, integers Assign ordered pairs
Probability, graphing	Read and make bar graphs Probability, using a spinner	Read pictograph, line graph, circle graph Read and make a bar graph Probability of an outcome: coin toss Graph points on a number line

ORGANIZING CURRICULUM CONTENT

After you have generally determined what the content of elementary school mathematics is, you must have equal concern about organizing it for learning. Children tend to organize their thinking in a fashion similar to the way they are taught. Relationships which are apparent are most easily accommodated into cognitive structure. From observations of the various relationships within a discipline, children organize sets of principles with which they construct what Gagné terms the "structure of organized knowledge about a topic."[1] Implicit within this organization is the assumption that every higher-level principle is based on certain

[1] Robert Gagné, *The Conditions of Learning* (New York: Holt, Rinehart and Winston, 1965), p. 149.

subordinate learnings, which must be grasped before higher-order learnings can be understood. To test this assumption, Gagné isolated a mathematical principle to be learned and identified the subordinate knowledge he believed necessary to the acquisition of that principle. Through testing, he found that students not having a grasp of the necessary subordinate skills were unsuccessful in demonstrating the competencies of higher levels. His study affirms the need for carefully structured, sequential mathematical experiences at the elementary level.

An Illustrative Addition Hierarchy

The notion of a learning hierarchy, as proposed by Gagné, was established under tightly controlled experimental conditions, during which a given learning hierarchy was successfully established and defended. The addition hierarchy about to be examined was not established under such rigorous experimental conditions, nor could it be. The operation of addition, with all its subordinate and superordinate learnings, is far too comprehensive to treat with such experimental rigor. What is presented is a hierarchy which reflects the logic and beliefs of the authors toward children's attainment of problem-solving behavior in addition. For example, addition is thought of as a joining of disjoint sets of concrete objects; the idea of addition as skips on the number line is not introduced until later. The hierarchy illustrated here reflects this bias. Each learning on the hierarchy implies meaning, not only in the understanding of a concept or principle but in its representation.

Notice that each subordinate learning in Figure 2.2 leads to some higher order of learning, culminating with a sample terminal objective—the child's ability to compute using a vertical algorithm. To attain this final behavior, a child must be able to compute addition exercises involving regrouping. This ability, in turn, is dependent upon his facility with basic addition facts through 9 and his understanding of the associative property. To build a hierarchy, teachers and children must repeatedly deal with the same question for each hierarchical level: "What subordinate learnings are needed to attain this particular objective?" Providing appropriate answers requires all the mathematical and organizational knowledge teachers and pupils can bring to bear.

Using the Hierarchy To Determine Specific Objectives

Although the illustrative addition hierarchy in Figure 2.2 provides a general sequence guide to content, it does not specify what the outcomes of instruction should be. Review a portion of the original hierarchy that is reproduced in Figure 2.3. The terminal statement, "Solve verbal problems with N addends" lacks specificity. It does not describe the type of problems to be solved, the conditions under which they are to be solved, or the desired level of learning to be achieved.

Robert Mager states, "Terminal behavior refers to the behavior you would like your learner to be able to demonstrate at the time your

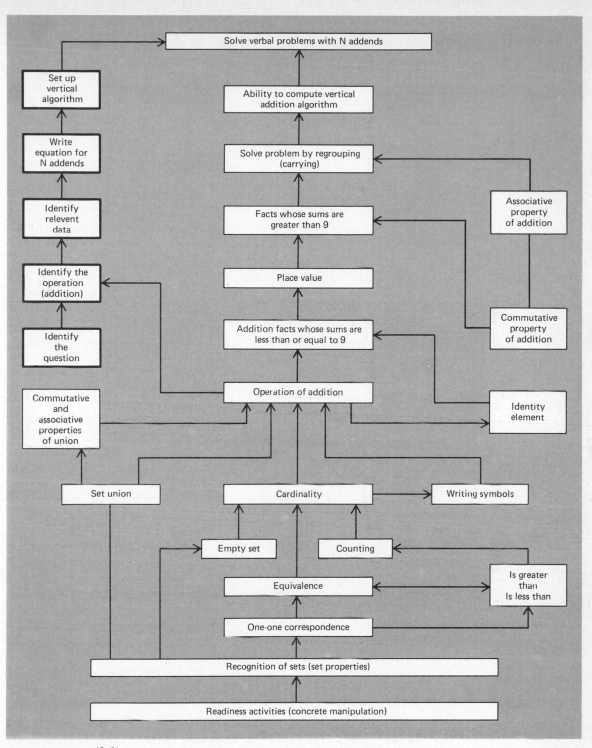

Solve verbal problems with N addends

Set up vertical algorithm

Write equation for N addends

Identify relevent data

Identify the operation (addition)

Identify the question

Commutative and associative properties of union

Ability to compute vertical addition algorithm

Solve problem by regrouping (carrying)

Facts whose sums are greater than 9

Place value

Addition facts whose sums are less than or equal to 9

Operation of addition

Associative property of addition

Commutative property of addition

Identity element

Set union

Cardinality

Writing symbols

Empty set

Counting

Equivalence

Is greater than Is less than

One-one correspondence

Recognition of sets (set properties)

Readiness activities (concrete manipulation)

(2.2)

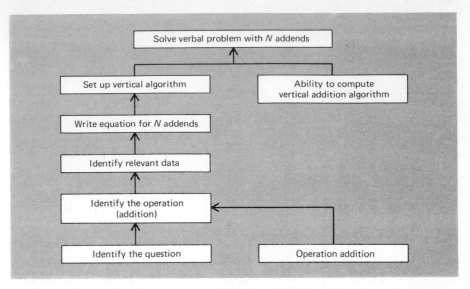

(2.3)

influence over him ends.''[2] To know that such a point has been reached, it is necessary that the desired behaviors be stated in terms that are both observable and measurable. Consider the original terminal statement recast as follows:

> Given a set of twenty one- and two-step written problems involving mixed practice, the learner must be able to do the following:
> 1. Recognize those problems which involve additive situations.
> 2. Correctly construct a number sentence for each additive problem.
> 3. Compute solutions to the number sentences with 90 percent accuracy.

How does this differ from what was originally stated as the objective of this addition unit? What are the components of this behaviorally stated objective?

The more general behavioral statement has been expanded to describe conditions under which the desired behavior must occur. Rather than simply indicating that children should be able to recognize addition problems, the statement now tells the teacher and students that the problems are one- and two-step problems. A child working with this unit would understand that the terminal behavior was performance on a set of written problems, not oral problems, and not simply a worksheet containing addition exercises in the usual algorithmic form. If a teacher and child want to define competency on the basis of active performance involving situations arising from the day's activities, they need only refine their criterion to include such performance.

[2]Robert F. Mager, *Preparing Instructional Objectives* (Palo Alto, Calif.: Fearon Publishers, Inc., 1962).

Some of the problems might not involve addition, since the statement quoted does not require this. Further precision would require revising the statement to indicate that a specified number of problems must involve other than additive situations.

Describing Subordinate Statements Behaviorally

The hierarchy we have been discussing forms a structure upon which to build mathematical understanding. As such, it is crucial to teaching. Thus far, however, we have considered only the terminal statement of the hierarchy. The subordinate statements of a hierarchy may also serve as guides to behaviorally stated outcomes of instruction. In Figure 2.3, consider the subordinate statement, "Set up vertical algorithm" and "Ability to compute vertical addition algorithm." Appropriate behavioral outcomes for these general statements might be, respectively:

> Given a set of five addition sentences involving n addends, the learner must be able to construct correctly a vertical algorithm for each.
> Given a set of five addition exercises aligned in a vertical algorithm, and including n addends, the learner will compute sums with 100 percent accuracy.

Notice that the behavioral description for each subordinate statement from the hierarchy clearly describes the condition under which the behavior is to be performed. Having defined the objectives of a lesson in behavioral terms, both teacher and child now have a clear concept of what needs to be done.

ASSESSMENT OF BEHAVIORALLY DESCRIBED OUTCOMES

As teachers have concerned themselves more with individual differences between students, they have moved away from the concept of evaluation as simply a means to assist in grading. Evaluation is now considered as one means used by a teacher to help children determine their learning levels and instructional needs. Through observation of test results, a child may be helped to see where additional competence is needed. Equally important, through a well-designed test the teacher may see where instruction has failed and determine what changes are needed in the mathematics teaching. Because these are the important objectives of evaluation, the criterion measures should be prepared before instruction takes place and should be generated by predetermined behavioral objectives. Evaluation then serves to guide the teacher in preparing a conditioned environment for learning; it becomes an integral part of the teaching act.

Consider the preparation of criterion tests to measure attainment of the terminal objective in an example cited earlier.

> Given a set of twenty one- and two-step written problems involving n addends, the learner must be able to do the following:
> 1. Recognize those problems which involve additive situations.
> 2. Correctly construct a number sentence for each additive problem.
> 3. Compute answers to problems with 90 percent accuracy.

It is relatively easy to construct twenty one- and two-step written problems to test for these skills, but teachers must be aware of the possible levels of response to objective assessment measures. Certain types of questions test for specific types of learning. A child may demonstrate his learning on four distinct levels: rote or associative learning, concept learning, principle learning, and problem solving. These distinctions are gross and further refinement may be desirable for specific situations. A more detailed consideration of the characteristics of the levels of learning may be obtained by reading *The Conditions of Learning* by Robert Gagné[3] and Benjamin Bloom's *Taxonomy of Educational Objectives: The Cognitive Domain.*[4] These four levels play a definite role in constructing goal-oriented evaluation.

Associative Learning and Assessment

Rote or associative learning might best be described through the use of examples. Assume that a teacher has spent a great deal of time giving instruction in multiplication facts. She has used flash cards such as that shown in Figure 2.4, and the children have spent additional time in both oral and written activities involving the basic multiplication algorithms.

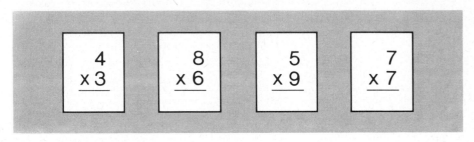

(2.4)

When children are asked to respond to examples such as these during a test, they are responding at a rote, or associative, level. To answer correctly they need only associate the correct response, 45, with the proper stimulus, 5×9. They need not have learned anything about the process of multiplication as addition of equal addends or Cartesian product, and so on. Assessment at the associate level is characterized by, but not limited to, computation portions of an objective measure.

Associative learning is *not always simple learning.* Not too many years ago it was common practice for teachers to advise their students to attack "story problems" by looking for certain key words. Having found the key word, the child would then be able to solve the problem. For example, the word *and,* when used in conjunction with a quantitative problem, often called for addition. Consider the problem:

[3]Robert Gagné, "The Acquisition of Knowledge," *Psychological Review*, Vol. 69 (July 1962), pp. 355–365.

[4]Benjamin Bloom, *Taxonomy of Educational Objectives: The Cognitive Domain* (New York: Longmans, Green & Co., Inc., 1959).

Mary had three dolls and her mother gave her four more. How many dolls does she have now?

Since the word *and* is used, the child is taught to respond three dolls and four dolls are seven dolls, and the problem would be correctly solved.

Other key words such as *of,* indicating multiplication, and *less,* indicating subtraction, were used in the same way at this time.

As children gained sophistication, they were taught to look for other keys to problem situations. They learned, for example, that the phrase *how many more* indicated a subtraction situation. These aids helped some students to solve story problems. Unfortunately, others became confused and forgot which key phrase applied, or did not associate the correct operation with the word or phrase. As a result, children's performance on written problems was often quite disappointing, and their performance on problems occurring in daily living was even worse.

Many tests are constructed almost exclusively of items testing at the associative level. The first four examples from the set of sample questions listed below test at the associative level since they require no understanding of the operations they demand.

1. 178
   +24

2. 59⟌579811

3. 1977
   76
   +561

4. 85
   ×19

5. Mary has eighteen cookies to share with her two friends. If she divides the eighteen cookies equally among the three persons, how many cookies will each person receive?

A child who has facility with the number facts for each operation, and who has learned the various steps to follow in computing an algorithm, is able to get the answer to the first four exercises without understanding the process involved. Many children with good memories are able to do complex exercises by simply following rote procedure. They have little or no comprehension of the meaning of their activities. The fifth example, a story problem, while potentially more penetrating than the other four, may still only be testing at the rote level.

Concept Learning and Assessment

Concepts are structures which exist in the mind. They are formed when experiences in the real world have a certain common bond that is recognized by the learner. Consider the schematic representation in Figure 2.5. On the left is a box called the sensory or real world. Represented within this box are those things a child can see, feel, smell, hear, and touch—in short, those things a child can experience with his senses. For example, a child may carefully examine a round ball, noting its shape and whether it can be compressed so as to form a different shape.

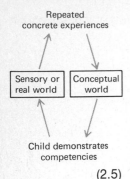

Repeated
concrete experiences

Sensory or real world

Conceptual world

Child demonstrates competencies

(2.5)

The second box of the figure is labeled the conceptual world. This box represents those ideas that a child cannot precisely define, yet which have a certain degree of common relationship to them. Despite the fact that one cannot precisely define those ideas occurring within the conceptual world, a child who understands a particular concept can discriminate those items which fall within the conceptual set from those that do not. For example, consider the concept "love." It cannot be precisely defined to everyone's satisfaction, yet one who has an understanding of the concept is able to discriminate examples of love from other experiences. A dog who greets his master with yips of joy and a wagging tail is said to love him. The same dog may snarl viciously at an intruder, and this behavior is not loving, which is recognized by the child with an understanding of the concept of love.

Piaget found that elementary school children understand only what they experience. Young children must rely upon repeated experiences with concrete materials which may appeal to several senses in order to gain concepts.

It is not a simple matter for a teacher to ascertain whether or not a child understands a concept. Carefully constructed tests involving a variety of problem situations and materials must be designed and utilized. The test examples shown in Figure 2.6 have one thing in common. They ask children to use their concept of 3 in performing a unique activity.

1. Circle the sets containing three objects (unfamiliar objects).

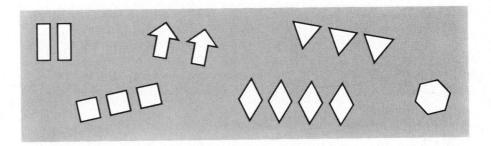

2. See the set of books on the shelf below. Color a set of three books.

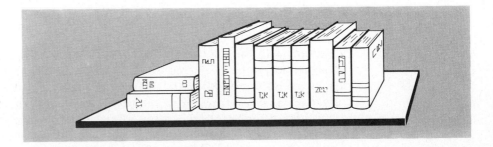

3. Draw a set of three objects. Your set should not have any of the objects shown on this page.
4. Do both of the pictures below contain a set of three objects? How do you know?

(2.6)

In the first question, the learner is asked to discriminate sets of three from sets containing more or less than three. Opportunity is given the child to make an error by including some sets which are similar in physical characteristics but different in number.

In the second question, the child is asked to select a subset of three from a total set, and to color the subset. This item gives the teacher further confirmation that the child's understanding of 3 exists independently from the particular physical objects represented.

In the third question, the child is asked to construct a set including three objects. Next, it is necessary to make use of illustrations which have not been previously encountered in instruction about cardinality.

From the fourth question, the teacher will gain insight into the child's notions regarding configuration and cardinality. Questions such as 3 and 4 above are rarely found in a mathematics text.

Principle Learning and Assessment

A mathematical principle is ordinarily generated out of the union of two or more related mathematical concepts. For example, a child perceives that forming the union of a disjoint set of two objects with a disjoint set of three objects forms a set of five objects. To understand this, the child must relate his previously formed concepts of 2 and 3 with his concept of union to perceive the rearranged set of five objects. This union describes the operation called addition and is illustrative of principle learning.

Further principle learning is involved in comprehending the operation of addition fully. To understand the addition sentence $3 + 2 = 5$, it is essential that the child have an understanding of the concepts of 2 and 3, and of the concept *plus* as it applies to mathematics. It is also essential that the child be able to discriminate instances where other concepts are incorrectly used to complete this statement. When children without adequate subordinate knowledge are forced into higher-order learning, they must soon rely on memory rather than understanding in order to be successful in mathematics. Consider this statement: "When operating with whole numbers, the operation of multiplication may be thought of as addition with equal addends." Many concepts are involved, and it is only when their relationships are fully understood that an understanding of the principle as a whole takes place.

It is easy to confuse principle learning with associative learning. The commutative property of addition, also called the order property, can be shown algebraically in the sentence "$a + b = b + a$," and it is possible for students to learn this by rote. Questions such as "The commutative property is stated ____" simply call for filling in the blank with "$a + b = b + a$." A teacher who consistently asks for and accepts this kind of answer as demonstrating understanding may be making a grave mistake. Subsequently, in settings which require an application of the commutative property in the context of other requirements, students who have merely memorized are frustrated. As an example, the addition sentence $18 + 14 + 2 = \square$ is more easily answered when the sentence is recast as $18 + 2 + 14$. It is when children can apply the commutative principle that a teacher may assume the principle is attained.

Carefully designed problem situations requiring a variety of responses give a good indication of a student's understanding of a mathematical principle. The following questions can be contrasted as to their relative effectiveness in determining understanding.

     Principle: In addition, the order of addends does not affect the sum (the commutative property).

    1. Which property was used in the following example?

$$5 + 6 + 9 = 6 + 9 + 5$$

        a. the associative property
        b. the closure property
        c. the commutative property
        d. the well-defined property
        e. the distributive property

    2. Explain how the commutative property helps you in the study of addition.

Each of the previous questions require a child to demonstrate knowledge in a unique situation. By contrast, the next questions permit only a limited view of the student's performance.

    1. Which equation shows the commutative property?
        a. $5 + 7 + 9 = (5 + 7) + 9$
        b. $a + b = b + a$
        c. $a (b + a) = ab + ac$
        d. $9 (5 + 6) = (9 \times 5) + (9 \times 6)$
        e. $a + (b + c) = (a + b) + c$

    2. Write a number sentence showing the commutative property.

A characteristic of the first set of questions was the requirement that students apply the principle in some unique situation. Questions such as these permit a teacher to identify areas of misunderstanding before long, arduous review is needed.

Testing Problem-Solving Behavior

The problem-solving level of learning is attained when a child is able to accommodate skills, concepts, and principles into a cognitive structure. Most of the problems children attempt to solve are called word problems, verbal problems, or story problems, because the situation is conveyed to the child in written form. The problems generally deal with quantitative situations—those which require a numerical solution—in a predominantly social, scientific, mathematical, or geometric setting. A typical example is:

> Ed and Joe each decided to share a Coke and a box of Crackerjacks. Cokes cost fifteen cents and Crackerjacks cost twenty-five cents. How much should each boy pay the clerk?

The problem focuses on amounts of money in a social setting. Others may involve finding area or volume (geometric setting) or making a precise measurement in grams (scientific setting). To solve problems, children need many subordinate capabilities. They must be able to read with understanding; they must be able to identify the mathematical question and the necessary operation from the relevant data; and they must be able to construct a number sentence either mentally or on paper. Finally, they must compute with accuracy. Each of these subordinate capacities is essential to problem-solving success.

To examine a child's problem-solving ability, a variety of problems which involve both paper and pencil solutions and solutions requiring some supporting activity on the child's part must be used.[5] The range of the problems should be such that the results provide a clear idea of any area of the child's misunderstanding. Consider the following example:

> A football costs $7.95. Joe has $5.00. How much more money does he need to buy the ball?

To the reader, this problem may be relatively straightforward. No irrelevant information is provided and the operation to be used is quite apparent; an adult knows a difference is being sought. An examination of the work done by a child may be revealing. If he writes $5.00 + $\square$ = $7.95 and then correctly computes the difference, he has come to a successful solution. However, an incorrect solution or the inability to write a number sentence indicates a need for further analysis. Was the error one of

---

[5]Anton Nickel, "A Multi-experience Approach to Conceptualization for Improving Problem Solving" (Unpublished Ph.D. dissertation, University of Oregon, June 1971).

computation? Did the child read the problem incorrectly? Was the number sentence correctly stated? Many such questions can be asked. The answers will provide valuable insights as the teacher assesses the pupil's progress in problem solving.

DESIGNING AN INDIVIDUAL INSTRUCTIONAL SEQUENCE
When a terminal objective has been identified and behaviorally defined, and a hierarchy has been constructed with projected evaluative measures, it is time to consider the preparation of instructional sequences to attain the objective. A sequence of instruction should be preceded by some form of diagnosis. This may be a well-prepared test designed specifically as a pretest for the particular unit, or it may be the test given for the terminal objective of the preceding unit. Careful examination of the results of the pretest will determine areas of instructional need for each child. Are there areas of deficiency which will interfere with a child's mathematical development in terms of the stated behavioral objective? If so, these must be attended to before a child can meaningfully progress to higher-order skills.

Assume that a hypothetical student, Kathy, could not discriminate additive and subtractive situations in a pretest setting. Before continuing, she must be given experience in discriminating additive situations. A logical first step is to begin her program by giving her repeated experiences joining sets of objects in response to both written and verbal statements. From that point on, her program would follow that part of the hierarchy (see Figure 2.3) which needs additional work. Initial sequential steps like those indicated below might appear.

1. Provide repeated experience in recognizing the union of disjoint sets of objects as an addition situation.
2. Have Kathy write a number sentence to describe the number action concretely demonstrated by the teacher or another child.
3. Provide repeated experience in manipulating sets to demonstrate the action called for by addition sentences prepared by the teacher or other children.
4. Have Kathy identify additive situations from story problems involving addition as well as other operations, and from problem situations in the classroom which the teacher has structured or which may occur incidentally. Once the addition problem has been discovered, Kathy must write a number sentence describing the action and must correctly manipulate concrete materials to demonstrate the action.
5. Have Kathy identify those quantities which are needed for the solution of a problem by including unnecessary data in problem situations.
6. Give Kathy experiences involving addition problems with more than two addends. Help her discover that order and grouping make no difference in the sum by having her repeatedly manipulate concrete materials and write number sentences to describe her actions.
7. Discuss why a vertical algorithm makes computation easier. Let Kathy demonstrate this is so by referring back to the horizontal algorithm.

Notice how this teaching plan can be carefully mapped along the lines of a hierarchy. Each step is plainly noted, yet a teacher is free to be creative in choosing instructional procedures.

SUMMARY

In the past decade, our public schools have been the subject of much attention as well as much criticism. Elementary school mathematics has not escaped notice, and the "mathematics revolution" of the 1960s has resulted in substantial changes in the commercially prepared curricular materials presently available to children and teachers. Familiarity with the particular content to be taught is a major responsibility for teachers.

In addition to the scrutiny of what topics should comprise elementary school mathematics, there has been a new thrust in how that content shall be sequenced for instruction. The latter has focused considerable attention on learning hierarchies and behavioral objectives. It is generally accepted that the hierarchical nature of mathematics offers the key for structuring its content during teaching. Once sequenced, the organized content is directly drawn upon to determine the specific outcomes of instruction.

Wisely used, behaviorally described outcomes can help diagnose academic difficulty, reflect desirable levels of learning, provide a sound basis for assessment, and guide the establishment of individual instructional sequences.

ACTIVITIES, PROJECTS, A POINT OF VIEW

1. Look at the scope and sequence of a textbook series printed during the late 1950s or early 1960s. Compare and contrast it with one from a contemporary series. Write a brief report on what you regard as significant changes.

2. Obtain a teacher's edition for a contemporary pupil text at the grade level of your choice. Analyze the text by applying the criteria questions in the section of this chapter entitled *Examining Student Textbooks*. State your findings in a written question-answer format.

3. Use the teacher's editions for grades K–3 from a contemporary elementary text series. Prepare an addition hierarchy. Compare and contrast your hierarchy with that found in Figure 2.2. Provide a brief report for the class.

4. State two subordinate behaviors that are necessary prerequisites for the following terminal behavior: Pupils can select two sets of three objects each when presented with several sets containing one to five objects.

5. Outline a sequential series of behavioral objectives that could guide instruction when utilizing the addition hierarchy you developed for Question 3 above.

6. Look at a mathematics test in a pupil's text or a test you have taken recently. Classify the items according to the four levels of learning. At what level did you find the most items?

7. Prepare some assessment items appropriate for the content of Chapters 1 and 2 of this text. Have at least one item applicable to each of the four levels of learning for both chapters. Present them to a classmate for agreement or disagreement.

8. Prepare a test item for each of the behavioral objectives you developed in Question 5 above. Specify the intended level of learning for each item.

9. Criticize or support this statement: Most learning failure in elementary school mathematics can be explained by the failure of teachers to employ the learning hierarchy principle.

10. What is the basis of your agreement or disagreement with the following statements?

a. Utilizing commercially prepared sets of behavioral objectives is the best way to assure that different pupils are working on different skills and at varying rates at all times.

b. The important principles of creativity and spontaneity are thwarted by the employment of predetermined outcomes for teaching.

c. The current "back-to-basics" trend for elementary schools is long overdue and behavioral objectives should be used to support the movement.

SELECTED READINGS

Bauer, G., and George, Linda. *Helping Children Learn Mathematics: A Competency-based Laboratory Approach.* Menlo Park, Calif.: Cummings Publishing Company, Inc., 1976, Chapters III, IV and V.

Bidwell, James K. "Learning Structures for Arithmetic." *Arithmetic Teacher,* Vol. 16 (April 1969), pp. 263–271.

Biggs, Edith F., and Hartung, Maurice L. "What's *Your* Position on the Role of Experience in the Learning of Mathematics?" *Arithmetic Teacher,* Vol. 18 (May 1971), pp. 278–295.

Green, G. F. *Elementary School Mathematics: Activities and Materials.* Lexington, Mass.: D. C. Heath and Company, 1974, pp. 15–33.

Lipson, J. I. "Hidden Strengths of Conventional Instruction." *Arithmetic Teacher,* Vol. 23 (January 1976), pp. 11–15.

Maertens, Norbert, and Schminke, Clarence. "Teaching—For What?" *Arithmetic Teacher,* Vol. 18 (November 1971), pp. 449–456.

McKeen, R. L. "Behavioral Objectives—Are They Restricting?" *Arithmetic Teacher,* Vol. 23 (April 1976), pp. 241–243.

Marks, J. L.; Purdy, C. R.; Kinney, Lucien; and Hiatt, Arthur. *Teaching Elementary School Mathematics for Understanding,* 4th ed. New York: McGraw-Hill Book Company, 1975, pp. 1–37.

CHAPTER 3

Teaching Strategy

PERSPECTIVE When teachers have a system which climaxes in unique strategies for a lesson, the resultant teaching is likely to be successful. The system must possess features that enable a teacher to make lesson plans in a manner consistent with modern learning theory, delineate clearly what is to be taught, and engage children in an active manner.

Teaching strategies vary in their complexity, depending on the nature of the material to be learned, the pupils involved, and the amount of time available. It is here that teachers must exert their professional prerogatives; they are the ones who must consider children, material, and environment as they prepare to teach. They must clearly understand the purpose of the lesson and develop an outline of the procedures to attain that objective. Each time teachers meet with students and attempt to help them learn, such decisions are made.

Educators have tried to develop a best method for many years. This work has helped us understand methodology but it has not been very successful in actually helping people to teach. Today, the many different settings in which teachers work make it unlikely that a best method of teaching mathematics will be found. Children attend open-space schools, free schools, and traditional schools. Teachers can be in self-contained classrooms with or without aides, working with another adult as a team, or be part of a multiple team arrangement. It is possible for a teacher to work effectively within many different settings. This chapter describes how a teacher can manipulate five components of teaching in order to help children learn in any situation. The important thing the teacher must remember in studying this chapter is that it does not describe a best method. Instead, it deals with a model which utilizes five components of method in order to help children learn.

After study of Chapter 3 you should be able to:

1. Outline a generalized model for a flow-charted lesson.
2. Name the five major components of teaching method.
3. List the essential characteristics of a behavioral objective and write an illustrative objective.
4. Identify five teacher moves and describe the pupil-teacher interaction promoted by each.
5. Enunciate clearly three principles of selection regarding choice of materials, exercises, and problems for use in a teaching sequence.
6. Describe the interrelated elements of a conditioned learning environment.

THE TEACHER'S ROLE IN PLANNING

The Context of Planning

The major role of the teacher pertains to instruction, the sequence of events initiated by a teacher for the purpose of enabling children to learn. Too often, planning for teaching does not reflect systematic, professional decision-making. What, then, is the practical task of planning to teach?

A learning activity, by definition, is one period of time during which children have certain experiences designed to help them learn something such as a concept, principle, or skill. Mathematics periods are usually twenty to forty-five minutes. Mathematics is usually taught each day and a school year is about 180 days long. This means that what children can learn, within their capabilities, is limited to about 180 twenty- to forty-five-minute periods. This is important because it helps teachers set up reasonable expectations for their mathematics program. Children learn rather deliberately, and it takes several related learning activities for them to master a skill or acquire some knowledge. In most schools, teaching mathematics consists of involving children in a series of related learning activities. This can be a unit, a chapter in a textbook, a section of a learning system, or a prescription.

To understand teaching and how it is done, the teacher should realize that certain things are done in order day-by-day. This is like a triangle that has at its vertices preparation, execution, and evaluation.

Examination of the teaching triangle in Figure 3.1 shows that a teacher constantly prepares, executes, and evaluates learning activities during each school year. Where the teacher begins this process is very important. Some teachers may prefer to focus on diagnosis (evaluation) first. After they identify what children need to learn, they prepare some learning activities. This is often called a prescription and such teaching is often called diagnostic and prescriptive teaching. Following diagnosis, the prescription is executed, the effects are evaluated, and the cycle begins anew. Other teachers, especially preschool and primary teachers, begin with planning activities. Then they involve children in the activities (execution) and observe children to determine what they learned (evaluation). One interesting kind of teaching begins with preparation that consists of setting up a laboratory which has manipulatives, games, and other materials. Children work in the lab and the teacher circulates to provide help, guidance, or offer suggestions (execution). At times children come together in groups to discuss discoveries or to take a test (evaluation). Coordinating all of these activities may have some local constraints, but it is a teacher's function to prepare, execute, and evaluate learning activities.

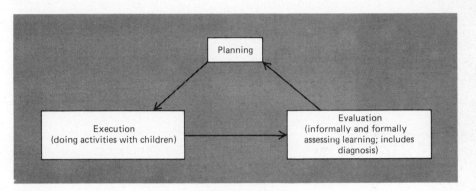

(3.1)

Flow-Charting a Lesson Plan

Decisions related to teaching are facilitated when the teacher employs a model for planning daily lessons which simply and comprehensively requires one to consider, write down, and relate details about preparation, execution, and evaluation. A generalized model for developing a flow-charted lesson plan is shown in Chart 3.1. Study the model carefully. It is a simple, yet systematic and thorough, design. In order to use the model effectively for developing lessons, a teacher must consider the major variables of the instructional setting. Take special note of the "performance check," because it must provide for evaluation in terms of the specified objective and learning level of the children. When results of the performance check are below criterion, children may be recycled within the plan of the flow-charted lesson plan.

To flow-chart a lesson, the teacher should select a desired objective in mathematics with which he is familiar and write it down in terms of what children should do. Next, the teacher must refer to a teaching strategy and think of several potential sequences of moves. After a moment or two, it is appropriate to write one down that seems to have potential for success. At the same time, consideration must be given to the examples, exercises or problems, and materials to be used. Good initial results are achieved if the lesson is simple and occurs in the classroom. As proficiency is gained, more complex lessons can be planned and taught. With a little practice and study, most teachers can become strategists who systematically vary

Chart 3.1 Flow Chart Lesson Plan Model—Generalized Form

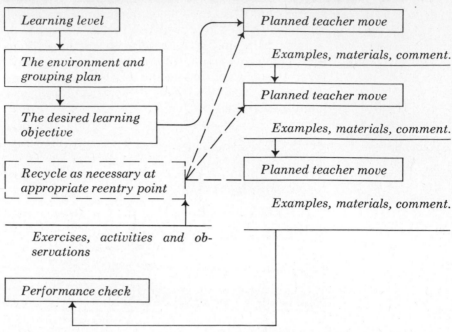

their teaching styles, exposing children in some manner to all of the mathematics curriculum allocated to them and making the instruction appropriate to the learning.

Model illustrative lessons are provided throughout the remaining chapters. These can serve as guides for the development of original flow-charted lessons.

THE MAJOR COMPONENTS OF METHOD

The variety of settings in which children learn and the increasing insistence on accountability mandates that teachers think carefully about what they do and how they do it. Teaching can be effective under nearly every circumstance when five components of method are carefully considered in the development of flow-charted lesson plans. The five components are: 1) the objectives for the lesson—that is, the knowledge and skills to be learned; 2) the conscious moves the teacher will make; 3) the materials, patterns, exercises, or problems to be utilized; 4) the environment in which the lesson will take place; and 5) pupil response. These five conditions can be viewed as the major components of the instructional setting and, as such, the crucial variables in a teaching plan. The distinctive feature of a teaching plan written as a flow chart is that the desired learning, the environmental setting, the teacher-pupil roles, and the conceptual referents to be used are sequenced in a clear, simple manner.

These features enable the teacher to use the plan effectively during instruction.

The Objectives for the Lesson

Society establishes goals for education. Curricular materials are used to translate these goals into what children are to learn in school. In developing a flow-charted teaching plan, the concepts and skills to be learned should be stated in terms which suggest behavior the child can demonstrate at the end of a lesson or sequence of lessons.

At present, most school districts employ behavioral objectives or semibehavioral objectives. Semibehavioral objectives which omit conditions and criteria and deal only with behavior are generally easier to work with. For example, suppose children are to master the skill of multiplying two whole numbers. An explicit behavioral objective for this would be:

> Given a test containing twenty items involving multiplication of two two-place whole numbers, the child employs the partial products algorithm to correctly solve at least sixteen items.

This objective is quite specific. The conditions are that the child use the partial products algorithm in relation to twenty multiplication items on a test. The terminal behavior is "solves." The criterion is sixteen out of twenty, or 80 percent mastery. In actual practice it is usually easier to state the objective simply as: The child multiplies two two-place whole numbers. The latter is not only easier, it is educationally sound for several reasons. First, conditions for the way a child demonstrates a behavior often relate more to the way a local school district evaluates children than to the behavior. Second, the criterion for minimally acceptable performance should not always be 80 percent. It has to vary somewhat in relation to what constitutes reasonable expectations. For example, severely intellectually limited children may never master pencil and paper computation but may learn to match objects one-to-one. Gifted children may demonstrate exceptional problem-solving ability.

Generally, the objective for a lessson should be stated without using terms such as know, understand, and appreciate. Terms such as recite, write, utilize, apply, interpret, describe, or discover should be used. Each objective should describe what the child ought to be able to do when the lesson is completed. For particular topics, the objectives to be achieved in a given lesson should be based on those of previous lessons and should lead to the development of higher-level objectives to be attained during future lessons in accordance with some planned hierarchy.

As an example, suppose the next ten pages to be studied in a fifth grade textbook deal with area measurement. There is no single sequence of lessons that could be developed by the authors of the textbook or any teacher which would enable pupils to learn this concept best. The following sequence of objectives to be achieved during five arithmetic periods is simply illustrative. Each objective is a declarative statement about what the child should be able to do.

1. Given directions to find the areas of three plane surfaces found within the classroom, the child is able to manipulate square-shaped tiles to find the number of square units in each surface.
2. Given four polygonal regions drawn on a sheet of paper, the child is able to use a transparent grid to determine the number of square units for each region.
3. The child is able to:
   a. Write and recite the area formulas for triangular and rectangular regions.
   b. Use the formulas to compute the area of triangular and rectangular regions drawn on a sheet of paper.
4. Given four irregular polygonal regions drawn on a sheet of paper, the child is able to partition each region into rectangular and triangular regions and determine their area.
5. Given directions to find the floor area contained in the school building, the child is able to use a steel tape to measure the dimensions in order to calculate the floor area.

Each of these objectives could be the basis for one or more lessons. The objectives are stated in such a way that learning is successively more abstract and complex. Ultimately, the pupils use what they have learned to solve a problem.

The teacher may not wish to record all details of the objective written on a flow-charted lesson. The fourth objective could be rewritten as, "Partitioning polygonal regions into rectangular and triangular regions in order to compute their area." In either case it is important that the objective state what the children should learn by identifying what they are to do. This practice suggests appropriate pupil-actions. The first objective implies that pupils can learn by manipulating tiles, while part of the third objective suggests that pupils can learn by applying formulas. When teaching is considered from this viewpoint, it becomes clear that objectives which deal with nothing more than tidiness and doing things in a rule-ridden way are unimportant. Here the teacher is able to become a skilled professional, as well as a warm and human person.

Teacher-Moves A large number of materials, textbooks, and teaching procedures have been made available because of the numerous approaches developed by educators for the improvement of the teaching of mathematics. To some extent, however, as new approaches have been conceived and research conducted to determine their relative effectiveness, little information has been made available to teachers regarding ways they can or should alter specific classroom behavior.

A teacher-move is a purposeful action initiated by the teacher to enable children to learn. Whether it is preplanned or not, a teacher does make a sequence of moves during any lesson. Consequently, the decisions about these moves are crucial to how well pupils can learn.

There are five basic moves a teacher can make. Each of these should directly facilitate learning. While classroom management is not among them, it is assumed the teacher will manage children in a human and sensible manner that will not make them feel inadequate as human beings.

To facilitate learning, the teacher can make an exposition move, an illustration move, a demonstration move, a discussion move, or an exploration move. By varying the use and sequencing of moves, the teacher can systematically and creatively make it possible for pupils to learn. A brief description of the moves is provided here without any implicit significance in the order of discussion.

Exposition Moves These are limited to auditory reception. The teacher makes an exposition move when he explains an idea. A lecture is the classic example of exposition, with the teacher verbally providing the information. The implicit assumption is that children can learn by listening and subsequently reinforcing what they have heard. This type of move has been soundly criticized in educational literature, yet the notion that people do not learn by listening is unrealistic. What needs to be understood is that exposition moves should not be used all the time or over long periods of time with young children. In deciding to use an exposition move, the teacher trusts that the child is capable of learning through listening. This means the child must have achieved a level of mental development advanced enough to profit from an idea in the absence of any other stimulus than an auditory one. Expository moves assume that children have acquired subordinate learnings needed for understanding new concepts or principles. They are often made near the end of a sequence of moves. The teacher should realize that nearly every idea which is initially explained will have to be subsequently reinforced.

Illustration Moves The teacher makes an illustration move when she shows children a physical model, a drawing, a picture, a filmstrip, or a motion picture. There may be some nominal accompanying talk, but emphasis is on visual presentation of an idea. The assumption in using an illustration move is that children can learn by looking and subsequently reinforcing what they see. The major difference between illustration and exposition moves is that information is acquired by the child via a different sensory mode.

Demonstration Moves The teacher makes a demonstration move when he simultaneously explains and shows a way of doing something. The basic assumption in using demonstration is that children can learn by listening and looking at the same time and subsequently reinforcing the technique that has been demonstrated. The teacher is explaining and showing at the same time, which may be more effective for certain objectives because the child receives information both aurally and visually.

Exposition, illustration, and demonstration moves are usually made when it is desirable to provide background information, move quickly through selected instructional material, clarify ideas, or fill informational gaps.

The assumptions underlying these three teacher-moves are important because each action places the teacher in a position where he imparts knowledge to his students. Although each move may provide an efficient mode for presenting some material, and the moves may be thought of as mutually supporting, the ideas presented must subsequently be reinforced by activities generated through additional teacher-moves. This is clearly indicated in each of the teaching strategies discussed. Exposition, illustration, and demonstration moves must be deployed carefully within time constraints in order to facilitate active learning. They must not constitute the major activity of instructional time.

Discussion Moves   The teacher executes a discussion move when she asks questions and encourages students to do the same; there is verbal interaction of an inquiry–response type between the teacher and children. This type of move is known to be effective for motivating new topics, conducting review, guiding discovery, and clarifying ideas.

Making productive discussion moves is complex. Still, a primary responsibility of every teacher is to develop his ability to conduct an effective discussion. One good way to do this is through the use of questions which elicit particular pupil-actions. Another is to ask questions which are open-ended.

The art of questioning during teacher discussion moves is probably nowhere more important than in teaching mathematics. Yet it is strangely true that while some teachers intuitively ask questions of high quality, most of us pose questions that rely on direct recall through memory. Consider the following pairs of questions that might be used during a mathematics discussion move and note their subtle differences.

Pair A
1. Nancy, the standard unit of English measure, the inch, is related to what metric unit of measure?
2. Nancy, what is the advantage of using a metric unit rather than the customary inch?

Pair B
1. Billy, what is the area of a plane figure whose length is 2 meters and whose width is 7 centimeters?

2. Billy, can you describe one way you might show us why .14 square meters is the area of a plane figure whose length is 2 meters and whose width is 7 centimeters?

Pair C

1. Terry, when the decimal point four, four, five [.445] is changed to a common fraction, how many zeros will there be in the denominator? Can you write the common fraction?

2. Terry, can you tell why there are three zeros in the denominator when the decimal point four, four, five [.445] is written in common fraction form as four hundred forty-five one-thousandths?

A careful reexamination of the first question in these pairs will reveal that each is principally a "memory" type of question. Each depends on direct recall of information through memory with the "right answer" as the only apparent objective. Unfortunately, such questions tend to encourage rote or associative learning and children can "learn" to do quite well in such discussions. Yet memory questions are most often considered ominous test questions by children and are not likely to encourage children to discuss mathematics. Discussion moves dominated by such questions provide little opportunity for learning because these inquiries require little thinking, and they leave a false and sometimes lasting impression on children about what is involved in learning mathematics.

Compare the second question of each pair with its counterpart in the set. Each question is phrased so as to cause a child to utilize information in a way that reflects both application and understanding. The "right answer" is not the primary focus. These inquiries are not highly dependent on computation. They tend to mirror teaching since they lead children to review processes and procedures that were used during the original learning process. As the questions provide feedback or insight, they review the process of learning conjunctively with content. At the same time they preserve the dignity of children while encouraging additional discussion.

The essence of a discussion move is that the teacher makes a planned inquiry which causes children to do such things as reflect on prior learning, seek further information, make comparisons, develop interpretations, solve new problems, or contribute opinions in order to achieve specific purposes. Throughout a person's teaching career there is a need to search continuously for a vocabulary, a rhetoric, a way to phrase inquiries during discussion moves so that discussion can develop as a crucial component of a planned teaching strategy.

Exploration Moves Exploration moves are made to afford children an opportunity to observe relationships, seek new data, discover ideas, look for solutions to various problems, or even practice an activity in order to achieve a desired level of performance. The essence of an exploration move is that the teacher develops a task with a student, a group of students, or the entire class which enables him or them to learn an idea or selectively utilize ideas to make a discovery or solve a problem. This is clearly indicated in the teaching strategies shown previously.

Exploration moves terminate direct teacher control of learning, thus setting children free to explore or guiding children to complete tasks sequentially in accordance with the teacher's instructions for developing extended understanding. The tasks may be as simple as studying a set of blocks to describe their physical characteristics or reinforcing an idea by completing a worksheet as a culminating activity. The task may be as complex as solving a new and difficult problem by conducting some original, active research.

One of the hallmarks of exploration moves is the focus on group activity. On many occasions it is more appropriate for a teacher to let pupils explore some task or problem as a group. Through this type of exploration move the mathematics program is made relevant and interesting for elementary-school pupils. For example, assume a group of primary-school children have spent several days learning how to count money. During this time the children may complete several worksheets dealing with the relative value of pennies, nickels, dimes, and quarters. These experiences are made more worthwhile by a trip to a local supermarket to make purchases, by developing a store for school supplies cooperatively and having pupils take turns as storekeeper, and by a host of other activities calling for group endeavor.

Suppose a group of intermediate-grade pupils has learned how to find the perimeter of polygons; to work with similar triangles and ratios; and to measure objects to the nearest centimeter or meter. All of these ideas can be reinforced and extended by dividing the class into small groups and encouraging them to survey the school building, the school yard, their classroom, and other sizes and shapes in their environment for the purpose of verifying that their new knowledge really works. In doing this, individuals within the group will assume various roles. One child might become the organizer. Another might do the measuring, while others perform the necessary calculations. This is important because it mirrors the kind of adult activity that puts men on the moon or that will win the battle against pollution. Letting pupils function in this manner involves what is called a variable-task assignment. Since each child himself determines what he actually learns, the extent to which the design of exploration moves are imaginative and suited to the intended learning will be the extent to which children's learning coincides with what the teacher hopes to teach.

Exposition, illustration, and demonstration moves differ from discussion and exploration in two very important ways. First, the intent of the former moves is usually to supply knowledge rather than provide an opportunity for guided discovery, and the learner is relatively passive. Discussion and exploration generate an active role for both teacher and children.

Second, of all teacher moves, discussion and exploration moves are most congenial for creating and maintaining a conscious awareness of mathematics in the child's environment. Creatively employed, these moves set the stage for discovering mathematical relationships in a meaningful manner and provide the opportunity for the child to use the mathematics he is learning. Each of these principles is a central feature of active learning and can effectively contribute to the establishment of an affective and effective learning environment.

The Materials, Patterns, Exercises, and Problems

During the establishment of a flow-charted plan for teaching, great care should be given to the selection of materials, patterns, exercises, or problems that will be used to promote learning. While the general task of learning mathematics is complex, it is comprised of many specific learnings which require the teacher to utilize effective examples in developing concepts and principles. A bewildering variety of materials with which to do this is available.

Manipulatives such as attribute blocks, base ten blocks, color rods, and fraction disks can be used for concrete representation of concepts. Their use is essential to abstracting mathematics and verifying that answers obtained via algorithms are correct. Audiovisual materials such as tapes, filmstrips, flash cards, records, and transparencies convey verbal and illustrative representations of mathematics to children. They can be effectively used to supplement and reinforce what children learn and for a refreshing change of pace. They are especially helpful for drilling children who need extra work. Pupil texts and learning systems materials contain a basic mathematics program for some level or grade. They usually order the concepts and skills to be learned and provide illustrative and symbolic representation. They are a useful resource and basic guide, but are never an adequate total program because they cannot represent concepts concretely and cannot relate to children in live, dynamic settings. Activity cards, problem cards, and assignment cards contain picture or word problems, puzzles, and situations that help children make discoveries or relate mathematics to real life. Worksheets and workbooks focus on drill (practice). Their use is essential to mastery of skills but most teachers employ them too much. Children should complete worksheets or workbook pages only after they have been involved in learning activities which enable them to understand abstract concepts and relationships. Games such as Yahtzee, Monopoly, Chess,

Checkers, and Triominos can reinforce skills and provide pleasure in using mathematics. They are an important part of enrichment.

Though there are many materials, the task faced by the teacher is always the same. It is to select and use a combination of materials consistent with the specific objective of the teaching plan such that children experience mathematics at concrete, illustrative, verbal, and written levels.

The Learning Environment Of paramount importance to your success in teaching mathematics will be your ability to organize the immediate learning environment, deciding how to tailor the total educational environment to the needs of children. For the teacher of integrity this "tailoring of the educational environment" is a complex operation. You must possess the requisite knowledge to form and test hypotheses regarding: 1) the kind of learning that is involved or desired; 2) the environmental arrangements that are most likely to promote that kind of learning; 3) the kinds of interaction that will promote the most productive involvement of a given learner or group of learners with selected content or courses of action; and 4) the materials that will facilitate learning.

Most teachers today have autonomy in deciding upon a grouping arrangement for children in their classrooms. There are essentially three ways children can be grouped for a learning activity. They can work independently at their own rates, be part of a small group, or work as a whole class. In the traditional self-contained classroom, teachers often involved the whole class in one or two activities each period. Teachers just "handled" individual differences. For some time ability grouping was popular, which enabled a class to be divided into high and low groups or high, middle, and low groups. More recently, the concept of individualized instruction has led teachers to have pupils work independently at their own rates through some material. Today's teacher is likely to find that within a single school district all these means of grouping are employed.

Irrespective of the grouping arrangement selected or required, the consideration for active learning of elementary-school mathematics are met by creating the opportunity for communication (discussion), maintaining a conscious awareness of the mathematics in the environment, and setting the stage for observing relationships and making mathematics useful. A few examples should provide a clear notion of the interrelatedness of these conditions.

Children have a natural proclivity to communicate. This tendency provides an opportunity to actively encourage language development and, at the same time, create an interest in the quantitative world which arises when a small group of children are given some new instructional materials with which to experiment—for example, Cuisenaire rods. Children will ask, "Why is this one longer?" and "Are all the yellow ones the same size?" In this setting an important concern is to avoid giving direct answers, to encourage discovery, and to elicit new questions. Other opportunities for discussion might arise in connection with plane figures that have been painted on a surface play area. Guided discussion can lead to such inquiries as "Are all the shapes in *four-square* the same?" "Is the ball field a true rectangle?" "How many steps will it take to cross the court?" As questions arise from the common experience, they can be made to lead to new lines of mathematical investigation by children.

Creating and maintaining a conscious awareness of mathematics in the school environment can be further generated within the framework of routine classroom business. Recording birth dates, noting time, maintaining attendance and monetary records, weather charts, and personal growth and achievement records are but a few examples. Others may involve noting relationships between the dimensions of windows and doors or between heights and shadows. Certainly these examples, when considered collectively, set the stage for discovering relationships in a meaningful manner and provide ample opportunity for children to use and enjoy mathematics.

All teachers encounter children who do not appear to understand or who do not look beyond the simple mechanics of an activity. Consider the recording of numerals on a height–weight chart. Here the teaching role must clearly be exercised. Instruction must not become ritualistic; the teacher must be an active partner with children in the educational process. Make subtle inquiries which demand further evaluation of data obtained ("What is the height in meters?"); suggest alternate procedures for recording the obtained data ("Can we group the data?"); or require the acquisition of additional relevant data ("Does relative size appear to be related to parent size?"). All these are key teacher actions which facilitate the active engagement of children in learning.

There are other important considerations involved in establishing a "conditioned environment" for learning. More than ever before, children have the opportunity to learn mathematics in environments other than the regular classroom. Teachers are required to develop resource centers, utilize programmed materials, send children to computer consoles, and establish "laboratories" for the purpose of learning mathematics. Within these alternatives, some educators have generalized an environmental consideration advocating a single approach such as programmed learning, a "laboratory" approach, or a responsive environment approach. This is unfortunate, because they are often misunderstood and tend to discount the inherent value of other single approaches as well as multiple approaches.

Suppose the teacher is told to use a general "laboratory" approach in teaching mathematics. Implicit in this approach is the notion that the children should learn in a setting which contains manipulative materials, tools, games, and other types of physical resources. There is much that children can learn in this environment, yet such an approach hardly considers the total range of environmental possibilities. Learning encompasses too many dimensions for the teacher to assume that it must always be generated by a single type of environmental arrangement. In many instances it *is* effective to explain something to children while they sit at desks. At other times it may be more effective to discuss and illustrate a mathematical idea as the teacher and children are grouped in a more informal arrangement around an overhead projector. Increasingly, programmed instructional materials may meet expository functions fulfilled earlier by the teacher. Not infrequently it is profitable for students to explore a mathematical idea in the library, cafeteria, or gymnasium, or on the playground, in the larger community, or at home. None of the previous possibilities is necessarily present in a narrowly conceived laboratory approach. The teacher should decide in advance which of several potential environmental arrangements will facilitate desired learning separately or collectively.

There are several useful criteria which may be applied to assess the potential of environmental arrangements for a lesson. First, does the choice really promote mathematics as a system of ideas? Second, does the choice stimulate pupil initiative and self-reliance? Third, does it encourage a unique teaching style and the unique learning style of the group of children? Fourth, does the choice accommodate discussion and exploratory responses? Fifth, is the choice generally appropriate for the desired learning? Within these criteria lie the crucial considerations which surround the arrangement of an appropriate learning environment for any lesson. Although current schemes of organization for instruction—such as staff differentiation, continuous progress, and utilization of paraprofessionals—may slightly alter a specific teaching setting, the crucial ingredients of the teaching act, the teacher and the children, remain relatively constant. It is the teacher who has the responsibility of making daily decisions regarding specific environmental arrangements for teaching from an ever-widening range of alternatives.

Pupil Response   For any teacher-move that is made, pupils will respond in some manner. Even if a teacher does nothing, pupils will eventually do something besides sit. Any pupil response such as listening, writing, or analyzing is a pupil-action. Just as there are levels of learning, there are levels of pupil-actions. For convenience they may be grouped as lower-level, intermediate-level, and higher-level actions. Some important pupil-actions are identified in Table 3.1.

TABLE 3.1   **Pupil-Actions**

Lower Level	Intermediate Level	Higher Level
a. Memorizing–recalling	a. Translating	a. Interpreting
b. Practicing	b. Comparing	b. Applying
c. Listening	c. Contrasting	c. Analyzing
d. Watching	d. Guessing	d. Generalizing
e. Manipulating	e. Verifying	e. Synthesizing
f. Drawing	f. Categorizing	f. Conceptualizing
	g. Classifying	g. Labeling
	h. Organizing	h. Evaluating
	i. Relating	
	j. Visualizing	

The actions listed in Table 3.1 do not require precise definition. There are, no doubt, other actions that could be identified. The important thing is that the actions clearly indicate the large number of things children can do in order to learn.

When different people engage in similar actions there will be different results. Teachers should expect children to vary. It is a normal condition when pupil response to a guided activity ranges from a lower-level memorizing–recalling response to a higher-level abstracting–generalizing response. For this reason it should be recognized that the previous categorization of pupil responses does not constitute a preferred hierarchy either vertically or horizontally. It is important that the teacher be conscious of the level of response that pupils make, both individually and collectively. Periodic analysis of pupil response can serve as a useful check for maintaining a desired balance in the nature of response that planned activities elicit.

SUMMARY   Regardless of movements that may be hailed as panaceas, success in teaching is always dependent upon careful planning. During periods of change, tampering with structure does not alter the fact that in teaching mathematics it is necessary first, to prepare; second, to execute; and third, to evaluate what has been accomplished. The teaching strategies recommended is this chapter offer guidelines for doing that.

Within the context of the flow-charted lesson plan, there are five major components of methodology that receive consideration. The model constitutes a vehicle that can be utilized to develop comprehensive, yet specific plans in a minimal amount of time. Of course, each of the major components may vary in intensity and importance directly in relation to the specific objective of a plan. The configuration of the model permits the teacher to consciously control a selected set of factors in order to enhance learning. The component termed teacher-moves exerts the greatest influence upon the immediate success of a period of direct instruction. This is because teachers make the major decisions regarding execution. These decision directly affect the quality of interaction between the child, the subject, and the teacher. Time spent in careful planning yields gratifying results.

ACTIVITIES, PROJECTS, A POINT OF VIEW

1. Teach a math lesson to a peer group or a small group of elementary school children. To do so, obtain a pupil's text and select a lesson. Translate it to flow-chart form using Chart 3.1 as a model guide. If with peers, distribute a copy of the flow-charted lesson plan prior to teaching.

2. Make a list of ten terms which describe observable mathematical behavior.

3. Review McKeen's article, "Behavioral Objectives—Are They Restricting?" Discuss its compatability with related recommendations in Chapters 2 and 3. In what important ways is it similar to and different from O'Daffer's article, "Individualized Instruction—A Search for a Humanized Approach"? Who is right?

4. Choose two mathematics concepts. Write a terminal behavioral objective for each. Have your work reviewed by a classmate.

5. Choose a course in which you are presently enrolled. Apply the criteria presented under *Discussion Moves* for the purpose of classifying kinds of questions utilized during discussion. What did you find? If possible, repeat the activity in an elementary school classroom. Compare the findings.

6. Describe a rationale that justifies employing a laboratory approach in teaching mathematics.

7. Make a list of commonly accepted classroom practices which you feel violate the active learning philosophy.

8. Criticize or support this statement: Pupil response is directly related to teacher behavior.

9. What is the basis of your agreement or disagreement with the following statements?

    a. There is probably a best method for every child.

    b. Teachers should relate the teaching of mathematics to the natural physical environment.

    c. The most serious limitation of the mathematics laboratory approach is that some teachers and many students do not work successfully in such a setting.

SELECTED READINGS

Arnold, William R., "Management By Learning Activities: An Alternative to Objectives." *Arithmetic Teacher*, Vol. 25 (October 1977), pp. 52–55.

Davis, Robert B. "Mathematics Teaching with Special Reference to Epistemological Problems." *Journal of Research and Development in Education*, Monograph No. 1 (Fall 1967), pp. 29–32.

Hunkins, Francis. *Questioning Strategies and Techniques.* Boston: Allyn & Bacon, Inc., 1972.

McKeen, Ronald L. "Behavioral Objectives—Are They Restricting?" *Arithmetic Teacher,* Vol. 23 (April 1976), p. 24.

O'Daffer, Phares G. "Individualized Instruction—A Search for a Humanized Approach." *Arithmetic Teacher,* Vol. 23 (January 1976), pp. 23–28.

Richardson, Lloyd I. "The Role of Strategies for Teaching Pupils to Solve Verbal Problems." *Arithmetic Teacher,* Vol. 22 (May 1975), pp. 414–421.

Tanner, Daniel. *Using Behavioral Objectives in the Classroom.* New York: The Macmillan Company, 1972.

Walbesser, H. H. "Behavioral Objectives, A Cause Célèbre." *Arithmetic Teacher,* Vol. 19 (October 1972), pp. 418f.

CHAPTER 4

Early Experiences
with Whole Numbers

PERSPECTIVE Children enter elementary school with a variety of environmental backgrounds. Some children have an amazing wealth of travel, participation, and planning experiences. At a very early age these children had collections of toys to play with and books to look at, and they were given many opportunities to exercise their natural inquisitiveness as well as their creative instincts. Contrast this picture with children coming from backgrounds that are socially, culturally, economically, or emotionally deprived. Such children often did not have a wealth of play experiences, and many did not have access to a variety of stimulating books and toys. They had not been involved in developing family plans, they had had few travel experiences, and no one had nurtured their proclivity to explore and learn. Unless mathematics is made both meaningful and relevant for these children, it is not very useful.

We also know that young children learn by experiencing. Experiencing includes acting, listening, observing, and expressing. It is in this manner that children learn mathematics and use it to interpret the quantitative world around them.

As a result of studying Chapter 4 you should be able to:
1. Prepare a variety of flow-charted lesson plans for use in the primary grades.
2. Develop original activity cards as an aid to instruction.
3. Distinguish between proportional and nonproportional materials for teaching groups.
4. Describe the use of three manipulative devices that can enhance children's learning of place value.
5. Illustrate appropriate use of the number line.
6. Specify several games, activities, or materials which can be used in helping children master the basic addition and subtraction facts.

USE OF SETS   Most young children who come to school have had prior experience with collections of things. These were probably in the form of dolls, baseball cards, hair ribbons, toy soldiers, and so forth. These early experiences with collections of concrete objects, which may be called sets, can form an important basis of early instruction in mathematics for children.

A set may be thought of as a definite collection. Sets are indicated by braces, [ ], and may be comprised of concrete objects having some common characteristic (see Figure 4.1). It is not necessary that members of sets be physical objects. They may be collections of ideas; for example, the natural number system, which is the collection of the counting numbers, can be represented as follows: [1, 2, 3, . . .].

A set of fruit   A set of furniture   A set of geometric shapes

(4.1)

From the study of Piagetian concepts in Chapter 1, the reader found that children's thinking at the early elementary-school level is dependent on what they can see. For this reason experienced elementary teachers have come to place heavy reliance on manipulation of sets of concrete objects. Such manipulation is essential to good mathematics instruction, both substantively and pedagogically. Instructional activities that might be used in developing set notions follow.

Activities To Bring About Set Awareness   Begin by placing some objects such as shown in Figure 4.2 on a table, and ask children what they notice about them. Let them use their own words to describe objects—for example, it rolls, it is made of rubber, the surface is smooth, it is round in shape and is colored red. To extend their thinking, ask the children how such an object might be used. Continue

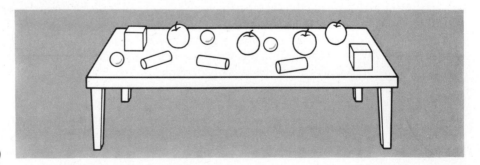

(4.2)

the experience by asking if there are other objects in the room which resemble selected objects. Ask them to explain what characteristic they have in common.

Next, children might be divided into groups of four or five, and asked to describe as many characteristics as possible of a different physical object provided to each group. Pupils could be asked to examine the new object for texture, color, size, shape, utility, and so on, with their findings reported orally to the class. Through experiences of this kind students become aware of the many characteristics of concrete objects. They begin to search for relationships which were not apparent to them earlier. Their growing perception of physical characteristics may be broadened through the use of other media such as flannelboards, art materials, student workbooks, articles of clothing, and so on. The purpose of the exploratory activities which require children to identify the common characteristics of physical objects is twofold: (1) children learn to search for physical characteristics not readily apparent in objects; and (2) children learn to search for the sometimes unique relationships among objects.

Children of about five to seven years begin to develop the ability to classify objects by their physical characteristics. They choose a particular object and select a characteristic with which to classify that object (for instance, green color). Subsequently they look for all other green objects and overlook the fact that all the objects may be round, while only a few are green. At this stage the child is unable to change his system of classifying and holds steadfastly to the color green as the class characteristic.

The child's ability to classify increases with age and experience. At about age eight many children are able to classify objects in a hierarchical fashion; that is, they are able to see that green shapes, red shapes, and black shapes may all be classified as round. However, the classifying being done at this stage is still tied to what the child can see or feel.

**Activities
To Bring About
Set Discrimination**

Once children have demonstrated their ability to discriminate similarities and differences of shape, color, size, utility, and so on, they are ready to classify by physical properties. Placing a set of objects such as those shown in Figure 4.3 on the desk and asking if the objects belong together is a good procedure. Have them tell *why* the objects form a group. Conclude that groups of objects with an identifiable common characteristic may be called sets. Have them discuss as many ways of classifying the objects into a set as possible—the objects are all solids; they are all capable of being rolled, and so forth. Reiterate that sets have one defined characteristic in common. If each object has the particular characteristic required for membership in the set, then that object is said to be a member of that set.

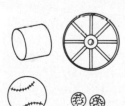

(4.3)

INITIAL UNDERSTANDING OF NUMBER

One way to describe a set is by using a number to tell how many objects there are. The same number may be used to describe every set with as many objects. Children do not automatically identify number as a property of sets. The number property of sets may not be as obvious to children as are the physical properties of the objects themselves.

Since most children today come to school with an intuitive understanding of cardinality for the first two or three ordinals, some simple activities may be used to reinforce the notion of number as a property of set. By matching any given group of objects and a "standard set," children begin to see that *three* is the number name given to all groups of objects that can be matched with ⬜△ ⊘ ✿⬜.

Following are several illustrative activities that may be employed to develop the concept of "five" as the number property of collections containing five elements. Notice that numerals need not be introduced. Later, similar activities may be used to develop the number property for sets representing all the numbers 0–9.

1. Have children place one hand, palm down, on the table or desk where they sit. After noting they have five fingers, see how many other groups of five they can name by glancing around the room. Record by listing the group on the chalkboard.

2. In directed discussion, give children pencils and paper and ask them to make a list of things that come in fives (toes on one foot, sticks of gum, days we go to school, and so forth).

3. Provide a pair of children with a small box of assorted toys and objects. Have them display as many groups of five objects as possible. Ask pairs of children to check the work, mix the objects, and form as many groups of five as they can. What were the results? Discuss.

4. Provide several children with a packet of picture cards, each card containing either one, two, or three objects. Display a "model set" card containing two objects and have children remove those picture cards from their packet which match the "model set." Discuss why certain picture cards were eliminated.

Relationships among Sets

Once children have developed an understanding of number as a property of sets, they are able to progress to a study of relationships such as greater than, less than, and equivalence. As they manipulate sets to form an understanding of these relations, children also develop an intuitive understanding of one-to-one correspondence.

As interesting learning experience may be generated from one of Piaget's[1] experiments to determine whether or not children have conceptualized the important attributes of conservation and reversibility. In his

---

[1]Jean Piaget, *The Child's Conception of Number* (New York: W. W. Norton & Company, Inc., 1965), pp. 41–43.

experiment Piaget arranged seven egg cups in a row and asked children to remove eggs from a nearby basket and arrange them (but not in the cups) so that each egg cup would subsequently contain exactly one egg, and so that no eggs would remain in the basket. One child of about five years made a row of eggs the same length as the row of egg cups. When asked to place the eggs into the cups he was surprised to see that there were more eggs than cups. The extra eggs were removed. The eggs that had been placed in the cups were then removed from the cups and placed in a compact group in front of the egg cups (see Figure 4.4). The child said that there were more egg cups than eggs, thus indicating a lack of conceptualization of conservation, an important attribute for a meaningful grasp of one-to-one correspondence. By about the age of five or six, children are often able to select the proper number of eggs to fill the egg cups, indicating an awareness of one-to-one correspondence. However, when the eggs are removed from the cups and spaced over a greater distance than the space occupied by the egg cups, children are often confused and indicate that there are more eggs than cups. They are not able to reverse the action and view the previous one-to-one correspondence as being intact.

(4.4)

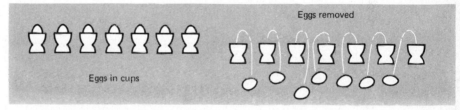

Finally, between the ages of five-and-a-half and six-and-a-half, most children are able to remove eggs from the cups and spread them into a variety of configurations while retaining the understanding that the eggs are related to the cups in a one-to-one correspondence. A child is able to conserve the number of eggs in the collection as the collection undergoes several transformations. Consequently, the child is now ready to grasp relationships such as equivalence, greater than, and less than more meaningfully.

The experiment described may be used to provide instruction in one-to-one correspondence. Further experiences may be had by asking children to place other sets of physical objects, with varying numbers of objects in each set, into one-to-one correspondence. If there are six children in a group, one person may be given the task of selecting an exact number of pieces of chalk so that each person would have one. The child would be encouraged to think: "A piece for Mary, a piece for Jim," and so on.

Other, similar exercises might involve children and baseball gloves, scissors, or rulers. You may also determine that each child has gained a functional conceptualization of conservation and reversibility by returning the objects to their original state and asking whether or not there are as many gloves as players. It is important that children be given adequate time to explore and refine these notions because an operational and meaningful understanding of one-to-one correspondence is essential to much of what they are to learn during their primary years.

Activities To Bring About Concepts of Equivalence, Greater Than, and Less Than

As children demonstrate competence in one-to-one correspondence, introduce them to equivalence relationships. Because these early concepts develop slowly and at varying rates, the teacher is urged to make use of a corner of the room and a math table where children can manipulate physical materials to attain concepts of equivalence, greater than, and less than. Some activities like those described below will help children shape their concepts of "more than," "less than," and "as many as," while they develop the vocabulary associated with these ideas.

1. Use the pupils and their chairs to illustrate the relationship between one child and one chair.
2. Make a bulletin board of pictures that illustrate various occupations and a tool associated with each occupation.
3. Place a group of green ink pens on a section of the table. Place a cap for each pen a short distance away. Children can match pens with caps. There are as many pens as caps. Now place six red pens on the table. Discuss. Remove two red pens. Discuss.
4. Place objects such as kernels of corn, beans, or bottle caps in small Dixie cups. Have children explore groupings which are equal, greater than, or less than.
5. Use counting discs in various arranged groupings on a table. Have children distinguish groups as equal, greater than, and less than.
6. Use some five-by-eight oaktag cards that display various groupings of geometric shapes. Have children select a card containing any grouping. Then have them select cards, containing groupings for "one-more-than" and "one-less-than." Have them arrange a set of cards according to relative size.

The Empty Set

It is curious that the notion we presently use to represent the empty set, an interpretation that makes zero a number in its own right, was originally used in our number system to indicate an absence of number. Because it is difficult to meaningfully visualize a set containing no objects, zero can be a troublesome concept. In fact, research has shown that most children do not fully understand the concept of the null class until the age of nine or ten years. For this reason, the idea needs some special attention in early informal activities. Oral foundation experiences that employ unusual examples can help. Here are a few discussion examples:

1. Name the members of the set of your classmates with three eyes.
2. Will the boys and girls with a driver's license please stand up?
3. Will the members of the class with green hair say hurray?
4. The set of children wearing lavender polka-dot shoes are excused for free time.
5. Name the members of our class who come to school on Saturday.

Utilizing Activity Cards for Teaching An activity card is simply a five-by-eight or other-sized card on which a particular day's activity is suggested. Each card lists the activity under study and the suggested level at which the card is to be used. Such cards may be purchased from several commerical sources, designed by cooperative writing teams, or written by an individual teacher. Their usefulness is dependent on the experience and resources of the teacher and the nature of the class which is to use the material. Every activity card should incorporate the following principles:

1. The children must do something: go out and measure, organize tables of facts, and so on.
2. The children must record their findings in some way that will communicate their procedures and conclusions.

A model activity card looks like this:

Activity Card: Topic Level

Activity—What is the child to do?

Activity—What should he do next?

Activity—What is his culminating activity?

Because activity cards are used to help the teacher promote active learning with children, it is important that the activities posed on the card be open-ended, allowing children to approach a problem in a variety of ways. Kidd, Meyers, and Cilley[2] provide an excellent example of such a question in a unit on ratio: "How can you measure the speed of a pitched baseball?"

This question provides no guidance as to the procedures to be followed, nor is any unit of measure specified. The child is free to explore various means of solving the problem and is thus given the opportunity of discovering a solution for himself. An illustrative activity card for equivalence relations might read as follows:

[2]Kenneth Kidd, Shirley Meyers, and David Cilley, *The Laboratory Approach to Mathematics* (Chicago: Science Research Associates, 1970), p. 254.

Activity Card: Equivalence relations   Level: Early primary

1. Find those sets which have the same number of objects as the set of red blocks. Which are they? Why are they equivalent?

2. Find the sets which have fewer members than the set of red blocks. Which are they?

3. Find the sets which have more members than the set of red blocks. Which are they?

4. Can you arrange the sets according to size? Do it.

Activity cards should be designed so children can be actively involved in manipulating objects and exploring relationships. At first the cards may be used under the direction of the teacher. Later they may be used independently by a single child, by children in pairs, or by small groups of children. The teaching suggestions found in the previous section could easily be transferred to activity cards for use with children when studying set properties. Numerous illustrative examples of their high utility are found throughout the remaining chapters of this book.

SYMBOLIZATION OF ABSTRACTIONS

There is an important distinction to be drawn between a symbol and that which it symbolizes. This is especially true in mathematics and has important implications for early number experiences. Consider the word *blue*. Certainly the symbols—the letters *b-l-u-e*—that are used to construct the word name *blue* are nothing like the attribute "blue." So it is in mathematics. The symbols, properly called numerals—1, 2, 3, 4, and so on—are not the respective ideas they symbolize. In truth, the numbers "one," "two," "three," and "four" exist only in the mind and are merely represented in a graphic and universally accepted set of symbols—1, 2, 3, 4. While the authors do not recommend that a stilted distinction continually be made during early instruction, children do need to become accustomed to this distinction naturally and along with the introduction of activities which require children to form the numerals.

Although children must necessarily be called on to use the abstractions that represent numbers relatively early, there is no need for the introduction of sophisticated symbolization to represent complex structures at the early primary level. To do so may be confusing and even harmful. For example, the symbols > and <, which represent greater than and less than, can be very confusing to many young children. At this early age, children often have a great struggle to avoid or correct "reversals" in letter and numeral formation. It is easy to see that the symbols > and < could readily be reversed and serve as one additional source of confusion. Since children have no need to know them at this time, such symbolism, as well as most formal set notation, should be deferred until later.

Numeration The number ability of children who can chant "One, two, buckle my shoe; three, four, shut the door," and other such rhymes must not be overestimated. Children can very often recite such interesting counting games at an early age, thus giving evidence of counting, possibly to 20 or beyond. Yet the young child who "knows" that 8 comes after 7 in this fashion often memorizes that the word *eight* comes after the word *seven* as, for example, in " . . . seven little, eight little, nine little Indians." He may not know that if he has seven pennies and someone gives him one penny, he will have eight pennies. The child fails to recognize that the next number is constructed in a number sequence by taking a number which is "one more" than the first number.

Numeration is basic to much that is fundamental in mathematical thinking. By associating numerals with objects, children are able to relate the sensory world to the abstract world of mathematics. Despite our understanding of the importance of such associations, attempts to teach them are often disappointing, and many children are left with numeration concepts of limited utility.

It is not enough that children have a sense of the abstractions underlying numeration. They must also have a good stock of visual images for embodying them. In a study of how third-grade children learn formal mathematics, Bruner and Kenney[3] found that even after children developed "example-free" abstractions, they used their enriched imagery to deal with new problems. Thus, it is important that children acquire sufficient visual imagery to support the development of useful numeration concepts. This may be especially important for the group of numerals we call the "teens." In all other decades the number name you hear first represents the first digit of the numeral—for example, *forty*-two (42) and *sixty*-one (61). However, consider *fourteen* and *sixteen*. Here, in the symbolic representation the order is reversed (that is, 14 and 16), and the first numeral named is second in the number. This is simply another reason why numeration must be carefully developed for children.

[3]Jerome S. Bruner and Helen Kenney, "Representation and Mathematics Learning," in L. Morrisett and J. Vinsonhaler, eds., *Mathematical Learning*, Monographs of the Society for Research in Child Development, No. 30 (Chicago: University of Chicago Press, 1965), pp. 50–59.

**Activities
To Introduce
the Numerals 1–4**

3
"Threeness"
Three

↓

(4.5)

(4.6)

Certain arrangements of objects appear to lend themselves to easy learning. Sets involving one, two, three, and four objects respectively are called elemental groups because their cardinality may be recognized at a glance.

Elemental groups may first be introduced by using a variety of concrete materials such as blocks, flannelboards, groupings of children, and the chalkboard. Pupils are exposed to several sets having equal numbers of objects as in Figure 4.5. Through this they are led to understand that each set shares one characteristic in common with the other sets shown, its cardinality. The particular name for the cardinal number of each set in 4.5 is three. It is important to recognize that this common characteristic, this attribute of "threeness," speaks *about* sets and not about the members of these sets. Children are given experiences in hearing the word *three* presented orally as well as both in reading and writing the word *three* and the numeral *3*. Be certain to vary the arrangement within sets. Children must understand that number is independent of arrangement. Exclusive use of three dots, ● ● ●, in a linear arrangement would be unwise. Later on, the arrangement ⦂• might not be recognized as three because the set of associations previously developed was too limited. Other numerals may be introduced in the same fashion by arranging several sets of objects to represent a particular cardinal and introducing its name.

To test for understanding of numeration, and to provide additional practice, the teacher may wish to write a numeral on the chalkboard and have children arrange sets of objects to represent that numeral. This gives children an opportunity to manipulate and explore. A manipulating device which lends itself to tasks such as that mentioned above is the flannelboard. Children may either manipulate materials which are placed on the teacher's large flannelboard or they may benefit from making one such as that shown in Figure 4.6. A cigar box (school box) serves nicely to hold sets of manipulative objects, while the inside of the cover has a piece of colored felt glued to it so that when the box is open the felt surface is ready to be used. Children may use an art period to cut pieces of felt for the boxes, or perhaps parents can be called upon to participate in the preparation of materials.

**Activities
To Introduce
the Numerals 5–9**

Sets representing the numbers 5 through 9 may be shown as using combinations of the elemental groups. Notice how the sets representing the numbers 5 through 9 in Figure 4.7 are grouped. Seven is represented as one row of three objects and one row of four, rather than a single row of seven objects. Because elemented groupings more easily allow children to form mental images of sets representing numbers, they are superior to ungrouped, randomly grouped, or linear grouped sets.

Chart 4.1 Flow Chart Lesson Plan—Numerals 1–4: Elemental Groups

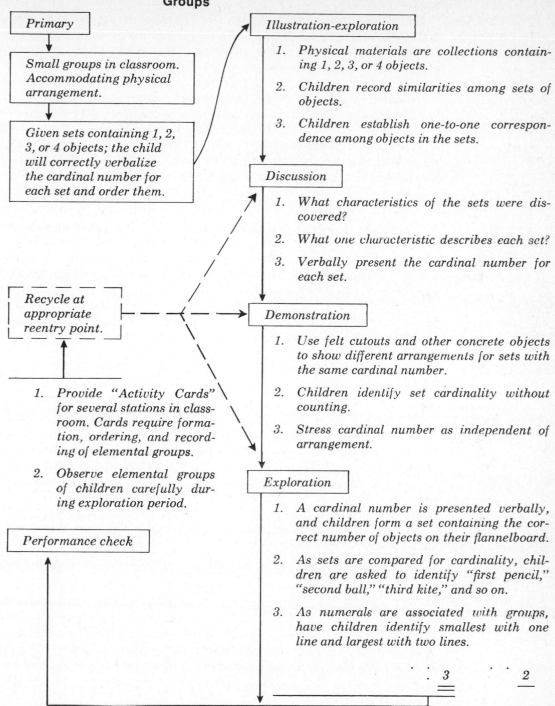

Primary

Small groups in classroom. Accommodating physical arrangement.

Given sets containing 1, 2, 3, or 4 objects; the child will correctly verbalize the cardinal number for each set and order them.

Recycle at appropriate reentry point.

1. Provide "Activity Cards" for several stations in classroom. Cards require formation, ordering, and recording of elemental groups.

2. Observe elemental groups of children carefully during exploration period.

Performance check

Illustration-exploration

1. Physical materials are collections containing 1, 2, 3, or 4 objects.

2. Children record similarities among sets of objects.

3. Children establish one-to-one correspondence among objects in the sets.

Discussion

1. What characteristics of the sets were discovered?

2. What one characteristic describes each set?

3. Verbally present the cardinal number for each set.

Demonstration

1. Use felt cutouts and other concrete objects to show different arrangements for sets with the same cardinal number.

2. Children identify set cardinality without counting.

3. Stress cardinal number as independent of arrangement.

Exploration

1. A cardinal number is presented verbally, and children form a set containing the correct number of objects on their flannelboard.

2. As sets are compared for cardinality, children are asked to identify "first pencil," "second ball," "third kite," and so on.

3. As numerals are associated with groups, have children identify smallest with one line and largest with two lines.

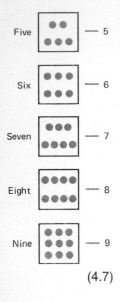

(4.7)

Activities similar to those used to help children learn the elemental groupings may also be used for groupings up to 9. Provide a variety of experiences involving mixtures of concrete and semiconcrete materials to insure that children acquire a meaningful representation of the numerals through 9.

Number block cards as shown in Figure 4.8 are useful for checking a child's mastery of numeration, and may be used as self-instructional materials for children having difficulty. Give children a stack of cards with the numerals revealed. For each card let them select the appropriate number of blocks to represent that numeral correctly. Later, have them arranged in order of magnitude. Additional teaching ideas include:

1. Deploying the children in elemental groups to actually form sets to represent the numerals 5–9.
2. Using sets of dominoes and asking children to find and arrange configurations according to relative size representing the numerals 5–9.
3. Obtaining an overhead projector. With small groups of children and counting discs or unit rods, utilize elemental groups to form and project configurations representing the numerals 5–9.

(4.8)

**Activities
To Expand
Numeration
Skills**

Although children are capable of learning numeration through 9 without counting, the value of counting in establishing and expanding numeration skills has been overlooked in some contemporary programs. Children may readily learn to count the members of a set by placing them into a one-to-one correspondence with the natural numbers as illustrated in Figure 4.9. As each object is touched or pointed to, the child calls out the appropriate number. It should be emphasized that such an exercise must be done with awareness. This implies that the child is aware he is pairing the term "one" with the first object, "two" with the second object, and so on.

The ability to understand that the words "three" and "five" describe the property of a set containing a certain number of elements evolves

(4.9)

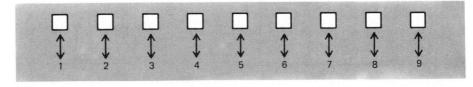

slowly. Meaningful counting experiences are achieved through activities such as taking a hot lunch count, collecting and passing out books and papers, and counting the days remaining before an event. Situations which arise naturally in the classroom provide additional counting experiences. Children count to determine whether there are more girls than boys in the room, or whether one team has enough members, or whether there is enough athletic equipment for the game. Other counting experiences come when teachers expand their instruction so that children are led to count by twos, fives, and tens. As new ways of counting are established, teachers may wish to create a counting chart similar to that shown in Figure 4.10. As children see patterns on the counting chart, they acquire the readiness for more advanced work. Encourage children to seek and discover additional patterns. Such patterns may be recorded by circling the appropriate numerals on pupil facsimiles of larger classroom charts.

```
1  2  3  4  5  6  7  8  9  10
2  4  6  8 10 12 14 16 18  20
3  6  9 12 15 18 21 24 27  30
4  8 12 16 20 24 28 32 36  40
5 10 15 20 25 30 35 40 45  50
 .  .  .  .  .  .  .  .  .   .

 .  .  .  .  .  .  .  .  .   .
 .  .  .  .  .  .  .  .  .   .
10 20 30 40 50 60 70 80 90 100
```

(4.10)

ADDITION AND SUBTRACTION WITH SUMS AND MINUENDS < 9

The operation of addition is commonly represented as the union of disjoint sets—that is, sets with no members in common. A child is led to see the operation of addition as the union of disjoint sets through sustained practice with physical sets of objects. In similar fashion finding the difference between disjoint sets lead naturally to the number operation of substraction. Subtraction is defined in terms of its relationship to addition.

Activities To Develop the Principles of Addition and Subtraction

Perhaps the most useful teacher aid in direct instruction for developing understanding of the process of addition and subtraction is the flannelboard. Through its use, teachers are able to show a physical joining action as in Figure 4.11. For example, it can be shown that by joining two people with the three people already standing in a group, you can form a group of five people. Orally describe the action: "We had three persons standing in

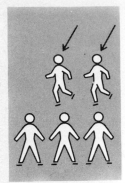

(4.11)

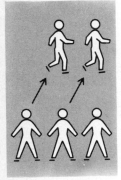

(4.12)

a group, and two more walked over to talk with them. Now how many are in the group?" Immediately following the introduction of each addition fact, the teacher may wish to show a related subtraction fact (see Figure 4.12). Begin by describing the original group of five. Then remove two while commenting that they have walked away. Summarize the action by an oral description: "Five people were talking in a group when two walked away. How many are left in the group?"

Lead children in your class to develop stories involving use of the flannelboard. As one child manipulates the flannel objects, you might ask another to describe the action verbally. Next, you might have a child state some desired action, and have the class manipulate objects on their individual flannelboards. By structuring situations which allow children to manipulate and describe action, you are helping them develop a sound concept of addition and subtraction as joining and separating actions.

Do not limit use of concrete representations to the flannelboard. Children may manipulate multibase arithmetic blocks, sets of erasers, color rods, playground equipment, and even themselves to represent joining and separating actions. As they experience activity, be certain children understand that the operations of addition and subtraction of numbers exist independently of the materials utilized.

Once children begin to see addition and subtraction as joining and separating actions, and when they can correctly manipulate and describe represented actions orally, it is time to describe the action in sentence form. For example, the action described in Figure 4.12 could be written: "Three people with two people equals five people." The separating action could be represented as, "Five people less two people equals three people." Written sentences are more descriptive of the action involved than are sentences using mathematical notation. However, soon the teacher will want to introduce children to the more common mathematical sentences.

An early introduction to number sentences might involve duplication of a familiar situation such as has been described above. After writing the sentence in the familiar all-word way, state that there is an easier way to show what has happened. Instead of writing, "Three people with two people equals five people," show children that $3 + 2 = 5$ describes the action. Emphasize that this sentence only describes the action; it does not tell the particular situation involved. That must be determined from the context of the problem. Illustrate other situations where the sentence $3 + 2 = 5$ correctly describes the action. Do the same with subtractive situations, stressing that the number sentence only tells the action, not the specific instance. A teacher-made activity card that looked like this might be employed for independent work or reinforcement:

Activity Card: Number sentences   Level: Early primary

Note: Provide students with partitioned containers plus five, six, and seven marbles respectively.

1. How many ways can you show 5? Write an addition sentence for each.

2. How many ways can you show 6? Write an addition sentence for each.

3. How many ways can you show 7? Write an addition sentence for each.

4. How many subtraction sentences can you write for Exercise 3?

After the idea of number sentences has been established, let children make up a story to describe the action indicated. For example, write the sentence $3 + 2 = 5$ on the board, and ask the class or small groups of children to make up stories to show this type of activity. Have the groups read their stories to the class. This serves as reinforcement, as well as acquainting them with diverse problem settings calling for the same number sentence. Children who can successfully perform activities of this type demonstrate a real knowledge of addition and subtraction as joining and separating situations. They are not likely to be confused with story problems they may encounter later.

Early Concepts of Place Value

Once a child has established concepts of addition and subtraction as joining and separating actions, and when he has learned to associate specific sets with the appropriate numeral, he is ready to begin systematic study of numbers greater than 9. To do this, some basic concepts of grouping must be developed.

Grouping is critical to our system of numeration. It would be impossible to symbolize and manipulate large numbers in our mathematics without grouping. For this reason, it is important for children to begin grouping objects when they are developing the concept of the numbers zero through nine. Because place value is of such great importance to our numeration system and grouping is fundamental to place value, extensive grouping work is essential for young children.

Chart 4.2 Flow Chart Lesson Plan—Addition Sentences

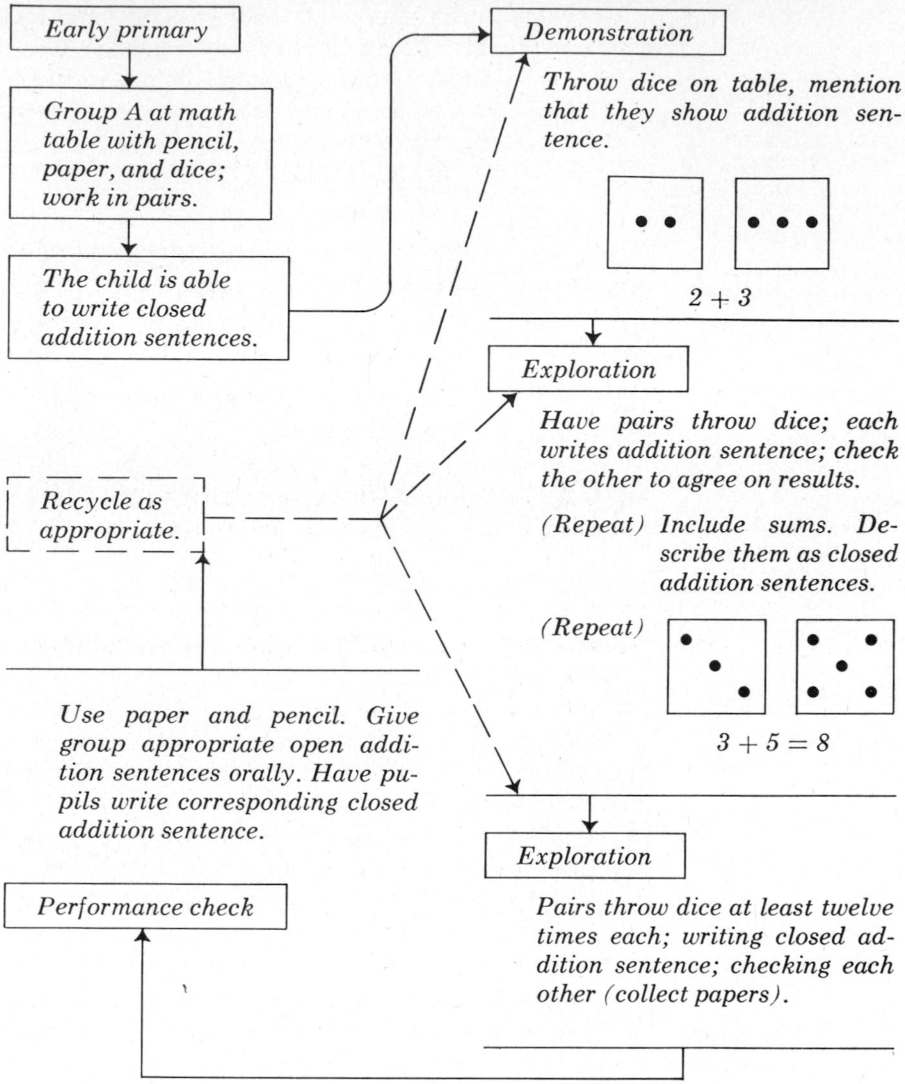

Early primary

Group A at math table with pencil, paper, and dice; work in pairs.

The child is able to write closed addition sentences.

Recycle as appropriate.

Use paper and pencil. Give group appropriate open addition sentences orally. Have pupils write corresponding closed addition sentence.

Performance check

Demonstration

Throw dice on table, mention that they show addition sentence.

2 + 3

Exploration

Have pairs throw dice; each writes addition sentence; check the other to agree on results.

(Repeat) Include sums. Describe them as closed addition sentences.

(Repeat)

3 + 5 = 8

Exploration

Pairs throw dice at least twelve times each; writing closed addition sentence; checking each other (collect papers).

Grouping materials may be proportional or nonproportional. Proportional materials are so constructed that if groupings are by 10, the material for 10 is ten times as large as one, the material for 100 is ten times as large as ten, the material for 1000 is ten times as large as one hundred, and so forth. Nonproportional aids do not show this consistent size distinction (see Figure 4.13). Proportional materials can include multibase arithmetic blocks, color rods, and bean sticks. Nonproportional material aids can be color chips, tongue depressors, and the abacus. Because of the relative size, some teachers have found it advantageous to explore the concept of grouping for larger numbers by utilizing proportional material representing collection points of powers other than 10. Figure 4.14 shows a set of multibase blocks representing a grouping point of three and a set of bean sticks representing a collection point of five.

(4.13)

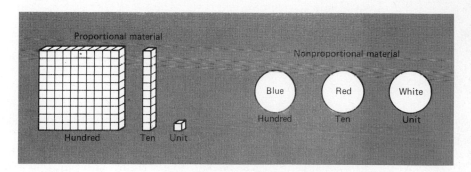

(4.14)

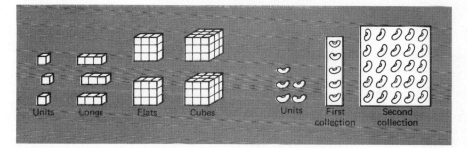

Activities To Develop Concept of Place Value

Since primary-grade children find it easier to understand what they can see and manipulate, the teacher would be well-advised to introduce children to place value concepts by utilizing representatives which involve sets of objects in both the ones and tens places, thus avoiding the need for the empty set. For example, the flannelboard might be utilized by placing a set of twelve objects instead of ten objects in the center of the field. Children would then be asked to tell how many objects were shown (see Figure 4.15). When they had responded with the correct number, the problem of writing a numeral to represent that number could be presented to the children. The base ten system of numeration has symbols only for 0 through 9. Representing larger numbers requires combining digits, prop-

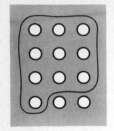

(4.15)

(4.16)

erly called numerals, in a particular way. In this case, a piece of yarn has been used to separate one group of ten from the two ones. Notice how much easier this is to illustrate than if ten items had been selected for the reference model. Children would not have a referent for the ones place. However, in this manner they are able to see that twelve objects may be thought of as one set of ten and one set of two.

Introduce the numeral for twelve by asking the group how they think the numeral for twelve is written. Undoubtedly several children will be able to respond correctly. The mere fact that they may respond properly does not, by itself, indicate understanding. Children must comprehend what is actually embedded in the printed symbol 12. Have them explain what they mean when they write 12. Using the illustration in Figure 4.16, illustrate that 12 may be chosen as 10 + 2, and that the numeral 12 actually may be thought of as an abbreviation for 10 + 2.

Pocket charts are also suited to the teaching of place value (see Figure 4.17). These charts may be used to show the relationship of ones to tens, hundreds, thousands, and so on. Children need experiences to develop the understanding that each pocket has a value that is exactly ten times the value of the pocket on its right. They must realize that one marker from the tens pocket equals ten markers from the ones pocket, and that it would take ten markers in the tens pocket to equal one of the hundreds markers, and so forth. To help them gain such understanding, the teacher may wish to have children place markers to demonstrate a written numeral. Later, they may write numerals to describe what the teacher has illustrated with the pockets.

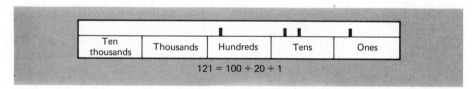

(4.17)

When arranged in groups of four or five, children in one group enjoy contriving situations for other groups to solve. For example, one group may present a series of manipulations which the other groups then describe with a numeral. Conversely, one group may write numerals for a second group to represent by manipulation.

The position value system of notation is based on the process of grouping, on grouping these groups, on grouping these larger groups, and so forth. Now to understand fully the idea of grouping in powers of base, which is what we really do, children must have concrete experiences involving powers of decimal notation. Bundles of sticks are often used in

Chart 4.3   Flow Chart Lesson Plan — Place Value

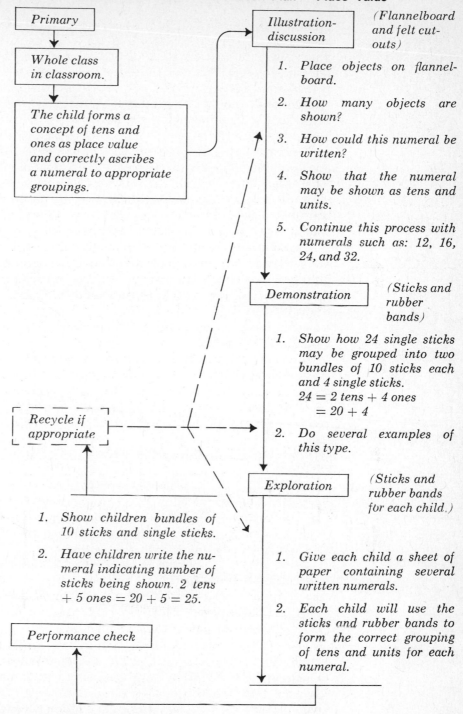

Primary

Whole class in classroom.

The child forms a concept of tens and ones as place value and correctly ascribes a numeral to appropriate groupings.

Illustration-discussion   (Flannelboard and felt cut-outs)

1. Place objects on flannel-board.

2. How many objects are shown?

3. How could this numeral be written?

4. Show that the numeral may be shown as tens and units.

5. Continue this process with numerals such as: 12, 16, 24, and 32.

Demonstration   (Sticks and rubber bands)

1. Show how 24 single sticks may be grouped into two bundles of 10 sticks each and 4 single sticks.
24 = 2 tens + 4 ones
    = 20 + 4

2. Do several examples of this type.

Recycle if appropriate

1. Show children bundles of 10 sticks and single sticks.

2. Have children write the numeral indicating number of sticks being shown. 2 tens + 5 ones = 20 + 5 = 25.

Exploration   (Sticks and rubber bands for each child.)

1. Give each child a sheet of paper containing several written numerals.

2. Each child will use the sticks and rubber bands to form the correct grouping of tens and units for each numeral.

Performance check

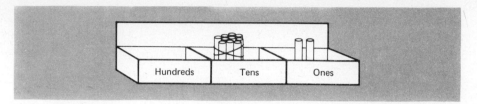

(4.18)

8
Hundreds

4
Tens

5
Ones

(4.19)

conjunction with a place value "box" (see Figure 4.18), so that children are able to comprehend differences in relative amounts and make the exchanges which are involved in the powers of our decimal system. When children have accumulated ten sticks, they are held together with a rubber band and placed in the tens box, where they represent one bundle of ten. It is equally effective to exchange the bundle of ten ones for a larger single "stick" and to place the latter in the tens "box." When ten bundles of ten are gathered, they are in turn bound together and put into the hundreds "box," where they represent one bundle of 100, and so on. Through activities of this nature, children are led to compare relative values of the digits.

To check whether or not pupils have attained a clear concept of place value, pass out cards to each student so that every child has a card similar to the ones shown in Figure 4.19. Write a numeral on the board and ask the members of the class to come forward if they have the appropriate representation of the numeral that has been written. Thus, if the numeral is 386, children with cards reading three hundreds, eight tens, and six ones would be expected to step forward. An integral part of this experience is that children arrange themselves in an order which correctly represents the numeral that was written.

ADDITION AND SUBTRACTION WITH SUMS AND MINUENDS > 9

Introduction of addition facts with sums above 9 requires concrete demonstration and manipulation. Just as students who study place value learn that ten ones may be grouped to form one ten, so too must students learn that adding requires regrouping if a combined quantity is to exceed ten. Consider the following quantitative setting:

> If seven rabbits are eating cabbage in a garden, and five rabbits hop over to join them, how many rabbits are now eating cabbage in the garden? Use the flannelboard to demonstrate the action of the rabbits (see Figure 4.20).

A set has now been formed which is five larger than the original set. In order to facilitate description of the new set, ten of the rabbits must be involved in a regrouping to form one set of ten. Thus, three rabbits may be added to the set of seven to form one set of ten. Two rabbits remain from the original set of five. There is now a set of 10 + 2 or twelve rabbits in the field. To solve this problem we had to employ the associative property of addition; we first grouped the seven with three to form ten, and subse-

(4.20)

quently added two to form twelve. In its applications in elementary-school mathematics, it is appropriate to think of the associative property as the grouping property. This property permits us to group or associate addends in the manner most appropriate to the quantitative setting. Subsequently, you will observe the great utility of the associative property in unit column addition as well as addition with two- and three-digit addends.

The ability to group to 10 is important in both addition and subtraction. Because of its importance, many teachers spend time working with children to assist them in this skill. One device which is used might simply be called a "group to 10" card. A teacher or child holds up a card displaying a numeral and asks the group how many more ones are needed to form 10. A variation of this procedure is to show one card with a numeral on it; then, as the group watches, turn over another stack of cards one at a time and ask, "Does this form 10?" "How many are left over?" Other oral activity may include inquiries like "Eight plus four equals ten plus what number?" "Three plus seven equals ten plus what number?" and so forth.

The abacus is a very useful physical device for representing addition concretely. Children must regroup to show numbers above 9 and for this reason an abacus has been popular when introducing children to sums greater than 9. The sum $8 + 4$ may be obtained and verified with an abacus by combining two beads with eight beads to form ten beads in the units column (see Figure 4.21). The ten beads that have been pushed forward are then exchanged for one bead in the tens column. That is, ten units beads are brought back to the base of the units column and a bead is pushed forward to the tens column. Finally, two beads are pushed forward in the units column and the abacus now records the sum 12. An abacus of the type illustrated in Figure 4.21 can be used with equal facility to solve and verify subtractions by making the regrouping exchange in reverse. Consider $12 - 9 = \square$. Begin by putting 12 "in" the abacus. That is, one tens bead and two units beads are moved forward in the appropriate columns. Now decomposition is begun by moving the two units beads back to the base. Since no units beads remain, a regroup-

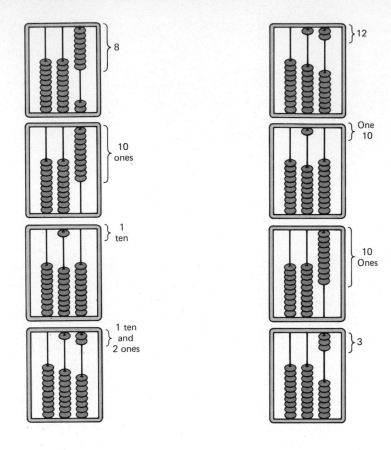

(4.21)

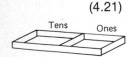

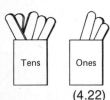

(4.22)

ing is necessary. To accomplish this, the tens bead is moved back to the base of the tens column (exchanged) and all ten units beads are moved to the top of the units column. The decomposition may subsequently be completed resulting in the difference, 3.

The type of abacus shown in Figure 4.21 has a disadvantage in that it is not "open-ended." In early work with primary children, simplified teacher-made devices may serve equally well. Those pictured in Figure 4.22 simply utilize counting discs, bottle caps, beans, or carrom rings. With these open-ended devices children can freely experience the concrete representation of regrouping required in addition.

AUTOMATIC MASTERY OF THE ADDITION AND SUBTRACTION FACTS

There are one hundred basic addition facts and one hundred subtraction facts. The one hundred addition facts are determined by combinations involving the digits 0 through 9, which are used in decimal numeration. Each basic addition fact has a subtraction combination which may be paired with it. Thus, the addition fact $9 + 4 = 13$ may be paired with the subtraction fact $13 - 4 = 9$. The one hundred basic addition and subtraction facts are commonly shown through the use of charts. Table 4.1 is an addition fact chart. The numerals appearing outside the heavy black lines are the addends, while the sums are represented within the squares in the interior of the chart. The addition chart thus represents a many-to-one mapping, whereby two addends (ordered pairs) are placed in a specific space through the operation of addition. This is represented mathematically by $(8, 6) \underset{\rightarrow}{+} 14$.

TABLE 4.1 Basic Addition Facts

						First Addend					
	+	0	1	2	3	4	5	6	7	8	9
	0	0	1	2	3	4	5	6	7	8	9
	1	1	2	3	4	5	6	7	8	9	10
	2	2	3	4	5	6	7	8	9	10	11
	3	3	4	5	6	7	8	9	10	11	12
Second Addend	4	4	5	6	7	8	9	10	11	12	13
	5	5	6	7	8	9	10	11	12	13	14
	6	6	7	8	9	10	11	12	13	14	15
	7	7	8	9	10	11	12	13	14	15	16
	8	8	9	10	11	12	13	14	15	16	17
	9	9	10	11	12	13	14	15	16	17	18

TABLE 4.2 Basic Subtraction Facts

						Subtrahend						*Minuend Represented Within the Squares of the Interior*
	−	0	1	2	3	4	5	6	7	8	9	
	0	0	1	2	3	4	5	6	7	8	9	
	1	1	2	3	4	5	6	7	8	9	10	
	2	2	3	4	5	6	7	8	9	10	11	
	3	3	4	5	6	7	8	9	10	11	12	
Remainder (or Difference)	4	4	5	6	7	8	9	10	11	12	13	
	5	5	6	7	8	9	10	11	12	13	14	
	6	6	7	8	9	10	11	12	13	14	15	
	7	7	8	9	10	11	12	13	14	15	16	
	8	8	9	10	11	12	13	14	15	16	17	
	9	9	10	11	12	13	14	15	16	17	18	

The subtraction facts are represented on a similar chart (see Table 4.2). If one considers the relationship of subtraction to addition, it is easy to note the relationship between the two charts. Whereas sums on the first chart were conceived as the mapping of two addends to form a sum—that is, $8 + 5 = 13$—subtraction may be thought of as the undoing of addition. Beginning with the sum (minuend in the interior of the chart), remove one of the addends (subtrahend at the top of the chart). The remaining addend is the difference (remainder). Thus $13 - 5 = 8$, the inverse of addition, because $8 + 5 = 13$.

Modern programs in mathematics do not, at first glance, appear to place much stress on learning addition and subtraction facts. Initial appearances can be deceiving, because what is actually missing is the heavy emphasis on isolated numer fact drill characteristic of traditional programs. Rather than giving children numerous examples to compute during each arithmetic period, today's teacher strives to incorporate number fact drills into other meaningful activities.

Using Addition Properties To Help Learn Addition Facts

The one hundred basic addition facts may be reduced considerably through application of some properties of addition. Perhaps the most helpful addition property is the order property—addition is commutative. That is, the order of the addends does not affect the sum. This property is often represented by the sentence "$a + b = b + a$." For example, $4 + 5 = 5 + 4$. If children understand and use this property they are able to reduce the one hundred basic addition facts by almost one-half. Children thus have only fifty-five basic facts to learn rather than one hundred. To help children discover the commutative property of addition, original activity cards can be used.

The number of independent facts which must be learned may be reduced still further by helping children use their knowledge of the identity element of addition—sometimes called the "zero property of addition." Simply stated, adding 0 to any number leaves the quantity unchanged. Once children know this, they have reduced the independent facts left to learn by ten.

Through the use of these properties children have now reduced the number of independent addition facts to be learned from one hundred to forty-five.

Facilitating Mastery of the Addition and Subtraction Facts

Perhaps the most widely used materials for practicing the addition and subtraction facts are sets of flash cards. These cards, including the one hundred number facts (see Figure 4.23), are flashed quickly by the teacher or by a student, and children respond to each fact in turn as it is shown. Flash cards have several advantages over repetitious testing of number facts by other means. They lend themselves well to small groups or individual work with students, whereby one child flashes the cards while others answer. Also, the use of flash cards allows the teacher, or child instructor, to remove those cards which do not cause trouble, thus giving

Activity Card: Commutative property   Level: Primary

Use the set of weights and balances to help you match each addition sentence under A with the addition sentence under B which correctly completes the equation.

A	=	B
3 + 5		9 + 4
7 + 1		5 + 3
6 + 2		5 + 6
4 + 9		1 + 7
6 + 5		2 + 6

1. What did you discover?
2. Are there other addition equations which also balance?
3. Describe how your discovery helps you in mastering the basic addition facts.

children more practice on difficult examples. This is a real advantage, for most children have much more difficulty with combinations involving 7, 8, and 9 than the other facts.

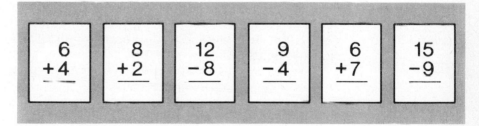

(4.23)

A square number matrix similar to a fact chart may also be a useful device for helping children master the addition facts. Simply create a number matrix as shown in Table 4.3, recognizing that all boxes would be empty on the matrix. Children may be asked to find the sum for a particular empty box. At first an empty box may be indicated by pointing at it, or by having a child point at it, and the other children may supply the appropriate sum. Simultaneously, a much more creative activity may be to have the children describe the location of the particular box they want through the use of number pairs. Using the base as the X axis and the vertical boundary as the Y axis, have a child indicate a desired box by listing a number pair, the X axis first, and the Y axis second. Other children may record the sum. Conversely, a child may give a sum and other children supply the number pair. Such activity provides children with early experience with ordered pairs, an opportunity to discover number patterns, and an excellent illustration of the commutative principle. Some numerals were placed in selected boxes in Table 4.3 so that the reader may observe these important notions.

TABLE 4.3   **Number Matrix**

Y	1	2	3	4	5	6	7	8	9
9	10	11	12	13					18
8		10						16	
7	8	9	10	11	12	13	14		
6		8				12	13		
5		7			10	11	12		
4		6		8	9		11	12	13
3		5	6	7			10		
2		4	5	6	7	8	9		
1		3					8		
X	1	2	3	4	5	6	7	8	9

After a number matrix has been filled with sums, it has additional utility for firmly establishing the relationship between addition and subtraction, and, as a consequence, mastery of the subtraction facts. An excellent activity with a small group of children and a plainly visible matrix of sums begins, "I am thinking of a number pair whose sum is 13 and whose difference is 5." Again, returning to Table 4.3 the reader can observe the number pair (9, 4) as the most appropriate response. Can you use the matrix to verify the difference 5?

Other types of number-fact practice may be found in the materials normally associated with common games. For example, by a minor modification of an inexpensive spinner children can construct a valuable and interesting practice game (see Figure 4.24). A number is selected as being one of the addends, and the pointer is then spun to determine the other addend. A variation of this practice may be gotten by using two spinners. Spinning one pointer locates the first addend; spinning the second pointer identifies the second addend. Two children may make a game of this by spinning their pointers simultaneously. When the pointers stop, each child tries to be first in naming the sum.

Another game can be made with inexpensive materials such as

(4.24)

wooden cubes with numerals painted on them. Children roll the cubes and respond to the number fact represented. These cubes are quite flexible since they allow the child to use several addends merely by increasing the number of cubes.

Activity cards are useful as an independent procedure for number-fact practice. They can also incorporate elements of problem solving. An illustrative model that will intrigue children has been provided.

Activity Card: Finding sums   Level: Primary

1. Complete the magic triangle using:

   (a.)   one digit numerals (1, 2, 3, 4, 5, 6, 7, 8, 9)

   (b.)   no numeral more than once so all sides equal 17.

2. Supply the missing digits in each table:

(a.)

+ 3		
	2	
7	12	

(b.)

+		3	7
8	9		
		7	
4		6	
			9

3. Make a magic circle by filling in each ◯ with a different numeral, using each numeral only once. Any three numerals on a straight line should have the same sum.

The ideas suggested here are only representative of the many ways in which to practice for mastery of addition facts. Use creativity to design interesting and useful materials for children, and, whenever possible, allow children to construct and use materials of their own; they thus remain constantly and actively involved in learning mathematics.

The Number Line In the late second or early third grade, after children have developed a basic understanding of the operations of addition and subtraction through the use of the union and separation of disjoint sets, the teacher may wish to extend understanding through the use of the number line. The number line is based on units of length (Figure 4.25). "Three" is more than just the number marking an equal distance between 2 and 4. Three describes the distance from the starting point, or 0, to the point marked 3, based on an arbitrary unit of measure. This can be a difficult concept for young children for two reasons. First, children are accustomed to associating numbers with groups of discrete objects. The number line is based on length rather than a number of objects. Second, many youngsters are unable to conserve length until at least age seven. It is difficult for them to understand that the distance from 0 to 2 on a number line is twice as long as the distance from 0 to 1.

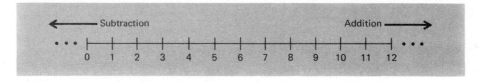

(4.25)

Early difficulty with the number line can be avoided and full understanding will develop through time and use. Following are some helpful, developmental activities.

1. Make a walk-on number line on the floor. Use masking tape. Mark uniform intervals the size of a normal step (child's) and have children take turns walking a given number of steps starting from zero.
2. Make desk-sized number lines for each child containing the numerals 0–20. Laminate and attach to desks so that children may mark on them with grease pencils. Use to count and verify.
3. Provide children with a small cricket or frog, and use the desk top number lines frequently to demonstrate number as "hops" on a line, to reinforce the notion of counting spaces rather than points.

Whatever setting is chosen for the introduction of the number line and its subsequent use, teachers must strongly consider the intellectual development of each child. When children are sufficiently mature to profit from the use of the number line, they will find it an important aid to their understanding and mastery of basic facts. Figure 4.26 portrays some appropriate variation, properly drawn, for use as an aid during study of addition and subtraction.

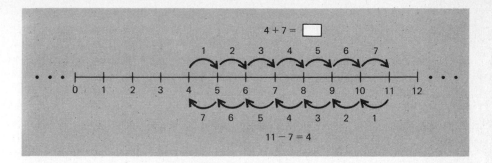

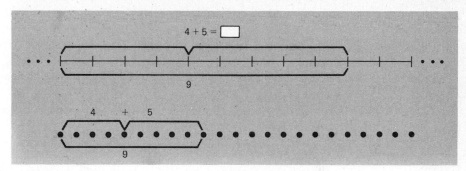

(4.26)

Using Expanded Addition Algorithms

Merely presenting an algorithm to children without helping them to see a need for it is not likely to be effective. Instead, children can be provided with a need to develop and use algorithms through carefully structured experiences in problem situations utilizing increasingly greater quantities of concrete materials. Pose problems such as the following:

"A boy has twelve blocks, and he finds fifteen more. How many blocks does he have in all?"

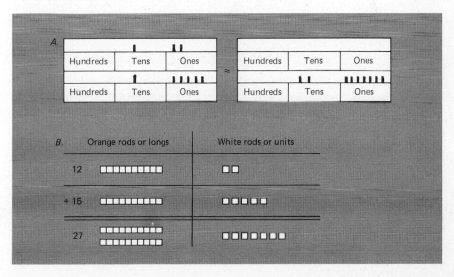

(4.27)

Using this problem setting, examine with the children both the vertical and horizontal addition algorithm. As you determine the function of the algorithm, demonstrate the concomitant number action through some concrete aid so that the children may review the number action at the same time as they study the algorithm. Place value pockets are extremely useful at this point, as are multibase arithmetic blocks or color rods. Notice that pupil manipulations are required to show the combining action in a concrete fashion. You may also observe from computation of the vertical algorithm that digits in the tens column are summed first, followed by the addition of the ones. The partial sums are then combined. When children are comfortable with adding the tens column first, they may be encouraged to add using the units place first. Of course, the major advantage of employing the horizontal algorithm is to gain a graphic portrayal of the "number action" in addition when regrouping is required. The horizontal algorithm, termed expanded notation in commercially prepared pupil materials, takes full advantage of the associative property for addition.

$$\begin{array}{r} 12 \\ +15 \\ \hline \end{array} \qquad 12 + 15 = \square$$

(4.28)

$$\begin{array}{r} 12 \\ +15 \\ \hline 20 \ (2 \text{ tens}) \\ 7 \ (7 \text{ ones}) \\ \hline 27 \end{array} \qquad \begin{array}{rl} 12 + 15 &= (10 + 2) + (10 + 5) \\ &= (10 + 10) + (2 + 5) \\ &= 20 + 7 \\ &= 27 \end{array}$$

When introduced to algorithms in this fashion, children see an algorithm as a pattern that accommodates computation. They understand that an algorithm is merely a convenience that permits us to record our thinking, and they learn that there is no special meaning inherent in the algorithm.

Using Expanded Subtraction Algorithms

For most children the algorithms for subtraction seem more difficult to manage than addition algorithms. This may be because subtraction often requires that quantities be regrouped in reverse, so that digits originally representing larger place values are used to increase the quantity of successively lower column values. Also, the subtraction algorithm is somewhat less flexible than the addition algorithm.

Because the subtraction algorithm is difficult for children, you must give children many opportunities to manipulate materials, to search for patterns, and to discuss the process. For example, examine the subtraction algorithm embedded in the following quantitative setting:

"Julie and Jeff had a total of 274 marbles to play with. Julie owned 36 of them. How many marbles did Jeff own?"

The algorithm may be written in vertical or horizontal form and the several ways to think about a solution are provided in Figure 4.29.

A. Decomposition (borrowing)

$$\begin{array}{r} 6\ 14 \\ 2\cancel{7}\ \cancel{4} \\ -3\ \ 6 \\ \hline 23\ \ 8 \end{array}$$

B. Compensation (adding like amounts to both terms before computation leaves the difference unchanged)

$$\begin{array}{rcr} 274 & & 278 \\ -36 & = & -40 \\ \hline & & 238 \end{array}$$

(4.29)

C. Expanded notation

$$\begin{aligned} 274 - 36 \ &= (200 + 70 + 4) - (30 + 6) \\ &= (200 + 60 + 14) - (30 + 6) \\ &= (200) + (60 - 30) + (14 - 6) \\ &= 100 + 30 + 8 \\ &= 238 \end{aligned}$$

In Figure 4.29 children are confronted with the problem of subtracting six ones from four ones, a task they understand is impossible with the set of numbers they have been given. Place value pockets are ideally suited to represent the needed action. A variation of the simple place value pocket to show subtraction more clearly might be used (see Figure 4.30). The minuend is represented by the markers in the upper pockets, while the subtrahend is represented in the pockets below. Children are able to see the regrouping as they remove a marker in the tens pocket and replace it with ten ones in the units pocket. A units column difference is then obtained by using a one-to-one correspondence comparison, moving one marker from the minuend for each marker in the subtrahend. The difference is then represented by the remaining markers. When available, commercially prepared color rods and multibase arithmetic blocks are also excellent materials to use for concrete illustration of the regrouping required in subtraction. The latter are especially appropriate with minuends less than 100.

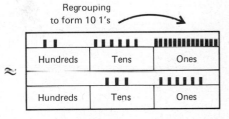

(4.30)

The expanded notation form of algorithm would appear to have certain advantages so far as rationalizing the "number action" is concerned. At the same time quick mental responses of the nonpaper and pencil variety can be given by children who gain facility with the compensation form of the algorithm, since it negates the necessity of regrouping. It should be clearly recognized that the usual decomposition form represents the most efficient notational way and thus illustrates the "number action" least appropriately.

SUMMARY The foundation experiences proposed in this chapter are exceedingly important to the mathematical future of children. Formulation of mathematical abstraction is a developmental process, the essence of which is concept formation, and both take place over a relatively long period of time. The most fundamental principles implicit in the recommendations include:

1. Learning proceeds from concrete to abstract.
2. Learning is most effective when based on experience.
3. Learning requires active participation of the learner.

Activities related to explorations with sets can introduce the idea of number as well as the essential characteristics of the operation of addition. Skill in addition and subtraction of whole numbers is highly dependent upon proficiency with basic combination. Having children work with concrete objects on the cardinal numbers 0–9 before working with groups of ten or more will facilitate an orderly and logical mastery of the basic facts as well as enhance later mastery of place value concepts.

Understanding properties in relation to operations helps children develop independence in solving quantitative situations and provides an appreciation of mathematics as a unified system of ideas. This can be vividly portrayed by a careful analysis of the algorithm employed for comptations with two- and three-digit numbers. However, since electronic means for calculation are increasingly available to children in life outside school, the greater emphasis is on flexibility and understanding of processes.

ACTIVITIES, PROJECTS, A POINT OF VIEW

1. Prepare a five- to eight-minute report for presentation to your class. The topic is use of manipulatives. The chief information source can be Robert Reys' article entitled, "Considerations for Teachers Using Manipulative Materials," *Arithmetic Teacher*, Vol. 18 (December 1971).

2. Write a behavioral objective for each of the following concepts that would be suitable for primary children at the level of your choice.

   a. set membership   d. ordinal number
   b. set equivalence   e. counting
   c. cardinal number   f. place value

3. The position of elements in a linear collection is specified by ordinal number—that is, first, second, third, and so on. Design an activity card for the purpose of helping children learn ordinal number concepts.

4. Prepare an activity card that utilizes color rods as a concrete aid to develop the addition property involved in $8 + 6 = 10 + 4$.

5. Write a nonmathematical illustration that demonstrates the associative principle. Prepare a nonmathematical illustration where it does not hold.

6. Make a list of occasions in daily life which naturally embody one-to-one correspondence. Do the same for the idea of set.

7. Obtain a pupil's text as the content source and design a flow chart lesson to teach a small group of children the concepts less than, equal to, and greater than. The plan should utilize one of the concrete aids mentioned in Chapter 4.

8. Design some simple model of an "open-ended" abacus to teach the basic facts whose sums are greater than 10.

9. Criticize or support this statement: It is neither possible nor necessary to teach primary children the *meaning* of the operations of addition and subtraction.

10. What is the basis of your agreement or disagreement with the following statement?

a. Children should learn to use counting discs, multibase arithmetic blocks, or color rods before using an abacus.

b. There is no real advantage to a pupil who perceives addition and subtraction as inverse operations.

c. The schools should supply a set of hand-held calculators to each primary classroom to be used as an aid in learning the basic facts.

d. Teachers would do well to be wary of too heavy reliance on concrete referents.

SELECTED READINGS

Ashlock, R. B. "Teaching the Basic Facts: Three Classes of Activities." *Arithmetic Teacher*, Vol. 18 (October 1971), pp. 359–364.

Bauer, G. R., and George, Linda. *Helping Children Learn Mathematics: A Competency-Based Laboratory Approach.* Menlo Park, Calif.: Cummings Publishing Company, Inc., 1976, Chapters 6, 7, and 8.

Goutard, M. *Experiences with Numbers in Color.* New Rochelle, N.Y.: Cuisenaire Company of America, Inc., 1974, Chapters 1–5.

Green, G. F., Jr. *Elementary School Mathematics: Activities and Materials.* Lexington, Massachusetts: D. C. Heath and Company, 1974, Chapters IV and V.

Heddens, James W. *Today's Mathematics.* Chicago: Science Research Associates, Inc., 1974, Units 2, 3, 6, and 7.

Hoppe, Ruth C. "Research on a 'New' Method of Subtraction." *Arithmetic Teacher*, Vol. 18 (October 1971), pp. 359–364.

Hubbard, Sherry P., and Ashlock, R. B. "Using Flowcharts with First Graders." *Arithmetic Teacher*, Vol. 24 (January 1977), pp. 23–28.

Marks, J. L.; Purdy, C. R.; Kenney, L. B.; and Hiatt, Arthur. *Teaching Elementary School Mathematics for Understanding.* New York: McGraw-Hill Book Company, 1975, Chapter IV.

Reisman, Fredricka K. *Diagnostic Teaching of Elementary School Mathematics Methods and Content.* Chicago: Rand McNally College Publishing Company, 1977, Chapters 8, 9, 10, 13, and 14.

Reys, Robert. "Considerations for Teachers Using Manipulative Materials." *The Arithmetic Teacher*, Vol. 18 (December 1971), pp. 551–558.

Rogers, Barbara Dillard. "The Basic Fact Bug." *Arithmetic Teacher,* Vol. 23 (April 1976), pp. 265–266.

White, Philip; Brownstein, B.; and Wagner, V. "Initiating Task Card Activities with Teachers." *Arthmetic Teacher,* Vol. 22 (April 1975), pp. 274–276.

CHAPTER 5

Extending Foundation Experiences through Multiplication, Division, and Rational Numbers

PERSPECTIVE   Merely presenting mathematical content to children is not sufficient to insure good teaching. Children need a meaningful model to see and work with. Mathematical models take many forms. For example, multiplication may be shown as constructions to form arrays, equidistant moves on a number line, or as Cartesian products of even repeated addition with equal addends. Wisely selected, mathematical models help children to understand the mathematical notion being taught, how the model relates to real-life situations, and how it can be used to advance their knowledge of other mathematical topics.

Mathematical models serve another purpose—involving the child. Children are unlikely to be positively involved if their tasks consist of endless computing. However, they can become quite eager to search for and describe rectangular arrays existing in the environment. They might also be excited when they find that they can use the model for ratio and proportion to determine the best purchase among choices for candy or toys.

As a result of studying Chapter 5 you should be able to:

> **1.** Describe an instructional strategy for teaching multiplication as repeated addition, moves on a number line, array constructions, or as a Cartesian product.

2. Write a flow-charted lesson plan for teaching division as repeated subtraction, hops on number lines, or array constructions.
3. Name some materials appropriate for developing children's readiness for fractions and describe their use.
4. Prepare a sequence of activity cards to enable children to discover a process for generating a set of equivalent fractions.
5. Describe an instructional sequence to involve children actively in learning how to use a ratio and proportion algorithm.

PRESENTING MULTIPLICATION

Multiplication, like addition, is undefined. It is possible to view the operation in a number of ways. For example, multiplication may be shown as the repeated addition of equivalent subsets. Multiplication may also be viewed as a Cartesian product or as skips on a number line, to name just two more. Each view has some utility for the classroom, and a particular child may favor one while rejecting another. Accept this—for each child should be given the opportunity to accommodate the process of multiplication into his own cognitive structure. Jerome Bruner states:

> In general, material that is organized in terms of a person's own interests and cognitive structures is material that has the best chance of being accessible in memory. . . . thus the very attitudes and activities that characterize figuring out or discovering things for oneself also seem to have the effect of conserving memory.[1]

Readiness for Multiplication

A child's understanding of multiplication depends on understanding correspondence or multiequivalence. Children must understand the invariance of each addend so that if $a = b$ and $b = c$, then $a = c$ (an illustration of the transitive property of equality). To study children's ability to understand multiequivalence, Piaget used two sets of ten flowers and a set of ten vases.[2] Each child was asked to put one flower from set x into each vase in set z (see Figure 5.1). Piaget then removed the flowers from the vases and put them into one large vase as shown in Figure 5.2. Next he placed one flower from set y into each of the ten vases of set z. He then removed these flowers from the vases and placed them into a differently shaped large vase. Piaget then asked the child to tell whether the number of flowers in vase x was the same as the number of flowers in vase y. He found that it is not until about age six that a child correctly states that $x = y$. Before that, his logic is distorted by his perception; and

---

[1]Jerome Bruner, *On Knowing Essays for the Left Hand* (New York: Atheneum Publishers, 1967), p. 96.
[2]Jean Piaget, *The Child's Concept of Number* (London: Routledge and Kegan Paul, Ltd., 1964), p. 208.

he most likely chooses vase y as containing more flowers. He does not realize that if set x = set y and set y = set z then x = z.

Set x   Set y   Set z

(5.1)

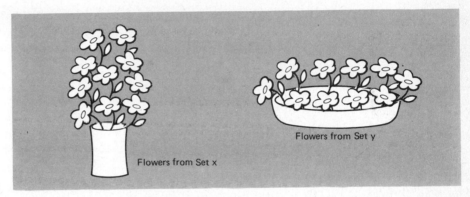

Flowers from Set x

Flowers from Set y

(5.2)

When the children had attained the ability to understand multiequivalence, Piaget determined whether they were also able to state other equivalence relations of flowers to vases as, for example, two to one. At about age six or seven most children understand that such a relationship of flowers to vases is $2 \times n$, and that additional sets may be described as $3 \times n$ (10 + 10 + 10), and so on. When this occurs, children are ready to understand the multiequivalence relations of multiplication. Their formal instruction in multiplication can begin.

Multiplication as Repeated Additions

Multiplication may be interpreted as a means whereby equal addends are summed a specified number of times without performing several additions. Children who have a sound background in addition and who have been encouraged to manipulate objects may be led to discover the need for multiplication. For example, divide children into groups of four or five. Provide each group with a box of blocks and ask the children to take twelve blocks from the box and place them on the table. Then use an activity card such as the following:

Activity Card: Introduction to multiplication   Level: Primary

Have children cut out twenty squares and place them on their desk.

1.   Place fourteen squares on your table, and put the remaining into an envelope. Now, arrange the squares to show as many addition combinations as you can. Stop when you reach ten combinations. Write an addition sentence for each.

2.   Using sets of equal size, find as many combinations as you can. Write an addition sentence for each.

3.   Now, add two more squares to your pile. Again, using sets of equal size, find as many combinations as you can. Write an addition sentence for each.

4.   Add another square to your pile. Again, using sets of equal size, find as many combinations as you can. Write an addition sentence for each. How many sentences did you find? Try again using thirteen squares. What did you find?

5.   Using the squares, find number sentences for two through twenty. How many more unusual numbers did you find?

2 sets of 3 = 6 objects

(5.3)

Through manipulation of physical objects, children are able to discover for themselves many patterns of multiplication. As the teacher, your role is to provide an opportunity for children to discover solutions. Accept responses, but do not hesitate to suggest alternatives for examination. Always try to open a new avenue of exploration which might lead a child to discover the concept or principle for himself. Left to their own initiatives, children will quickly discover patterns for themselves. Children who have been encouraged to make discoveries will gain the background needed to understand properties such as the commutative property and its usefulness, the identity element, and the zero property, for they will already have used them in their work.

Introduction of the operation of multiplication as equal additions might involve the flannelboard (see Figure 5.3). On the flannelboard, arrange several sets of objects of equal number at random. Ask children to arrange these objects into sets according to some described characteristic, as, for example, color. When done, ask them to write a number sentence and demonstrate how to find the sum. Be certain that children show the number of sets that are formed and the cardinality of each set. If children have individual flannelboards, these activities can be performed at their desks. One activity that might be suggested is to have each child find as many ways as possible of showing a given number by using sets with an equal number of objects. Ask what would happen if another set of equal number were available. For example, if a child shows 8 as 4 + 4, another set of 4 would increase the sum to 12, another to 16, and so forth. Continue with questions of this nature, either verbally presented or on activity cards, until children perceive the pattern. They may record their findings by use of the chart form shown in Figure 5.4.

Sets of 2	Sets of 3	Sets of 4
2 + 2 = 4	3 + 3 = 6	4 + 4 = 8
2 + 2 + 2 = 6	3 + 3 + 3 = 9	4 + 4 + 4 = 12
2 + 2 + 2 + 2 = 8	3 + 3 + 3 + 3 = 12	4 + 4 + 4 + 4 = 16

Sets of 5	Sets of 6
5 + 5 = 10	6 + 6 = 12
5 + 5 + 5 = 15	6 + 6 + 6 = 18
5 + 5 + 5 + 5 = 20	6 + 6 + 6 + 6 = 24

(5.4)

Multiplication as an Array

Children are often helped to perceive relationships among sets of objects when these objects are arranged in some systematic fashion. Because of this, mathematics teachers frequently align objects or drawings to form a rectangular array.

Children determine that four rows of three objects equal twelve objects (part A of Figure 5.5). They see that three rows of four objects also equals twelve objects (part B). Initially, most children either add or count to determine the product. Counting behavior may be kept to a minimum if the first examples employ a limited number of sets, and if each set contains objects whose numerousness may be perceived at a glance. Another activity card might be a useful aid to instruction.

A	B
○ ○ ○ 3	○ ○ ○ ○ 4
○ ○ ○ 3	○ ○ ○ ○ 4
○ ○ ○ 3	○ ○ ○ ○ + 4
○ ○ ○ + 3	———— 12
———— 12	

(5.5)   4 sets of 3 = 12   3 sets of 4 = 12

Activity Card: Beginning multiplication   Level: Primary

1. Write addition sentences to find a sum for each of the arrangements shown below.

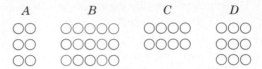

2. The array shown under *A* may be described as three sets of 2. How could you describe the other arrays?

3. Write a multiplication sentence for each array.

Multiplication as a Cartesian Product

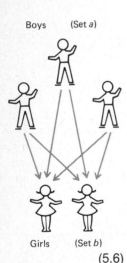

Boys   (Set *a*)

Girls   (Set *b*)

(5.6)

The Cartesian product of two sets is the number of ordered pairs formed when members of one set are joined with members of the other set. Set *A* in Figure 5.6 represents a set of boys and *B* a set of girls. The Cartesian product of the two sets, read *A* cross *B*, is found by forming as many ordered combinations of set *A* with *B* as possible. In this example there are six possible combinations, and the Cartesian product of the two sets is shown as 6.

Piaget[3] found that most children develop the ability to classify two dimensions (that is, blouses of brown and red and dresses of orange and green) by the age of seven or eight. Thus, the use of the Cartesian product to introduce multiplication appears to be feasible. However, Piaget found that seven-to-eight-year-old children were confused when a third attribute was added. Even by the age of eight to nine, only about 60 percent of the children could successfully classify three attributes. From this research it appears that introductory work with the Cartesian product should be kept basic. Later, extension to a third attribute can be given as enrichment.

Appropriate activities with the Cartesian product can be performed by having three boys stand across from two girls. Pieces of colored yarn can then be used to join the members of one set with the members of another. Someone from outside the set can be assigned the task of counting the number of pairings.

[3]Bärbel Inhelder and Jean Piaget, *The Early Growth of Logic in the Child* (New York: W. W. Norton & Co., Inc., 1969), p. 151.

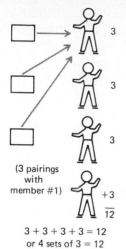

(3 pairings
with
member #1)

+3

12

3 + 3 + 3 + 3 = 12
or 4 sets of 3 = 12

(5.8)

A further extension of the idea of ordering pairings may be obtained by giving children two sets of objects, such as two differently colored blocks and three toy trucks of a different shape (see Figure 5.7). An activity card can give such directions as: "Find as many combinations as you can where one truck carries one block. Record your answer. How many combinations did you have in all?" Other objects involving other numbers might then be used to extend children's understanding to more complex combinations. Urge children to search for a pattern to make their work easier. They should discover that each item in set A of Figure 5.7 is matched with one item in set B. The product can be computed by finding the number of pairings between the sets (see Figure 5.8).

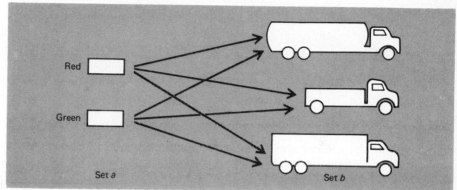

Red

Green

Set *a*

Set *b*

(5.7)

Confirmation of the process of multiplication as a Cartesian product is facilitated by recording observations in some systematic manner. Most children develop the ability to perform the operation of multiplication as a Cartesian product at about the same time as they learn union of sets. To attain most stated objectives, this ability must be translated into discovery of patterns and generalization of process. Without systematic recording of data, these discoveries are often delayed or even overlooked. One popular method of recording is through the use of a matrix or grid (see Figure 5.9).

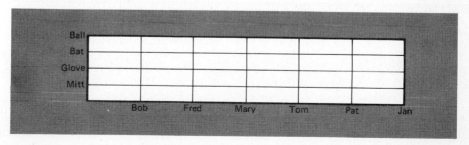

Ball
Bat
Glove
Mitt

Bob   Fred   Mary   Tom   Pat   Jan

(5.9)

One axis of the grid carries the members of one set as entries (in this case the set of baseball materials used in a game). The other axis has entries of the members of the other set (the team). The Cartesian product can be found by having children place a dot to show each combination. A dot would be placed at the intersection of lines leading from mitt and Bob, indicating that one possible combination would be Bob with the mitt, and so forth. You will notice that the intersections formed by this procedure resemble the formation of rectangular arrays with sets of objects. The intersection formed by the mitt and each player resembles a set of six, the ball and players a set of six, and so on. Systematic recording in this fashion relates the Cartesian product to the rectangular array. Rather than two distinct and unrelated interpretations of multiplication, children see one operation demonstrated by more than one procedure.

As children work with multiplication, they begin to see that many sets can be described in more than one way. For example, 6 can be described as three sets of 2 or as two sets of 3. Having children record their findings in a fashion similar to that in Figure 5.10 not only gives a child a chance to see beginning number facts, but also helps him observe that multiplication is commutative. An easy transition to the notation of multiplication may be made by providing children with an alternative. If they prefer, they may write their addition sentences in an abbreviated form by counting the sets and indicating the quantity of each set. For example, 2 + 2 + 2 + 2 can be written as four sets of 2, and so on (see Figure 5.10). Finally, children may substitute the symbol x for "set of."

Sets of 2	Sets of 3	Sets of 4
2 sets of 2 = 4	2 sets of 3 = 6	2 sets of 4 = 8
3 sets of 2 = 6	3 sets of 3 = 9	3 sets of 4 = 12
4 sets of 2 = 8	4 sets of 3 = 12	4 sets of 4 = 16

(5.10)

A child's surroundings may provide many concrete materials to use as representations for the operation of multiplication. Items overlooked earlier may prove to be excellent media. For example, consider using a deck of playing cards. There are exactly four jacks, four queens, four tens, and so on. Within each set of 4 are two subsets of two black cards and two red cards. There are also thirteen hearts or twenty-six red cards, and so forth. Questions should be structured to serve as a challenge to children; they can gain a great deal of valuable experience by writing an addition or multiplication sentence to show the number of face cards as 4 jacks + 4 queens + 4 kings or three sets of 4, or the number of red cards below 6 as 2 + 2 + 2 + 2 + 2 = 10.

PRESENTING DIVISION   Preparation for understanding division may be facilitated early in the study of multiplication, again with the aid of concrete materials. Consider Figure 5.11. It is simply a strip of oaktag which is folded in alternating directions to separate either the equal addends of multiplication, or the equal subgroups of division. The illustration shows that two groups of 4 equal 8, three groups of 4 equal 12, and so on. After dealing with multiplication, one merely has to count equal subgroups in the opposite direction to illustrate division. The utility of such an aid to each child should be clear.

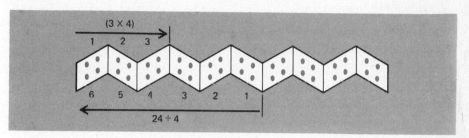

(5.11)

There is an additional inexpensive and sound procedure which will help children rationalize the relationship between operations. Simply duplicate "dot pages" on regular 8 1/2-×-11 paper. Examine Figure 5.12. The sheets contain an arbitrary number of dots, in this case seventy-two. On the left side of the figure a multiplication quantitative situation has been solved:

> There were three children at a table and each one needed four sheets of paper for art. How many sheets of paper should Billy leave at the table?

Children must simply circle three groups of four dots and then count the "equal addends." Conversely, on the right side of Figure 5.12, pupils are to circle as many subsets of six as are indicated in the quantitative setting.

> Twenty-four cookies were to be placed in sacks, six cookies per sack. How many sacks will Janet need?

The quotient may be obtained by counting the circled subsets.

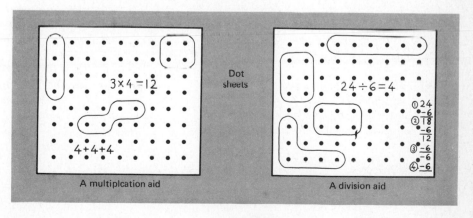

(5.12)

Chart 5.1 Flow Chart Lesson Plan—Division as Repeated Subtractions

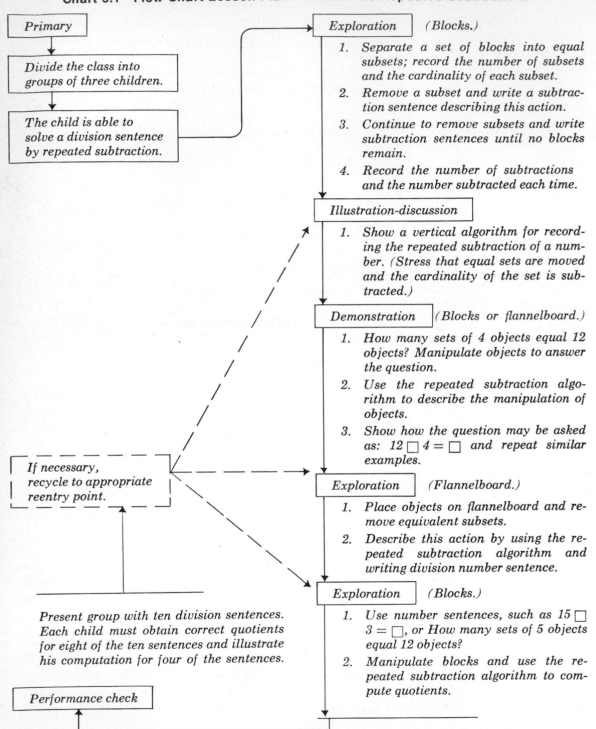

Primary

Divide the class into groups of three children.

The child is able to solve a division sentence by repeated subtraction.

Exploration *(Blocks.)*

1. Separate a set of blocks into equal subsets; record the number of subsets and the cardinality of each subset.
2. Remove a subset and write a subtraction sentence describing this action.
3. Continue to remove subsets and write subtraction sentences until no blocks remain.
4. Record the number of subtractions and the number subtracted each time.

Illustration-discussion

1. Show a vertical algorithm for recording the repeated subtraction of a number. *(Stress that equal sets are moved and the cardinality of the set is subtracted.)*

Demonstration *(Blocks or flannelboard.)*

1. How many sets of 4 objects equal 12 objects? Manipulate objects to answer the question.
2. Use the repeated subtraction algorithm to describe the manipulation of objects.
3. Show how the question may be asked as: $12 \square 4 = \square$ and repeat similar examples.

Exploration *(Flannelboard.)*

1. Place objects on flannelboard and remove equivalent subsets.
2. Describe this action by using the repeated subtraction algorithm and writing division number sentence.

If necessary, recycle to appropriate reentry point.

Exploration *(Blocks.)*

1. Use number sentences, such as $15 \square 3 = \square$, or How many sets of 5 objects equal 12 objects?
2. Manipulate blocks and use the repeated subtraction algorithm to compute quotients.

Present group with ten division sentences. Each child must obtain correct quotients for eight of the ten sentences and illustrate his computation for four of the sentences.

Performance check

Division as Repeated Subtractions

Division is the inverse of multiplication. Because of this inverse relationship and a mutual dependence on multicorrespondence (a many-to-one situation) the operations of multiplication and division may be taught simultaneously after reversibility of thought is attained by the child. It is apparent that a child who conceptualizes one operation can readily understand the other.

Just as multiplication is shown by a union of several equivalent sets, division may be illustrated as a separation of a given set into equivalent subsets. Once a child has performed the required separation, the action may be illustrated with a series of subtractions as shown in Figure 5.13.

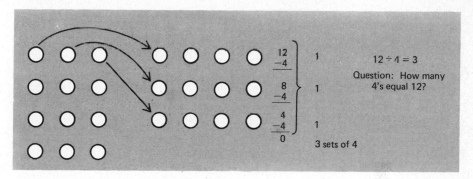

(5.13)

In a quantitative setting, division is represented by one of two types of number action, measurement or partition. At the concrete level each of these situations is distinct from the other, and each may create a slightly different conceptual image of the process of division.

Measurement and Partition

The authors recommend using measurement situations during initial instruction. Both types are best illustrated through story problems.

> George has twelve candy bars to share. He decides to place three candy bars in each of the May baskets of some friends. How many friends will receive candy bars in their May baskets?

A child may solve this measurement problem by successively removing groups of three candy bars each from the set of 12 until they are all gone. He then observes how many subsets of 3 have been formed (see Figure 5.14).

> George has twelve candy bars to give away. He wants to give them to his four friends. How many candy bars will each friend receive?

A child solves this partition problem by passing one candy bar to each person in turn until all are gone. He then counts the number of candy bars given to each child (see Figure 5.15).

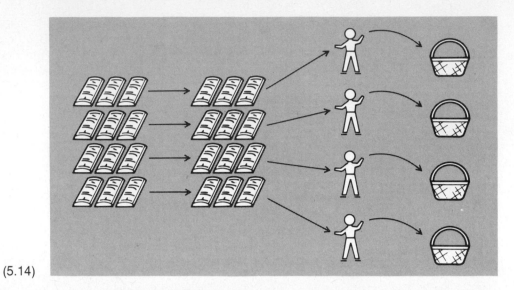

(5.14)

(5.15)

Measurement situations are most easily understood by the child, for he is able to gain quickly an image of division as a repeated separation of equivalent sets and can later describe it as repeated subtractions. This is consistent with his early experience with multiplication. Conversely, the partition process, as used to represent division, is generally more difficult for children to understand. Rather than being observable as a separation of equivalent sets, partition division appears to be a dealing out or matching process. For this reason most mathematics educators recommend that children work with and understand division as a measurement situation before partitioning is introduced. Nevertheless, young children need experience with both kinds of division settings because much conceptualization with fractions is embedded in the partition notion.

After children have a concept of division as a separation of equivalent subsets, have them manipulate objects to demonstrate the solution to problems which have been provided. Following this, children might write stories to describe a computation performed in the classroom (see Figure 5.16). Such activities help children develop an understanding of division at the problem-solving level.

(5.16)

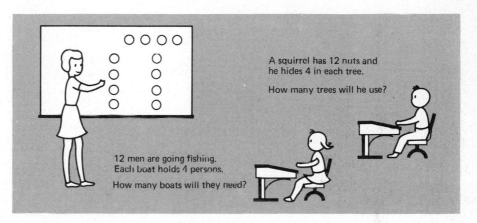

When children can demonstrate their competence in the activities already described, introduce them to the abstract mathematical sentence "to shorten their work." Thus, the action of problems posed may be described through the sentence 12 ÷ 4 = 3, read "How many 4s equal 12?" Children who have engaged in a developmental process such as the one just described can relate a division sentence to a real problem. With such a background, failure at the problem-solving level is unlikely.

Division as an Array   Since division is the inverse operation of multiplication, the array model with which children are already familiar may be used again. Use blocks and string to construct some rectangular arrays or let some drawings represent them.

To understand the process of division, children determine that the joining action of multiplication may be reversed. Twelve objects may be separated to form four rows of 3 as in part *A* of Figure 5.17, or three rows of 4 as in part *B*.

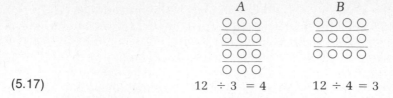

(5.17)

Like multiplication, the abstract notation for division should follow understanding of the process. Initially, children manipulate objects and write stories to describe actions. Finally, they are introduced to, and work with, the division sentences derived from quantitative settings.

THE NUMBER LINE IN MULTIPLICATION AND DIVISION

As they progress through school, children should be exposed to several interpretations of multiplication and division. Because of the ease with which the operations of multiplication and division and their relationship can be shown, many teachers use the number line (see Figure 5.18). To find the answer to the exercise $3 \times 4 = \square$, a child is told to consider that he has a $^+4$ cricket. Each time that the cricket jumps, he jumps four spaces to the right. The other factor tells the child how many jumps the cricket is going to take. The product is shown as the point where the cricket lands after his final jump.

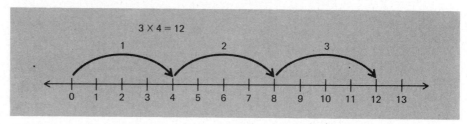

(5.18)

Division is easily shown as the undoing of the previous action. To solve a problem such as $12 \div 4 = \square$, a child is told to consider that he has $^-4$ cricket. Each time the cricket jumps, he moves four spaces to the left. He keeps on jumping until he reaches 0. The number of jumps that he has taken represents the quotient (see Figure 5.19). Once again, be aware that

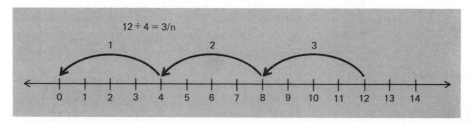

(5.19)

the number line is abstract, and that some younger children may not be able to accommodate the process of multiplication and division as both equal additions or separations and as skips on the number line. You may avoid confusion for some children by delaying work with the number line until these other concepts are well established.

Experience involving the use of a number line need not be confined to paper-and-pencil activities. Many interesting activities involving various media may be devised to make participation more exciting. For example, instead of using a number line made of paper, the teacher might make one of square pieces of carpeting remnants or samples. When stitched together these form an interesting number line. Children can then perform actions from directions by the teacher or by the class. In response to the exercise $3 \times 4 = \square$, a child would take three jumps covering four carpeting squares with each jump. A variation of this procedure is to have a child perform a certain action on the number line, while each child attempts to write a number sentence to describe the action just completed.

Other variations of the number line include making a line of chalk on a blacktop playing surface, using the squares in the floor tile as units, and so on. Children enjoy the opportunity to become physically involved, and such involvement may actually reinforce the relationship of division to multiplication, since one requires a movement which is the inverse of the other.

PRESENTING FACTS FOR MASTERY   Typically, many elementary school teachers place great emphasis on multiplication and division facts. This is understandable, since for years the only real test of a teacher's competence in mathematics teaching was ability of the class to compute rapidly. Modern programs place equal emphasis on computation and understanding. Educators recognize that early computational facility without the ability to solve problems is of little use to children. When they understand the processes of multiplication and division and are able to utilize these processes in problem situations, they must then commit the multiplication and division facts to memory. By giving children time to accommodate processes and relate these to problem situations, the teacher reduces the frustration and confusion often accompanying these two operations. With such teaching, children need not slight either understanding or computational facility.

There are one hundred basic multiplication facts, but only ninety basic division facts. The hundred multiplication facts are determined by combinations involving the digits 0 through 9 (see Table 5.1). The numerals appearing outside the heavy black lines are the factors, and the products are within the squares.

The division facts may be shown on a similar chart (see Table 5.2), where a dividend rather than a product is found inside the heavy black lines.

TABLE 5.1   **Basic Multiplication Facts**

×	0	1	2	3	4	5	6	7	8	9
0	0	0	0	0	0	0	0	0	0	0
1	0	1	2	3	4	5	6	7	8	9
2	0	2	4	6	8	10	12	14	16	18
3	0	3	6	9	12	15	18	21	24	27
4	0	4	8	12	16	20	24	28	32	36
5	0	5	10	15	20	25	30	35	40	45
6	0	6	12	18	24	30	36	42	48	54
7	0	7	14	21	28	35	42	49	56	63
8	0	8	16	24	32	40	48	56	64	72
9	0	9	18	27	36	45	54	63	72	81

TABLE 5.2   **Basic Division Facts**

÷	1	2	3	4	5	6	7	8	9
0	0	0	0	0	0	0	0	0	0
1	1	2	3	4	5	6	7	8	9
2	2	4	6	8	10	12	14	16	18
3	3	6	9	12	15	18	21	24	27
4	4	8	12	16	20	24	28	32	36
5	5	10	15	20	25	30	35	40	45
6	6	12	18	24	30	36	42	48	54
7	7	14	21	28	35	42	49	56	63
8	8	16	24	32	40	48	56	64	72
9	9	18	27	36	45	54	63	72	81

The relationship of division to multiplication is observed through examining this chart and comparing it to the previous chart. Each multiplication fact has a corresponding division fact. One basic restriction applies to division which reduces the number of facts to be learned from one hundred to ninety. Division by 0 is not possible. Mathematicians say that division by 0 is undefined. This is easily understandable when you ask the question: "How many sets of 0 are there in 8?" There is an infinite number of 0's in 8, therefore no answer correctly solves the equation. This fact is reflected in the chart by eliminating 0 as a divisor.

The hundred basic multiplication facts may be reduced considerably through the application of some of the properties of multiplication. Like addition, a very useful property of multiplication is the commutative property. This property is often shown algebraically by sentences such as $a \times b = b \times a$. For example, $3 \times 2 = 2 \times 3$. By applying this property children are able to reduce muliplication facts to fifty-five rather than one hundred.

Use of the zero property of multiplication further reduces the number of facts to be learned. When children understand that any multiplication fact having zero as one of its factors always has a product of zero, they have reduced the facts to be learned by ten, leaving forty-five facts in all.

Finally, application of the identity element (any number times 1 leaves that quantity unchanged, or $a \times 1 = a$), allows a child to further reduce the facts to be memorized to thirty-six.

Because division is not commutative, children are not able to reduce the number of division facts to such a large extent. Each child should understand that the division of any number by 1 leaves that quantity unchanged ($a \div 1 = a$). They should also understand that any number divided by itself equals 1 ($a \div a = 1$).

Relating Multiplication and Division Facts   During mastery, it is important that children perceive multiplication and division as inverse processes. For this reason, teachers often introduce related multiplication and division sentences together (see Figure 5.20). Children might be given one of the number sentences shown below and asked to complete the other three sentences which are missing. This not only provides practice on the facts but emphasizes relationships among facts.

(5.20)
$$5 \times 3 = 15 \qquad 15 \div 3 = 5$$
$$3 \times 5 = 15 \qquad 15 \div 5 = 3$$

Children need not be given the related multiplication and division facts through some rote process. By providing them with the opportunity to work with materials and record their answers, the teacher can help children master related facts. Using the rectangular array portrayed in Figure 5.21, children readily discover the related multiplication and division facts for 12. They see that four sets of 3 equal 12 and that three sets of 4 equal 12 (an illustration of the commutative property). They are able to see that $12 \div 3 = 4$ and that $12 \div 4 = 3$, thus noting the relationships among the four number sentences.

(5.21)
$$12 \div 4 = 3$$
$$0\ 0\ 0\ 0$$
$$4 \times 3 = 12 \quad 0\ 0\ 0\ 0 \quad 12 \div 3 = 4$$
$$0\ 0\ 0\ 0$$
$$3 \times 4 = 12$$

1	2	3	4	5	6	7
8	9	10	11	12	13	14
15	16	17	18	19	20	21
22	23	24	25	26	27	28

(5.22)

Arrays need not be artificially contrived by the teacher. There are many familiar arrays which occur in the pupil's surroundings and which may be used to help maintain the classroom as a conditioned environment for active learning. For example, a calendar makes a useful array. By judicious cutting, children can make several different arrays from one calendar. Figure 5.22 is a 4 × 7 array. Children could by given this calendar page and asked to write the related multiplication and division sentences describing the array. They might then be asked to bring old calendars from home which may be cut to form arrays representing given division and multiplication facts. The related multiplication and division facts could be recorded on a card.

Egg cartons also make useful arrays. They can be used in combination with other cartons to form several rows of 6 (see Figure 5.23). Or they can be cut out and joined together to form a variety of different arrays. Let children explore the many different arrays. They should describe each array with the appropriate number sentences for division and multiplication. Groups may wish to meet and discuss what they have discovered or to show their arrays to one another.

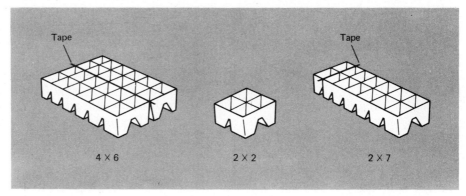

(5.23)

Arrays appear everywhere in children's natural environment. They are in the ordered spacing of panes of glass on a school window, rows of bricks in the wall, rows of tiles on the floor, rows of fruit trees, and so on. It is a rewarding and interesting experience for children to search for arrays on a field trip or on their way to and from school. They might be encouraged to sketch what they have found, or simply report their findings to the group. A contest might be held to see which group discovered the most arrays. Be alert to the possibilities of the school and neighborhood, for children enjoy discovering patterns and relationships, including arrays, outside their classrooms.

To be a truly successful teacher, your influence and teaching must not stop at the door of your classroom. if you actively seek the many opportunities offered in the immediate environment, both you and your class will be rewarded for it. By being actively involved, children will find your teaching interesting and challenging.

Competitive Games

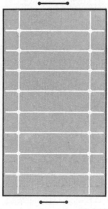

(5.24)

(5.25)

A limited use of competitive games is also appropriate for the learning of basic facts. For example, it might be possible to make use of popular sports to form the basis of the competition. Many such activities were designed and successfully used in the elementary school by Essig.[4] In one game, using a model of a football field for the playing surface, students competed against one another (see Figure 5.24). Children were paired by the teacher so as to avoid a complete overmatch. Thus students of low ability were not matched with students of higher ability. The game consisted of mathematical exercises which the child had to answer correctly. For example, the teacher would say: "9×7"; then, after a slight pause, "63." If a child wrote the correct answer on a sheet of paper before the teacher called out the answer, he was allowed to move one space on the football field. If both children answered correctly, they were both allowed to move.

Children find game situations such as this exciting. Only a little ingenuity is required to develop games around holidays, the sports seasons, and other events appropriate to the school life of children. Use game situations to stress those facts causing children the greatest difficulty, rather than repeating previously learned facts. One example is a chart or chalkboard drawing of a duck and some slices of bread. On each slice of bread, a combination (multiplication or division) is written for which practice is needed. Players take turns to see if they can "feed the duck" by giving answers for all the combinations. A slight but useful variation of this activity is making a chart with pictures of ducks on which the hard-to-master combinations are written. Make a slot or pocket under each in which cards in the shape of slices of bread can be placed. The cards should have numerals representing answers to the combinations (see Figure 5.25).

Other forms of instruction involve self-competition, where children compete against their own prior performance. To do this, periodically pass out a sheet of number facts and time your class as they work them.

[4]Donald Essig, "Using Competitive Math Games with Elementary Children" (Unpublished manuscript, Eugene Public School District 4J, 1968).

After a specified period of time, usually two minutes, you halt the work and examine the papers. Children record their results on some form of graph paper. Through careful scrutiny of children's performance, as indicated by their graphs, you can vary the instruction sheets. For example, when children have reached criterion performance with the facts below 5 × 5, you may wish to include facts through 6 × 6 and eliminate some of the easier facts which were previously learned. Typically, as each new set of facts is introduced, the graph shows a decline in performance. Notice that as the facts through 7 × 7 were introduced in Figure 5.26 Janet showed a decline in performance.

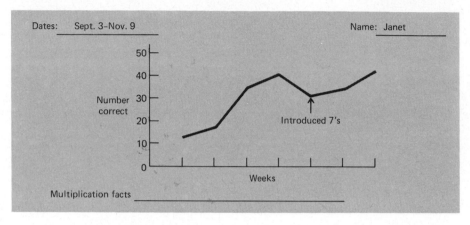

(5.26)

A third type of number fact drill employs a cassette recorder. This activity is becoming more common in schools, and in homes as well. It serves as a very useful drill device for individual children. The teacher may simply place those facts which cause trouble on tape. The preferred language would be "six nines," pause, "54," and so on. Children can play the tapes and merely listen or play the tape and record the products during the pause.

Children can also learn by actually programming the recorder themselves. By reading number facts from a sheet, they gain some practice in these facts. In addition, since this is an example of immediate knowledge of results, it can be highly motivating. Dramatic improvement is generally the result especially when children keep individual graphs of self-improvement.

PROPERTIES IN MULTIPLICATION AND DIVISION

The Commutative Property

Multiplication is commutative—that is, "the order of the facts does not affect the product." Arrays lend themselves ideally to the discovery of the commutative property, and teachers are urged to make extensive use of them by having children compare the product shown by one array with another. For an example, see Figure 5.27. Children notice that 3 × 2 = 2 × 3. As they are given the opportunity to search for arrays, they should be encouraged to notice that the order of the sets does not affect the product.

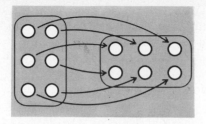

(5.27)

$$3 \times 2 = 2 \times 3$$

The Associative Property When children begin work with problems involving more than two factors, they must employ the associative property of multiplication. Because multiplication is a binary operation, only two numbers may be multiplied at any time. The exercise $3 \times 4 \times 7 = \square$ involves two multiplications, not one. It makes no difference which numbers are multiplied first; the product is the same.

The associative property of multiplication can be discovered by using physical objects. For example, a group of children may be given a set of blocks and an activity card, which reads as follows:

Activity Card: Associative property   Level: Primary

1. Solve the following multiplication exercise with block arrangements in as many different ways as possible:

    $$4 \times 2 \times 3 = \square$$

    Record your answer.

2. Solve the following multiplication exercise:

    $$5 \times 2 \times 4 = \square$$

    Which two factors did you multiply together first? How can you show this? Now solve the exercise in another way. Which two factors did you multiply together first this time? How can you show this?

3. Write a multiplication sentence to show what has been done with the blocks in the illustration below. Use your blocks to show another way to attain the same product.

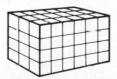

Multibase arithmetic blocks are extremely useful in helping children extend their understanding of the associative property of multiplication. The teacher might pose a problem by asking children to show the solution to the following exercise: $(4 \times 4) \times 3 = \square$. The group would then find three 4×4 "flats" and arrange them into some kind of order (see Figure 5.28). Work with arithmetic blocks can be quite creative if children are encouraged to make different configurations with their blocks. The only stipulation placed on them is that they must be able to describe the block configurations with a multiplication sentence.

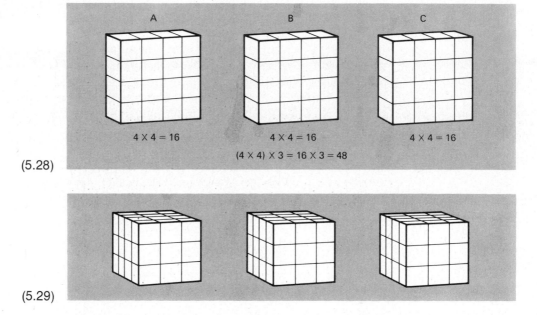

(5.28)

A   B   C

$4 \times 4 = 16$ $4 \times 4 = 16$ $4 \times 4 = 16$

$(4 \times 4) \times 3 = 16 \times 3 = 48$

(5.29)

Do not limit your class to multiplication sentences involving only three factors. Let children discover that the associative property of multiplication extends to any number of factors. For example, you might use an activity card with the following instruction: "Write a multiplication sentence to show what has been done with the blocks in this illustration (see Figure 5.29). Use your blocks to show another way you might attain the same product."

The Distributive Property

Both multiplication and division are distributive. The distributive property implies that a factor or dividend may be broken into component addends and multiplied or divided without affecting the product or dividend. This is shown algebraically for multiplication as $a \times (b + c) = ab + ac$; and for division as $(b + c) \div a = (b \div a) + (c \div a)$.

Help children discover the distributive property of multiplication by having them work in small groups using concrete materials to form arrays. For example, a calendar array can be accompanied by the following activity card.

Activity Card: Distributive property   Level: Late primary

1. Write a multiplication sentence to describe the array you have before you. What is the product?

2. Cut the last three rows to form two arrays and write a number sentence to describe each. Determine the product of each.

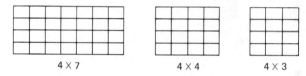

  4 × 7   4 × 4   4 × 3

3. What relationship is there between the two small arrays and the one large array? Write a multiplication sentence to show how the two arrays are related to the one large array.

Children should quickly discover that $4 \times 7 = (4 \times 4) + (4 \times 3)$.

After children develop a beginning awareness of the distributive property of multiplication, you may wish to do some direct teaching involving the use of arrays. For example, write 5×9 on the chalkboard and have the children in your class arrange objects on their flannelboards or their desks to represent that array. Have them record the answer to the number sentence on their papers. Next ask them to split the array to show 5×4 and 5×5, and ask them to find the product of each. After the children have found the products indicated, let them tell you whether the sum of the two products is equal to the product of the original array. Finally, ask them to write a number sentence describing what they have done.

Further practice may be obtained by having the class make arrangements with objects to depict a particular array. Then have them see how many different multiplication sentences they can derive from the given array. Ask if the multiplier may also be distributive and why.

Chart 5.2   Flow Chart Lesson Plan—Distributive Property of Multiplication

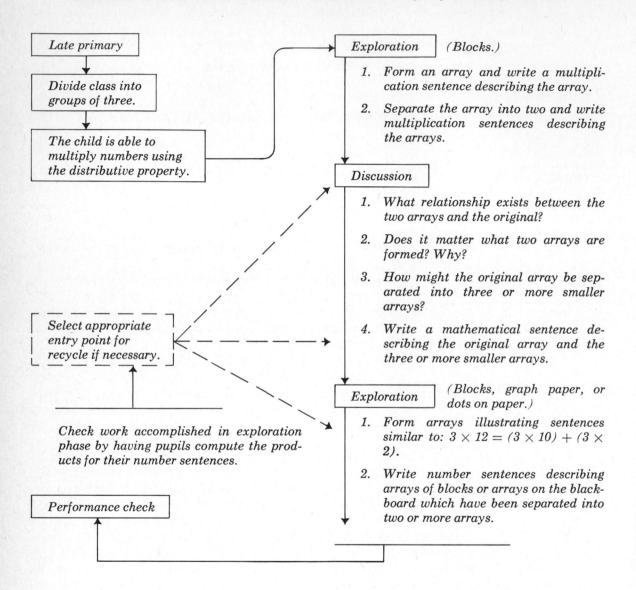

Similar procedures to those already discussed can be used to illustrate the distributive property of division. For example, pass out a sheet of graph paper to the children and ask them to make two 4 × 7 arrays. Next have them cut one of the arrays to form a 4 × 4 array and a 4 × 3 array, a further illustration of the distributive property of multiplication. Now provide an activity card such as this one:

Activity Card: Distributive property of division   Level: Late primary

1. Using your 4 × 7 array, show 28 ÷ 4. Write a division sentence to illustrate the action.

2. Use your 4 × 4 and 4 × 3 arrays to show 16 ÷ 4 and 12 ÷ 4. Write division sentences to show your action.

3. What can you say about the quotient of 28 ÷ 4, and the quotients of 16 ÷ 4 and 12 ÷ 4?

Children may need some help to discover that 28 ÷ 4 = (16 + 12) ÷ 4. By using arrays, arranging blocks, and so on, the teacher can help children relate the distributive property of multiplication to that of division. Children with a sound understanding of the distributive property of division are not as easily confused when they attempt a division algorithm. For example, they can understand that 6/108 may be rewritten using multiples of ten to read 6/60 + 6/48. Thus, the distributive property of division provides children with another illustration of how properties of mathematics are interrelated, a primary goal of contemporary mathematics.

COMMON FRACTIONS   A fraction may be thought of as a relationship which exists between a whole and some portion of the whole. This relationship may be demonstrated through the use of a part of a unit, or it may be demonstrated through the use of a subset as compared to the parent set. When assimilated by a child, these two concrete interpretations of a fraction form a meaningful concept of fraction.

Part–Whole Relationships   Children's constructions of part–whole relationships develop slowly, with constructions relating to halves evolving first. To the child, "one-half" means something has been separated into two parts, irrespective of the size of each part. When children explain, "Your half is bigger than mine," they are exhibiting a fair amount of intuitive understanding. Simple instructions in the meaning of halves, thirds, and fourths may now begin. Several foundation experiences are appropriate and equivalent parts should be stressed.

Structural materials such as color rods are ideal for teaching fractions. If such materials are available, children may be allowed to discover fractional relationships for themselves. For example, give several children a sack of rods and ask them to work with the purple, red, and white rods. Their first task might be to see how the purple, red, and white rods are related, and to record their observations. After discussion, the next task might be to determine how the purple rods are related to the brown rods. This observation may also be recorded.

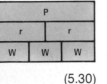

(5.30)

Among other things children will quickly discover that two white rods are equivalent in length to one red rod (see Figure 5.30). They will notice that two red rods equal one purple rod, and so on. Ask them to find other cases where two rods of one color equal one rod of a different color. Have them record their answers.

After children have perceived the relationship of white rods to red rods, ask them to tell how long one white rod is in comparison to the red rod. Children with extensive out-of-school experience will respond that the length of the white rod is half that of the red one, but others will probably not know the proper terminology. The word *one-half* will have to be introduced.

Use other materials to extend the understanding of the class to include thirds, fourths, and other unit fractions. Children can work with their desk flannelboards, they can cut string or fold paper, and they can cut objects to develop these concepts.

Fold each of several sheets of paper into two equal parts. Fold some other sheets. Have the children identify which sheets are folded in half. Give the children paper to fold into halves. Let them check each other. Are any papers folded into two unequal parts? Repeat this with thirds and fourths.

Another useful procedure is to draw pictures of several familiar objects. Separate them into two pieces in several ways as shown in Figure 5.31. Let the children find those objects separated into halves. If they identify the halves, give them pictures of objects which are not divided. Let them show halves. This may be repeated later for thirds and fourths.

(5.31)

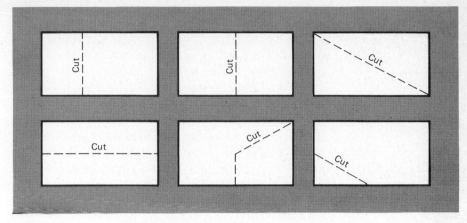

(5.32)

Once again, examples of objects that do *not* apply can be helpful. Separate several rectangular pieces of oaktag into two pieces in different ways as illustrated in Figure 5.32. Mix them. Pairs of children are to share a rectangular shape so each will get the same amount. Let the children manipulate the oaktag to show solutions. Have the children compare those chosen as one-half with those not chosen. Later, repeat the activity with one-third and one-fourth.

Figures created on the geoboard lend themselves well to exploring fractions. Make an activity card using the following directions: "How many ways can you use a rubber band to separate the geoboard in half? See how many ways you can separate the geoboards into fourths. Copy the figure (Figure 5.33) on your geoboard. Make a figure one-half the size. Make a figure one-third the size. Make three other figures with which you can show one-fourth."

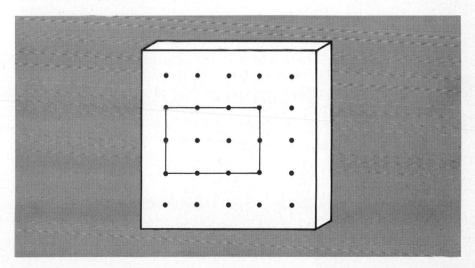

(5.33)

Part–Group Relationships

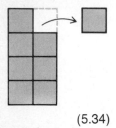

(5.34)

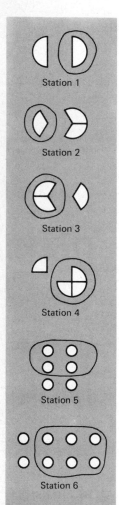

Station 1

Station 2

Station 3

Station 4

Station 5

Station 6

(5.35)

After children have developed a concept of fraction as some part of one unit, they may expand their understanding to include the concept of a fraction when working with sets of objects. Using blocks, color rods, and so forth, children can be provided with a purpose for counting out eight objects. Next, tell them to use only one-half the objects at first and ask them to find half of the set. Expect a wide variety of response from such directions. Many children will intuitively separate the set into two subsets of equal size. Others who have not reached the Piagetian level of class inclusion may have difficulty. Instead of comparing the part to the unit, they compare one part to the other parts. Have them arrange their blocks into an array (see Figure 5.34). Take one block and ask, "Do I have one-half the blocks?" It should be readily apparent to children that you do not. Ask them to explain why. They may state that it does not look right or that you need to take more blocks. Ask how many more blocks you should take. Help children to realize that one-half of a set implies equality of number or size, and so forth, just as one-half of a unit does.

If some children are still confused at this point, give them additional experiences where they are helped to identify a set of blocks, and so on, as one whole. A lesson might begin with a story such as:

> You are going to build a coal barge. It takes eight blocks to build one barge. Show how you would put your eight blocks together to build a barge.

A second story or card might say:

> Suddenly your coal barge is hit by a large wave and breaks in half. Show how your barge looks when it is broken in half.

Provide additional experiences where children are given the impression that many discrete objects may be joined to form one whole. Have them search for illustrations of this outside the classroom. For example, six panes of glass form one window, twelve classrooms form one hallway of a school, or three hallways unite to form one wing.

Through additional developmental experiences children can be led to discover the role of the numerator and the denominator of a fraction. Before this, they have become accustomed to recognizing and naming fractions such as 1/3, 1/2, and so on. Now divide them into groups and let them approach a series of experience stations. For each station, arrange materials in a particular order; the group or individual can record activities for each station (see Figure 5.35).

The only directions for the entire series of stations might be: "Describe the fraction circled with red yarn. Record your answer."

As the children encounter each station, they will recognize the need for symbolic representation when more than one fractional part is being considered. Often the correct numeral which describes fractions with more than one part considered is discovered without any help. Some children may need a reminder that a single part is called 1/3, 1/4, and so on. Then inquire:

> How do I describe the circled set? (See Station 3 of Figure 5.35.) How many thirds are circled? How can I write two-thirds?

Whenever it is necessary to help children by asking a leading question or moving a piece of material, keep directions to a minimum. Allow children to discover for themselves the exciting relationships of mathematics. Do not spoil it for them by being overly directive or too helpful.

Equivalent Fractions

1/2

2/4

4/8

?/16

(5.36)

In order that children will be able to solve addition problems with fractions, it is essential that they have an understanding that a fractional number may be represented by many other fractional numbers which are equivalent. In the beginning, it is perhaps best to help children attain such understanding by using equivalent figures, such as circles, rectangles, and the like. Children might first be asked to identify the unshaded part of the first circular region shown at the left in Figure 5.36. Following this, a second circular region of equivalent size could be exposed on the flannelboard. The regions would be divided into one-fourths. Children in the class would be asked to identify the unshaded portions of the second circular region and would respond "two-fourths." A third circular region indicating a division by eighths could then be exposed. Once again children would be asked to identify the indicated part of the region, and they should respond "four-eighths." Children may also engage in this process on an exploratory basis with individual fraction kits.

When children correctly identify the parts of circles in Figure 5.36, ask them to identify the similarities among the three regions. Record their answers on the board. Next, expose a circular region which has been divided into sixteenths and inquire how many sixteenths are needed to make that circular region equivalent to the others. Record that answer on the board.

Repeat this procedure beginning with thirds and/or fifths, and using other figures such as rectangles. At each point, be certain that children recognize the equivalence of all the fractions in the set. Have them record their work on a sheet of paper or on the board.

Once children have grasped the idea of equivalent fractions derived from a unit, introduce them to the number line (see Figure 5.37). Initially, teachers may prefer to use a number line with only the points from 0 to 1 identified. Ask children to divide the space from 0 to 1 in half, and label the point of division. Next, ask the class to divide the line into fourths and to label each point of division. Let them discover that 1/2 and 2/4 are equivalent fractions. Next, ask them to place a point between 1/4 and 0. Ask them to label that point. To label the point midway between 0 and 1/4 as an eighth successfully, a child must understand that the whole of this

Chart 5.3 Flow Chart Lesson Plan—Equivalent Fractions

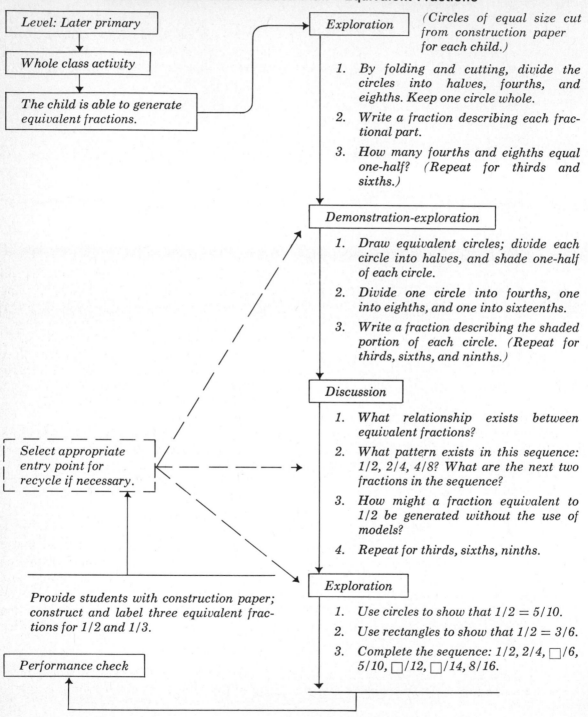

Level: Later primary

Whole class activity

The child is able to generate equivalent fractions.

Exploration *(Circles of equal size cut from construction paper for each child.)*

1. By folding and cutting, divide the circles into halves, fourths, and eighths. Keep one circle whole.
2. Write a fraction describing each fractional part.
3. How many fourths and eighths equal one-half? (Repeat for thirds and sixths.)

Demonstration-exploration

1. Draw equivalent circles; divide each circle into halves, and shade one-half of each circle.
2. Divide one circle into fourths, one into eighths, and one into sixteenths.
3. Write a fraction describing the shaded portion of each circle. (Repeat for thirds, sixths, and ninths.)

Discussion

1. What relationship exists between equivalent fractions?
2. What pattern exists in this sequence: 1/2, 2/4, 4/8? What are the next two fractions in the sequence?
3. How might a fraction equivalent to 1/2 be generated without the use of models?
4. Repeat for thirds, sixths, ninths.

Select appropriate entry point for recycle if necessary.

Provide students with construction paper; construct and label three equivalent fractions for 1/2 and 1/3.

Exploration

1. Use circles to show that 1/2 = 5/10.
2. Use rectangles to show that 1/2 = 3/6.
3. Complete the sequence: 1/2, 2/4, □/6, 5/10, □/12, □/14, 8/16.

Performance check

unit is now to be divided into eight parts. Ask him to complete the dividing and labeling using eighths. Do the same with sixteenths. After each new division, stress the equivalence of the fraction to the basic unit. Sets of ordinary classroom rulers may often be used with efficacy in this procedure.

(5.37)

```
        · · ·←————————————————————————→ · · ·
          0       1/4       1/2       3/4       1
                            2/4
```

(5.38)

```
        0       1/6       1/3       3/6       2/3       5/6   1
                          2/6                 4/6
        0               1/4       1/2               3/4       1
                                  2/4                        4/4
```

When children appear comfortable working with halves, fourths, and so on, give them another number line of equivalent size and have them repeat this procedure with thirds. When they have completed the number line through ninths or twelfths, have them compare it with the previous completed number line of halves, fourths, and so on (see Figure 5.38).

Let them discover that the distance on congruent unit number lines represented by 3/6, 2/4, and 1/2 are equivalent. Discussion should disclose the conclusion that they have worked with fraction lines for 1/2 and 1/3, and have formed equivalent fractions for these. Next, let them discover other number lines for fractions not previously included.

Each child should have some means of keeping a record to show the equivalent fractions he has discovered on the number line. He may record his findings in a fashion similar to that shown in Figure 5.39.

(5.39)
$$1/2 = 2/4, 3/6, 4/8, 5/10. \ldots$$
$$1/3 = 2/6, 3/9, 4/12, 5/15. \ldots$$

The systematic recording of the numeral for equivalent fractions provides the teacher with the opportunity for structuring several interesting lessons. For example, divide the class into several small groups and provide each with a set of materials including a unit number line, several circular regions, several rectangular regions, and so on. Each station would have an activity card similar to the following and most children will easily detect the indicated patterns.

Ratio and Proportion   Many of the problems that a child encounters in his everyday world imply some form of proportional relationship. For example, if Jimmy is able to

Activity Card: Equivalent fractions   **Level:** Later primary

1. Notice that Richard has recorded a set of fractions which are equivalent to 1/2. Predict which fraction he will record next.

    1/2 = 2/4, 3/6, 4/8, 5/10, _____

2. What fraction will he record below?

    1/3 = 2/6, 3/9, 4/12, 5/15, _____

3. What fraction is missing from John's list below?

    1/4 = 2/8, _____, 4/16, 5/20

4. What did you notice about the pattern of the fractions in each previous series? Predict the next fraction in any of the series. Check your work on your number line.

buy two pieces of bubble gum for five cents, how much will it cost to buy bubble gum for himself and his three sisters? Originally he will perhaps solve this problem by asking the storekeeper if he has enough money to buy the bubble gum he needs. Such early naiveté quickly disappears as he begins questioning similar transactions. Because he sees the need for knowledge, the child will rapidly assimilate the idea of a proportional relationship and how it can be used to help solve problems in real life.

To introduce children to the idea of problems involving proportional relationships, structure a problem situation in one corner of the room where a child or group of children could be given an envelope containing three 25-cent pieces and a set of tickets. On an assignment card write the following instructions:

Merry-go-round rides cost two for twenty-five cents. How many rides will you receive for seventy-five cents?

Children may solve this problem through two-to-one correspondence (see Figure 5.40). For each 25-cent piece that a child has, he knows that he may buy two rides. When he has matched all three quarters with tickets to indicate two rides, he has merely to count the number of tickets to find the solution to his problem.

Give the class additional experience involving proportional relationships by structuring problems such as:

(5.40)

6 rides for 75¢

If it costs $1.00 for three cans of beans, how many cans of beans may I buy with $4.00?

When children understand the proportional relationship of the previous problems, more difficult or abstract relationships are likely to be handled with ease. For example, use physical objects to encourage children to solve the following problem:

Two large sacks hold five bushels of leaves when they are both full. Your father told you that it normally takes six sacks to hold all the leaves from your lawn. How many bushels of leaves can you expect to rake?

This implies a somewhat more complex comparison. Objects must be put into correspondence with more than one object (see Figure 5.41).

(5.41)

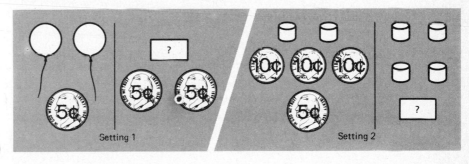

(5.42)

Setting 1   Setting 2

By varying these procedures, some interesting responses can be obtained from children. For example, on a flannelboard or other medium, construct a series of physical settings with sets of objects in a proportional relationship (see Figure 5.42). As a child approaches each of these settings, he is to write a story to describe the action indicated by the setting. The story which he has written may then be used with another child who constructs a one-to-one correspondence of sets to solve the problem.

Children soon tire of writing stories to describe activities such as these. They will probably ask if there is an easier way to write the story—just as there was for addition, subtraction, multiplication, and division. If the children in the class seek a "shorthand" system, introduce them to the notation used. If not, delay teaching this notation until after they are a bit older. Until problems become more complex they actually have little use, other than convenience, for the number sentence of proportional relations.

When the occasion demands that children be introduced to the number sentence associated with ratio and proportion problems, first introduce children to the notation for a ratio. Use a procedure such as the following in your introductory lessons. On a table have several sets of objects in a many-to-one correspondence (see Figure 5.43). Discussion questions like these can serve to interest the children:

1. Which number pair would you choose to describe the relationships shown on the table? (1,2), (1,3), (3,2), (2,4)
2. With a set of materials show a relationship of physical objects indicated by the number pair (1,3).

Subsequent inquiries might provide experience for the child with more complex relationships such as (2,5) and so forth.

(5.43)

These ordered pairs are not the only ways that ratios are written, nor perhaps are they the most common. Other, equally acceptable notations for ratios are 1/2 and 1:2. Each is read as *one per two*, or *one is to two*. The determination of whether or not the symbol 1/2 represents a ratio or a fraction must be made from the context of the problem situation. Each describes an entirely different concept. For example, compare the fraction 5/10 to the ratio 5/10 within the context of a recording of baseball results. If a team wins five-tenths of their games (a fraction), this indicates that half their games have been won. It does not tell you how many games have been played, or the total number won. That must be derived from the context. The fraction 5/10 also does not tell you in what order the games have been won. On the other hand, the ratio five per ten indicates that for every ten games played, five were won. The fraction then denotes the number of games won for each part of the whole season. The ratio indicates an ongoing relationship up to a particular period of time. If the ratio correctly predicts the proportion of games to be won during the rest of the season, the manager knows that every time he plays ten games, he will win five of them. If the fraction 5/10 correctly describes winning, the manager has no idea which games will be won or lost. The team might win the first fifty and lose the last fifty. No indication of order is implied.

Once children understand the concept of ratio and its notation, proceed to the number sentence 1/2 :: x/6. The sentence reads, "One per two is proportional to x per six." The proportional relationship is described by the sign (::) rather than the equality symbol (=). Because the ratio describes physical quantities, this kind of notation is essential. One ice cream cone for two boys is not the same as three ice cream cones for six boys. The relationship is proportional but not equal.

At this early level of development, ratio and proportion problems are still solved through one-to-one correspondence of sets. The use of a number sentence is primarily a convenience for describing action.

Foundations for Decimal Fractions

Just as the earlier development of the numeration system built up to the grouping point of ten, the development of fractions builds up to the fractional part tenths. For example, the orange color rod or ten egg carton cups are named the unit or one. Thus, a white rod or a single egg cup represents one-tenth. Once activities are presented to highlight tenths, the place value concept with a grouping point at ten can be expanded to decimal notation. The following activities will help develop the concept of decimal fractions.

The earlier activities recommended for color rods may be extended to include the idea of tenths. The orange rod has the value of one. What value does one white rod have? Because it takes ten white rods to make an orange rod, each white rod is one-tenth of the orange rod. What would be the value of three white rods? What is the value of seven white rods? What is the value of nine white rods? What is the value of five white rods? What is another way to express this amount? How many white rods make a green rod? If the orange rod has the value of one and the white rod is one-tenth, what is the value of the green rod? Can you find another way to represent three-tenths?

The egg carton can be quickly converted to tenths by cutting two sections from one end. By placing beans or buttons in the remaining ten cups, the concept of tenths can be explored. When seven of the cups have beans, seven-tenths is the focus of attention. The concept of tenths is developed in a manner similar to the other fractional parts discussed earlier with egg cartons. The tenths sequence is similar to that previously outlined for color rods.

Money provides a practical example of tenths and hundredths. The values of a penny compared with a dime and a dime compared with a dollar are one-tenth. If a dime has the value of one, four pennies have what value? If a dollar has the value of one and a dime is one-tenth, what is seven-tenths?

As the children become comfortable with the concept of tenths and the common fraction forms 1/10, 2/10, 3/10 and so forth, the teacher should introduce decimal notation. The value of the green rod when the orange rod is one and the white rod one-tenth can be expressed as .3. All rod relationships should be symbolized with the decimal notation. Considerable practice may be necessary to master the new notation, but very soon .3, .4, .5, .6, and so on, will become as natural as the common fraction notation.

SUMMARY   As children progress through the elementary school, they are introduced to an ever increasing collection of abstract ideas related to number and operations. For this reason there must be a continued emphasis upon concrete representations of ideas during the foundation period.

In the introductory phases, it is well for children to have experience solving multiplication and division quantitative settings through counting and utilizing their prior knowledge of addition and subtraction. Subsequently arrays, Cartesian products, and set partition are used as models. Understanding the structure of the numeration system, the inverse relationship, and the idea that the operations of multiplication and division are distributive over addition increases comprehension of the algorithms for multiplication and division. Again, ultimate ability with the respective operations is closely allied to proficiency with basic combinations.

In most elementary school programs, children in the primary grades encounter their first formal experience with numbers beyond the whole numbers. This initial work on "parts" of numbers includes key notions related to the *concept* of fractional numbers as well as the equivalence of fractions and their relative size. Because the topics of fractions, ratio and proportion, and decimals are so interrelated, foundation experience and concomitant activities for teaching them must reflect this relationship.

ACTIVITIES, PROJECTS, A POINT OF VIEW

1. Make a list of five addition activities that could be used as foundation experiences for multiplication.

2. Devote one class period to a mathematics fair. Each class member must invent and design the materials necessary to make a self-instructive visual display of one of the concepts or properties mentioned in Chapter 5. If appropriate, provide a two-minute exposition to your classmates.

3. Design an original activity card that will provide a student or small group of students experience in rationalizing the operation of multiplication as mapping order pairs.

4. Imagine you have gathered a small group of children and you are displaying a relatively large multiplication fact chart in your lap.

    a. Your purpose is to demonstrate that there are only thirty-six "unrelated" multiplication facts to master. Write what you would say and do.

    b. Your purpose is to demonstrate the inverse relationship between multiplication and division. Write what you would say and do.

5. Use some chalk or masking tape and design a number line on the floor of your classroom. Demonstrate to the class (using classmates) how the number line can be used to introduce division as the inverse of multiplication.

6. Write an instructional objective which specifies the appropriate pupil behavior involved in understanding that muliplication and division are distributive over addition.

7. Survey some recent issues of *The Arithmetic Teacher*. Find a teaching game, idea, or activity that would be useful for drill and practice with the basic multiplication or division facts. Record directions as appropriate on a cassette tape. Have some classmates perform the activity.

8. Obtain a contemporary pupil's text designed for the third grade. Examine the quantitative settings or word problems used to introduce division. Decide whether they are measurement or partition. Make a list of each.

9. Design an activity card for independent use by pupils that utilizes color rods for developing the notion of equivalent fractions.

10. Use the teacher's edition of a pupil's text as a content source. Develop a flow chart lesson plan suitable for introducing decimals in the primary grades.

11. Provide a brief report which includes the supporting rationale on the recommendations of Donald Firl's essay, "Fractions, Decimals and Their Future," *Arithmetic Teacher*, Vol. 24, No. 3 (March 1977).

12. Develop a set of three or four real life settings taken from the local newspaper that could be used to introduce ratio and proportion.

13. What is the basis for your argument or disagreement with the following statements?

a. Multiplication and division facts should be introduced simultaneously.

b. The distributive property is not as important in the operation of division as in multiplication.

c. Because there will soon be little need to use common fractions in life outside school, they should receive decreasing emphasis in elementary school mathematics programs.

SELECTED READINGS

Ashlock, Robert B. "Introducing Decimal Fractions with the Meterstick." *Arithmetic Teacher,* Vol. 23 (March 1976), pp. 201–206.

Bruni, James V. and Silverman, Helene. "An Introduction to Fractions." *Arithmetic Teacher,* Vol. 22 (November 1975), pp. 538–545.

Davidson, Jessica. *Using the Cuisenaire Rods.* New Rochelle, N.Y.: Cuisenaire Company of America, Inc., 1969.

Englehardt, Jon M. "Basic Facts-Alternative Activities for Mastery." *School Science and Mathematics,* Vol. 76, No. 5 (May–June 1976), pp. 371–376.

Green, G. F., Jr. *Elementary School Mathematics Activities and Materials.* Lexington, Mass.: D. C. Heath and Company, 1974, Chapter VI.

Heddens, James W. *Today's Mathematics.* Chicago: Science Research Associates, Inc., 1974, Units 8, 12, and 13.

Marks, J. L.; Purdy, C. R.; Kinney, L. B.; and Hiatt, Arthur. *Teaching Elementary School Mathematics for Understanding.* New York: McGraw-Hill Book Company, 1975, Chapter V.

Rappaport, David. "Multiplication is Repeated Addition." *Arithmetic Teacher,* Vol. 12 (November 1965), pp. 550–551.

Spitzer, Herbert F. "Measurement or Partition Division for Introducing Study of the Division Operation." *Arithmetic Teacher,* Vol. 14 (May 1967), pp. 369–372.

Trafton, P. R., and Suydam, M. N. "Computational Skills: A Point of View." *Arithmetic Teacher,* Vol. 22 (November 1975), pp. 529–537.

Developing Measurement Concepts through Metric Measures

PERSPECTIVE   "A hectogram of prevention is worth a kilogram of cure" (1 hectogram = 3.5279 ounces and 1 kilogram = 2.2046 pounds).

"That was more fun that 119.24 liters of monkeys!" (119.24 liters = 1 barrel [U.S. liquid]).

"Give them 2.54 centimeters and they will take 1.609 kilometers" (2.54 centimeters = 1 inch and 1.609 kilometers = 1 mile).

"Don't hide your light under 3.52 dekaliters" (3.52 dekaliters = 1 bushel).

The previous statements could appropriately be termed "metric follies." They represent what some old sayings might sound like when translated into metric terms, and metric measurement is what Chapter 6 is about.

There are two central notions about which we should be absolutely clear before beginning a serious study of teaching measurement to children. First, the basis of measurement is comparison and comparison is a natural activity. Children and adults embrace it daily, for example:

> Janet drops two racquet balls an equal distance to see which bounces higher.
> Bill simultaneously tests several Hot-Wheels cars on his track to see which is fastest.
> To complete her "do-it-yourself" task, Linda first sorts through, then selects several tiles from a box containing miscellaneous sizes.
> In the school cafeteria, Aaron glances across all eleven pieces of cake before making a selection.

Certainly, it is not difficult to recall engaging in activities similar to the previous examples. It is equally likely you could give parallel instances from your daily life. In fact, most adults are aware that the inclusion of measurement in the elementary school mathematics program provides an opportunity for exceedingly practical experiences with activities that may have high utility at any time in one's life.

The previous condition prompts the second, equally important though somewhat less obvious, notion. It is completely possible that a superior elementary school mathematics program (in the abstract sense) could exist without the inclusion of study of denominate numbers. Unfortunately, teachers and others have often failed to recognize the full significance of either of the above notions. Such failure has undoubtedly contributed to a teaching of measurement to children which emphasized some memorization from "tables" of unrelated and illogical "standard" English units of distance, volume, and mass and which underscored computation. The latter consisted principally of reducing units of measure to the same class and subsequently performing the required basic operation.

Four fundamental concepts associated with measurements are as appropriate for prospective teachers as they are for children in elementary school classrooms. These concepts may be written as generalizations and stated as follows: 1) measurement involves comparison; 2) measurements are approximations and, as such, vary in precision; 3) measurement may be indirect as well as direct; and 4) universally standard as well as logical units of measure are necessary for efficient communication.

After study of Chapter 6 you should be able to:

1. Explain the unique use of number in measurement.
2. Outline a brief history of the metric system.
3. List the basic metric units and name their important subunits.
4. Demonstrate the interrelatedness of standard metric measures.
5. Write a statement of personal philosophy for teaching measurement.

BASIC CONCEPTS

Describing Measurement

For purposes of your study as well as a study of measurement by children, it is well to understand at the outset how numbers are involved with measurement. When numbers are used in the study of measurement, they are often referred to as denominate numbers. A denominate number is one whose referent *represents* a unit of measure—for example, six centimeters, three liters, or two kilograms. Numbers associated with measurement are termed "denominate" because in order to perform the four basic operations, it is necessary to reduce the units of measure represented by the number to the same denomination or class. For instance, how many square meters would be needed to cover an area 34.6 decimeters by 127 centimeters? The edges in meters are 3.46 and 1.27. Thus, the required area is 3.46 × 1.27 or 4.39 square meters.

Measurement may be described as a process that uses numbers to quantify observations regarding such physical properties or characteristics as length, area, volume, mass or weight, and temperature. Generally, the defined referent of the physical property is called a *unit*. We then find how many units of the physical property are required to be equal to that same physical property in the object of our concern. As an example, in the matter of length or distance, we transpose the question "how far?" to the question of "how many units of distance?"

As an essential part of our understanding of how numbers are used in measurement, it is important to make a practical distinction between counting and measuring. Counting is generally thought of as an exact procedure because it involves the assignment of number to discrete elements of a set—for example, pieces of candy in a dish, dolls in a collection, or birds on a feeder. When the counting is completed we know there were exactly eight pieces of candy in the dish, exactly six dolls in the collection, and exactly four birds on the feeder.

Measurement, on the other hand, is generally viewed as an inexact process or approximation because it involves ascribing numbers to physical qualities or characteristics of a continuous nature. As an example, suppose on an ordinary personal scale your weight is about 62 kilograms insofar as you can judge from the indicator. Of course, as a practical matter it is perfectly acceptable to tell others your weight is 62 kilograms. In truth, however, 62 kilograms is very likely only an approximation of your weight. First, the physical quality measured is subject to measurement in continuously refined basic units—that is, hectograms, decigrams, centigrams, and so forth. Thus, it is extremely unlikely that your weight is exactly 62 kilograms. Second, the distance and angle from which the indicator was read as well as the width of the indicator lines virtually assume human variance in the original reading of the scale. The consequences of these examples (and they permeate all ordinary measurement activities) are the reasons for the related generalizations that measurements are inexact and vary in precision.

THE METRIC SYSTEM IN THE UNITED STATES

A Brief History

The metric system is now the official system of measures and weights in almost all pursuits between and within nations of the world. Strangely enough, England, Canada, and Australia were among the last English-speaking countries that decided to convert, and America has, until very recently, lagged behind them.

During the eighteenth century, the French proposed a base-ten system of length founded upon a permanent referent. The meter was named as the basic unit of length and the referent was defined as one ten-millionth of the quadrant passing through Paris and extending from the earth's equator to either pole. Even though the metric system became "official" in France late in the eighteenth century (about 1795), nearly fifty years passed before the French government declared the system mandatory. Certainly this early reluctance in France has been paralleled in the United States.

Metrication in America has been a persistent idea, but it certainly is not a new one. Scientists and statisticians have long recommended its exclusive utilization. At the time the French were making the metric system official though not mandatory, our own Thomas Jefferson was suggesting that Congress adopt the idea of decimal measurement. Still later, around 1821, John Q. Adams met with little success recommending national action on the matter. Finally, in 1866, Congress legalized the use of the metric system in America but did not make it mandatory, nor was there any firm commitment to an ultimate changeover. Nonetheless, Senator Charles Sumner of Massachusetts, Chairman of the Senate Select Committee on Coinage and Weights and Measures, had this to say after guiding the legalization:

> By these enactments the metric system will be presented to the American people, and will become an approved instrument of commerce. It will not be forced into use, but will be left for the present to its own intrinsic merits. Meanwhile it must be taught in schools. Our arithmetics must explain it. They who have already passed a certain period of life may not adopt it; but the rising generation will embrace it and ever afterwards number it among the choicest possessions of an advanced civilization.[1]

In spite of Senator Sumner's evident enthusiasm, the promise of his rhetoric was not fulfilled. There was, however, a minor flurry of activity following the passage of the 1866 Act. The activity was prompted by an accompanying resolution which authorized the printing and distribution of literature explaining the system and making available tables of English–metric equivalents. Still, passage of the act did little to change people's daily lives or habits, and our citizens were generally free to totally ignore the metric system unless, of course, they were engaged in some kind of formal study beyond the early grades.

The legalizing effort of 1866 prompted some new attention to the metric system in popular arithmetics of the day. Ray's *New Practical Arithmetic* published in 1877 is one example. Whereas Ray's *Practical Arithmetic* of 1857 failed to mention the metric system and a later version contained only an appendix reference, the 1877 revision contained a seven-page chapter complete with exercise set near the center of the book. It was noted in the preface:

> . . . All obsolete tables of weights and measure, such as beer measure and cloth measure, and all obsolete denominations, such as drams, roods, etc., are discarded. The Metric System of Weights and Measures is presented in accordance with its now widely extended usage, and is assigned its proper place immediately after Decimals.[2]

---

[1]U.S. Department of Commerce, *A History of the Metric System Controversy in the United States*, NBS-SP 345-10, August 1971, p. 46.
[2]Joseph D. Ray, *Ray's New Practical Arithmetic* (Cincinnati: Van Antwerp, Bragg & Co., 1877), p. iv.

THE METRICAL SYSTEM. 321

APPENDIX.

THE METRICAL SYSTEM

OF WEIGHTS AND MEASURES.

333. The **Metrical System** is so called because the **Meter** is the base, and the principal and invariable unit, upon which the system is founded.

This system was first employed by the French; and, hence, is frequently called the *French System of Weights and Measures*. Great confusion formerly existed in the weights and measures of France. Each province had its particular measures, which caused great embarrassment in commerce.

Government vainly endeavored to establish a uniformity, and to regulate all measures by those used in Paris.

In 1790, the French Assembly proclaimed the necessity of a complete reform, and invited other governments to join them in establishing a simple system, to be common to all nations.

The coöperation of other nations could not at the time be secured, and a commission, nominated by the Academy of Sciences, and composed of eminent scholars, was instructed to prepare a general system of measures.

The new system was adopted, and declared obligatory after Nov. 2, 1801. But its introduction was gradual. It had to struggle against the local customs, and, for a time, only increased the confusion by adding the new measures to the old.

In 1837, the Assembly enacted a law, rendering the *exclusive* use of the new system obligatory after Jan. 1, 1841; and imposed penalties against the further use of the old system.

It has since been adopted by Spain, Belgium, and Portugal, to the exclusion of all other weights and measures; and is in general or partial use in nearly all the states of Europe and America, and by scientific men throughout the world.

In 1864, the British Parliament passed an act allowing the metrical system to be used throughout the Empire; and in

3d Bk. 21.

(6.1) Page 321 in *Ray's Practical Arithmetic,* by Joseph Ray, M.D. (Cincinnati: Van Antwerp, Bragg & Co., 1872).

THE METRIC SYSTEM.

DEFINITIONS.

155. 1. The **Metric System** is so called from the *meter*, the unit upon which the system is based.

REM.—The French originated this system of weights and measures at the close of the last century, and its use in France became obligatory in 1841. The metric system is now legal in nearly all civilized countries, and, in several, it is making its way rapidly into general use. In 1866, its use was legalized, in the United States, by act of Congress. It is in general use by scientific men throughout the world.

2. All the units of the other measures are derived in a simple manner from the meter. Thus,

1st. The **Meter** is the unit of Length. It is the base of the Metric System, and is very nearly one ten-millionth (.0000001) part of the quadrant extending through Paris from the equator to the pole.

2d. The **Ar** is the unit of Land Measure. It is a square whose side is 10 meters.

3d. The **Liter** is the unit of capacity. It is a vessel whose contents are equivalent to a cube the edge of which is .1 meter.

4th. The **Gram** is the unit of Weight. It is the weight of a cube of pure water whose edge is .01 meter.

(189)

(6.2) Page 189 in *Ray's New Practical Arithmetic,* by Joseph Ray, M.D. (Cincinnati: Van Antwerp, Bragg & Co., 1877).

Nonetheless, there is little evidence that the Act of 1866 had any significant impact on school curriculum. The added metric sections of the popular arithmetics shown in Figures 6.1 and 6.2 were ordinarily placed in an appendix or inserted with an existing chapter on denominate numbers. There was no integration of the metric system in applications. Further, grammar school texts of the period continued to present measurement problem sets in customary units.[3]

[3]Robert G. Clason, "When the U.S. Accepted the Metric System," *Arithmetic Teacher,* Vol. 24, No. 1 (January 1977), p. 58.

After nearly a century of debate, the United States has taken the necessary action which could lead to a truly universal system of weights and measures. It was not until 1975 that the Ninety-fourth United States Congress approved a Metric Conversion Act and set aside two million dollars for the purpose of helping the country with metric conversion. Awards totalling that amount have been given to four types of projects: school-based programs of local education agencies; interstate cooperative programs under the jurisdiction of state departments of education; teacher preparation and inservice programs conducted by colleges; and national metric programs. There is speculation that 1983 will be the date for mandatory changeover. Should this date become firm, it means that all of our nation's present elementary school population (1978 K–6) will live in a totally metric academic world before high school completion.

STANDARD UNITS IN THE METRIC SYSTEM

It is now clear that the school's responsibility is no longer to decide whether we shall teach the metric system, but rather how we shall teach it. Further, from a practical standpoint it is difficult to understand nearly two centuries of resistance, for it is certain children will learn the metric system much more quickly and thoroughly than most of us have learned the English system.

The English and Metric Systems of Measurement

In support of the previous statement, use a piece of scratch paper and complete this quiz relating to our "familiar" English system of measures. The answers to the quiz are given at the bottom of the page.[4]

1. ____ teaspoons = 1 tablespoon
2. ____ ounces = 1 pound
3. ____ quarts = 1 peck
4. ____ pecks = 1 bushel
5. ____ square inches = 1 square yard
6. ____ yards = 1 rod
7. ____ square feet = 1 acre
8. ____ acres = 1 square mile

You probably discovered you did not do well, despite the fact that each one of the measures is rather common and you have probably used several of them repeatedly in your adult life.

It may be that our lack of familiarity with the English system is traceable to the essentially unrelated units. For example, many of us may recall a certain distress from our own study of linear measurement when it was often necessary to remember the number of inches in a foot, the number of feet in a yard, the number of yards in a rod, and both the number of feet and number of rods in a mile. Even when we obtained a table of standard English measures, we were confronted with a host of conversions within and between the standard units before a practical problem could be solved. Further, complete familiarity with the unrelated standard elements of linear measurement provided no logical foundation for study of volume and mass.

[4]Answers to quiz: 1) 3; 2) 16; 3) 8; 4) 4; 5) 1,296; 6) 5 1/2; 7) 43,560; 8) 640.

**Metric Units:
Meter, Liter,
Gram, Celsius**

For successful adoption of the International System of Units (formally abbreviated SI, but synonymous with the metric system), it will be important that you have confidence in your understanding of the system. The metric system is based on the decimal system with which you are very familiar. Consequently, beyond recognizing the terms meter, liter, and gram as the basic units for distance, capacity, and weight (mass), and becoming familiar with a few unusual sounding temperatures, you acquired the important foundation for the metric system when you learned the place value scheme of our decimal number system.

TABLE 6.1   **The Metric Primer**

kilo	meter*	(km)			
	liter	(kl)	=	1000	(10^3)
	gram*	(kg)			
hecto	meter	(hm)			
	liter	(hl)	=	100	(10^2)
	gram	(hg)			
deka	meter	(dam)			
	liter	(dal)	=	10	(10^1)
	meter*	(m)			
	liter*	(l)	=	1	(10^0)
	gram*	(g)			
deci	meter	(dm)			
	liter	(dl)	=	0.1	(10^{-1})
	gram	(dg)			
centi	meter*	(cm)			
	liter	(cl)	=	0.01	(10^{-2})
	gram	(cg)			
milli	meter*	(mm)			
	liter	(ml)	=	0.001	(10^{-3})
	gram*	(mg)			

*Frequently used units.

TABLE 6.2

Prefix	Basic Unit	Decimal Ratio
(Greek)		
kilo		$1000\ (10^3)$
hecto		$100\ (10^2)$
deka		$10\ (10^1)$
	meter, liter, gram	
(Latin)		
deci		$0.1\ (10^{-1})$
centi		$0.01\ (10^{-2})$
milli		$0.001\ (10^{-3})$

Table 6.2 summarizes basic metric referents for measuring length, capacity, and weight. The prefix name establishes its relation to the unit of measure. Ratios within a single unit are determined through multiply-

ing the basic units by integral powers of ten; thus, larger or smaller units may be easily identified by "moving" the decimal point. As an example, suppose a student in your class is 1.26 m tall. The student's height would also be 32.6 dam. But it could also be given as 12.6 dm or 126 cm as well as 1260 mm. Furthermore, the prefixes of the metric system are used consistently "across" the basic units. As an example of this, a milli*meter* is 1/1000 (10^{-3}) of a liter, a centi*liter* is 1/100 (10^{-2}) of a liter, and a deci*gram* is 1/10 (10^{-1}) of a gram.

As with English measures, metric surface measures are derived from the square of linear measures. Volume or capacity measures are obtained from the cube of linear units. Further, these decimally derived cubic measures of capacity arbitrarily define the standard metric unit for mass. This basic and important relationship is demonstrated in Figure 6.3 which illustrates how the meter provides the foundation of the metric system.

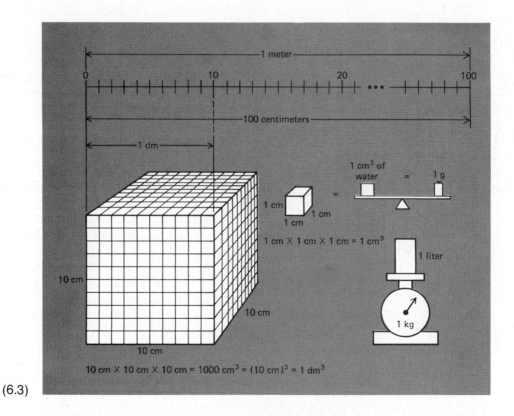

(6.3)

For its measures of temperature, the metric system uses the Celsius scale. Until recently this scale was referred to as the centigrade scale. Its present designation comes from Anders Celsius, the Swedish astonomer who originally devised the centigrade scale of temperature. In Celsius, the familiar referents of freezing and boiling points for fresh water are arbitrarily set at 0°C and 100°C respectively. Normal human body temperature is found to be 37°C when the 98.6°F is converted. Although recommendations for the teaching and study of the metric system in elementary school do not include conversion activities, it may be useful for you to know how Celsius–Fahrenheit conversions are obtained. This is especially true since the National Weather Service currently provides local radio and television stations with Celsius and Fahrenheit readings and forecasts. The Celsius–Fahrenheit conversion formulas are $F = 9/5\ C + 32$ and $C = 5/9\ (F-32)$. As a consequence, you can determine outdoor swimming is appropriate at 25°C $(F = 9/5\ (25) + 32 = 45 + 32 = 77°F)$.

THE METRIC SYSTEM IN THE CLASSROOM

General Considerations

An initial consideration for teachers is whether or not there shall be a dual approach in the classroom. A dual approach suggests a balance between the metric and English systems when organizing classroom measurement experience. Such an approach is not advocated here. To be sure, as children advance through the transitional period, they will need some knowledge of traditional measures, but they can and will be gained through daily life experiences outside school. In fact, it would very likely be impossible to prevent this from happening.

There are several good reasons for discarding a dual approach. Contemporary experience from classrooms where a dual approach is practiced indicates a tendency to become involved in the computation of conversion between systems. This perpetuates a real interference for children who would naturally, through a variety of exclusively metric experiences, have little difficulty learning the metric system. Further, experience from the recent past in Great Britain and other countries provides testimony that our society, including school age children, would not likely be serious about the metric system until they are required to go "cold turkey." Of course, if immediate circumstances call for direct teaching of elements from the traditional English system, then the metric system should be taught as *another* measuring system such that no conversions are required.

A second crucial consideration in teaching measurement is the perceptual development of children. There are illusive subtleties involved with understanding basic measurement concepts. As examples, if we desire to know the height of a classmate or the distance from our own seat to the classroom door, we may use a measure such as a meterstick or tape and count the number of times it is applied. While this example of direct measurement may seem rather straightforward to us, it requires sufficient maturation from children to understand what is accomplished by unit iteration and the transitive property relative to the measuring relation. The former is the repeated application of the selected unit of measure— for instance, one meter—and the latter is the belief that each application measures the same length with the resultant separate measure forming a measure of the entire object.

When you recall that conservation of quantity was a crucial prerequisite for understanding number (Chapter 1), it should not be surprising to find the quality equally crucial for understanding measurement. The research of Piaget[5] and subsequent analysis by his followers[6] clearly reveals conservation—in this case, recognition of the invariance of distance and length—as an essential for meaningful measuring. Turn your thoughts back to the two examples given above. How can a child measure if he perceives the measuring instrument as variable in length from application to application, or if he cannot view the distance from his seat to the classroom door as being the same as the distance from the door to his seat?

There are several simple, informal performance activities you can use to determine a child's ability to conserve length and area. In the matter of length, use colored rods or strips of oak tag of equal length. By positioning, have the child demonstrate to his satisfaction that the objects are of equal length. Next, move one of the objects an appropriate distance right or left of one that is fixed and have the child describe their relative length. Children who cannot conserve will declare one or the other longer.

For area, use an ordinary sheet of centimeter paper, equally divided, and four one-centimeter chips for each half of the paper. Again, by *initial* positioning, have the child determine that an equal amount of space is occupied on both sides of the line. Subsequently, utilize positions B and C as illustrated in Figure 6.4 and ask the child to describe the relative amount of occupied space on each half of the paper. A child who cannot conserve area, or two-dimensional space, will generally claim the respective halves of positions B and C no longer contain equal amounts of occupied space.

Repeated application of the previous tests will reveal that most children do not acquire ability to conserve length or area until they are at least eight years of age. Since few children in grades one and two are conservers of length and area, formal teaching of measurement should not be initiated until the latter half of grade three. Planned instruction in earlier grades should be on *exploring* measures. Experiences in grades one and two can focus on simple problem settings where children work individ-

[5]Jean Piaget, "How Children Form Mathematical Concepts," *Scientific American*, Vol. 189 (November 1953), pp. 2–6, 78.

[6]John A. Flavell, *The Developmental Psychology of Jean Piaget* (Princeton, N.J.: D. Van Nostrand Co., Inc., 1963).

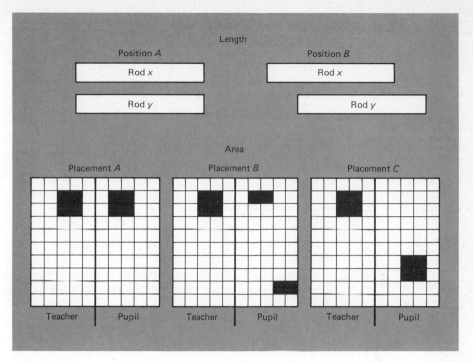

(6.4)

ually or in small groups to obtain solutions for presentation to classmates without the aid of standard units. Repeated foundation experiences will lead children to discover the need for standard units, and the first introduction to selected standard units is appropriate for the latter portion of third grade. The measurement program in grades four, five, and six should extend the intuitive generalizations of the foundation period as they are applied to the remaining topics of measurement—that is, the standard units for area, volume, capacity, and mass.

The final general consideration centers around why we include metric measures in elementary school mathematics and what the processes and content shall be. There are two principal reasons for including the study of metric measure in elementary school mathematics. First, it is a logical context for an introduction to measurement processes that have great social utility. Second, it provides a foundation for subsequent study of more complex measurement concepts in mathematics and science. Table 6.3 presents a suggested outline for the content of metric measurement in the first grades. In addition, ten foundation processes provide a methods framework for the teaching activities displayed in the final portion of this chapter. It should be noted that the ten foundation processes are considered crucial to teaching measurement at all levels.

TABLE 6.3

Foundation Process	*Metric Topic*	*Unit*	*Grade* 1	2	3	4	5	6
Exploring	Length	Centimeter			√	√	√	√
Sorting		Meter			√	√	√	√
Comparing		Kilometer				√	√	√
Matching		Millimeter					√	√
Estimating	Area	Square Centimeter			√	√	√	√
Substituting		Square Meter				√	√	√
Equalizing	Volume	Cubic Centimeter					√	√
Describing		Cubic Meter						√
Recording	Capacity	Liter			√	√	√	√
Measuring		Milliliter					√	√
	Weight/Mass	Kilogram				√	√	√
		Gram				√	√	√
		Milligram						√

HELPING CHILDREN MEASURE METRICALLY

Active Learning

No other area of elementary school mathematics offers a more natural opportunity to exploit an active learning philosophy than does measurement. Also, no phase of the elementary school mathematics program offers a better opportunity for a topic to become a favorite one. Preferred teaching procedures are embedded in the series of activities which follow. Although related areas of measurement are listed together, an order of difficulty is not intended for the activities. They are structured only by the limits of the specific activity. The activities are intended to exploit the ten measurement foundation processes in Table 6.3. Of course, it is always possible and even desirable that you adjust the described condition or invent an original procedure to carry out an activity.

Linear Measurement

The child comes to school with gross conception about length. At the same time, the concepts associated with linear metric measure are the most important children will learn. This is because the meter, a linear distance, is the basic unit from which all other metric concepts derive. As a consequence, the early gross notions must be carefully nurtured and systematically refined through first-hand experiences that will lead to both confidence and competence in metric measuring.

1. Give each child one-half of a discarded manila folder, a pencil, and a pair of scissors. Have them trace or draw one or more body measures—for instance, a "hand" or a "foot." (Invent one.) Working in pairs, direct the children to discover and record the measurements ("hands" or "feet") of a variety of classroom objects. Compare. Discuss.

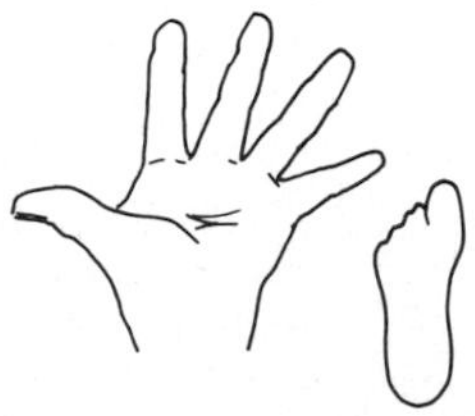

(6.5)

2. Have children take turns measuring a selected distance in the classroom using a normal, consistent "stride." Record on the chalkboard. Discuss.

TABLE 6.4

West Wall

Stride	Number
Richard	17
Janet	22
Nancy	17
Terry	19
Jim	20

3. It is possible to refine the concept of linear measurement through the consideration of possible solutions to simple problems. Propositions like the following may be presented. Direct measurement is not an alternative.
   a. Can our aquarium be placed in the sink for cleaning?
   b. Does Miss Brown's chair fit under the table where Jill, Nancy, and Tim sit?
   c. Will the cord from our record player on the shelf reach the electrical outlet?
   Let children give possible solutions. Record. Discuss. Have children try the solutions. What were best? Why?

4. Have children construct their own measurement tools. Both rigid and flexible models are appropriate. String, thin wire, window shade sticks, tongue depressors, adding machine tape, and strips of tag board are a few examples. Calibrate them (invent) in nonstandard units—for example, "fingernail," "three fingers," "foot arm," and so forth. Use the tools to measure a variety of objects such as the record player, books, desks, doors, heights, and room size. Comparison of results should lead to a discussion of the desirability and efficacy of standard units. Later these model tools may be calibrated in standard units.

(6.6)

5. Since all measure is not in fixed lines, children may use some length of string to measure the circumference of a basketball, the globe, a piece of chalk, a light bulb, or a hat size. Using a string to measure a friend can also be fun. Compare and establish a class record for each of the following:
   a. the longest thumb.   d. the smallest wrist.
   b. the widest shoe.   e. the largest waist.
   c. the shortest arm.   f. the tallest class member.

6. A classroom reference chart relating customary units to metric units can be important as you guide children through early metric measurement activities. Such a chart can eliminate unnecessary confusion and help create confidence as children become comfortable with metric measures.

7. During early applications of standard length, children may also construct inexpensive measuring tools. Calibrated in standard metric units, these must be more sturdy than previous nonstandard tools. Initial emphasis is on the centimeter, but a tag board decimeter rule, as well as a meterstick, should be

available. Use the student-constructed models in estimating and measuring all sorts of objects in and out of the classroom. Children may keep individual records.

Things We All Know

1 cm is about 1/2 inch
30 cm is about 1 foot
1 m is a little more than a yard
1 km is a little more than 1/2 mile

(6.7)

TABLE 6.5

Item	Est.	Actual
Width of eraser	____	____
Length of these words	____	____
Height of desk	____	____
Length of paper clip	____	____
Width of button	____	____
Height of door	____	____

8. Longer distances and larger objects should also be estimated and measured. This can include distances children might:
   a. span with both arms outstretched.   d. throw a ball.
   b. jump straight up.   e. jump with both feet.
   c. hop on one foot.   f. skip.
   Construct a "folding meter" by using transparent mending tape to fasten ten decimeter rulers together.

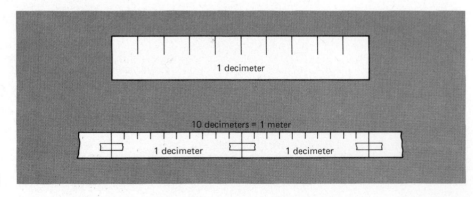

(6.8)

9. Have some children prepare a classroom wall chart. It should portray the decimal relationship between common linear metric units. Let them explain it. An example is provided.

Linear Measure
1 centimeter = 10 millimeters
(1 cm = 10 mm)
1 decimeter = 10 centimeters
(1 dm = 10 cm)
1 meter = 10 decimeters
(1 m = 10 dm)
1 kilometer = 1000 meters
(1 km = 1000 m)

(6.9)

10. Have each child locate a "secret object." It should be visible to all. The children (sometimes) measure and record the length (height or width) of the "secret object" in centimeters. Take turns revealing the dimension in centimeters to the class. See who can identify the "secret object." (Permit a maximum of ten guesses for the class.)

11. Just as with one-dimensional measurement, it is possible to develop the important concepts associated with surface measurement through exploration of possible solutions to simple problems. Estimation, prediction, and guessing are key activities. Conduct exploration with problems like these:
    a. Do we have enough sheets of blue construction paper to cover the library stand?
    b. Will the arithmetic books from our room cover the reading table?
    c. Do we have enough wrapping paper for our room mother's gift?
    Solicit guesses and predictions. Ask why. Record. Try them. Which ones worked? Which were best? Why?

12. Obtain samples of small-sized, square ceramic tile from a floor covering shop. Have children use them to fill common, regular shapes drawn on a sheet of paper. Count the total number used. Count the number used on two sides. What conclusion can be reached? Centimeter chips and centimeter grid paper may also be used.

13. Provide each child or small groups of children with a sheet of square centimeter grid paper. Have them estimate and record the area of their hand in centimeters. Next have them place their hand over the grid and make an outline. Compare the estimate to the actual surface.

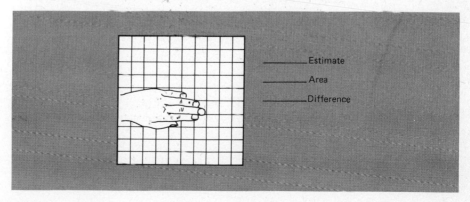

(6.10)

14. Have children use a meter stick, some old newspapers, and some mending tape to make a square meter. Use it to estimate and then determine how many unit applications would be necessary for covering:
    a. the classroom door.   d. the library table.
    b. a classroom window.   e. the hopscotch grid.
    c. the teacher's desk.   f. the floor in your classroom.
    Make up three other things to do.

15. Provide children with some pieces of twenty-by-twenty square centimeter grid paper. Ask them to cover the square meter they made for Activity 14. How many pieces did it take? What conclusion can be reached? Is there a "short way" to determine area?

16. As in one-dimensional measurement, a chart for easy reference on the classroom wall or bulletin board can be an important aid to children while studying surface measure.

Area Measurement
1 square centimeter = 100 square millimeters
$(1 \text{ cm}^2 = 100 \text{ mm}^2)$
1 square decimeter = 100 square centimeters
$(1 \text{ dm}^2 = 100 \text{ cm}^2)$
1 square meter = 100 square decimeters
$(1 \text{ m}^2 = 100 \text{ dm}^2)$

(6.11)

Volume/Capacity Measurement[7]

Volume is the measure of space occupied or enclosed. It is three-dimensional in nature and thus a more advanced concept of measurement. Since linear measure provides the foundation for volume measures, length and area need to be thoroughly understood prior to the introduction of capacity measurement. Further, formal study of the standard metric liter is preceded by conceptual experiences with cubic measure as a natural extension of square measure.

17. Children's early experiences with the measurement of volume can include making gross discrimination through comparisons where it is determined which of similar objects are larger and therefore occupy more space. Collect pairs of common objects for such comparisons.
    a. marble to golf ball.   e. baseball to volleyball.
    b. cigar box to radio.   f. piece of cloth to crayon.
    c. arithmetic book to dictionary. g. comic book to reading book.
    d. waste basket to garbage can.   h. brick to cement block.
    Discuss, speculate. Compare other sets of things.

18. Exploration with water displacement is useful for illustrating that solids immersed in water will displace an amount of water equal to the volume of

---

[7]Throughout these activities the terms "volume" and "capacity" will be used interchangeably. Functionally, volume refers to the amount of space an object occupies while capacity refers to the amount a container will hold.

the solid. It is also the foundation for the idea of a unit of volume. Two procedures may be used and children can perform both activities.

Procedure A: Select a large clear container and determine its volume by recording the measure of liquid required to fill it. Empty the container, place a solid (rock, egg, figurine, brick) in it, and refill. Remove only the solid and record the measure needed to fill it. The latter will be the volume of the solid.

Procedure B: Select a small clear container and fill it only half full. Mark the original level clearly. Successively place golf balls in the container, each time marking the new water level. When the container is filled, remove the golf balls and return the water level to its origin. The series of marks on the container vividly portrays the unit volume of the golf balls.

Variation: Use either of the above procedures and let children determine the volumes of their hands through water displacement.

19. The need for standardization of the "space occupying" unit is important. Children need experience examining situations requiring cubic units. The students may construct and handle standard cubes. Initially they can estimate, then count, the number of cubes required to fill small spaces such as crayon, thumb tack, paper clip, and cassette tape boxes.

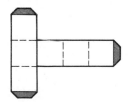

(6.12)

20. Unit blocks can be arranged to form a variety of shapes. The invariance of volume with changes in shape must be established. Since this kind of exploration requires *many* cubes, commercially prepared cubic centimeters (wood or plastic) are appropriate. Initially, children may simply stack blocks, noting how many different patterns they can obtain with a given number of blocks.

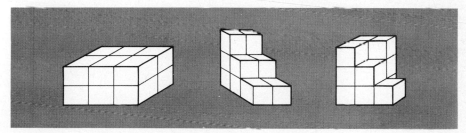

(6.13)

Variation: Construct several small open-top boxes using uniform centimeter measurement; for example, 2 cm × 5 cm × 3 cm and 4 cm × 7 cm × 3 cm. As children fill them, attention may be directed to the generalization, l × w × h.

21. Use commercially obtained wooden or plastic centimeter blocks and have children stack them for the purpose of gaining a perception of the relationship between volume and surface measures. Children may work in pairs with a set of thirty-six (or some other number) cubes and a series of instructions like these:

a. Make a single story house six blocks long and six blocks wide.
b. Make a single story house eighteen blocks long and two blocks wide.
c. Make a two-story house that uses all the blocks.
d. Make as many two-story houses as you can.
e. Repeat (c) and (d) with three- and four-story houses.

Have each pair of children record the results on a chart. Discuss. What do you notice?

TABLE 6.6

Stories	Height	Length	Width	Area	Volume
1	1	6	6	36	36
1	1	18	2	36	36
2	2	6	3	18	36
3					
4					

22. To help pupils form ideas of quantity, establish a collection of common containers of varying but unknown capacities. The collection can include milk cartons, coffee cans, jelly jars, frozen orange juice containers, baby food jars, peanut cans, and Dixie cups. Let children freely investigate the capacity of the various containers by pouring water from one container to the next. Guess which hold the most, the least, twice as much, and so forth. It may be convenient, on occasion, to substitute a dry material for exploratory activities. Use rice, sand, beans, dried coffee grounds, dried peas, or kernels of corn.

23. Choose a specific set of graduated containers (four or five) from your collection. Have pairs of children guess the relative order of the containers according to "holds more or less." Have them check their guesses by establishing the correct relative volume through a pouring activity.

Variation: After initial experiences, the procedures of this activity and the preceding one may be repeated or extended by checking individual guesses, estimations, and perceptions through the introduction of a standard liter container that is appropriately calibrated.

24. The notion of cubic measure as an extension of square measure can be reinforced through the construction and application of a meter cube. Have children use the square meter patterns designed for Activity 18. Provide some reasonably rigid cardboard from which they may measure and cut six square meters. Fit the edges and tape as shown.

Children in pairs or small groups may now estimate and then measure the volume of larger, familiar spaces such as the classroom closet, the storage space, the classroom, the principal's office, and the nurse's room.

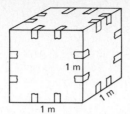

(6.14)

25. The interrelationships of standard metric measure can be studied through design and exploration with a liter cube. Children may use their decimeter rules and the previous instructions but cut only five square decimeters. The open liter cube may subsequently be used to pour dry materials back and forth between standard liter measures.

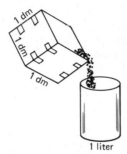

(6.15)

Variation: Line the liter cube with a plastic bag and use water. How many liter cubes are necessary to fill the meter cube in Activity 24?

26. During a study of volume and capacity in grades five and six, a classroom visual can be an important aid to children in gaining confidence with standard units while arriving at important generalizations about metric relationships.

$$1 \text{ cubic centimeter } (1 \text{ cm}^3) = 1 \text{ milliliter } (0.001 \text{ l})$$
$$1 \text{ cubic decimeter } (1 \text{ dm}^3) = 1 \text{ liter}$$
$$1 \text{ cubic meter } (1 \text{ m}^3) = 1 \text{ kiloliter } (1000 \text{ l})$$

Weight/Mass Activities

Mass is anything that occupies space, and weight is a gravitational pull exerted on the mass by earth. Mass can be compacted but its quantity does not change. Gravitational pull varies by location. Further, the density of objects directly affects weight in a manner such that we cannot tell by the mere observation of volume which of two objects is heavier. For these reasons, children can encounter serious difficulty in fully comprehending concepts associated with mass.

Teaching strategies should parallel those used in linear and capacity measurement. Children need physical experience handling and feeling weight. As before, exploration and estimation precede actual measurement. Familiarity with basic units should be an outgrowth of developing skill with selected measuring devices.

27. Children need tactile and visual experience to realize that size (volume) and shape do not determine mass. Collect a series of pairs of objects for comparison that have both equal and varying volume and mass. Some examples are:
   a. a lead sinker and a filbert.
   b. a clay brick and a cleansing sponge.
   c. an apple and a styrofoam ball.
   d. a pumice and an ordinary stone.
   e. a measure of Wheaties and a measure of water.
   f. a glass marble and a plastic cube.
   Without lifting, have children predict "which is heavier," "which is lighter," and "which are about the same." Next, have children handle the objects to verify judgments. Discuss. Choose a set of objects from the above and let children order them light to heavy, independent of volume.

28. A student-made pan balance (balance scales) has many uses. Involve several small groups of children in the construction of a balance scale. You will need such materials as clothes hangers, string, scissors, paper plates, Dixie cups or a plastic tube, some pieces of wood, a drill, a bolt, and some glue. Two examples are provided. Initial use should involve experimentation and comparison in seeking balance for common objects—for example, how many blackboard erasers equal a shoe, pieces of chalk equal a cup, thumb tacks equal a gum eraser, and so forth. Use the student-made pan balance to verify the order of weight of the set of objects in Activity 27.

(6.16)

29. Use the student-made balance (or a commercial one) to provide experience in estimating the mass of objects, compared with a nonstandard but constant mass—for instance, a nickel, a marble, a large or small washer, or some other appropriate constant mass. Place the constant in one pan and utilize some of the objects collected for the previous activities. Children can first estimate, then weigh.

30. A two-pound coffee tin, when closed and entirely filled with dried, used coffee grounds, approximates one kilogram. To help children gain familiarity with this important metric unit, prepare several of these nonstandard models. Have children hold the model in one hand and a chosen object in the other to determine if the object is less, about equal to, or more than one kilogram. A wall chart is appropriate for recording the results.

TABLE 6.7 **How Much Is a Kilogram?**

Item	Less	About Equal	Greater
brick			×
football	×		
box of chalk	×		
quart of water		×	
————			
————			
————			

31. First-hand experience in developing concepts about standard metric mass may be obtained by having children make prototypes of some common metric weights. You will need an accurate pan balance, a set of standard pan weights, some sand, and clear pill boxes or plastic vials. Fill the boxes or vials until they balance a selected standard weight. Label clearly and let children have their own sets of "standard" metric weights. (Plasticine may also be used to assemble a set of gram masses). Use them to estimate, then weigh, assorted common objects. A chart for recording the estimates and actual mass would look like this:

TABLE 6.8

Item	Est.	Weight	
		g	kg
two pencils			
paper clip			
nickel			
scissors			
lunch sack			
dictionary			

32. The metric system relates volume and weight by defining the gram as the mass (weight) of one cubic centimeter of distilled water at 4°C. Consequently, a liter of water weighs one kilogram. Children can have actual experience with this relationship by lining the open liter cube constructed for Activity 25

with a strong plastic bag, filling it with water, and verifying with the pan balance. Construct a half-liter measure and do the same.

33. Obtain a metric scale or recalibrate an old bathroom scale in five-kilogram units. Have children work in pairs to estimate and then obtain their mass. Plot the results for the class on a graph as shown.

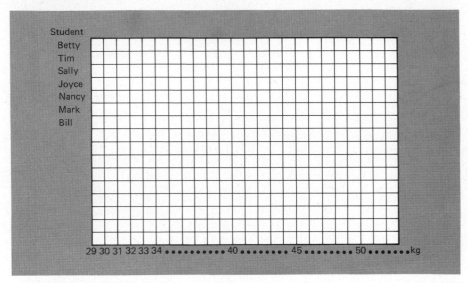

(6.17)

34. Prepare a series of pictures of things to be measured. Ask children to make judgments regarding the measure required, the instrument, and the most appropriate unit for reporting the measure. A record of the activity would look like this:

TABLE 6.9

Picture	Measure	Instrument	Unit
rice	weight	scale	kilograms
milk	volume	meas. container	liters
winter day	temperature	thermometer	degrees Celsius
counter	area	metric tape	square meters
cloth	length	tape	meters
cement	volume	variable	cubic meters

36. Simple recipes provide an interesting avenue for application of smaller units of metric measure. They also provide additional experience in the conversion convenience of volume and mass. Some basic metric measuring instruments are required but a chart of approximate equivalents can help.

1 teaspoon = about 5 ml   1 cup shortening = about 225 g
1 tablespoon = about 15 ml   1 ounce = about 30 g
1/2 cup = about 125 ml   1/2 cup butter = about 115 g
1/3 cup = about 80 ml   1 cup sugar = 250 g
4 cups = about 1 liter   Moderate oven = 180° Celsius

a. *Art Garden*

Mix these ingredients:

32 ml salt   32 ml water

32 ml liquid bluing   7 ml ammonia

Find a shallow pan, 20 cm × 20 cm, and cover the bottom with small pieces of tile, pumice, cinder, or sponge. Add the mixture and observe for several days. Add some food coloring.

b. *Cool Cookies*

Mix in medium pan:

480 ml white sugar   100 g margarine or butter

50 ml cocoa   110 ml milk

Cook over medium heat and bring to 100° C for one minute.

Add: 750 ml quick-cook oats   1–2 ml salt

       100 g peanut butter   5 ml vanilla

Stir until mixed well. Drop amounts of about 5 ml each onto wax paper. Cool and eat!

c. *Finger Fudge*

Mix in a large bowl:

1 egg, well beaten   3–4 ml salt

40 ml cream   400 g confectioner's sugar

5 ml vanilla

Melt in saucepan at 70° C

112 g unsweetened chocolate   15 ml butter

Add melted ingredients and stir in:

240 ml chopped walnut meats or marshmallows cut in pieces, or some of both.

Spread in buttered pan 20 cm × 20 cm. Cool and cut. Makes about 65 kgs.

Temperature Measures

Temperature scales are very arbitrary. Children learning to read a Celsius scale must relate the unit measurement of the scale to temperature conditions they experience in everyday life. Anyone who has used the Fahrenheit system will find the warmth of 32° C rather strange. The several activities which follow may be introduced any time appropriate to the developmental level of children and are generally independent of the previous measurement activities.

37. Young children need the opportunity to "feel" different temperatures. Assemble four containers of water, one hot, one warm, one room temperature, and one containing water with ice cubes. Invent other experiences.

a. Have children place hands simultaneously in containers where temperatures vary. They may describe what they feel.

b. Estimate the temperature of each container.

c. Place both an F and C scale in the containers. Read and record.

38. A large classroom visual can provide focus for orientation to common comparative temperatures in degrees Celsius. Discussion can center around: a) the point at which water freezes; b) a nice day; c) a very cold day; d) a heat wave; e) normal body temperature; f) comfortable room temperature; and g) the point at which water boils.

Variation: Ask children what would happen if:

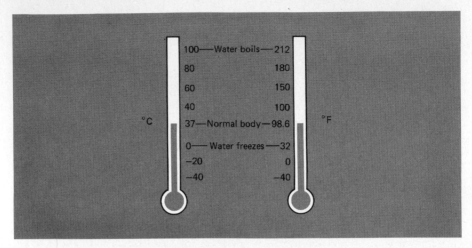

(6.18)

    a. the temperature of your bath water became 44°C?
    b. the doctor says your body temperature is 55°F?
    c. your ice cream stick was placed in the refrigerator at 32°C?
    d. the temperature in our classroom became 55°C?
    e. you played a baseball game when the temperature is 19°C?
    f. you baked a cake at 200°F?

39. An interesting class project consists of relabeling an ordinary thermometer. Tape a light strip of tagboard opposite the F scale on the old thermometer and make marks at 50°F and 95°F. The marks correspond exactly to 10°C and 35°C respectively and are thus twenty-five Celsius degrees apart. Remove the tagboard strip, label the two points, and use a rule to calibrate the distance between them into five equal segments. Now use the marks between 10°C and 35°C as a referent and extend the scale from 15°C to 100°C. Tape the strip over the F scale, making certain 10°C and 35°C correspond exactly to 50°F and 95°F.

40. Use student-made models (recalibrated) of the Celsius scale to obtain and record the outdoor temperature for ten consecutive days. Compare the record to an F record for the same days (see Figure 6.19).

41. Have a small group of children use a Celsius thermometer to take the temperature of liquid (water) that has been brought to the boiling point and then placed in three different containers. Take the temperature every three minutes for a period of eighteen minutes. Graph the results (see Figure 6.20). Discuss.

SUMMARY Concepts of measure surround us. We use our understanding of measure to quantify and interpret the world around us. Many of the things we do and enjoy in our daily lives are possible because of measurement. Without it, there would be little mass production resulting in inexpensive goods, no weather reporting or projections, no scheduled public transportation, and certainly no ocean or space exploration.

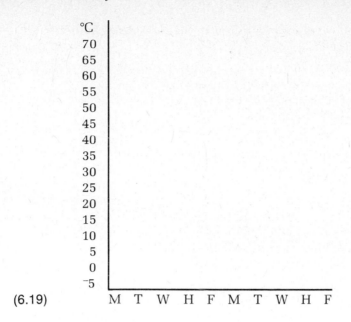

(6.19)

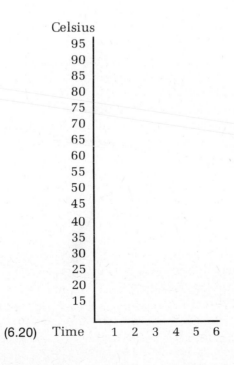

(6.20)

Our work with children in measurement should result in three basic outcomes:

1. Children should obtain appropriate knowledge regarding measures and concomitant skills in using measuring instruments.
2. Children should appreciate the role that measurement plays in their lives and in society generally.
3. Children should enjoy measuring and being able to measure for themselves.

The view expressed regarding the implementation of metric measure is that the schools should vigorously lead in the move to educate society in the metric system. The activities provided are not intended as an exhaustive list or as a complete guide to curriculum. For the former you can refer to a metric anthology,[8] and for the latter the most appropriate guide is the commercially prepared text from your arithmetic series. The principal intent is to provide a sound conceptual framework for understanding measurement principles.

ACTIVITIES, PROJECTS, A POINT OF VIEW

1. Obtain a printed copy of the goals for mathematics in your state. Are goals for metric education included? Does your state have any special metric publications for elementary teachers? Obtain a copy. Does the highway department in your state have any plans to go metric? Discuss.

2. Select a school or school district familiar to you. Obtain a list of the goals and objectives for the elementary school mathematics program. Are goals for metric education included? Record a brief outline of the topics and skills by recommended grade level.

3. Select a grade level of your choice. Compare a pupil's text published since 1975 with one published prior to 1971. Compare the units on measurement. How do they differ in content? How do they differ in process? Prepare a brief class report.

4. Estimation skills are exceedingly important in mathematics. Practice can help you become familiar and comfortable in thinking metric. Try the following, then divide items with two or three classmates and obtain the actual measurement. Share your findings.

Estimate		Actual
_____	Length of postage stamp	_____
_____	Circumference of orange	_____
_____	Width of kitchen sink	_____
_____	Length of baseball bat	_____
_____	Height of coffee cup	_____
_____	Surface area of dollar bill	_____
_____	Surface area of baseball infield	_____
_____	Volume of shoe box	_____

[8]Gary Bitter, Jerald Mikesell, and Kathryn Maurdeff, *Activities Handbook for Teaching the Metric System* (Boston: Allyn and Bacon, Inc., 1976).

_____   Volume of queen-size mattress   _____
_____   Volume of walk-in closet   _____
_____   Weight of this book   _____
_____   Weight of liter of water   _____
_____   Weight of ten-speed bike   _____
_____   Weight of average adult female   _____

5. Obtain a copy of the *Guinness Book of Records*. Select five unusual records that are appropriate to report in kilometers. Do them.

6. For the fast workers: Take a map of your area (city, county, defined suburb). Estimate its area, then calculate the area in appropriate metric units. Record and report.

7. Devise an original measurement project from the classroom environment that calls for determining volume. Record it in the form of an activity card. If possible, try it with a small group of school age children or some peers.

8. Select one of the activities from each area of measurement in Chapter 6. Translate them to activity cards, making whatever creative adjustments you think desirable. If possible, try them with some children or peers.

9. What is the basis of your agreement or disagreement with the following statements?

   a. Since parents and other adults are so uncomfortable with the metric system, the schools ought be very cautious in any metric campaigns.

   b. Growing up with a dual system will only result in "blocks" to gaining proficiency in one or the other.

   c. The entire matter of measurement has become so "popularized" among educators that it is assuming an inflated role in current elementary school mathematics curriculum development.

SELECTED READINGS

Ashlock, Robert. "Introducing Decimal Fractions with the Water Stick." *Arithmetic Teacher*, Vol. 23, No. 3 (March 1976), pp. 201–206.

Bitter, Gary; Mikesell, Jerald; and Maurdeff, Kathryn. *Activities Handbook for Teaching the Metric System.* Boston: Allyn and Bacon, Inc., 1976.

Clason, Robert G. "When the U.S. Accepted the Metric System." *Arithmetic Teacher*, Vol. 24, No. 1 (January 1977), pp. 56–62.

Dumos, Enoch, and Schminke, C. W. *Math Activities for Child Involvement.* Boston: Allyn and Bacon, Inc., 1977, Chapter 7.

Nelson, Doyal, ed. *Measurement in School Mathematics.* Reston, Va.: National Council of Teachers of Mathematics, 1976.

Ostergard, Susan; Silvia, Evelyn; and Wheeler, Brandon. *The Metric World—A Survival Guide.* St. Paul: West Publishing Company, 1975.

Pottinger, Barbara. "Measuring, Discovering, and Estimating the Metric Way." *Arithmetic Teacher*, Vol. 22, No. 5 (May 1975), pp. 272–277.

Shumway, Richard, and Sachs, Larry. "Don't Just Think Metric—Live Metric." *Arithmetic Teacher*, Vol. 22, No. 2 (February 1975), pp. 103–110.

Kurtz, Ray. *Teaching Metric Awareness.* St. Louis: C. V. Mosby Company, 1976.

CHAPTER 7

Reintroduction of Addition and Subtraction
Early Experiences with Integers

PERSPECTIVE   Several methods of introducing children to the operations of addition and subtraction were discussed in Chapter 4. In that chapter, early experiences in promoting arithmetical readiness were the basis for later manipulations with sets of objects, culminating with the introduction of algorithms for addition and subtraction and selected procedures for mastering the basic facts of addition and subtraction. For the study of addition and subtraction in the upper grades, the teacher's task is essentially one of providing new and challenging settings for the reintroduction of those processes for further study. This must be done in a manner that requires children to use what they have already learned to gain increased understanding of the fundamental operations.

The material in Chapter 7 helps teachers select methods to lead children to an extended understanding of the basic concepts underlying selected algorithms of addition and subtraction. Some consideration of the addition and subtraction of both positive and negative integers is provided, and the relationship of these operations to similar operations with whole numbers is stressed.

As a result of studying Chapter 7 you should be able to:

1. Describe teacher moves appropriate for teaching a contemporary addition algorithm.

2. Prepare an original activity card requiring children to use addition in a problem-solving setting.
3. Write a flow-charted lesson plan for teaching one of the following subtraction algorithms: decomposition or equal additions.
4. Describe a unique contribution of subtraction to early facility with problem solving.
5. Prepare a flow chart lesson which utilizes a "new" process for the reintroduction of either addition or subtraction for further study.
6. Illustrate a teaching strategy that will enhance student growth in mental arithmetic.
7. Write a behavioral objective indicating student behaviors necessary to demonstrate understanding of addition and subtraction with integers.

ADDITION ALGORITHMS

Chapter 4 discussed how the digits in a vertical algorithm could be summed in any order without affecting the result as shown in Figure 7.1. Because an algorithm is only a computational convenience, it is all too often learned in rote fashion. The algorithm alone will not enhance understanding of the basic properties of addition. In fact, the continued separation of the algorithm from meaningful mathematical situations may contribute to the disparity between problem-solving performance and computational skill.

$$
\begin{array}{ccc}
634 & 634 & 634 \\
+153 & +153 & +153 \\
\hline
700 & 7 & 80 \\
80 & 700 & 700 \\
7 & 80 & 7 \\
\end{array}
$$

(7.1)

Constructing Addition Algorithms

During the formative part of their mathematical experience, children learn to describe the action of additive situations through the use of horizontal mathematical sentences. Thus, Joseph knows that if he has eight pigeons and then buys one more, he now has nine pigeons. He can show this action by the number sentence $8 + 1 = 9$.

Children must be helped to realize that as mathematical situations become more complex and involve larger numbers, they require more comprehensive procedures. Consider the following problem:

Nancy sold thirty-five tickets for the Halloween party, while Susan sold seventy-eight tickets. How many tickets have the two girls sold?

A mathematical sentence may be written $35 + 78 = \square$. However, the computation is not so simple. To solve this problem, children may be led to use the commutative and associative properties of addition. Thus $35 + 78 = \square$ may be rewritten in expanded form as illustrated in Figure 7.2.

$$35 + 78 = (30 + 5) + (70 + 8)$$ Expanded form (relies on knowledge of decimal system)

$$= 30 + 70 + 5 + 8$$ Commutative property

$$= (30 + 70) + (5 + 8)$$ Associative property

$$= (100) + (13)$$

(7.2) $$= 113$$

This is an acceptable algorithm for the solution of problems of this magnitude if the child is comfortable with it.

Until a problem becomes so cumbersome that efficacy dictates use of a more efficient algorithm, children do not need an introduction to the traditional short-form vertical algorithm. More important, introduction of the vertical algorithm before children become proficient in using other, more meaningful algorithms, may detract from the meaning and interest of mathematics experiences for them.

The research and writing of psychologists such as Bruner emphasize the importance of allowing a child to discover her own algorithm. The need for this does not diminish as she advances through the upper grades.

Some children, given the opportunity to analyze the quantitative setting in Figure 7.2., may solve the problem using another algorithm— perhaps one devised by them. For example, once the addition sentence 35 + 78 = □ has been generated, it might be solved by either of the forms shown in Figure 7.3.

$$35 + 78 = (35 - 2) + (78 + 2) \quad \text{or} \quad 35 + 78 = (35 + 5) + (78 + 2) - 7$$

$$= 33 + 80 \qquad\qquad\qquad = 40 + 80 - 7$$

$$= 113 \qquad\qquad\qquad = (40 + 80) - 7$$

$$= 120 - 7$$

(7.3) $$= 113$$

Appearance of such algorithms in the work of children is evidence of an awareness of many basic properties of equality. However, it may not be wise to present these algorithms to *all* children. They can be discouraging to children who are not completely confident.

A Vertical Algorithm Once children recognize the properties discussed in the examples shown above, it is time for them to transfer to a vertical algorithm. An efficient way to introduce the vertical algorithm is through direct instruction to the group. Pose a problem to the class such as the following:

> The end-of-the-year program is scheduled for next week. Mrs. Smith, the principal, says they need to borrow all the chairs from the fourth, fifth, and sixth grades in order to have enough for the program. The school has 87 fourth-graders, 112 fifth-graders, and 93 sixth-graders. How many chairs will have to be put in place?

Have the children solve the problem using the algorithms previously learned, then observe:

> "I noticed that it took most of you at least two or three minutes to solve this one problem. Most of your time was spent in writing the problem down. Since I know you know your basic addition facts very well, and you also know how to rename numbers to find sums, I thought you might be interested in an easier way to show your work. Look at what I've written on the chalkboard."

The illustration you place on the board will look like that shown in Figure 7.4. Discuss A first, then B and C.

	A	B	C
$87 + 112 + 93$	$= (80 + 7) + (100 + 12) + (90 + 3)$	87	87
	$= (80 + 90) + (100) + (7 + 12 + 3)$	112	112
	$= (170) + (100) + (10 + 12)$	$+93$	$+93$
	$= (170 + 100) + (20 + 2)$	12	292
	$= (270) + (20 + 2)$	180	
	$= (270 + 20) + 2$	100	
	$= (290) + (2)$	292	
(7.4)	$= 292$		

Emphasize that the final vertical algorithm places the addends into correct alignment so that tens may be added to tens, and ones to ones, and so on. Be certain to show how the algorithms relate to the horizontal number sentence.

Once children understand the relationships, they must be given additional opportunities to translate quantitative settings described in words into computational algorithms. All too often we have seen children compute with remarkable facility when examples are presented in algorithmic form, yet fail to perform satisfactorily on tests of problem-solving. These children are not able to translate real life or story problems into a mathematical algorithm. Many mathematics educators tend to blame this failure on reading competence. Although reading is crucial to the solving of verbal problems, attempts to increase mathematical performance by reducing the vocabulary in story problems have yielded little real improvement in performance. Also, blaming mathematical failure upon reading inability fails to explain the apparent lack of facility in solving problem situations arising from the daily activities of children. It seems logical to assume, then, that practice in translating real life and story problems into algorithmic form is as crucial as practice in computation. Neither can be overlooked.

Activities Involving the Use of Addition   The classroom, the school building, and the play yard comprise a vast potential environment for mathematics learning. For example, is there a music room in your school? A group of four or five children may be sent to the music room with an activity card such as the one which follows.

Activity Card: Using addition   Level: Early intermediate

1. Describe and count the musical instruments you find.

2. Arrange them in sets. How many sets did you find? How many instruments are in each set? How many are there in all?

3. How else might you classify the instruments you found?

4. How many are in each set?

5. Find as many other ways of forming sets of instruments as you can. How many are in each?

While one group is classifying and adding sets of musical instruments, another group might be outside the room describing, classifying, and recording quantitative data regarding the environment as requested on another card you have prepared.

Activity Card: Using addition   Level: Early intermediate

1. Describe and count the evergreens in the playground.

2. Describe and count other playground plants and bushes

3. Arrange the material into sets according to your classification.

4. How many other items could you fit into each set?

5. Compare your results with others using the same card. Were there differences? Why?

A third group might be examining the books in the classroom library and classifying them by content, size, shape, and length in number of pages, and adding those on shelf one to shelf two, and so on. Other groups might look at the physical education equipment, the number of boys and girls eating the hot lunch surveyed by grades, and so forth. When one group finishes a problem they might move on to a problem previously completed by another group to "see if the first group missed anything." The two groups could then meet and discuss their findings.

Number sequences can provide children an independent challenge in a problem solving setting. Provide an activity card like this one.

Activity Card: Problem solving   **Level:** Early intermediate

1. Place the numerals 1, 2, 3, 4, and 5 in the circles of the formation so the sum of three numbers in each direction is the same. How many different ways can you do it? Record them.

2. Place each of the numerals 1, 2, 3, 4, 5 in one of the circles so that no two consecutive numerals are connected.

3. Now try these using the same number of consecutive numerals as circles.

Computing with Addends in a Column   Addition is a binary operation. Because of this, only two addends may be summed at any one time. Therefore, when a number of addends are arranged in a column, children must understand that not one but a series of additions is required (see Figure 7.5). When three addends are involved, it is necessary to make use of the associative property by grouping two of the addends to find their sum, and then combining the third addend.

$$
\begin{array}{c}
6 \\
3 \\
+8 \\
\hline
\end{array}
\begin{array}{c}
9 \\
\end{array}
\qquad
\begin{array}{lcr}
(6 + 3) + 8 = \square & \text{or} & 6 + (3 + 8) = \square \\
9 + 8 = 17 & & 6 + 11 = 17
\end{array}
$$

(7.5)   17

Initial Algorithm	Step One	Step Two—Adding Ones	
14	10 + 4	10 + 4	13
29	20 + 9	20 + 9	>16
63	60 + 3	60 + 3	>21
+35	30 + 5	30 + 5	
		21	

Step Three—
Regrouping and
Adding Tens
10
20
60
30
+(20) + (20) + 1 = 141

(7.6)   140   1

Provide children with exercises involving numerals with more than one digit. An effective technique is to make use of expanded notation (see Figure 7.6). Notice that the same ideas previously used in the introduction of the addition algorithm are equally applicable with column addition.

Estimation and Mental Addition   A great deal of useful and meaningful practice may be had through mental addition. One purpose for mental arithmetic is to provide children with an opportunity to appreciate the commutative and associative properties. Suppose children are asked to mentally find the sum for the following addition problem: 14 + 19 + 16 = □. Many would quickly discover that 14 and 16 are easily added to form 30. Once this is done, it is a quick decision for them to add 30 + 19. Other children will discover alternate methods which they prefer and which are effective for them. Mental exercises such as these do more than provide children with an opportunity for practice. They will generally contribute to increased agility with numbers, as well as with problem-solving facility.

Activity Card: Mental arithmetic   **Level:** Early intermediate

1. You have $15 which you are to spend. Buy as many items from the table as you think you can. You have three minutes.

2. Check your purchases by summing the cost. How close did you come?

3. Is there some other combination of items which would have come closer to the $15?

4. Estimate sums for each of the following exercises. You have one minute.

    a. 14 + 17 + 23 + 16 + 8 = □
    b. 5 + 81 + 12 + 9 + 18 + 6 = □
    c. 3184 − 562 = □
    d. 24693 − 8821 = □

5. Compare your estimate with the true sums by doing the required computation. How close were you? Do you have a system for estimating? How is estimation useful to you?

Estimation and mental arithmetic go hand in hand. Construct a chart for display like the one in Figure 7.7 which assigns a dollar value to each letter of the alphabet. Initially, children may view the chart, estimate the value for their name, then compute its actual value. Here children can use estimation and then addition to make a variety of interesting computations.

Many opportunities for mental arithmetic and estimation are found in life outside school. Have the class estimate the miles from home or school to their favorite place of entertainment, the cost of refreshments for a party, the number of "rows" it will take to mow the lawn, and so on. With a minimum of experience children will quickly learn to use gross or precise estimates, whichever the problem setting calls for. An activity card can structure useful exercises for children so that the functional value of estimation skill, as well as its usefulness to computation, is evident.

SUBTRACTION ALGORITHMS   Most elementary schools in the United States and Canada currently teach a subtraction algorithm called the decomposition method. Generally,

A = $1   H = $8   O = $15   U = $21
B = $2   I = $9   P = $16   V = $22
C = $3   J = $10   Q = $17   W = $23
D = $4   K = $11   R = $18   X = $24
E = $5   L = $12   S = $19   Y = $25
F = $6   M = $13   T = $20   Z = $26
G = $7   N = $14

Example: Nancy Drew
$$14 + 1 + 14 + 3 + 25 + 4 + 18 + 5 + 23$$

1. Famous people
2. The school name
3. The teacher's name
4. The principal's name

5. Their sisters' names
6. The most expensive three-letter word
7. $100 words
   ($50 words, etc.)
8. Least expensive words

(7.7)

most mathematics educators support the teaching of this method because it is apparently easier for children to rationalize. One other subtraction algorithm, the equal additions method, is occasionally used. Each approaches subtraction from a different perspective.

The Decomposition Method The decomposition method involves the use of regrouping (or borrowing). When children observe that they cannot "take 8 from 2" in Figure 7.8 (in the system of natural numbers), they are taught to regroup one of the tens to form ones. The regrouped value is now six tens and twelve ones. Next, they are told to subtract eight ones from twelve ones. The difference, four ones, is recorded below the line in alignment with the ones column. Looking at the tens column, a child subtracts three tens from six tens and records his answer below the line in alignment with the tens column. The same procedures are used as larger numbers are encountered. Such quantitites are renamed to facilitate computation (see Figure 7.9).

$$
\begin{array}{r}
72 \quad (72 = 6 \text{ tens plus 12 ones}) \\
-38 \\
\hline
\end{array}
$$

$$
\begin{array}{r}
6 \ (12) \ \text{ones} \\
7\ 2 \\
-3\ 8 \\
\hline
4
\end{array}
$$

$$
\begin{array}{r}
6 \ (12) \ \text{ones} \\
7\ 2 \\
-3\ 8 \\
\hline
3\ 4
\end{array}
$$

(7.8)

$$
\begin{array}{cc}
& \quad\quad 3 \\
1643 & 1\ 6\ 4\ \textcircled{13} \quad \text{ones} \\
-865 & -\ 8\ 6\ 5 \\
\hline
& \quad\quad\quad\quad 8 \\
\end{array}
$$

$$
\begin{array}{c}
5\ \textcircled{13} \quad \text{tens} \\
1\ \cancel{6}\ 4\ 3 \\
-\ 8\ 6\ 5 \\
\hline
7\ 8 \\
\end{array}
$$

$$
\begin{array}{c}
\textcircled{15} \quad \text{hundreds} \\
\cancel{1}\ \cancel{6}\ 4\ 3 \\
-\ 8\ 6\ 5 \\
\hline
7\ 7\ 8 \\
\end{array}
$$

(7.9)

The Equal Additions Method

Unlike the decomposition method, there is no regrouping with the equal additions method. When children observe that they cannot subtract eight ones from two ones without using negative numbers, they are taught to add 10 to the minuend in the ones column immediately. It is now possible to subtract eight ones from twelve ones, with a difference of four ones. This is then recorded below the ones column. However, since 10 was added to the ones column of the minuend, it is necessary to add 10 to the subtrahend. Subsequently, the 3 in the tens column of the subtrahend is crossed out and a 4 is put in its place. Four tens are then subtracted from seven tens and the difference recorded below the tens column. Since adding equal amounts to number pairs does not change their difference, the correct answer is obtained. Identical procedures are used with digits of larger value.

$$
\begin{array}{c}
7\ 2 \\
-3\ 8 \\
\hline
\end{array}
$$

$$
\begin{array}{c}
7\ \textcircled{12} \quad \text{ones} \\
-3\quad 8 \\
\hline
4 \\
\end{array}
$$

$$
\begin{array}{c}
7\ 12 \\
\textcircled{4} \quad\quad \text{tens} \\
-\cancel{3}\quad 8 \\
\hline
3\quad 4 \\
\end{array}
$$

(7.10)

ANALYZING THE PROBLEM- SOLVING POTENTIAL OF SUBTRACTION

When it is determined that children have a knowledge of the operation of subtraction at the principle level (children can subtract accurately and explain and demonstrate the processes involved), it is time to move to the problem-solving level. Three types of subtraction problem situations occur naturally in the real world. The rationale underlying each procedure differs greatly, as does the appropriate teaching procedure. The three situations, called subtractive subtraction, comparative subtraction, and additive subtraction are described below.

**Subtractive
Subtraction**

The setting which follows is easily recognized as a subtraction situation because the problem is stated in such a way that a separation is obviously indicated.

> George's father owns a farm which has five tractors. One night a fire destroyed the shed containing two of the tractors. How many tractors did George's father have left?

From the statement of the problem it is easily seen that one must subtract 2 from 5.

This type of subtractive situation may easily be shown through use of the flannelboard, blocks, and so on (see Figure 7.11).

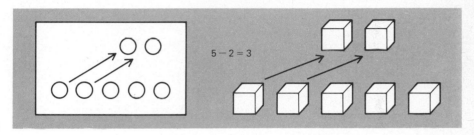

(7.11)

Place five objects on the felt board or on a table. While the child watches, remove two objects from the five and ask the child to tell you what you have just done. Finally, have him write the subtraction sentence 5 − 2 = 3 to describe the action just taken. You may anticipate little trouble with this phase of subtraction.

**Comparative
Subtraction**

The comparative subtraction situation is more difficult to understand than subtractive subtraction. Rather than calling for a simple separation of one set from a greater set, comparative situations require that one set be compared to another and the difference of their relative sizes determined.

> Nancy has twelve stuffed toys while Sally has seven stuffed toys. How many more stuffed toys does Nancy have than Sally?

To solve this particular problem it is necessary for children to understand that two sets are being compared with each other to determine their numerical relationship (see Figure 7.12). Through the use of one-to-one correspondence, children will find that after matching Sally's stuffed toys with Nancy's several of Nancy's toys remain unmatched. Sally does not have enough dolls to match each of Nancy's. Therefore, the difference between Nancy's set and Sally's is found by counting the unmatched toys in Nancy's set. However, this solution does not lead directly to the writing of a number sentence to show the action encountered.

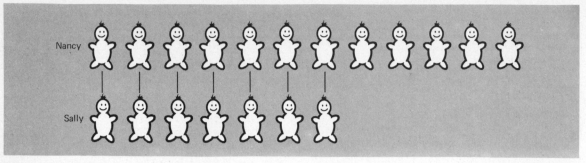

(7.12)

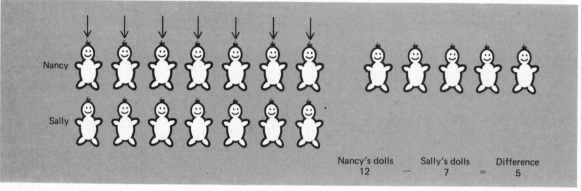

Nancy's dolls		Sally's dolls		Difference
12	—	7	=	5

(7.13)

Rather than having children place toys from Nancy's and Sally's sets into a one-to-one correspondence, show what would happen if enough dolls were removed from Nancy's set to match Sally's (see Figure 7.13). Children may then be asked to describe this action with the number sentence $12 - 7 = 5$. This procedure may be repeated with several other problems to insure understanding of the subtraction situation and its description in algorithmic form.

Additive Subtraction   The additive subtraction situation is encountered when a given quantity is less than a desired quantity. Like the comparative subtraction problem, the additive subtraction problem requires a knowledge of one-to-one correspondence.

> Janet has made a bargain with her mother. She has agreed to rake twelve bushel baskets of leaves from the front lawn. By noon she had raked nine baskets of leaves. How many more baskets of leaves does she need to rake?

The situation is called additive subtraction because the required thought is additive in nature. To solve the problem, the child needs to add

Chart 7.1 Flow Chart Lesson Plan—Comparative Subtraction

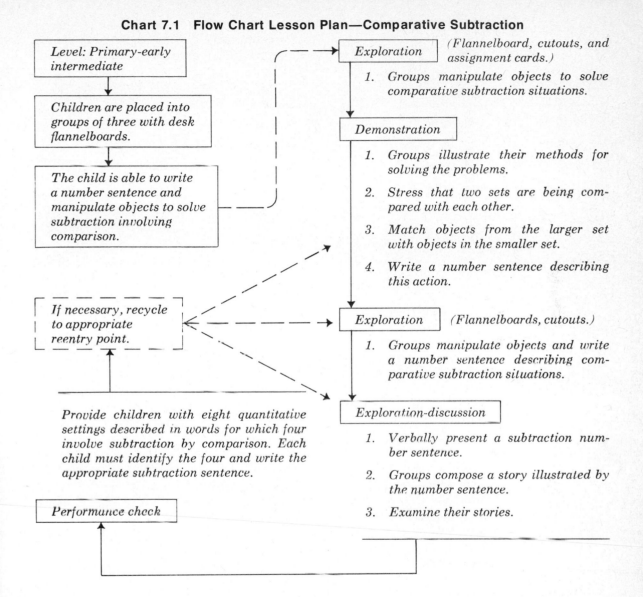

Level: Primary-early intermediate

Children are placed into groups of three with desk flannelboards.

The child is able to write a number sentence and manipulate objects to solve subtraction involving comparison.

If necessary, recycle to appropriate reentry point.

Provide children with eight quantitative settings described in words for which four involve subtraction by comparison. Each child must identify the four and write the appropriate subtraction sentence.

Performance check

Exploration *(Flannelboard, cutouts, and assignment cards.)*

1. Groups manipulate objects to solve comparative subtraction situations.

Demonstration

1. Groups illustrate their methods for solving the problems.

2. Stress that two sets are being compared with each other.

3. Match objects from the larger set with objects in the smaller set.

4. Write a number sentence describing this action.

Exploration *(Flannelboards, cutouts.)*

1. Groups manipulate objects and write a number sentence describing comparative subtraction situations.

Exploration-discussion

1. Verbally present a subtraction number sentence.

2. Groups compose a story illustrated by the number sentence.

3. Examine their stories.

several baskets of leaves to the nine baskets she already has, so that she may attain her goal of twelve baskets. She must be shown that although the situation is additive the most efficient way of solving the problem is to subtract the number of baskets raked from the number of baskets needed.

A teaching example using a directed approach is as follows. Have the class write the problem in a number sentence, 9 bushels + □ bushels = 12 bushels. Provide the children with an opportunity to explore various ways of finding a solution to the problem. Many will immediately answer that the problem can be solved by simply counting the number of objects from 9 to 12 and placing that numeral into the frame. Ask individual children to demonstrate this action by showing you on the flannelboard.

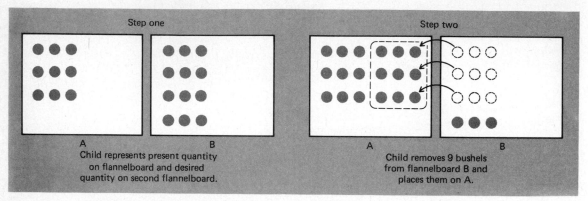

(7.14)

Demonstration of the action may be attained more quickly if two flannelboards instead of one are used (see Figure 7.14). One flannelboard represents the desired quantity and one is used to represent the quantity already on hand (Step One). As members from the set representing the desired quantity are matched on the flannelboard containing the members representing the quantity already on hand, children easily see that this problem, although additive, may be solved by taking from the desired set a quantity of members equal to those already on hand (Step Two).

Although children may have an intuitive grasp of the idea that additive subtraction problems may be solved by subtracting the quantity on hand from the quantity desired, they still have not been led to transfer this knowledge to performance with an algorithm. Since objects are taken from one set and mapped on another set, children might easily feel that a quantity has merely been subtracted from one side of an equation and added to the other. This may be avoided by continuing instruction with one additional transitional step. Using the two flannelboards again, explain that the same result may be obtained by removing equal quantities from both flannelboards until the board representing the number of objects on hand is empty (see Figure 7.15). Have them compare the results of this manipulation with that previously demonstrated in Figure 7.14. After several comparisons they will agree that both activities produce the same result. At this point they are ready for the horizontal algorithm. They can understand that a child having twelve baskets of leaves to rake who has already raked nine baskets may use a subtractive process to make the computation of this problem easier (see Figure 7.15). Notice that each step of this procedure is demonstrated in Figure 7.16. The number sentence clearly describes the action previously completed on the flannelboard or with other manipulative materials.

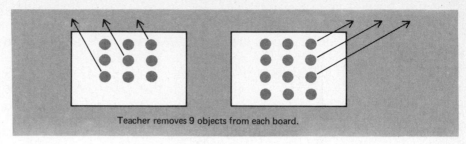

Teacher removes 9 objects from each board.

(7.15)

$$9 + \square = 12$$
$$9 - 9 + \square = 12 - 9$$
$$\square = 3$$

(7.16)

As with addition, pattern and sequence may be used in a problem-solving format for subtraction. Use the following instructions on an activity card for the formats provided below.

Activity Card: Subtraction puzzles   Level: Intermediate

1. Place the numerals 1–6 around the circumference of the circle in a manner such that the difference between neighboring numbers will never be greater than 2.

2. Try the same thing with seven numerals and a circle. What happens? Can you do it?

3. Place the numerals 1 to 7 in the circle of the H format so that for any three in a row, the sum of the end numbers minus the middle is always the same. Will it work with the numerals 11 to 17? 121 to 127?

Another form of problem-solving practice in subtraction is found in supplying children with sheets that contain several grids in which selected cells are blank. The task is to fill in the missing numbers in some orderly, logical manner. In the example shown (a subtraction grid), the first row is differences, the second row is minuends, and the bottom row contains subtrahends. The children should simply be encouraged to begin. Grids can be constructed for combined operations, so answers may vary.

(7.17)

6	10	8		42	21	
8		12	9	49		24
2	5		4			

An activity card is a useful means for providing further practice or reviewing recently acquired skills and concepts. As an example, this activity card might be used following several days of instruction with subtraction during which several new algorithms were introduced.

Activity Card: Subtraction review   Level: Intermediate

1. Solve each of the subtraction examples below using the equal-additions algorithm. Check each computation using the decomposition method *or* the Austrian method.

1000	981	1837
−872	−86	−954

2. Rewrite one of the above examples and solve it using the method of complements.

3. Record three different situations where you or someone you know has had to use subtraction. Classify each situation according to whether it was subtractive, comparative, or additive.

EXTENDED SETTINGS FOR REINTRODUCING ADDITION AND SUBTRACTION

It is an unsettling fact that after the third grade there is very little "new" material that can be presented to children regarding the operations of addition and subtraction. This presents a serious challenge for intermediate grade teachers. Providing children with the same familiar exercises and formats for the study of basic operations in each succeeding grade level does not generate much interest in mathematics. Those pupils who did not acquire the main ideas previously will not be stimulated by a reintroduction in the familiar fashion. Likewise, pupils who did acquire some main ideas the first time will be unimpressed. There are intrinsic values in devising new settings for reintroduction of the operations, and they may be summed as follows:

1. The new procedure may create interest for the talented students as well as the less able.
2. The new procedure may be presented as a challenge for pupils to figure something out for themselves.
3. The new process provides a setting for illustrating the superiority of the "old" or "new" way.
4. The new procedure provides an opportunity to consider the operation from a broader perspective, thus extending understanding.

Rapid Addition

Reintroduction of addition in problem settings which require the use of column addition provides a great deal of meaningful practice for children as reinforcement for the basic addition facts; it also creates another opportunity to employ the commutative and associative properties of addition in a meaningful way. Early in fourth grade, prior to systematic study in pupil texts, give children a problem situation requiring them to find the sum of five addends. Ask them to look for ways to make their computation more efficient. They may look for pairs of addends which total 10, or look for number pairs such as $6 + 6$, and so on. Actively searching for patterns allows them to overcome the drudgery of adding long columns of figures one addend at a time, and enhances accuracy as well. Help them to see that what they have actually done is change the order of the addends (commutative property) to find sums for those addends totaling 10 (associative property). During subsequent study, have children apply the process and discuss its advantages.

$$
\begin{array}{r}
7 \\
4 \\
5 \\
6 \\
+3
\end{array}
\qquad (7 + 3) + (6 + 4) + 5 = 25
$$

(7.18)

Simultaneous Addition

A setting which places an emphasis on mental arithmetic is also appropriate for reintroducing the study of addition in grade five or six. Again, prior to using textbooks, present a problem setting like the following:

"It was about 2:00 P.M. one day this summer as we were driving on our vacation. We knew we could drive about 150 miles before evening and we wondered what city we would reach by that time. On our map were these distances between the next four towns: 46, 64, 23, 18. My father read the names of the towns, the distances, and said, 'We will stop here because that is 151 miles.' I was amazed and asked how he did it. He just smiled, then took paper and pencil and made a diagram like the one I have on the board. From the diagram, can you tell how he thought to get the answer so quickly?"

$$
\begin{array}{r}
46 \\
64 \\
23 \\
18 \\
\hline
151
\end{array}
$$

(7.19)

During a brief guided discussion of the algorithmic form shown in Figure 7.19, children can be lead to recognize the nonpencil and paper sum is obtained by thinking 46 (and 60), 106 (and 4), 110 (and 20), 130 (and 3), 133 (and 10), 143 (and 8). The expressions in parentheses are written as an explanation. The addition should actually be thought: 46, 106, 110, 130, 133, 143, 151. While not all children will readily accept this "new way of thinking" because most of us are mentally lazy, with a bit of practice a surprising number of pupils will apply it with enthusiasm to subsequent addition tasks.

The Scratch Method of Addition

A "new check" can often be utilized as the reason for introducing a unique procedure. The scratch method of addition lends itself nicely to that rationale. When children learn to add using the vertical algorithm, they commonly began by first adding the ones column, followed by the tens, hundreds, and so on. Examine the possibility of adding by beginning with the place having the greatest relative value, and progressing from it to places of lesser value (see Figure 7.20). The scratch method of addition involves first finding the sum of the thousands column by adding $7 + 1 = 8$. Next find the sum of the hundreds column by adding $6 + 1 + 1 = 8$. The sum of the tens column is 15; enter the 5 under the tens column and add 1 to the hundreds column. Scratch out the 8 and record 9 below it. Now, add the ones column to total 23. Set the 3 below the ones column and add 2 to the tens column, making 7 tens. Scratch out the 5 and place a 7 in the tens column. The unscratched digits, 8973, represent the desired sum.

Properly used as a setting for reintroduction, the scratch method of addition brings a new perspective to the understanding of place value necessary for the use of the addition algorithm. Often, those children who

$$
\begin{array}{r}
7\,6\,5\,4 \\
1\,8\,3 \\
1\,0\,9 \\
1\,0\,2\,7 \\
\hline
8\,8\,5\,3 \\
9\,7
\end{array}
$$

(7.20)

do not truly understand the role of place value and regrouping in addition will discover it, and the need for reteaching will be made clear. Still other children may obtain a clear notion of regrouping for the first time from this new perspective. The scratch method provides children with an opportunity to study the characteristics of place value and how the algorithm commonly used in addition might derive from it.

Utilizing Compensation in Subtraction

Through the principle of compensation it is often possible to make subtraction "easier." Because such an approach appeals to children, it provides an ideal setting for the reintroduction of subtraction in the fourth grade.

On the day subtraction is to be reintroduced for further study, place on the chalkboard several verbal problem settings requiring the operation of subtraction. Abstract the subtraction equation from at least two of the settings and place each beside its respective word problem. Then recast the number sentence into a vertical algorithm as shown in Figure 7.21.

$$
\begin{array}{cc}
37 + \square = 65 & \square + 55 = 125 \\
\downarrow & \downarrow \\
68 & 130 \\
-\,40 & -\,60
\end{array}
$$

(7.21)

Through guided discussion, lead children to observe that an arbitrary amount was "added" to both terms of each example to make computation easier. They should also not that the source of the amount in both examples was the difference between the subtrahend and the next even tens number. Before proceeding to their regular work, provide children with a work sheet containing ten subtraction problems. The students should write the number sentence, recast the problem, and "just think the answer." Subsequently, discuss the advantages and disadvantages of this new procedure. Conclude that adding like amounts to number pairs leaves their difference unchanged.

The Complementary Method of Subtraction

The complementary method of subtraction offers a welcome format for the reintroduction of a study of subtraction in fifth or sixth grade. The complement of a number is the difference between a given number and the next largest power of 10. Thus the complement of 7 is 3, the complement of 25 is 75, and the complement of 98 is 2. In each case the second number is the difference between the given number and the next highest power of 10.

Beyond the obvious method of inspection, the complement of a number can easily be obtained by subtracting the first digit on the right that is other than zero, from 10, and all other digits of the given number from 9. For example, to obtain the complement of 240, subtract 4 (which is the first digit on the right that is other than zero) from 10, obtaining 6; then, 2 from 9 leaves 7. The result, 760, is the complement of 240. Similarly, the complement of 13,420 can be found; starting at the left, $9 - 1 = 8$, $9 - 3 = 6$, $9 - 4 = 5$ and $10 - 2 = 8$. The result, 86,580, is the complement of 13,420.

At first, children can simply "have fun" obtaining complements. In the process, they will obtain much mental practice in reviewing basic subtraction facts. Subsequently, recalling the principle—if the same quantity is added to the minuend and to the subtrahend, the difference remains unchanged—it is easy to see that adding the complement of the subtrahend to both the minuend and the subtrahend leaves the difference unchanged.

For all practical purposes, the complementary method is an extension of compensation, but there is a "short" method of applying it to obtain differences for subtraction algorithms. Consider $546 - 83$. We can simply think "546, 563, 463" (see Figure 7.22).

(7.22)

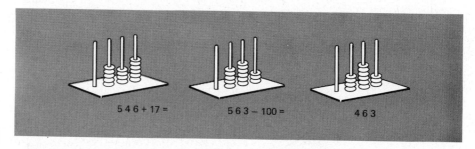

$$546 + 17 = \qquad 563 - 100 = \qquad 463$$

The solution consists of adding 17 (the complement of 83) to 546, resulting in 563, and then subtracting 100, the next power of 10 (10^2) larger than 83. It should be clear that adding 17 to a number and subsequently subtracting 100 is the same as subtracting 83.

Children enjoy using an abacus like the one shown in Figure 7.22 to obtain or verify the results of solving subtraction examples by the complementary method.

Checking Subtraction   As with addition, utilizing a new check provides an appropriate setting for the reintroduction of subtraction for further study. Since subtraction is the inverse operation of addition, the check of subtraction most often used is summing the obtained difference and the subtrahend, resulting in the original minuend. While this is useful, it can become routine, and children grow careless in repeated applications. One useful procedure for reintroducing subtraction is giving children a work sheet containing ten or fifteen subtraction examples with the differences provided. Several should be incorrect. Tell them their only task is to check the answers with the restriction that they cannot sum the difference and minuend to obtain their check. Most children will discover they can check subtraction in an "all subtraction way." That is, the minuend minus the difference equals the subtrahend. Discuss the advantages and disadvantages of the new procedure after children have applied it for several days in their subtraction work.

These examples are representative of the many varied settings that may be employed to make the reintroduction of basic operations on the intermediate level meaningful and fun.

ADDITION AND SUBTRACTION OF INTEGERS By the fourth or fifth grade, children have had an introduction to the positive integers. They have manipulated materials, written number sentences, solved common everyday problems, and so on. Their exposure to the negative integers, while not as varied, is much more extensive than was once believed. Children at this age normally understand what is meant when one owes five cents, what −5° Celsius means, and what is meant by "going into the hole" when playing a game. These concepts, while rudimentary and undeveloped, form a basis for introducing addition and subtraction of integers to children. It is often useful to discuss a simple problem using a number line to present a visual picture (see Figure 7.23).

There were some counting disks in a box. Joseph placed twelve more in the box. Charles was then asked to remove fifteen. How many less are in the box than when Joseph added twelve?

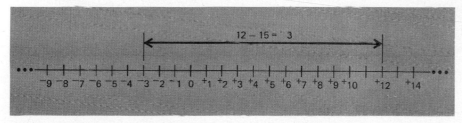

(7.23)

When it appears that several children in the class are ready for future work on negative integers, design a series of experiences for them and allow them to explore and manipulate and thus discover relationships for them. This is an ingredient of active learning. A typical learning experience might go like this:

A group of four or five children at a table in one corner of the room may be given some materials and an activity card such as the following. The materials might include some paper, a ruler, and a crayon or pencil.

Activity Card: Rationalizing integers   Level: Intermediate

1. How many days are there until Easter? Can you make a number line to show this? How many days will there be until Easter tomorrow?

2. Can you make a number line to show how many minutes it is until (*lunch*)? What happens when you get to 0?

3. Extend the number line you just made to show minutes after lunch. Show 5 minutes after lunch. Show 8 minutes. Make your line long enough to show 15 minutes after lunch.

4. Now if I look at the number line, how can I tell whether a time is before or after lunch?

5. Where would you place the mark to show that I have 8¢ in my pocket? Where would you place the mark to show that I owe 5¢ (*And other questions of similar kind.*)

6. Show what would happen if I owe 5¢ and someone gives me 8¢. Make up another problem and show it on the number line.

7. Make a thermometer and show 6° below zero. Show what happens when it warms up 15° during the day.

Addition with Integers Assignments can be changed or extended to obtain desired objectives. Through experiences such as the previous activity card, children may be shown that quantitative expressions represented on the number line are expressed in terms of their relationship to 0. A man with no money who

Chart 7.2   Flow Chart Lesson Plan—Discovering Integers

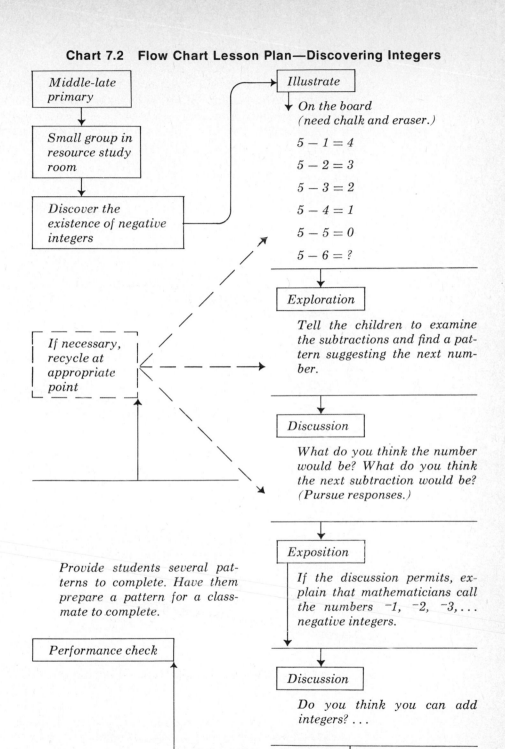

Middle-late primary

Small group in resource study room

Discover the existence of negative integers

If necessary, recycle at appropriate point

Provide students several patterns to complete. Have them prepare a pattern for a classmate to complete.

Performance check

Illustrate

On the board (need chalk and eraser.)

$5 - 1 = 4$

$5 - 2 = 3$

$5 - 3 = 2$

$5 - 4 = 1$

$5 - 5 = 0$

$5 - 6 = ?$

Exploration

Tell the children to examine the subtractions and find a pattern suggesting the next number.

Discussion

What do you think the number would be? What do you think the next subtraction would be? (Pursue responses.)

Exposition

If the discussion permits, explain that mathematicians call the numbers $^-1$, $^-2$, $^-3$,... negative integers.

Discussion

Do you think you can add integers? ...

suddenly finds a five-dollar bill might be shown as now possessing the quantity of five dollars. Conversely, a man with no money might be browsing in a store and accidentally break a five-dollar piece of glassware, for which he is subsequently billed. He now possesses a negative quantity of money which may be expressed as ⁻five dollars. Other quantities are expressed in the same manner.

Once children understand the meaning of signed numbers (sometimes called directed numbers), they are ready to perform the operation of addition using both positive and negative numbers. Through the use of examples familiar to children, give the class an opportunity to add using both positive and negative addends. Problems such as this are useful in helping to develop such understanding.

> In a "spin game" which requires twelve points to win, Mary lost three points on her first turn and four points on her second turn. How many points did Mary lose?

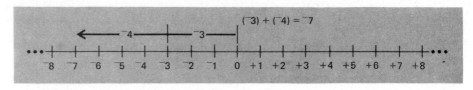

(7.24)

When solving problems, children must understand that the direction of the moves is indicated by the sign of the numbers. In this example, since two negative quantities are being added, the move is toward the left. Such examples become more complex when they involve a combination of positive and negative addends.

> During the day the temperature reached a high of 6° Celsius. By late afternoon the temperature had dropped 11°. How cold was it in the late afternoon?

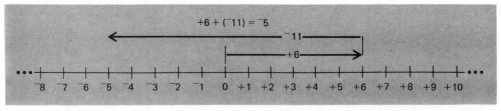

(7.25)

Additive Inverse Understanding the additive inverse is dependent on a child's attainment of the Piagetian concept of reversibility. He must understand that a one-to-one relationship exists between a number and its inverse, and that the effect of adding a quantity of an equation may be nullified by moving in reverse (by adding a negative quantity).

You may easily demonstrate with the number line that any number plus its inverse equals 0. Examples may be drawn from the everyday activities of the classroom. For example, consider the problem in Figure 7.24. Mary is down seven points for her third turn. Have each group show an action such as this on the number line. Several similar problems may be necessary to help children realize that adding the inverse of any number yields a sum of 0. To further their understanding, you may wish to have them develop stories of their own which they represent by actions on the number line.

Subtracting Integers   Just as with the natural numbers, the operation of subtraction with negative integers seems more difficult for children to rationalize than addition. It is important that you provide children with a great deal of experience involving subtraction so that they envision the operation of subtraction as a separating or "taking away" action. This background of experience is essential to an understanding of subtraction with negative integers, and is necessary if one is to overcome reliance upon associative learning typified by rote memorization of the rule: "To subtract a negative number, change its sign and add."

Help children understand subtraction of negative integers by providing instructions such as: "Solve this problem using the number line. Write a number sentence to show your action."

> Jerry owes fifteen cents at a candy store. The owner of the store tells Jerry that he will set aside ten cents of the debt if Jerry will deliver a package for him. How much will Jerry owe after he delivers the package?

To solve this problem, children must recognize that they are actually decreasing a part of the debt. They cannot solve it by counting in a negative direction, as they have been able to do with other subtraction problems, because to do so will increase the debt to twenty-five cents. Since they are decreasing the debt, they must represent this on the number line by moves in the direction of 0. Thus, the direction of the moves on the number line is determined by context (see Figure 7.26).

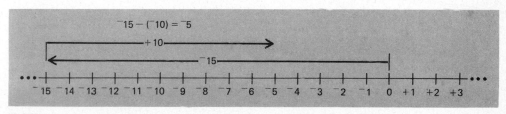

(7.26)

To help children understand the nature of the problem and the required action, you may wish to use media other than the number line. But because the number line is such an integral part of later teaching with integers, it is a good policy to refer to it. Set up problems such as:

> Your father has an account for $36.00 at the department store. Just before he pays it, he gets a second notice telling him they overcharged him $15.00. How much does he now owe? Can you show this on the number line?

The task is made more interesting if actual bills are prepared. Children enjoy being "store manager" and preparing their own bills (see Figure 7.27).

	Truax Mercantile		
Mr. Joe Brown			
May statement		*Bal.*	*00.00*
Item	*Charges*	*Credits*	*Net*
Sweater	36.00	Credit on overcharge 15.00	
		Pay this amount	?

(7.27)

A more difficult idea of subtraction with negative integers occurs when both positive and negative integers are involved. Consider the following problem.

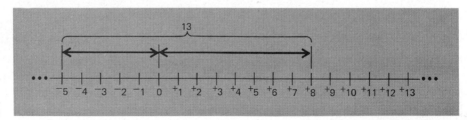

(7.28)

It is crucial that children understand precisely what they are being asked to find in examples of this kind. They are actually being asked to find the difference between $^+8$ and $^-5$. This is shown by the sentence $^+8 - {}^-5 = \square$. By plotting the two points on the number line, children can easily see that the distance between the points is thirteen spaces. This appeals to them intuitively, since the distance is apparent.

When you are satisfied that the children visualize the process of subtraction with negative numbers, introduce them to the algorithm whereby they change the sign and add. This may be done meaningfully by use of the addition property of equality in a problem such as the one in Figure 7.29.

$$5 - (^-8) = \square$$
$$5 - (^-8) + (^-8) = \square + (^-8) \quad \text{[Add } (^-8) \text{ to both sides]}$$
$$5 = \square - 8$$
$$5 + 8 = \square \ ^-8 + 8 \quad \text{[Add } (^+8) \text{ to both sides]}$$
$$5 + 8 = \square$$
(7.29) $$13 = \square$$

The quantity 8 is added to both sides of the equation and the sum computed. When this is done, the 5 is left on one side while $\square - 8$ is left on the other. It is a simple matter to add 8 to both sides of the equation leaving the common equation $5 + 8 = \square$. Have the children work several of these problems independently and ask them to look for a pattern. Help them see that the application of the addition property of equality actually allows the use of the common shortcut algorithm exemplified by "When subtracting a negative integer, change the sign and add."

There is a useful teaching guide that may be followed when using vectors to represent moves on the number line. For addition of signed numbers, both vectors travel in the directions indicated by the signed numbers. In subtraction of signed numbers, the minus sign reverses the direction of the vector following the operation sign. Study Figure 7.30 and observe how relating this reversal of the vector to the inverse operation might help children during their early experiences with addition and subtraction of integers.

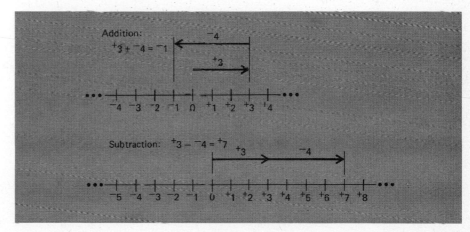

(7.30)

GROUPING NUMBERS Because it is difficult to read numerals when they are written without punctuation marks, mathematicians divide numerals into grouping for easy reading.

Help the class discover the need for "mathematical punctuation" by asking them to read a large ungrouped numeral such as 3458632. Just as is the case with elementally grouped objects (Chapter 4), children and adults have difficulty in attaching meaning to such symbols. For this reason, punctuation is used to designate different periods. Using place-value pockets or an abacus, help children see that there are certain natural groupings which lead to easy punctuation.

Place some markers on the place-value pockets to indicate a numeral and ask the class to read the numeral aloud. Begin with a small numeral such as 324, and put the markers into appropriate pockets to show that the numerals represent hundreds, tens, and ones in each period; attach the appropriate label of the period to the various pockets in Figure 7.31, so children can read it as 204 billion, 13 million, 102 thousand, 41. Check their understanding by writing a numeral on the board and asking them to represent that numeral using place-value pockets or an abacus.

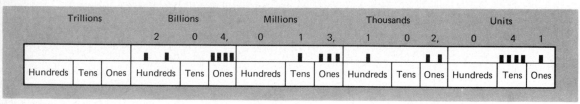

(7.31)

Student interest in large numbers can be enhanced through utilization of projects, facts, and activities that help make large numbers meaningful. Here are a few.

1. Make a wall chart of the period names for large numbers.

Table 7.1

Name	Relative Size	Zeros Required
Million	1000 thousands	6
Billion	1000 millions	9
Trillion	1000 billions	12
Quadrillion	1000 trillions	15
Quintillion	1000 quadrillions	18
Sextillion	1000 quintillions	21
Septillion	1000 sextillions	24
Octillion	1000 septillions	27
Nonillion	1000 octillions	30
Decillion	1000 nonillions	33
Undecillion		
Duodecillion		

2. For practice in writing numerals for large numbers, suggest that children write a numeral for a number larger than 5000; between 150,000 and 300,000; less than 1,000,000 but greater than 500,000; greater than 10,000 but containing no zeros; and so on.

3. Make a wall display of 1 million zeros on butcher paper.

4. Have the class collect 1 million bottle caps. If there are 30 students in the class and each student brings 100 per day, it will take about 8 weeks to collect them. If each student brings 100 per week, it will take about 35 weeks to collect them. Design a place to display them as they are accumulated.

5. Large number facts: Did you know that:
   a. one million seconds is about 11 days?
      one billion seconds is about 32 years?
      one trillion seconds is about 32,000 years?
   b. One million dollar bills laid end to end would be about 1000 miles long. How many dollar bills would it take to go around the earth at the equator? (25 million) How many dollar bills is the moon from the earth? (225 million) The sun? (93 billion)
   c. A train traveling nonstop at 100 km per hour would take 1140 years to travel 1 billion km.
   d. You probably have more than 100,000 hairs on your head.
   e. If you spent $1 million per day for 1000 days (a little over 3 years), you would spend $1 billion.

SUMMARY Teaching children how to perform whole number computations with efficacy and understanding is one major objective of elementary school mathematics programs. Any algorithm is a process involving some repetition of certain steps, culminating in that result for which the algorithm was invented. The algorithm of larger numbers for the operations of addition and subtraction generally involves manipulations with basic facts, together with the application of a few generalizations made possible by the properties of arithmetic. The essential challenge is one of doing this in a setting where children can use what they have previously learned. This is because there is fundamentally very little new about the operations of addition and subtraction that can be presented to boys and girls in the intermediate grades.

When the set of whole numbers is extended to include the negative numbers, this new set is referred to as the set of integers or signed numbers. Consideration of signed numbers is generally exploratory in the elementary school. Few contemporary elementary programs exploit signed numbers to the extent the "new mathematics" movement once forecast. Still, children very naturally experience concepts involving negative numbers in their lives, and to that extent selected formal experiences are appropriate. The love of large numbers provides another opportunity for enrichment and increased pupil interest in the enjoyment of mathematics during the intermediate grades.

ACTIVITIES, PROJECTS, A POINT OF VIEW

1. The extended algorithms of addition and subtraction have a logical rationale. Write the name of the appropriate principle or property for each step in the following example:

$$35 + 72 = [3(10^1) + 5] + [7(10^1) + 2]$$ _____
$$= [3(10^1) + 7(10^1)] + [5 + 2]$$ _____
$$= [(3 + 7)(10^1)] + [5 + 2]$$ _____
$$= 10(10^1) + 7$$ _____
$$= 77$$ _____

2. Imagine the examples reproduced below were taken early in the year from a fourth-grade student paper involving mixed practice with addition and subtraction. Write a brief analysis of the pupil's difficulties. Your analysis should include reasons that support the statements you have made. Several students should present an analysis to the class.

$$\begin{array}{r} 178 \\ + 52 \\ \hline 120 \end{array} \qquad \begin{array}{r} 524 \\ -262 \\ \hline 382 \end{array}$$

3. Pupils in the intermediate grades often need to experience reteaching of fundamental concepts in concrete terms. Use multibase blocks, color rods, or some form of open-end abacus to "explain" the subtraction example $503 - 268$. Record the results in expanded notation form.

4. Use a contemporary pupil text for the intermediate grade level of your choice. Prepare a flow chart lesson plan that could serve to reintroduce the operation of addition or subtraction for further study.

5. Write a brief critique of "The Odometer in the Addition Algorithm," *Arithmetic Teacher*, January 1977, p. 18. If you believe it worthwhile, design a model of the odometer and present a brief to the class.

6. In the same issue of *The Arithmetic Teacher*, Mr. Wenner describes a "base subtraction" method. Criticize or support this statement: The "base subtraction" method is clearly superior to either the decomposition method or the equal additions method.

7. For the subtraction example $394 - 85 = 209$, list three reasons why $394 - 209$ is a superior subtraction check.

8. Use the number line to illustrate with vectors the solution for $^-4 - {}^+3$.

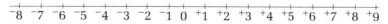

9. What is the basis of your agreement or disagreement with the following statements?

    a. It is important to develop the technical vocabulary of properties and principles when they are first introduced.

b. Most children and adults exhibit a natural disdain for checking their arithmetical computations.

SELECTED READINGS

Copeland, Richard W. *Mathematics and the Elementary Teacher*, 2d ed. Philadelphia: W. B. Saunders Co., 1972, Chapter 6.

D'Augustine, C. H. *Multiple Methods of Teaching Mathematics in the Elementary School*, 2d ed. New York: Harper & Row, 1973, Chapters 6 and 7.

Green, G. F., Jr. *Elementary School Mathematics—Activities and Materials*. Lexington, Mass.: D. C. Heath and Company, 1974, pp. 186–208.

Grossnickle, Foster E., and Reckzeh, J. *Discovering Meanings in Elementary School Mathematics*, 6th ed. New York: Holt, Rinehart and Winston, 1973, pp. 164–179.

Hall, Donald E., and Cynthia, T. "The Odometer in the Addition Algorithm." *Arithmetic Teacher*, Vol. 24 (January 1977), pp. 18–20.

Heddens, J. W. *Today's Mathematics*, 3d ed. Chicago: Science Research Associates, Inc., 1974, Unit 16.

Kramer, Klaas. *Teaching Elementary School Mathematics*, 3d ed. Boston: Allyn and Bacon, Inc., 1975, Chapters 10 and 11.

King, Irv. "Giving Meaning to the Addition Algorithm." *Arithmetic Teacher*, Vol. 19 (May 1972), pp. 345–348.

Murray, Peter J. "Addition Practice through Partitioning of Sets of Numbers." *Arithmetic Teacher*, Vol. 23 (October 1976), pp. 430–431.

Schwartzman, S. "A Method of Subtraction." *Arithmetic Teacher*, Vol. 22 (December 1975), pp. 628–630.

Wenner, William J. "Compound Subtraction—An Easier Way." *Arithmetic Teacher*, Vol. 24 (January 1977), pp. 33–35.

CHAPTER 8

Reintroduction of Multiplication and Division
Extended Operations with Integers

PERSPECTIVE   There are at least two conditions necessary in the discovery process. First, in order to make a discovery, a child must purposefully explore something. Second, she must accommodate this new knowledge into an existing structure in order that it serve some new purpose. As an example, the commutative, associative, and distributive properties of multiplication can be discovered and later generalized to form the basis for simple computational algorithms. These simple algorithms can then be refined through discussion, observation, or direct instruction until they most effectively fit the particular needs and abilities of the child.

Computation should be a function of a child's need to apply quantitative procedures in order to describe or generalize concrete experiences or observed number patterns. The use of new settings and expanded algorithms in the reintroduction of multiplication and division at successive levels of the intermediate grades is an efficient way to employ a problem-solving process while providing an opportunity for extended understanding of the operation.

The material included in this chapter expands the concepts and principles introduced in Chapter 5 by providing children with additional experiences which have wider application, and by introducing algorithms which make computation more efficient. The chapter also extends children's knowledge of operations with integers.

As a result of studying Chapter 8 you should be able to:

1. Design a sequence of activities enabling children to discover an algorithm for multiplication.
2. Utilize concrete material to demonstrate teaching the standard multiplication algorithm.
3. Describe a unique setting for the reintroduction of multiplication.
4. Design a sequence of teaching activities that will enable children to discover a division algorithm.
5. Prepare an activity card designed to analyze the standard division algorithm.
6. Design an original setting for the reintroduction of the study of division.
7. Write a flow chart lesson plan enabling children to abstract the processes of multiplication for directed numbers.

THE MULTIPLICATION ALGORITHM Children who have developed facility with the basic multiplication facts and who are able to perceive the usefulness of the distributive property of multiplication should be provided with experiences designed to introduce them to a natural algorithm for multiplication.

Initially, alignment of the multiplicand into frames is an efficient representation of the way in which place value and the distributive property are used in solving multiplication examples. In working with Figure 8.1, children may observe that a correct response to the exercise requires that they consider the relative value of the tens and ones, and that the product of the exercise may be found by regrouping the partial products formed through multiplication by tens and by ones. It becomes clear that 4×3 really means 4×3 tens and equals 12 tens, not simply 12.

$$4 \times 36 = \square$$
$$(4 \times 30) + (4 \times 6) = \square$$
$$4 \times \boxed{3}\boxed{6} = \boxed{12}\boxed{24}$$

tens ———┘
ones ———————┘   └——————— ones
                  └——————— tens

$$= 120 + 24$$
$$= \text{(renaming of tens and ones)}$$
(8.1) $$= 144$$

Examples which utilize formats similar to that shown in Figure 8.1 gives children the background they need in developing natural multiplication algorithms for themselves. To provide a setting for helping children to discover an algorithm for multiplication, give a problem such as this one:

Jim found it was 424 steps from the back door of his house to his rabbit hutch. In order to care for the pets properly, Jim made three round trips daily. How many steps did he travel?

After multiplication has been identified as the necessary operation, children may be guided to utilize several options for recording the manner in which they can obtain a product (see Figure 8.2).

	A	B	C
	424	424	424
	× 6	× 6	× 6
	2400	120	24
	120	24	2400
	24	2400	120
(8.2)	2544	2544	2544

As illustrated in Figure 8.2, some children may choose to multiply the hundreds first, while others may decide to multiply in the alternative ways shown in B and C. Once children have computed products, additional beneficial learning may take place through group discussion of the results. The children will observe that each product is the same, despite apparently dissimilar procedures in computation.

Standard Multiplication Algorithm The rationales for teaching the standard multiplication algorithm are that 1) it is efficient; 2) it simultaneously forces an organizational pattern for computation and thinking, because each partial product is not fully recorded; and 3) it is familiar to most adults. In fact, omission of this particular algorithm can cause parental concern as well as concern to another teacher a child may encounter later.

	A	B	C
	2	12	424
	424	424	× 6
	× 6	× 6	2544
(8.3)	4	44	

When teaching the standard multiplication algorithm, several restrictions must be noted (see Figure 8.3). For one thing, to be most efficient, computation always begins with the units column and then proceeds sequentially through the tens, hundreds, and so on. It is appropriate to observe that this procedure insures that regrouping always proceeds to the next larger place value. A second restriction must be observed: the ones must be aligned under the ones column, tens under tens, and so on, so that partial products may be summed. You may wish to discuss with the children what would happen if the alignment were altered.

In the example shown in Figure 8.3 children must recognize that multiplying by a factor in the ones column results in twenty-four ones or two tens and four ones. The tens are then regrouped to the tens column, as in *A*. A child may either write the 2 to represent the tens he has regrouped, or he may retain it mentally. Children who choose to write the numeral to indicate regrouping, should be encouraged to do so. When such a "crutch" no longer has utility, a child will probably discard it without the teacher's insistence. Actually, there is little real need for children to discard the crutch.

	Natural	*Standard*
✓	7 8 4	7 3
	× 2 9	7 8 4
	3 6	× 2 9
	7 2 0	7 0 5 6
	6 3 0 0	1 5 6 8
	. 8 0	2 2 7 3 6
	.1 6 0 0	
	1 4 0 0 0	
(8.4)	2 2 7 3 6	

Using Multipliers of Two or More Digits

The greater the number of digits in a multiplication activity, the greater the need for the efficiency of the standard algorithm (see Figure 8.4). Notice that the natural algorithm involves six partial products—that is, three digits (multiplicand) each considered twice (multiplier). The standard algorithm does not record as many partial products because the summing of partial products is accomplished along with computation.

Experiences which encourage the use and comparison of the natural and standard algorithms are both interesting and worthwhile to children. They can employ both algorithms to find the product of examples, as shown in the problems of this chapter. When this has been done, whole group participation in a lively discussion can be encouraged by comparing the two algorithms to determine how they are related. One child may notice that the first three partial products in the natural algorithm sum to the value of the first partial product in the standard algorithm. Another child may observe that the second set of three partial products in the natural algorithm sums to the second partial product in the standard algorithm. Others may call attention to the number of partial products in each algorithm. Experiences such as these help children understand the rationale of both algorithms. Through utilization, examination, and discussion, children are able to observe for themselves the role of place value in these algorithms and to understand the contributions of the distributive property to the solution of multiplication exercises.

Extended Settings for Reintroducing Multiplication The reintroduction of basic operations for additional study in the upper grades can be uninspiring for both teachers and children. This is because the form and setting of the reintroduction is generally identical to that of the original study. Thoughtful reexamination of basic operations within unique algorithmic formats can create new interest, provide additional practice, and extend pupil understanding. These new formats may simply involve novel practice; sometimes they may be introduced in the form of a new check; other times the principal advantage may be reliance on mental arithmetic. Whatever purpose is chosen to accompany a selected format, children can always compare the efficacy of the need procedure to "the way we did it last year."

The Lightning Method or Cross Multiplication When it is necessary to review or reteach the multiplication process, one good setting for this is provided by mental cross multiplication, sometimes called the "lightning method." This method was one of eight to appear in Paciali's *Suma*, 1494. Earlier (c. 900 A.D.) it appeared in an Arab manuscript. Consider the multiplication 39 × 43. Figure 8.5 shows how it works.

Step 1
9 × 3 = 27
Write 7 ones and carry the 2 tens.

$$\begin{array}{r} 43 \\ \times\ 39\ \uparrow \\ \hline 7 \end{array}$$

Step 2
9 × 4 tens = 36 tens
3 tens × 3 = 9 tens
36 + 9 + 2 = 47 tens
Write the 7 in the tens' place and carry the 4 hundreds.

$$\begin{array}{r} 4\ \ 3 \\ \times\ 3\ \ 9 \\ \hline 7\ 7 \end{array}$$

Step 3
3 tens × 4 tens = 12 hundreds
12 + 4 = 16 hundreds
Write the 16 hundreds.

$$\begin{array}{r} 43 \\ \times\ \uparrow 39 \\ \hline 1677 \end{array}$$

(8.5)   Multiply as usual for a check.

After this procedure has been introduced to children and discussed by them, an appropriate follow-up is to present a series of multiplication exercises with two-digit multipliers where children are asked to do one half the "old way," the other half the "new way," and to determine which is more efficient. An alternative strategy is to present the "lightning method" as a "new and shorter check."

It should be emphasized that the value of these "other ways to multiply" will be lost unless children are engaged in lively discussions regarding the advantages and disadvantages of each, the knowledge they need to use them effectively, and the contribution each process makes to an extended understanding of the number action in multiplication.

Finger Multiplication Children enjoy this historical procedure in which one needs to know only the facts up to 5. Once common, finger multiplying is fun to use if one forgets the products of pairs of numbers between 5 and 10. Consider 8 × 7. First, give numbers to the fingers of each hand beginning with "6" for the thumb. To multiply 8 × 7, place the "8" finger of one hand against the "7" finger of the other hand, holding the hands with thumbs up. Bend down the fingers below the "8" and "7" fingers. Count the pointed fingers (the two touching and those above them) for the tens' digit and multiply the number of bent fingers on one hand by the number of bent fingers on the other hand for the ones' digit. This activity involves more than just review of basic facts because with some pairs of factors it will be necessary to mentally regroup. Complete the multiplication 6 × 7 according to the above instructions and see why this is so.

(8.6)

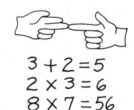

$$3 + 2 = 5$$
$$2 \times 3 = 6$$
$$8 \times 7 = 56$$

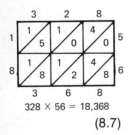

328 × 56 = 18,368

(8.7)

Lattice Multiplication In 1478, a book printed in Triviso, Italy, showed a method of multiplying called the Gelosia (lattice) method. Wisely used, the lattice method of multiplication provides children with a great deal of meaningful practice with the multiplication facts. As a unique multiplication algorithm for whole numbers, it is also an effective means of reemphasizing place value. Figure 8.7 shows how one would use this method to multiply 328 × 56. Note that in the upper right square is the product of 8 and 5, 40. To its left is the product of 2 and 5, 10. Others are done in a similar manner. The final product is found by summing numbers along diagonals starting with the lower right square, and regrouping to the next diagonal where necessary.

In the sixteenth century, a Scotchman, John Napier, improved on the lattice method by inventing strips (originally made of bone or ivory and therefore known as Napier's bones) on which products from a multiplication array were shown. You may wish to study Figure 8.8 and use it as a model to make a set of "bones." The strips can be arranged so as to make

Chart 8.1 Flow Chart Lesson Plan—Lattice Multiplication

Level: Upper intermediate

Whole class with pencil and paper, need overhead projector or chalkboard, worksheet.

The child will correctly solve several multiplication exercises using the lattice method.

Illustration-discussion

Write on board:

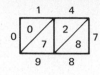

98

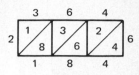

2,184

Pupils study examples. Ask what they think is happening. (Pursue with examples until children "catch on" — don't tell them.)

Demonstration-exploration-discussion

Expand to: *(Teacher and pupils do exercise.)*

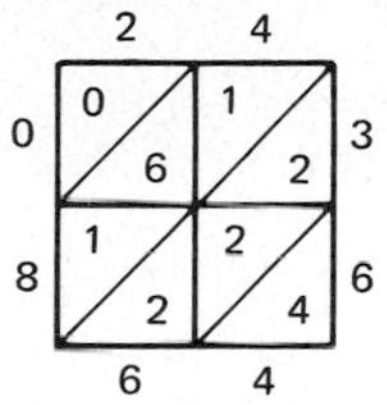

(Check with regular algorithm.)

864

How is the multiplication done? (Pursue) Direct pupils to suggest some; solve as a class; check.

- - - - - - - - - - - -
Recycling not appropriate for this lesson.
- - - - - - - - - - - -

Exploration

Distribute worksheet (10 exercises) such as:

| 36 | to | 347 |
| $\times$ 4 | | $\times$ 261 |

in lattice form. Pupils do any five — make up two of their own! (Circulate as children work). Examine responses on assigned exercises.

Informal only   *Observe pupils work. Are they enthusiastic in their tasks? Note whether their original exercises are simple or complex. Examine at least one response for each child on assigned exercises.*

Performance check

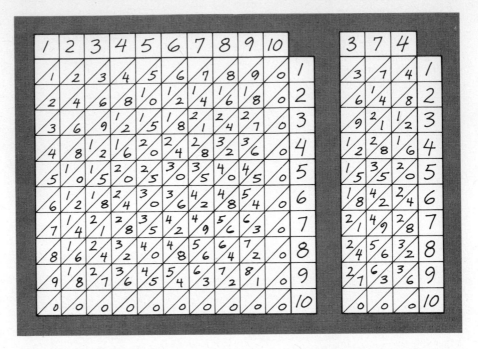

(8.8)

multiplication easy. The array shown indicates how Napier marked his strips. On the right are shown three strips (and multipliers) for multiplying 374 by another number, in this case, 89. The products of 9 and 3, 7, and 4 are 27, 63, and 36, as shown to the left of 9 as ⟨²⁶³⟩⟨⁷³⁶⟩. Adding diagonally as in the lattice method, we have 9 × 374 = 3366. Similarly, 8 × 374 is seen as 2992. These products should be recorded as 3366, 2992 and 33286 added in the usual way.

$$
\begin{array}{r}
3366 \\
2992 \\
\hline
33286
\end{array}
$$

$$
\begin{array}{r r}
\cancel{4\,2}\text{--------}\cancel{2\,9\,4} \\
2\,1 \qquad 5\,8\,8 \\
\cancel{1\,0}\text{------}\cancel{1\,1\,7\,6} \\
5 \qquad 2\,3\,5\,2 \\
\cancel{2}\text{------}\cancel{4\,7\,0\,4} \\
1 \qquad 9\,4\,0\,8 \\
\hline
1\,2,3\,4\,8
\end{array}
$$

(8.9)

Halving and Doubling A multiplication procedure employing halving and doubling was common in early commerce. To multiply 42 × 294, first set the factors side by side as shown in Figure 8.9. Next, successively halve 42 and double 294 (ignore remainders). Cross out all "products" opposite even numbers (left) and sum the remaining numbers on the right. The product is 12,348. In early times the summing was usually done on an abacus.

This activity, when thoughtfully executed, provides an excellent setting for reintroducing multiplication because, although the solution is simple, a great deal of thought is required to discover why the remainders are dropped and why all the even divisors are scratched out. Upper-grade children will spend a great deal of time searching for patterns before they finally arrive at the solution. In fact, the problem may challenge you! See if you can determine why the remainders are dropped before you read on.

The slight variation of the process shown in Figure 8.10 reveals that you can also double both factors, beginning on the left with 1 and continuing until there are numbers in the left column that will total exactly 42. Note that in doubling beginning with 1, binary numeration place values will be generated.

$$
\begin{array}{rr}
\cancel{1} & \cancel{2\,9\,4} \\
2 & 5\,8\,8 \\
\cancel{4} & \cancel{1\,1\,7\,6} \\
8 & 2\,3\,5\,2 \\
\cancel{1\,6} & \cancel{4\,7\,0\,4} \\
3\,2 & 9\,4\,0\,7 \\
\hline
4\,2 & 1\,2,3\,4\,8
\end{array}
$$

(8.10)

THE DIVISION ALGORITHM

Division is considered as the inverse of multiplication. Since multiplication was introduced as repeated addition of equal quantities, it is logical to introduce division as repeated subtractions of equal quantities. The algorithms for division form an extension of the earlier division experiences of Chapter 5, and become useful, perhaps essential, as quantitative settings call for dividends and divisors with more than one digit.

During the reintroduction of division for further analysis, multibase arithmetic blocks are superior materials to use as an aid to reviewing the serial subtraction model as well as the inverse relationship between multiplication and division. After children have completed a series of experiences such as those presented on the following activity card, they are ready to move to an explicit consideration of division algorithm.

Observe the children as they work with their activity cards to see that each child is participating in the activity of the group and that he understands what has transpired. Provide ample opportunity for groups to hold discussions among themselves and to share their discoveries. Be certain that the advantages and disadvantages of each group's methods for recording subtraction are illustrated and discussed so that each child has the opportunity of evaluating the work and modifying procedures as the need arises.

During the study and analysis of division, there are several other procedures that can help children rationalize the strategy of the division process. The strategy of the division algorithm is different from the strategy of all the other algorithms in this way. In every other operation we start with units—that is, the smallest part—but in division, if children

Activity Card: Natural division algorithm   Level: Intermediate

1. Using your multibase blocks, show 63. Now divide 63 into equivalent sets with seven members in each set. How many sets of 7 do you have? Write a subtraction sentence to show what you did. What could you do to put the blocks back together? Write a sentence to show this action.

2. Using your multibase blocks, show 84. Now divide 84 into equivalent sets with twelve members in each set. How many sets of 12 do you have? Write a subtraction sentence to show what you did. Next put the blocks back together and write a sentence to show what you did.

3. Using multibase blocks, show 192. Now divide 192 into equivalent sets with eight members in each set. How many sets of 8 do you have? Write a subtraction sentence to show what you did. See if your group can discover an easier way to write the subtraction sentence. Write a subtraction sentence using your new way.

4. Can anyone discover a way to do division without using blocks? Show how you would do this. Discuss your results. Can you write a multiplication sentence for any of the above?

are to become efficient, they need to be taught to "take the largest part" first. There are several ways this idea can be taught and both rely upon prior pupil learning.

One method may simply be termed "add and circle." For this activity children may be provided with columns of numbers generated by powers of two as shown in Figure 8.11. The only direction accompanying the activity would be, "Circle the addends you need to reach the sum at the bottom of each column." Such exercises will help familiarize children with the idea of taking the largest part first.

Another procedure builds upon pupils' prior knowledge of multiplication and, to some extent, place value. Since this activity is somewhat more time consuming, it lends itself well to an activity card for use during independent investigation. Study the illustrative activity card that has been provided.

Chart 8.2   Flow Chart Lesson Plan—A Natural Division Algorithm

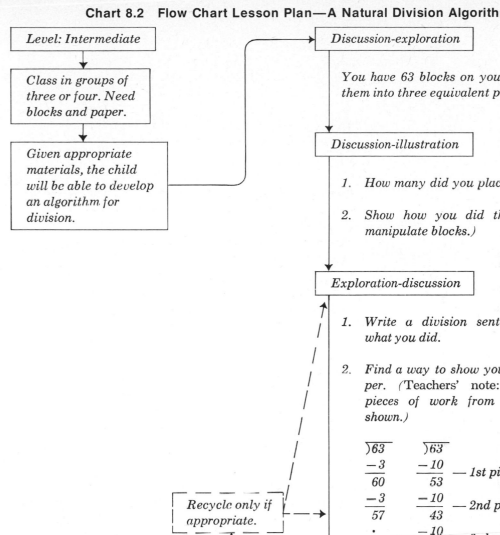

Level: Intermediate

Class in groups of three or four. Need blocks and paper.

Given appropriate materials, the child will be able to develop an algorithm for division.

Recycle only if appropriate.

Provide three division exercises. Encourage children to devise and use their own unique algorithm for computation. Share algorithms and observations about them.

Performance check

Discussion-exploration

You have 63 blocks on your desk. Divide them into three equivalent piles.

Discussion-illustration

1. How many did you place in each pile?

2. Show how you did this. (Children manipulate blocks.)

Exploration-discussion

1. Write a division sentence to show what you did.

2. Find a way to show your work on paper. (Teachers' note: *Two actual pieces of work from a lesson are shown.*)

$$\begin{array}{r})63 \\ -3 \\ \hline 60 \\ -3 \\ \hline 57 \\ \cdot \\ \cdot \\ \cdot \end{array} \qquad \begin{array}{r})63 \\ -10 \\ \hline 53 \\ -10 \\ \hline 43 \\ -10 \\ \hline 33 \\ \cdot \\ \cdot \\ \cdot \end{array}$$

— 1st pile

— 2nd pile

— 3rd pile

3. (Exchange papers.) Can you tell what was done? How does it differ from your work? Can you improve your method? (Use additional examples.)

$$
\begin{array}{cccc}
① & 1   & 1   & 1   \\
② & 2   & 2   & 2   \\
4   & 4   & 4   & 4   \\
8   & 8   & 8   & 8   \\
16 & 16 & 16 & 16 \\
㉜ & 32 & 32 & 32 \\
64 & 64 & 64 & 64 \\
\underline{128} & \underline{128} & \underline{128} & \underline{128} \\
35 & 43 & 92 & 176 \\
\end{array}
$$

(8.11)

Activity Card: Finding sixes in a number   Level: Intermediate

1.   Complete the first list:

1 × 6 ___	10 × 6 ___	100 × 6 ___
2 × 6 ___	20 × 6 ___	200 × 6 ___
3 × 6 ___	30 × 6 ___	300 × 6 ___
4 × 6 ___	40 × 6 ___	400 × 6 ___
5 × 6 ___	50 × 6 ___	500 × 6 ___
6 × 6 ___	60 × 6 ___	600 × 6 ___
7 × 6 ___	70 × 6 ___	700 × 6 ___
.	.	.
.	.	.
9 × 6 ___	90 × 6 ___	900 × 6 ___

2.   Fill the second and third lists.

3.   Complete the box below. First, pick the largest number from the list above that is < 5634. Enter it in the box and record the number of sixes it represents.

4.   Subtract and find the largest number on the lists that is less than the difference. Enter it below and record the number of sixes it represents.

5.   Can you find 54? How many sixes equal 5,634?

	5	6	3	4
900	5	4	0	0
___	_	_	_	_

A Natural Division Algorithm

An algorithm is simply a computational tool, nothing more. Mathematical concepts giving meaning to an algorithm must be found elsewhere. For this reason, teachers are well advised to help children acquire a meaningful division algorithm through a carefully planned sequence of steps. Use concrete materials as you demonstrate "your" algorithm (see Figure 8.12).

As you remove each set of seven blocks from the pile of thirty-five blocks, show how you record your work in the appropriate place. Do not become concerned if a child wishes to continue to use his own algorithm in his work. If his procedure leads him into later difficulty, you may then suggest the more efficient recording system.

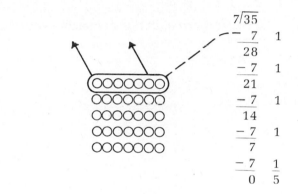

(8.12)

$$
\begin{array}{r}
15\overline{)360} \\
-150 \quad 10 \\
\hline
210 \\
-150 \quad 10 \\
\hline
60 \\
-60 \quad 4 \\
\hline
24
\end{array}
$$

(8.13)

Some children quickly learn additional, more sophisticated techniques for estimation of the partial quotients. For example, after some experience with an algorithm like that shown in Figure 8.13, alert children will discover that they can subtract more than 150 at a time. Observation reveals that there are at least twenty sets of 15 in 360, and so his first estimate is 20, not 10 as shown in the first step. Given encouragement, some children become extremely sophisticated in such estimates. Teacher-made activity cards can enhance this process.

The Standard Long Division Algorithm

The standard long division algorithm requires a series of carefully structured moves by the person attempting to solve an exercise. The skills and moves necessary for success with the algorithm are fully discussed in the following paragraphs (see Figure 8.14).

Activity Card: Estimation with division algorithm   Level: Intermediate

1. Solve the following exercise using no more
than six subtractions:

$$15\overline{)360}$$

2. Can you reduce the number of subtractions
you need to three or less? Show your work.

3. Solve each of the following exercises using the
fewest number of subtractions possible.

$$20\overline{)480} \qquad 32\overline{)672} \qquad 27\overline{)1156}$$

4. Prepare two division exercises and solve each
exercise with the fewest number of subtractions possible.

	A	B	C
	3	32	328
	$27\overline{)8856}$	$27\overline{)8856}$	$27\overline{)8856}$
	81	81	81
	7	75	75
		54	54
		21	216
(8.14)			216

To solve exercises such as that shown in Figure 8.14, children were
once told to decide which numerals in the dividend are to be considered
first by asking the question, "Are there any twenty-sevens in 8? 88?" and
so on. When a numeral containing at least one twenty-seven was found,
children then estimated the number of twenty-sevens contained in 88.

This procedure, although accurate, gives no direct tie either to the child's concept of division or to his prior experience with a natural algorithm. Without such a relationship, performance with the division algorithm becomes a rote process.

Estimating Partial Quotients Use children's past experiences with a natural division algorithm as a means of introducing the long division algorithm. Begin by writing a division exercise on the board and asking the group how it might be solved. Because of their extensive experience with a natural division algorithm, the children's initial attempts will likely be similar to that shown in Figure 8.15.

	Child A		Child B	
(8.15)	27⟌8856	100	27⟌8856	300
	2700		8100	

Children who make a response similar to that of child *A* should be encouraged to estimate how many twenty-sevens (in even hundreds) are contained in 8856. If they experience difficulty in making such a sophisticated estimate, provide several exercises where the partial quotient is more readily apparent than in the exercise being discussed. If the children have further difficulty in estimating the partial quotient, consider carefully whether or not they are ready to transfer to the standard long division algorithm.

Children who demonstrate their ability to make precise estimates, such as child *B* in Figure 8.16, should be ready to begin work with the standard algorithm. Illustrate a different method of recording results by having students examine and compare the similarities of the two algorithms shown in Figure 8.16. Be certain that each child observes that this "new" method of recording is really no different from the old way except that the partial quotients are recorded above the exercise rather than alongside it.

	A		B
	27⟌8856		8
	8100	300	20
	756		300
	540	20	27⟌8856
	216		8100
	216	8	756
		328	540
			216
(8.16)			216

Tests of Divisibility and a Table of Divisors There are tests of divisibility which can help children deal efficiently with certain kinds of problems and add insight regarding number relationships. Although memorizing the rules of divisibility may be of doubtful validity, they are useful to intermediate grade children as an aid in checking estimated quotient figures and determining whether a common fraction is in its lowest terms. The tests are as follows:

1. A whole number is divisible by 2 if its ones digit is divisible by 2.
2. A whole number is divisible by 3 if the sum of its digits is divisible by 3.
3. A whole number is divisible by 4 if the number named by its tens and ones digits is divisible by 4, or if the ones digit plus two times the tens digit is divisible by 4.
4. A whole number is divisible by 5 if its ones digit is divisible by 5.
5. A whole number is divisible by 6 if it is divisible by 2 and by 3.
6. A whole number is divisible by 8 if the partial number named by its hundreds, tens, and ones digits is divisible by 8.
7. A number is divisible by 9 if the sum of its digits is divisible by 9.
8. Any number is divisible by the product of two or more of its prime divisors; for example, a number divisible by both 2 and 3 is also divisible by 2 × 3, or 6. A number divisible by a composite number is also divisible by the prime factors of the latter; for example, a number divisible by 6 is also divisible by 2 and 3.

A useful teaching idea for children who have continued and persistent difficulty in estimating quotient figures is the development of a table of divisors. Consider the example $864 \div 17 = \Box$. In this case, the divisor is 17 and is often troublesome to estimate because of the proximity of the value between the tens digit and the ones digit. Children can quickly be shown, through a doubling process, division by 2, and the simple addition or subtraction of 17, how to develop a division table. Study the example in Figure 8.17.

$$864 \div 17 = \Box$$

(1)	17
(2)	34
(3)	51
(4)	68
(5)	85
.	.
.	.
.	.
(8)	136
(9)	153

(8.17)

Possible quotient figures for the divisor 17—that is (2), (4), and (8)—were generated by simple doubling. Potential quotient digits for other multiples of 17—namely (3), (5), and (9)—were obtained by adding 17 to 34, 68, and 136 respectively. While this process does not develop all products for the divisor, it certainly develops enough to enable the child to proceed with division. The procedure reemphasizes in an obvious manner the relationship between multiplication and division, while providing the child with added confidence as an independent learner.

Extended Settings for Reintroducing Division Just as with multiplication, there needs to be variety in the settings used to reintroduce division for further study. Reexamination of the operation of division can also use new algorithmic formats to create interest, provide review, and extend pupil understanding of the process.

Dividing with Factors Since a "new way to check" has previously been recommended as an appropriate setting for reintroduction, a word about checking is in order. Because multiplication is the inverse of division, checking an answer in division is accomplished through multiplication. Children use the process: "Divisor times quotient plus remainder equals dividend." A limited amount of formal checking of this type serves to encourage accuracy as well as to promote an awareness of division and multiplication as inverse operations. However, existing evidence implies that other methods of checking division are probably superior to the multiplication check. Research suggests that pupils using an "inverse" often "force" the check. That is, when the product of divisor and quotient plus remainder do not equal the dividend, children will change the product in the check to have the result equal that dividend without reworking the division example.

The function of checking is twofold. Its first, and most obvious, use is to determine the accuracy of a computation that has been performed. This is a legitimate function. However, equally important and often overlooked is the fact that the checks employed can serve as an aid to growth in understanding the specific process, as well as the relationship between operations and an understanding of number in general.

There is an interesting process for checking division with two-digit divisors that can extend pupil understanding of the operation of division, as well as reinforce notions regarding the relationship between multiplication and division. This idea might be introduced in fourth grade in the following manner:

> "Boys and girls, you know it always seems easier to divide by one digit than by two. My father showed me a way to divide that I think we could use as a check for division. I've placed an example on the board and then used my father's check. See if you can figure out what I've done."

The example shown in Figure 8.18 had been placed on the board by the teacher.

$$468 \div 12 = \boxed{39}$$

$$
\begin{array}{c}
3 \\
4\overline{)12} \\
\underline{12}
\end{array}
\qquad
\begin{array}{c}
117 \\
4\overline{)468} \\
\underline{4} \\
6 \\
\underline{4} \\
28 \\
\underline{28}
\end{array}
\qquad
\begin{array}{c}
39 \\
3\overline{)117} \\
\underline{9} \\
27 \\
\underline{27}
\end{array}
$$

(8.18)

In the ensuing discussion it was determined that the process called for arbitrarily dividing both the divisor and dividend by 4, a factor of the divisor, and then dividing the resultant quotients. It was also noted that knowledge of the basic multiplication facts was necessary in order to begin the process, and it had the advantage of being an all-division check. Following a discussion of the process and its relative merits, activity cards could be given to individual children or small groups.

Activity Card: Verifying a new check   Level: Intermediate

$$300 \div 12 = \boxed{25} \quad \ldots\ldots\ldots / \ldots\ldots / \ldots\ldots$$

$$630 \div 15 = \boxed{42} \quad \ldots\ldots\ldots / \ldots\ldots / \ldots\ldots$$

$$432 \div 24 = \boxed{18} \quad \ldots\ldots\ldots / \ldots\ldots / \ldots\ldots$$

$$1190 \div 14 = \boxed{85} \quad \ldots\ldots\ldots / \ldots\ldots / \ldots\ldots$$

Latin Division Utilizing a shortened form of the division algorithm serves as excellent practice for reinforcement of the defined operation of division, while providing the opportunity for mental practice with all the operations necessary to complete division. Such an algorithm is used extensively in Latin America. An example is provided in Figure 8.19.

(8.19)
$$
\text{Step 1} \quad
\begin{array}{r|l}
567 & 27 \\
2 & 2
\end{array}
\qquad
\text{Step 2} \quad
\begin{array}{r|l}
567 & 27 \\
27 & 21
\end{array}
$$

Initially, fifth-grade children may simply be presented with an example of the new algorithm to see if they can "figure it out." Subsequently, it may be utilized in problem-solving exercises requiring computation, and "last year's way" can be used as a check.

To use this algorithm, the initial quotient figure is estimated by whatever manner the children have learned. The quotient figure is set immediately below the tens digit of the divisor and the computation 2 × 27 × 54 is performed mentally. The obtained difference, in this case 2, is recorded appropriately beneath the dividend. Subsequently the 7 is brought down and the computation is completed by thinking how many twenty-sevens equal 27. The resultant units digit of the quotient, in this case 1, is recorded beneath the units digit of the divisor, and since this example is one of even division the computation is complete. Again, the main feature is that it requires completion of the necessary multiplication/ subtraction computation of division in one operation. In short, pupils are required to use mental arithmetic and work with unseen digits. Try it with 432 ÷ 24.

The Galley Method The galley method of dividing is an adaption of a Hindu procedure. It was widely used across Europe from the twelfth to the seventeenth centuries. The process utilizes additive subtraction and illustrates the distributive principle with respect to division. When employing the format illustrated in Figure 8.20, teacher-directed discussion should focus on advantages and disadvantages. The format is an appropriate setting for the reintroduction of the study of division in grade six.

$$7704 \div 24 = \square$$

Step 1
```
     5
   7704 )   3
    24
```
Write the divisor under the dividend, align on the left. Determine how many 24s equal 77. This first quotient figure is set to the right and the necessary computation—77 − (3 × 24)—is done mentally. The difference is recorded above the 77 and the appropriate digits are scratched.

Step 2
```
    52
   7704
    244     32
     2
```
Shift the divisor one digit to the right and set it. Repeat the procedure of Step 1—that is, how many 24s equal 504? Complete the computation 50 − (2 × 24) and record the difference as before.

(8.20)

Step 3
```
    52
   7704     321
   2444
    22
```
Set the divisor one digit to the right and complete the division as before—that is, how many 24s equal 24? 24 − (1 × 24) and record the difference.

Casting Out 9s While not providing a new division setting, the "excess of 9s" check is one that all intermediate grade children can enjoy, and it does avoid forcing the check as can be the case when inverse processes are used as a check. It is relatively easy for children to learn to check division through a process of finding the excess of 9s in the divisor, dividend, and quotient. To do so, the digits in each of these are summed and the excess beyond 9 is noted.

$$
\begin{array}{r}
328 \\
27\overline{)8863} \\
81 \\
\hline
76 \\
54 \\
\hline
223 \\
216 \\
\hline
7
\end{array}
$$

Excess of 9s in divisor $= 2 + 7 = 9 = 0$

Excess of 9s in quotient $= 8 + 2 + 3 = 13 = 1 + 3 = 4$

8863 dividend   0 divisor

$-$ 7 remainder $\times$ 4 quotient

8856   0

(8.21)   Excess of 9s in dividend $= 8 + 8 + 5 + 6 = 27 = 2 + 7 = 9 = 0$

The product of the excess of 9s in the divisor and the quotient must equal the excess of 9s in the dividend. Note, however, in this example the remainder, 7, was subtracted from the dividend before the excess of 9s in the dividend was found. Note also that there is no excess of 9s in the dividend after the remainder was subtracted: $8 + 8 + 5 + 6 = 27$ and $3 \times 9 = 27$.

Other procedures for checking division by casting out 9s are also available and involve only a modification of the manner in which the remainder is treated. Some children may enjoy working with this procedure and may decide to attempt to determine the "why" on their own. Casting out 9s can be explained via modular arithmetic where $9 \equiv 0$.

All of the previous settings can be profitable learning experiences for children as they compare, discuss, and weigh the relative merits of these new procedures against the more familiar formats of computation.

MULTIPLICATION AND DIVISION WITH INTEGERS

Unless a child has attained the formal operations stage described by Piaget, he is probably not ready to work with signed numbers at the principle or problem-solving level. However, in the belief that selected children in the later intermediate grades will have the necessary subordinate abilities for success in operations with signed numbers, and will benefit from them, a brief discussion and some illustrative teaching procedures have been included here.

**Multiplying
Directed Numbers**   Number patterns can be used as an initial activity to help students develop an intuitive idea of the multiplication of integers. This might be done by employing an activity card like the following:

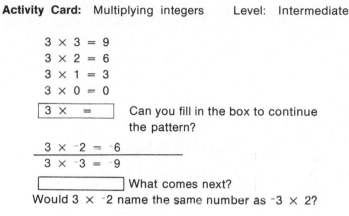

Activity Card: Multiplying integers   Level: Intermediate

$3 \times 3 = 9$
$3 \times 2 = 6$
$3 \times 1 = 3$
$3 \times 0 = 0$

$3 \times \boxed{} = \boxed{}$ Can you fill in the box to continue the pattern?

$3 \times {}^-2 = {}^-6$
$3 \times {}^-3 = {}^-9$

$\boxed{}$ What comes next?
Would $3 \times {}^-2$ name the same number as ${}^-3 \times 2$?

In addition to utilizing number patterns, children can be helped to gain an understanding of multiplication of integers by recalling the relationship of multiplication and addition. Children have previously learned that 3×2 means $2 + 2 + 2$. Consequently, $3 \times {}^-2$ should naturally mean ${}^-2 + {}^-2 + {}^-2$, or ${}^-6$. At this point, the number line may be used to advantage for interpreting the multiplication of a positive integer and a negative integer. As an example, $3 \times {}^-2$ may be pictured as in Figure 8.22.

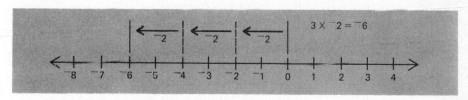

(8.22)

As was the case with the multiplication of whole numbers, the commutative property is valid for multiplication of integers. Consequently, if we wish the commutative property to reamin valid, then $3 \times {}^-2$ will have to name the same number as ${}^-2 \times 3$.

It is sometimes profitable to have a small group of children actually prepare a number line on the blacktop playing surface outside or in the gymnasium. When this is done, give the group a set of exercises to solve. Have them appoint crickets from their group and perform the actions indicated by each exercise physically. Later, have them record their work. The combination of mental thought, physical action, and adequate record-keeping is very effective for learning. Active children need experiences that keep them physically and mentally involved in learning. In this case the classroom no longer serves as a boundary.

After children have had sufficient experiences with signed numbers involving only one negative factor, they are ready to rationalize multiplication with two negative factors. Again, it is advantageous to utilize an activity card involving number patterns. An illustrative activity card for children has been presented. It would be instructive to work through the pattern.

Activity Card: Negative integers   Level: Intermediate

$$^-3 \times \ 3 = \ ^-9$$
$$^-3 \times \ 2 = \ ^-6$$
$$^-3 \times \ 1 = \ ^-3$$
$$^-3 \times \ 0 = \ 0$$

| $^-3 \times$ | $=$ |

Can you determine what to write in this box?

$$^-3 \times \ ^-2 = \ 6$$
$$^-3 \times \ ^-3 = \ 9$$

| $^-3 \times$ | $=$ |

Can you determine what to write in this box?

The mathematical sentences resulting from the pattern on the activity card make it appear reasonable that the product of two negative integers is a positive integer. In short, for the pattern to prevail we must accept the products $^-3 \times \ ^-3 = 9$, $^-3 \times \ ^-4 = 12$, and so on. Children enjoy building patterns such as those shown in the activity card. Other patterns may look like the one in Figure 8.23 and contain the simple direction: "Complete the table." Through directed discussion, the children will conclude that patterns for other numbers would be similar.

Second factor (Model chart)

					5					
					4					
			⁻6	⁻3	3					
					2		4	6		
					1					
⁻5	⁻4	⁻3	⁻2	⁻1	0	1	2	3	4	5
					⁻1					
					⁻2		⁻4	⁻6		
					⁻3					
	16	12			⁻4					
					⁻5					

First factor — Model chart

Second factor (Completed chart)

⁻25	⁻20	⁻15	⁻10	⁻5	5	5	10	15	20	25
⁻20	⁻16	⁻12	⁻8	⁻4	4	4	8	12	16	20
⁻15	⁻12	⁻9	⁻6	⁻3	3	3	6	9	12	15
⁻10	⁻8	⁻6	⁻4	⁻2	2	2	4	6	8	10
⁻5	⁻4	⁻3	⁻2	⁻1	1	1	2	3	4	5
⁻5	⁻4	⁻3	⁻2	⁻1	0	1	2	3	4	5
5	4	3	2	1	⁻1	⁻1	⁻2	⁻3	⁻4	⁻5
10	8	6	4	2	⁻2	⁻2	⁻4	⁻6	⁻8	⁻10
15	12	9	6	3	⁻3	⁻3	⁻6	⁻9	⁻12	⁻15
20	16	12	8	4	⁻4	⁻4	⁻8	⁻12	⁻16	⁻20
25	20	15	10	5	⁻5	⁻5	⁻10	⁻15	⁻20	⁻25

First factor — Completed chart

(8.23)

Table 8.1

Factor	Factor	Product
2	⁻7	
1	⁻7	
0	⁻7	
⁻1	⁻7	
⁻2	⁻7	
⁻3	⁻7	
⁻4	⁻7	

Another useful activity is to provide students with a table like the one shown in Table 8.1. Since it is in the form previously utilized with whole numbers, children will not have difficulty with the row/column idea. Study the model a few moments to determine for yourself how useful it would be for rationalizing the multiplication of integers.

Dividing Directed Numbers

In studying division of directed numbers, children are often confused as to whether the quotient is positive or negative when either the divisor or the dividend is negative. This becomes even more confusing to some children if *both* divisor and dividend are negative. Parenthetically, even the best elementary school teachers are frustrated at times when they try to teach children division with negative integers. Because concrete models are difficult to present, and are to a large extent ineffective, be certain that each child has entered the formal operations stage of development before beginning this topic.

By having children examine number patterns, you can help them gain an intuitive understanding of division with negative integers. For example, divide the class into groups of three or four and present them with a series of activity cards. Circulate among the children; observe their work; listen to their discussions.

Activity Card: Division integers (A)   Level: Intermediate

1. Complete the following number pattern:

$$6 \div 2 = 3$$
$$4 \div 2 = 2$$
$$2 \div 2 = 1$$
$$0 \div 2 = 0$$
$$^-2 \div 2 = \underline{\hspace{1cm}}$$
$$^-3 \div 2 = \underline{\hspace{1cm}}$$
$$^-6 \div 2 = \underline{^-3}$$

2. What did you observe when you divided a negative integer by a positive integer?

3. Will your answer be the same if you divided 6 by ⁻2?

Since children are usually introduced to rational numbers prior to integers, and since division can now be thought of as multiplication by a reciprocal, the problem of a negative divided by a negative becomes a logical extension of $a \times {}^-b$. Let $b = 1/c$; then ${}^-a \times {}^-1/c = a \div c$.

When beginning work with integers, we need new definitions for the four basic operations. This requires new foundational experiences for children so that they can develop ways of thinking about these operations. Again, an original developmental activity card is a superior device for helping children discover and explore these "ways of thinking."

SUMMARY As was the case with extended algorithms in addition and subtraction, teaching the extended algorithms of multiplication and division should utilize the fundamental properties. This is because properties are the unifying elements for all of the operations and as such are excellent tools for building understanding of the operations. Beyond this, the steps involved in the algorithms are cumulative. That is, success is dependent upon knowledge and skill with previously learned operations. As an

Activity Card: Division with integers   Level: Intermediate

1. Complete the following by writing a related number sentence:

a. 8 ÷ 2 = 4   8 = 2 × 4
b. 6 ÷ 2 = 3   6 = 2 × _____
c. 6/2 = 3   6 = 2 × _____
d. ⁻6/2 = ⁻3   ⁻6 = 2 × _____
e. ⁻8/N = ⁻2   ⁻8 = N × ⁻2 thus N = _____
f. ⁻6/⁻2 = 3   ⁻6 = 3 × _____

2. What did you observe with the exercises in Problem 1?

3. Complete the following exercises:

a. ⁻12/⁻3 = _____ because ⁻12 = _____ × ⁻3
b.   8/⁻4 = _____ because
c. ⁻4/2 = _____ because

example, few children will experience success with division if they lack confidence in subtraction and multiplication. Further, because of the unique nature of the division algorithm, it deserves special consideration during development.

As children experience more sophisticated aspects of multiplication and division, they should be presented with explorations of alternative methods for seeking solutions. So long as a solution system results in the desired outcome and the child is satisfied, then that method is appropriate. The developmental character of alternative solutions can provide chidren with a great deal of confidence in their ability to do mathematics during the intermediate grades.

When work in the elementary school mathematics program is extended to include the integers, the previously learned whole number properties will be useful. It follows, generally, that the properties which hold for the set of whole numbers also hold for the set of integers.

ACTIVITIES, PROJECTS, A POINT OF VIEW

1. We say that multiplication is distributive over addition. Name the appropriate properties, principles, or operations, that justify the algorithm below.

$$
\begin{aligned}
8 \times 172 &= 8 \times (100 + 70 + 2) \\
&= (8 \times 100) + (8 \times 70) + (8 \times 2) &&\underline{\hspace{2cm}} \\
&= 800 + 560 + 16 &&\underline{\hspace{2cm}} \\
&= 800 + (500 + 60) + (10 + 6) &&\underline{\hspace{2cm}} \\
&= (800 + 500) + (60 + 10) + 6 &&\underline{\hspace{2cm}} \\
&= 1300 + 70 + 6 &&\underline{\hspace{2cm}} \\
&= 1376 &&\underline{\text{product}}
\end{aligned}
$$

2. Invent your own way of rewriting the example $5634 \div 6$ in expanded notation form. Explain to a classmate why you are able to construct such an algorithm.

3. Practice finger multiplication so that you know it well enough to show it to someone. Demonstrate it to someone where you live or to a friend in another class.

4. Design an activity card for use with a small group of children. It must utilize the exploration of the halving and doubling algorithms as the basis for the reintroduction of the study of multiplication. The activity card should be sufficiently clear so that it could be used independently by children as well as under teacher guidance.

5. Imagine the examples reproduced below were taken early in the year from a sixth-grade student paper. Write a separate analysis of the pupil's difficulties in each example. Are they related? Describe concisely your *first* step in reteaching. What would you do second?

$$
\begin{array}{r}
2803 \\
\times\ 27 \\
\hline
64691 \\
50626 \\
\hline
560951
\end{array}
\qquad
\begin{array}{r}
428 \\
4\overline{)1628} \\
16 \\
\hline
28 \\
28 \\
\hline
\end{array}
$$

6. Create and record three verbal problems that could serve as a setting for introducing division as the inverse of multiplication. Have a friend review them for quality of idea, pupil interest, and plausibility.

7. Survey some recent issues of *The Arithmetic Teacher*. Find an unusual algorithm for multiplication or division. Translate the activity into a flow chart lesson plan designed to either reintroduce the chosen operation for further study or to provide pupils with a new and useful check.

8. Defend or reject this statement: For the division example, $8\overline{)264}$, the instructional vocabulary, "There are no eights in 2," is confusing and misleading.

9. What is the basis of your agreement or disagreement with the following statements?

a. In the final analysis, intermediate-grade pupils should be required to commit the multiplication and division facts to memory.

b. A hand-held calculator is an appropriate learning aid for the extended algorithms of multiplication and division.

c. The ability to estimate the first quotient figure in long division is a real asset to children during the introductory phases.

d. The distributive property cannot really help a child rationalize the steps in the long division process.

SELECTED READINGS

Bauer, G. R., and George, Linda. *Helping Children Learn Mathematics: A Competency-Based Laboratory Approach.* Menlo Park, Calif.: Cummings Publishing Company, Inc., 1976, Chapter 8.

D'Augustine, C. H. *Multiple Methods of Teaching Mathematics in the Elementary School,* 2d ed. New York: Harper & Row, Publishers, 1973, Chapters 8, 9, and 16.

Dumas, E., and Schminke, C. W. *Math Activities for Child Involvement,* 2d ed. Boston: Allyn and Bacon, Inc., 1977, Chapter 4.

Fass, A. L., and Newman, C. M. *Unified Mathematics: Content, Methods and Materials for Elementary School Teachers.* Lexington, Mass.: D. C. Heath and Company, 1975, Chapter 8.

Kindle, E. G. "Droopy, the Number Line, and Multiplication of Integers." *Arithmetic Teacher,* Vol. 23 (December 1976), pp. 647–650.

Kramer, Klaas, *Teaching Elementary School Mathematics,* 3d ed. Boston: Allyn and Bacon, Inc., 1975, Chapters 12 and 13.

Peterson, J. C. "Fourteen Different Strategies for Multiplication of Integers or Why $(-1)(-1) = + 1$." *Arithmetic Teacher,* Vol. 19 (May 1972), pp. 386–403.

Riedesel, C. Alan, and Burns, P. C. *Handbook for Exploratory and Systematic Teaching of Elementary School Mathematics.* New York: Harper & Row, Publishers, 1977, Sections 11, 12, and 17.

Spitler, Gail. "Multiplying by Eleven—A Place Value Exploration." *Arithmetic Teacher,* Vol. 24 (February 1977), pp. 122–124.

Thornton, C. A. "A Glance at the Power of Pattern." *Arithmetic Teacher,* Vol. 24 (February 1977), pp. 154–157.

CHAPTER 9

Rational Numbers, Ratio and Proportion, and Percent

PERSPECTIVE   Rational numbers both include and extend the system of natural numbers. Therefore, they generate the same axioms and postulates as natural numbers, and they demonstrate the same logical order. Further, in a comprehensive mathematics program rational numbers provide teachers with a means of demonstrating the interrelatedness and logic of number.

Of all the mathematical concepts encountered by elementary school children, those dealing with fractional numbers seem to remain the most bothersome and least understood. Why is this so? First, two numerals are used to name one number. Later, the child is confronted with something called equivalent fractions and overwhelmed by their apparent size. Furthermore, all of this seems cumbersome, since the child was dealing orally with fractions ("Give me half your apple!") long before he met fractional notation in the formal setting of school. Admonitions such as "invert and multiply" are given but are then followed by a discussion of ratio and proportion. The latter simply requires an understanding of the relationships involved. The fraction 16/64 yields 1/4 easily by canceling the sixes, but 13/39 fails to equal 1/9 and bewilderment builds when $1 \div 2/3$ does not become 1 1/3. Finally, the fractional number in the form of 2/5 seems unclear and ambiguous to the child because it is used in the physical world to represent several different ideas. Teachers and other adults often have difficulty in helping children interpret and ascribe meaning to fractional numbers; the root of the problem for the child is most often the lack of ample exploration and discovery experiences to determine and internalize fractional relationships. Once children have grasped the fundamental relationships of fractional numbers, computational skills will increase markedly, because all the properties of operations with whole numbers hold for fractional numbers.

In retrospect, perhaps it is true that nine-tenths of our population use rational numbers in less than one-fourth of their quantitative interactions. But then we would have to use rational numbers to say that, wouldn't we?

As a result of studying Chapter 9 you should be able to:
1. Differentiate two models appropriate for demonstrating an interpretation of common fractions.
2. Prepare an activity card for pupil use which explicates the process of generating equivalent fractions.
3. Describe a process for use with children in determining common denominators.
4. Prepare a flow chart lesson for use with pupils in the introduction of multiplication of fractions.
5. Describe the use of reciprocals in division of fractions.
6. Write a clear rational for the common denominator algorithm.
7. Prepare an activity card which will lead children to use decimal names for fractional numbers.
8. Write a flow chart lesson for use in teaching children to graph and solve proportion problems.
9. Illustrate and explain two approaches to solving percentage problems.

ADDITION OF RATIONAL NUMBERS

For many years, it has been common practice to introduce addition of rational numbers by selecting exercises having common denominators. These were termed "like" fractions. Parts of a circle or other figures were shown and their fractions written below the figure (see Figure 9.1). However, this kind of practice had to be repeated when addition with fractions not having common denominators was introduced. Much reteaching was required and children who had developed the understanding that "you add the numerators, but not the denominators" were confused over a "new process." For this reason, many teachers introduce the addition of fractions by using fractions whose denominators are not common. Consider the following quantitative setting with the children:

> Mary's candy recipe called for one-half of a cup of cream and one-fourth of a cup of melted butter. How much liquid was required in this candy recipe?

In the ensuing discussion, children should be encouraged to use concrete representations from their flannelboard boxes in solving the problem, and when the appropriate joining action is completed, a new name should be attached to the sum.

Demonstrate the joining of the physical parts as in Figure 9.2. Physical joining may be shown using materials to represent 1/2 and 1/4. However, the sum 3/4 requires the quantity 1/2 to be renamed as 2/4 before the appropriate sum may be ascribed. Since children should have had prior experience generating equivalent fractions through physical representation of rational numbers, they have the necessary prerequisite learnings to "discover" that part C may be represented by the numeral 3/4.

Because a majority of the children in the intermediate grades can conserve quantity, the number action of this problem and the accompanying discovery sought may be effectively promoted through the use of multiple sets of measuring cups, as illustrated in Figure 9.3.

The number line is also a useful device for teaching children to add rational numbers. For example, consider the addition example in Figure 9.4. Children who have had extensive experience using the number line to generate equivalent fractions will probably need little more direction than: "Use the number line to solve the exercise. Write your results in the proper space." They should immediately recognize that the distance marked "1/2" is also labeled "2/4". Adding another 1/4 will move them to the distance marked "3/4."

Arrays can also be used by children in understanding about the addition of rational numbers. When using an example like the one in Figure 9.5, have children discuss how the fractional part of the set is shown, and be certain to use an appropriate array to avoid the conceptual error of that representation. Notice that two objects of four objects is clearly half the objects in set A, and one of four objects is clearly one-fourth of set B. However, when these objects are joined, either conceptually or physically, they form a set which may easily be perceived as outside the context of the original sets. The apparent answer to the exercises is 3, when it ought to be 3/4. Through judicious care in selecting models for illustration, it is possible to avoid such confusion (see Figure 9.6).

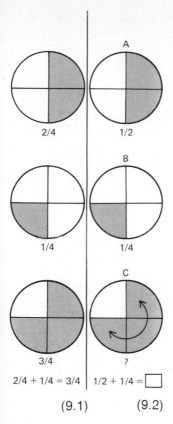

2/4   1/2

1/4   1/4

3/4   ?

2/4 + 1/4 = 3/4 | 1/2 + 1/4 = ☐

(9.1)   (9.2)

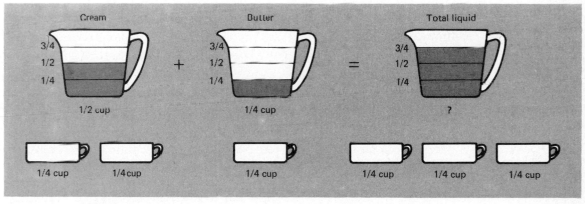

(9.3)

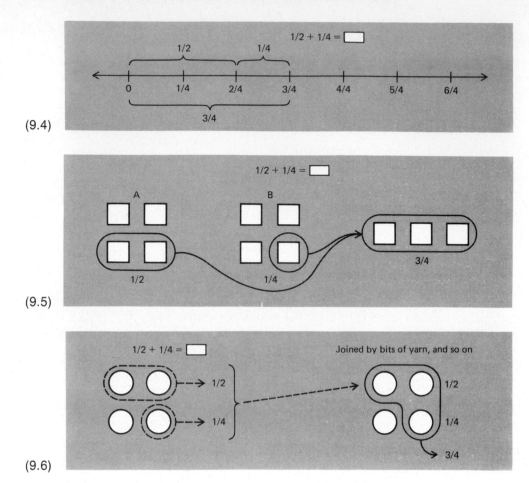

(9.4)

(9.5)

(9.6)

Use only one array to demonstrate the idea of addition of rational numbers, and perform each manipulation within the context of the original set, including the solution. When you do this, children are able to visualize the action as it relates to the original quantities being discussed and maintain the reference to the unit set.

An activity card may be used to structure experiences which develop an awareness of fractions used to describe parts of a set.

Generating Equivalent Fractions   Experiences such as those suggested earlier give children an intuitive understanding for the process of adding fractions, but when used extensively to solve exercises, such procedures are rather time-consuming and relatively inefficient. As an example, it is often necessary to deal with fractions where both the addends must be renamed as equivalent fractions in order to solve the exercise. This is extremely difficult when employing

---

Activity Card: Fractions describing a set   Level: Intermediate

1. Arrange 6 blocks in an array. Use a piece of green yarn to enclose half of the blocks. Use red yarn to enclose one-third of the blocks. How many did you enclose with each piece of yarn? What fraction describes the blocks enclosed by *both* pieces of yarn?

2. Write a fraction which describes the blocks enclosed by the dotted line. Write a fraction which describes the blocks enclosed by the solid line. What fraction would be used to describe the quantity enclosed by both lines?

3. What fraction describes each section of chalkboard in your schoolroom? The panes of glass in a window in your schoolroom? The ratio of girls to boys in your room?

---

any of the previous models. A much more efficient procedure is the method of expanding sets to form equivalent sets. The model in Figure 9.7 was utilized in solving the following problem:

> In a number game requiring partners, Janet's instruction card told her to move an object one-fourth of the distance between the spot marked "Go" and "Level One." Sherri's card told her to move the object one-seventh of the same distance. What single number (basic fraction) may be used to name the combined distance moved by Janet and Sherri?

$$1/4 + 1/7 = \square$$
$$1/4 = 2/8,\ 3/12,\ 4/16,\ 5/20,\ 6/24,\ 7/28,\ 8/32$$
$$1/7 = 2/14,\ 3/21,\ 4/28,\ 5/35$$
(9.7) $$7/28 + 4/28 = 11/28$$

Accompanying teacher comments should suggest that the solution may be found by determining an equivalent fraction for each addend. Beginning with the two addends, children can generate equivalent fractions for each until a common denominator is found. When this occurs, it is a simple matter to add the numerators and record the sum. It is essential

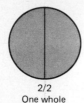

2/2
One whole

3/3
One whole

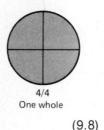

4/4
One whole

(9.8)

that each child understand that expansion of fractions involves repeatedly multiplying by a rational number equal to 1. This is an extremely important and fundamental notion and may be reexplored by children through examples embedded in quantitative settings. As an example, present children with two or three problems similar to the following:

> When picking strawberries, Henry could pick three pounds in an hour to Bob's four pounds in an hour. After ten hours of work how many pounds of strawberries will each boy have picked? Can you express your answer as a fraction? What did you do?

Subsequently, children should be encouraged to seek a solution through discussion and exploration, and illustrate the number action through appropriate number sentence recording.

If children remain uncertain of the process of multiplication by fractions equivalent to 1, it is best to review prior work through direct instruction to insure understanding of the identity element before going on. You may plan to begin direct review by asking for another name for 2/2, for 3/3, and so on (see Figure 9.8). Children must understand that each of these fractions is in the same equivalence class as the rational number 1, which may be shown by the fraction 1/1. Once this is understood, demonstrate to children that multiplying any number by 1 leaves the original quantity unchanged, although the form used for naming the original quantity has changed. Expanding a graphic representation often clarifies the development of a set of equivalent fractions (see Figure 9.9).

(9.9)

  1/4 is partitioned into 2 pieces, and 2 pieces are to be used, showing that 1/4 is equivalent to 2/8.

1/4   2/8

Have the children create representations, such as that shown in Figure 9.9, so they may observe that 1/4 is equivalent to 2/8, and so on. Understanding may be further strengthened through the use of the number line, where equivalent fractions are represented by the same point.

Discovering Common Denominators

Children may discover the necessary common denominators for the addition of fractions by inspection in cases where one denominator is a multiple of the other (see Figure 9.10). Through inspection, most children can rationalize that the denominators in this example may be made common by multiplying the denominator in the fraction 1/2 by 2, since the denominator 2 is a factor of the denominator 4. The task is completed when the numerator of 1/2 has been also multiplied by 2, thus yielding the equivalent fraction 2/4.

Chart 9.1 Flow Chart Lesson Plan — Discovering an Identity Element for Multiplication

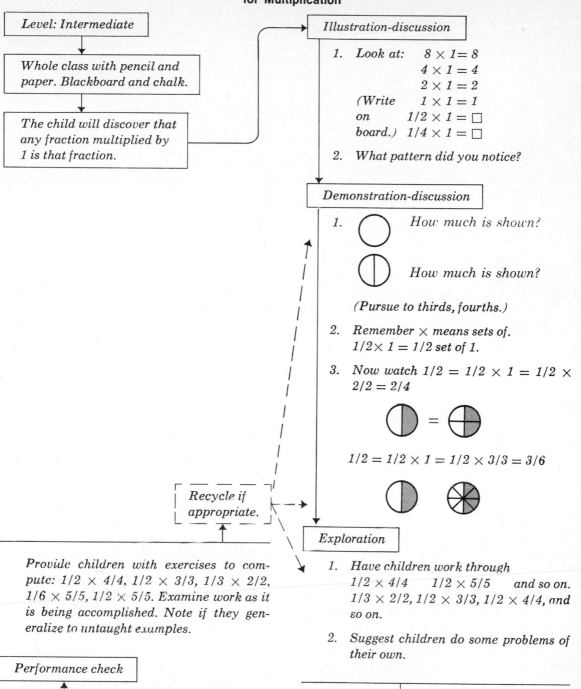

Level: Intermediate

Whole class with pencil and paper. Blackboard and chalk.

The child will discover that any fraction multiplied by 1 is that fraction.

Illustration-discussion

1. Look at: $8 \times 1 = 8$
                        $4 \times 1 = 4$
                        $2 \times 1 = 2$
   (Write $1 \times 1 = 1$
   on $1/2 \times 1 = \square$
   board.) $1/4 \times 1 = \square$

2. What pattern did you notice?

Demonstration-discussion

1. ◯   How much is shown?

    ◐   How much is shown?

    (Pursue to thirds, fourths.)

2. Remember $\times$ means sets of.
   $1/2 \times 1 = 1/2$ set of 1.

3. Now watch $1/2 = 1/2 \times 1 = 1/2 \times 2/2 = 2/4$

    ◐ = ◳

    $1/2 = 1/2 \times 1 = 1/2 \times 3/3 = 3/6$

Recycle if appropriate.

Exploration

Provide children with exercises to compute: $1/2 \times 4/4$, $1/2 \times 3/3$, $1/3 \times 2/2$, $1/6 \times 5/5$, $1/2 \times 5/5$. Examine work as it is being accomplished. Note if they generalize to untaught examples.

1. Have children work through
   $1/2 \times 4/4$ $1/2 \times 5/5$ and so on.
   $1/3 \times 2/2$, $1/2 \times 3/3$, $1/2 \times 4/4$, and so on.

2. Suggest children do some problems of their own.

Performance check

225

(9.10)

$$\frac{1}{2} + \frac{1}{4} = \square \qquad \left(\frac{2}{2} \times \frac{1}{2}\right) + \frac{1}{4} = \frac{2}{4} + \frac{1}{4} = \frac{3}{4}$$

Although the procedure described is easy for children to use, it has very limited utility—that of observing the relationship among denominators by inspection. When such relationships are apparent, it is quite efficient. Its main use lies, however, in demonstrating the process involved in creating and adding equivalent fractions.

One certain way of finding a common denominator involves multiplying denominators by each other. This is a basic mathematical rule for the addition of fractions, and because of its utility most children should become familiar with it (see Figure 9.11).

$$\frac{a}{b} + \frac{c}{d} = \left(\frac{a \times d}{b \times d}\right) + \left(\frac{b \times c}{b \times d}\right) = \square$$

$$\frac{(a \times d) + (b \times c)}{b \times d} = \square$$

$$Example: \frac{1}{3} + \frac{4}{7}$$

(9.11)

$$\left(\frac{7}{7} \times \frac{1}{3}\right) + \left(\frac{3}{3} \times \frac{4}{7}\right) = \frac{7}{21} + \frac{12}{21} = \frac{19}{21}$$

Because this algorithm is easily understood by most children having a background similar to that already discussed, activity cards such as the following are especially effective. Allow children to work in groups of two or three, and confine interaction with them to posing questions which suggest an approach to solutions.

Least Common Denominator   A characteristic of the algorithm of Figure 9.11 is that the common denominator is often larger than it needs to be. When this occurs, the size of the denominators may lead to computational errors. Further, in using this procedure, the sum is often not shown as a basic fraction, so that the numerator and denominator must have common factors removed to make it a basic fraction. To avoid some of the problems associated with this procedure, children may be introduced to an algorithm that employs the least common denominator in computation.

Before introducing the least common denominator method, ascertain that children have a basic understanding of prime and composite numbers. They must use this knowledge to find primes which are common to both denominators, and in so doing reduce the size of the denominator (see Figure 9.12). Because 3 is a factor in both denominators, it need only be

---

Activity Card: Adding fractions   Level: Intermediate

1. Use your flannelboard cutouts to help you find common denominators for each of the following exercises. When you have found a common denominator compute the sum.

   1/2 + 1/3 = _____   1/5 + 2/3 = _____
   1/8 + 1/3 = _____

2. Look closely at the common denominators you found for each exercise. See if you can discover a simple way to find a common denominator for each of the exercises. How were the numerators changed? Were they multiplied by the same number as the denominator?

3. Use your new algorithm to solve the following exercises. Check your work by expanding fractions to solve each exercise.

   1/3 + 1/7 = _____   1/5 + 1/2 = _____
   2/7 + 1/4 = _____

$$1/12 + 1/15 = \square$$
$$12 = 2, 2, 3$$
$$15 = 5, 3$$
$$(12 \times 15 = 180)$$
$$\text{Common denominator} = 2 \times 2 \times 5 \times 3 = 60$$
$$5/60 + 4/60 = 9/60$$

(9.12)

used once as a factor in determining the common denominator. Thus, the common denominator represents the product of the unique prime factors of each denominator. The numerator is then determined by finding what multiple was necessary to bring each denominator to 60. In the case of twelfths the multiple 5 was necessary, and in the case of fifteenths the multiple 4 was utilized. Notice that each multiple is comprised, inversely, of those prime factors unique to each original denominator. In finding the prime factors to use in determining the least common denominator, the multiples for obtaining the appropriate numerators must be determined at the same time. An illustrative flow chart lesson has been included to suggest an introductory instructional sequence for using primes to determine the least common denominator.

Chart 9.2   Flow Chart Lesson Plan—Least Common Denominator

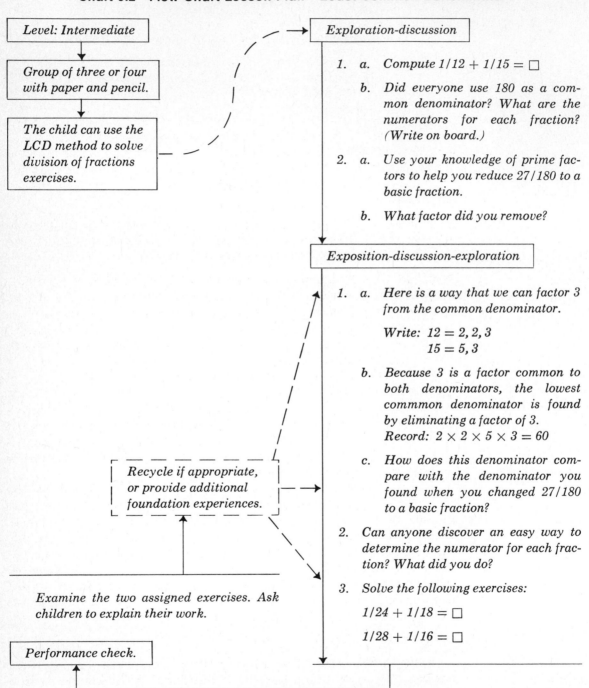

Level: Intermediate

Group of three or four with paper and pencil.

The child can use the LCD method to solve division of fractions exercises.

Recycle if appropriate, or provide additional foundation experiences.

Examine the two assigned exercises. Ask children to explain their work.

Performance check.

Exploration-discussion

1. a. Compute $1/12 + 1/15 = \square$

    b. Did everyone use 180 as a common denominator? What are the numerators for each fraction? (Write on board.)

2. a. Use your knowledge of prime factors to help you reduce 27/180 to a basic fraction.

    b. What factor did you remove?

Exposition-discussion-exploration

1. a. Here is a way that we can factor 3 from the common denominator.

    Write: $12 = 2, 2, 3$
    $15 = 5, 3$

    b. Because 3 is a factor common to both denominators, the lowest commmon denominator is found by eliminating a factor of 3.
    Record: $2 \times 2 \times 5 \times 3 = 60$

    c. How does this denominator compare with the denominator you found when you changed 27/180 to a basic fraction?

2. Can anyone discover an easy way to determine the numerator for each fraction? What did you do?

3. Solve the following exercises:

    $1/24 + 1/18 = \square$

    $1/28 + 1/16 = \square$

MULTIPLICATION OF RATIONAL NUMBERS

Unit Fractions

Elementary school children are often confused when they learn that the product obtained when multiplying a fraction by a fraction is a number which is of lesser value than the multiplicand. For example, $1/2 \times 1/3 = 1/6$, which is less than $1/2$ or $1/3$. Often, children's limited understanding of the $\times$ sign as meaning *times* is responsible for the confusion. For them, the literal interpretation for the meaning of multiplication with whole numbers has been *to increase*. Children who have had a great deal of experience in manipulating and observing rectangular arrays, regions in paper folding, sets, and number lines are less likely to have unsatisfactory experiences when multiplication of fractions is begun. This is because their concept of the meaning of the $\times$ sign will be *sets of* rather than *times*. Conceptual understanding is further enhanced when the introductory examples are embedded in problem settings such as the following:

> Jim's blueprint called for one-third of a pound of sixpenny nails for a raft with the dimensions four by eight feet. Since he decided to construct a raft only one-half that size, what fraction of a pound of nails will be needed?

Thus, $1/2 \times 1/3 = \square$ is read one-half of the set of $1/3$. Children with such an orientation are not surprised when they observe, for example, that $1/2 \times 1/3$ equals $1/6$, for the product is logical to them. Mentally, they can construct an image of $1/3$ and identify half of it to find the product. Because the interpretation of the $\times$ symbol as *sets of* facilitates children's learning, the teacher is well advised to undertake a brief review of multiplication of whole numbers before beginning multiplication of fractions.

Many teachers introduce multiplication of fractions by using nondirective procedures. To do so, proceed in the following manner. Group the class into sets of three or four children each. Pass out an activity card, a sheet of paper with several circular regions drawn upon it, and a set of blocks. The activity card might read like this:

Vary the problem situations by using one whole number for the multiplier and a rational number for the multiplicand. Have children describe the procedure. When satisfied that each child is able to demonstrate these processes satisfactorily, extend understanding to include multiplication when both factors are rational numbers. You may wish to continue with activity cards, or if necessary, do more direct teaching. The following example of a flow-charted lesson plan was generated by this word problem:

> Richard lived half a mile from school. Patty lived only one-half that distance from school. How far did Patty have to walk to get to school?

The set illustrating $1/2$ is found first, and then children are to show one-half of $1/2$, either at their seats or on a large demonstration flannelboard where appropriate fractional cutouts are available. To insure under-

Activity Card: Multiplying fractions   Level: Intermediate

1. Using both your blocks and your sheets of paper, show how you find the answer to $2 \times 4 = \square$. Record your work.

2. Using both your blocks and your sheets of paper, show how you find the answer to $1 \times 4 = \square$. Record your work.

3. Using only your sheets of paper with circular regions drawn upon them, show $1/2 \times 4 = \square$. Record your work.

4. Using your sheets of paper with circular regions drawn on them, show $1/4 \times 4 = \square$. Record your work.

standing of the process, the teacher may desire to perform the manipulations as a culmination of experimentation, while the group records the appropriate number sentence.

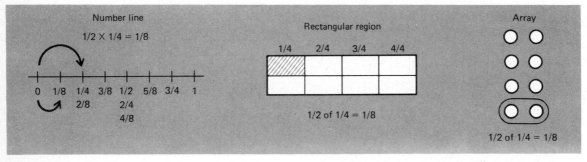

(9.13)

Do not limit the presentation to one model. Multiplication of rational numbers may also be effectively illustrated by the number line, by the use of rectangular regions, and through the use of arrays of objects (see Figure 9.13). Each representation gives children a broader perspective of the process, and the use of several materials insures that the representation models do not become "stimulus bound"—that is, bound to only one situation.

Chart 9.3   Flow Chart Lesson Plan — Multiplying a Fraction by a Fraction

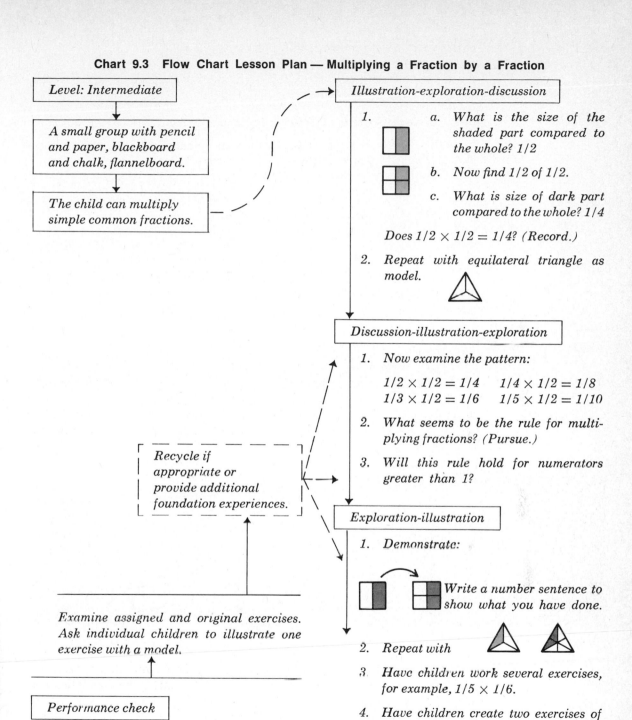

Level: Intermediate

A small group with pencil
and paper, blackboard
and chalk, flannelboard.

The child can multiply
simple common fractions.

Illustration-exploration-discussion

1.
   a. *What is the size of the shaded part compared to the whole? 1/2*
   b. *Now find 1/2 of 1/2.*
   c. *What is size of dark part compared to the whole? 1/4*

Does 1/2 × 1/2 = 1/4? (Record.)

2. *Repeat with equilateral triangle as model.*

Discussion-illustration-exploration

1. *Now examine the pattern:*

$1/2 \times 1/2 = 1/4$ $1/4 \times 1/2 = 1/8$
$1/3 \times 1/2 = 1/6$ $1/5 \times 1/2 = 1/10$

2. *What seems to be the rule for multiplying fractions? (Pursue.)*

3. *Will this rule hold for numerators greater than 1?*

Recycle if
appropriate or
provide additional
foundation experiences.

Exploration-illustration

1. *Demonstrate:*

Write a number sentence to show what you have done.

2. *Repeat with*

3. *Have children work several exercises, for example, 1/5 × 1/6.*

4. *Have children create two exercises of their own.*

Examine assigned and original exercises. Ask individual children to illustrate one exercise with a model.

Performance check

**Nonunit
Fractions**

Teachers often find it difficult to provide a simple model for multiplication examples with numerators greater than 1. Yet through the use of a problem setting children can often be led to develop an effective model for themselves. Provide children with a problem such as the following:

> Jeff's motorboat uses three-fourths of a tank of fuel to circle the lake. The fish hatchery is only two-thirds of the way around the lake. How much fuel will Jeff use to get to the hatchery?

Before they begin work, remind the children that they are discussing two-thirds of the set of 3/4, and ask them to provide a model which shows this action. An orderly means of attack on such an exercise is to have each child divide the unit into the parts called for by the multiplicand and shade them lightly. A second step is to divide the area of the multiplicand into the parts called for by the multiplier, shading these with a different color or design. The intersection of the shaded sets represents the product (see Figure 9.14).

(9.14)

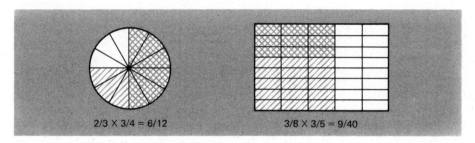

$2/3 \times 3/4 = 6/12$ $3/8 \times 3/5 = 9/40$

Despite the apparent visual complexity of these models, which effectively show multiplication of fractions with numerators greater than 1, they are often used by children. When they construct a model such as the one in Figure 9.14, children often have little trouble in interpreting the exercise. They usually follow the procedure outlined earlier and arrive at a correct product. Such explorations are prerequisites to generalizing an algorithm for multiplication of rational numbers. Again, assessment of pupil growth and independence may be observed through the use of original activity cards.

Through repeated concrete and semiconcrete experiences involving multiplication of rational numbers, children can discover an algorithm. Assist them by giving several exercises and the instructions: "Try to find a pattern so that you don't need to use materials to solve each exercise. Explain what you have done." By systematically keeping records, most children are able to see that multiplication of rational numbers involves a rather simple algorithm (see Figure 9.15).

Activity Card: Multiplication of fractions   Level: Intermediate

1. Use a set of six blocks to show 1/3 × 1/2 = ☐. Record your answer and explain what you did with the blocks.

2. Draw an array to show 1/4 × 1/2 = ☐. Record your answer.

3. Use a set of twelve blocks to show 2/3 × 1/2 = ☐. Record your answer.

4. Use a number line to show 2/5 × 1/2 = ☐.

5. What did you observe when you solved each of these exercises?

(9.15)

$$\frac{3}{4} \times \frac{5}{7} = \frac{15}{28} \qquad \frac{2}{5} \times \frac{8}{1} = \frac{16}{5}$$

$$\frac{3 \times 5}{4 \times 7} = \frac{15}{28} \qquad \frac{2 \times 8}{5 \times 1} = \frac{16}{5}$$

ADDING AND MULTIPLYING MIXED NUMBERS   Adding mixed numbers requires that a child apply the commutative and associative properties of addition and that he be able to add fractions. During the introduction, direct teaching should be kept to a minimum, with children working in small groups to solve the problems presented. For example:

> Janet needed 2 1/3 yards of blue silk and 1 3/6 yards of white cotton to complete a skirt and blouse. How many yards of material must she purchase?

As the groups work to solve this problem, take note of their deliberations, and present questions which provide direction for them. As children work and discuss, it must become apparent to them that they are applying both the commutative and associative properties of addition, and they must understand what they have done (see Figure 9.16).

$$2\ 1/3 + 1\ 3/6 = \square \qquad \text{(Statement of problem in sentence form.)}$$
$$(2 + 1/3) + (1 + 3/6) = \square \quad \text{(Simple restatement.)}$$
$$(2 + 1) + (1/3 + 3/6) = \square \quad \text{(Apply commutative and associative properties.)}$$
$$3 + (1/3 + 3/6) = \square \qquad \text{(Add 2 + 1.)}$$
$$3 + (2/6 + 3/6) = \square \qquad \text{(Find common denominator.)}$$
$$(9.16) \qquad 3 + 5/6 = 3\ 5/6$$

Activity Card: Addition of mixed numbers   Level: Intermediate

1. Use your flannel cutouts to show 2 1/3. Leave these cutouts on your board and show 1 3/6.

2. Use your flannel cutouts to show 2 1/3 + 1 3/6 = $\square$. Find a sum.

3. What did you do with your whole circular regions?

4. What did you do with your fractional circular regions?

5. Write a number sentence to show what you did with the cutouts.

6. Repeat steps 1 through 5 to find the sum for each of the following:

   1 3/5 + 1 1/5 = $\square$ 2 1/2 + 1 1/3 = $\square$

7. Make up an exercise and solve it without using concrete materials.

As they work, individual children can demonstrate their sequence of actions and explain what they have done (see Figure 9.17).

Multiplication of mixed numbers can present more of a problem for children than addition. It is often easier to convert mixed numbers to improper fractions before multiplying them. This makes computation an extension of the algorithm used with proper fractions.

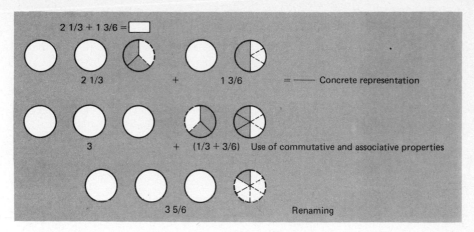

(9.17)

A simple statement is often enough to provide direction for children in attacking problems with mixed numbers. For example: "Can you rename the following numbers so that you can compute the product? You may use your cutouts to help you with the renaming." Observe to see that children understand what is needed (see Figure 9.18).

$$2\ 1/3 \times 1\ 3/6 = \square$$

$$\frac{7}{3} \times \frac{9}{6} = \square$$

$$7 \times 9 = 63$$

(9.18)

$3 \times 6 = 18$ which may be renamed 3 9/18 or 3 1/2.

Children first rename the numbers 2 1/3 and 1 3/6 to form thirds and sixths respectively (2 1/3 = 7/3 and 1 3/6 = 9/6). The rational numbers thus formed are then multiplied, using the algorithms for multiplying fractions which have been learned previously. The product may or may not be reduced to a mixed number, depending on the particular objectives the teacher has for such activities. For children who could still profit from it, graphic representation of the number action involved in renaming for addition and multiplication of mixed numbers is possible through the use of the number line and paper-folding activity.

RECIPROCALS   Any number multiplied by its reciprocal is equal to 1. This generalization is important in helping children solve division problems involving rational numbers because it allows them to understand the process involved in clearing denominators.

Children who are not able to reason abstractly should not be introduced to work with multiplication involving reciprocals, since it is difficult to develop a model which represents the process accurately and yet simply enough to be helpful to a child. Models should be carefully selected and used to reinforce the generalization by providing a visual representation of what has previously been discovered.

Introduce children to the study of reciprocals by presenting a problem which they can easily solve. For example:

> Nancy has several friends who have each been given one-fourth of an apple. How many fourths must Nancy have to get one whole apple? Show this by a number sentence (see Figure 9.19).

	Solution A	*Solution B*	*Solution C*
(9.19)	$1/4 + 1/4 + 1/4 + 1/4 = 1$	$4/1 \times 1/4 = 1$	$4 \times 1/4 = 1$
	4 sets of 1/4	4 sets of 1/4	4 sets of 1/4 = 1

Children performing work like that in solution *A* of Figure 9.19 should be encouraged to rewrite their addition sentences into multiplication sentences. When children using solutions *B* and *C* have completed their work, ask them if they notice any pattern in what they have done. Continue the lesson by providing other examples, such as $2/7 \times \square = 1$. When the situation warrants, reinforce the children's work with other concrete models (see Figure 9.19). Continue with other examples until children verbalize the generalization that "any number multiplied by its reciprocal equals 1."

Because it is a relatively simple matter to substitute rote performance for understanding, you may wish to test the level of class comprehension by including some examples which have not been used previously (see Figure 9.20). Be certain to include several exercises utilizing factors which are not reciprocals, to insure that the children are not merely reciting a pattern.

	$\square \times 4/5 = 1$	$x/y \times y/x = \square$
	$a/b \times \square = 1$	$1/4 \times 2/3 = \square$
(9.20)	$9/2 \times 2/9 = \square$	$1/4 \times 1 = \square$

DIVISION OF RATIONAL NUMBERS Division of rational numbers often causes children difficulty, perhaps because concrete representations are so difficult. However, because division of rational numbers is essential to the understanding of algebra, and because division of fractions is an important segment of children's understanding of mathematics, it has been retained in the elementary school program. Indeed, it would be difficult to explain the omission of one of the basic operations from the mathematics curriculum.

Before teaching children the division algorithm for rational numbers, present them with a variety of experiences which will help them gain an understanding of the process of division of rational numbers. Such experiences should be carefully selected and structured, since an ill-chosen problem or exercise can confuse children and cause them to miss significant relationships.

An excellent way to introduce division with rational numbers is through a carefully chosen story problem which lends itself to concrete representation. Have the children form groups of three or four and provide each group with paper strips. Next, present them with a story problem similar to the following (see Figure 9.21):

George is a carpenter and he needs some boards which are of a certain length. They must reach one-fourth of the distance between the floor and ceiling. However, the only boards available are longer. They reach one-half of the way to the ceiling. If George needs two boards which reach one-fourth of the way to the ceiling, how many boards should he buy?

(9.21)

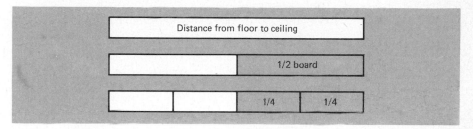

To solve this problem the children must find out how many one-fourth length boards there are in each one-half length board. Remind them that they have previously learned to consider $6 \div 3 = \square$ as an exercise asking the question, "How many 3s equal 6?" If this is well established, they need only substitute the phrase, "How many 1/4s equal 1/2?" and write the division sentence $1/2 \div 1/4 = \square$. Encourage each group to keep one unit strip to represent the total distance from floor to ceiling, and have them fold strips of equivalent length to determing how many 1/4s equal 1/2. Continue with other illustrations of the division process until chil-

(9.22)

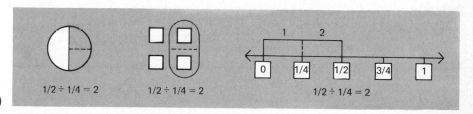

dren recognize the questions asked by the division sign—that is, "How many 1/4s equal 1/2?" Do not limit teaching to a single representation. Use other models, such as those suggested in Figure 9.22, to reinforce teaching.

Division of Fractions Algorithm

According to Piaget, children enter the formal operations stage at about eleven years of age. When this occurs, they are no longer bound to concrete representations. They can deal with the abstract if they have previously attained a concrete and intuitive level of understanding of a selected concept.

The child's ability to reason abstractly is of great pedagogical significance to the teacher, for one may not use abstract rather than concrete models in teaching. This is not to suggest that concrete representations be eliminated from teaching, but now there can be added flexibility in choosing models, patterns, or illustrations.

There is some evidence to suggest that due to the influence of contemporary living, including television, many children enter the formal operations stage somewhat earlier than was shown by Piaget. It is equally true that some children may never be able to reach the abstract level in regard to a specific concept. Use your awareness of children's intellectual development to help you decide on the appropriate time and means of teaching division of fractions to your class.

Rather than develop an algorithm for division of fractions through concrete media, many teachers introduce the algorithm in abstract fashion, using concrete models only for checking the validity of a child's early responses. This approach is preferred, since models are generally unsuitable to show all but the most elementary division exercises.

	Multiplication
Division	*as inverse*
$8 \div 4 = n$	$8 = 4 \times n$
$8 \div 2 = n$	$8 = 2 \times n$

(9.23)

One useful approach to the division of fractions algorithm is having children review their earlier understanding of multiplication and division of whole numbers as inverse processes. Provide a series of related multiplication and division exercises—for example, $4 \times 2 = 8$ and its inverse $8 \div 4 = 2$, as well as $2 \times 4 = 8$ and $8 \div 2 = 4$. Following the review of several related multiplication and division facts, place a model, such as is shown in Figure 9.24, on the chalkboard and, through discussion, determine that the children can rationalize that the N merely represents the products or dividends of the previous examples. When the relationship is firmly established, use the chalkboard to represent whole numbers as rationals and determine with the children that the previous generalizations apply (see Figure 9.24). When children can rationalize the relationship of multiplication and division in whole numbers, they are ready to rationalize an algorithm for division involving fractions. An outline of the suggested steps which would enable children to discover a division of fractions algorithm appears in Figure 9.25.

	Division	*Multiplication as inverse*
	$8/1 \div 4/1 = n$	$8/1 = 4/1 \times n$
(9.24)	$8/1 \div 2/1 = n$	$8/1 = 2/1 \times n$

	$8/1 \div 4/1 = n$	(Statement of exercise.)
Step 1	$8/1 = n \times 4/1$	(Multiplication as inverse of division.)
Step 2	$1/4 \times 8/1 = n \times 4/1 \times 1/4$	(Multiplying both sides of the equation by the reciprocal of 4/1 to clear n.)
Step 3	$1/4 \times 8/1 = n \times 1$	
Step 4	$1/4 \times 8/1 = n$	
Step 5	$8/4 = n$ or $n = 2$	
Step 6	$8/1 \div 4/1 = n$ implies that	(Generalizing from above results.)
(9.25)	$8/1 \times 1/4 = 2$	

Although the process may appear to be laborious and time-consuming, children gain a great deal of meaningful mathematical practice by applying their knowledge of such generalizations as the inverse property, the identity element, and so on. Such active involvement in learning, with the concomitant generalization it affords, is consistent with the philosophy of combining students' environment and experience in the creation of a conditioned environment for learning. Appropriate teacher moves are outlined in the flow chart lesson plan on page 240.

Complex Fraction Algorithm   Initially, the appearance of the complex fraction causes many children to be apprehensive and confused. This undesirable reaction is often further strengthened if adequate time is not taken to relate the complex fraction to prior work with division. To explain that the complex fraction is merely a different way of indicating a division is not enough. Children must see the need for changing the denominator to 1, and they must understand the process to be used.

Children can be helped to understand the complex fraction algorithm

Chart 9.4 Flow Chart Lesson Plan — Division of Fractions Algorithm

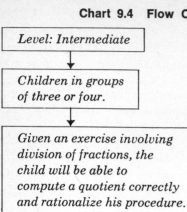

Level: Intermediate

↓

Children in groups of three or four.

↓

Given an exercise involving division of fractions, the child will be able to compute a quotient correctly and rationalize his procedure.

Exploration-discussion

1. a. Solve the following:

    (1) $8 \div 4 = N$ (1) $8 = N \times 4$

    (2) $12 \div 6 = N$ (2) $12 = N \times 6$

   b. How are these exercises related?

2. Can you solve the following exercises? Why?

    $8/1 \div 4/1 = N$ $8/1 = N \times 4/1$

Illustration-discussion-exploration

1. a. Here is a way to solve exercises such as the ones we just did:

    $8/1 \div 4/1 = N$ $8/1 = N \times 4/1$

   b. What don't we know?

    $8/1 = N \times 4/1$

   c. How can we find N? Show on board:

    $8/1 \times 1/4 = N \times 4/1 \times 1/4$

    $8/1 \times 1/4 = N \times 4/4$

    $8/1 \times 1/4 = N$ What have I done?

   d. Do the following:

    $12/1 \div 6/1 = N$

    $1/4 \div 3/5 = N$

    $2/3 \div 1/2 = N$

Recycle to appropriate entry point as indicated.

2. Can anyone discover an easy way to solve exercises involving division of fractions?

3. a. Write: $2/3 \div 1/2 = N$

            $2/3 \times 2/1 = N$

                   $4/3 = N$

   b. Explain why this algorithm is correct.

Have children find a quotient and explain their work as they solve five exercises involving division of fractions.

Performance check.

for division of rational numbers by illustrating a series of sequential steps on the chalkboard (see Figure 9.26).

$8 \div 4 = \square$ (Asks the same question—"How many 4s equal 8?"
$8/4 = \square$ —but rewrites the number sequence.)
$2 = \square$

$8/1 \div 4/1 = \square$ (Same problem, but the numbers are shown as
                              fractions.)

$$\frac{8/1}{4/1} = \square$$

$$\frac{8/1 \times 1/4}{4/1 \times 1/4} = \square$$ (Use of reciprocal to "clear" denominator.)

$$\frac{8/1 \times 1/4}{4/4} = \square$$ (Review that $4/4 = 1$.)

$8/1 \times 1/4 = \square$ (Rewritten without a denominator of 1.)
(9.26) $8/4 = \square$

Begin by writing $8 \div 4 = \square$ on the board and explaining that this may be rewritten as 8/4. Solve by dividing 8 by 4 and writing the quotient 2. At this point, ask the children to rewrite two or three exercises into the form already shown. When they understand that their work up to this point has merely involved a change in form, ask them to solve $8/1 \div 4/1 = \square$. Again, discuss with them the fact that this exercise calls for a change in form.

Continue through each step illustrated in Figure 9.26, talking over each step and observing the reactions of the class. Provide several additional examples until you are satisfied that the children understand the algorithm.

Inversion Algorithm   Children who have had extensive experience with either of the previous two teaching procedures will often discover a computational shortcut. Through repeated work and a sensitivity to arithmetical patterns, they detect that in every case the divisor becomes inverted and the sign changes from division to multiplication. From this observation they generalize: "When dividing rational numbers, you may invert the divisor and multiply" (see Figure 9.27).

	Step 1	$1/2 \div 2/3 = \square$		Step 3	$\dfrac{1 \times 3}{2 \times 2} = \square$
(9.27)	Step 2	$1/2 \times 3/2 = \square$		Step 4	$3/4 = \square$

It is extremely important that this generalization be based upon children's understanding of the process involved. The effect of rote learning is often observed in children and adults who have memorized the generalization represented by this algorithm. They will likely forget which to invert, the divisor or the dividend, and as a consequence, problem-solving is seriously impeded. When children can work through the process, even if the generalization is forgotten, they will be able to use it in problem-solving.

Common Denominator Algorithm

Because the common denominator method is similar to the method previously used in the addition of fractons, many teachers initiate the division of fractions with it (see Figure 9.28).

$1/2 \div 2/3 = \square$

$(3/3 \times 1/2) \div (2/3 \times 2/2) = \square$ (Multiplying by 1, the identity property.)

$3/6 \div 4/6 = \square$

$(6/1 \times 3/6) \div (4/6 \times 6/1) = \square$ (Equality property of multiplication.)

$18/6 \div 24/6 = \square$ (Dividing by six.)

$3 \div 4 = 3/4$

When using this method, children initially inspect the division exercise to determine what procedure is needed to form a common denominator. For example, in Figure 9.28, children easily see that $2 \times 3 = 6$ and that $3 \times 2 = 6$, forming a common divisor. Both the numerator and the denominator of each fraction are multiplied by 3 and 2 respectively. The division exercise thus formed is then easily solved by "clearing the denominators."

Although the common denominator method is consistent with a child's previous learning, it does not culminate in an understanding of the "invert and multiply" algorithm for the division of fractions. This need not concern the teacher. While the "invert and multiply" algorithm is efficient, you need not feel that you have omitted some mathematics content if you neglect to introduce it, for it is (as are all algorithms) simply a computational tool, not an essential component of learning.

RATIO AND PROPORTION

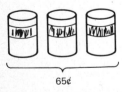

65¢

3 cans of beans / 65¢   or $\frac{3}{65}$

(9.29)

Relationships between two numbers may be shown by stating a comparison of one of the numbers to the other. This statement is called a ratio and may be expressed in many ways, although 2:4 and 2/4 (read "two is to four") are the most common. For example, the price relationship of three cans of beans to sixty-five cents may be shown by the ratio 3/65 (see Figure 9.29).

Contained within Chapter 5 is an introduction to the concept and notation for proportional relationships. The activities introduced there parallel the first activities presented in this chapter. However, because of the age and accompanying maturational differences of children, and because many children have not been exposed to the concept of proportional relationships, similar but more advanced ideas and activities are presented again in this chapter.

Ratios are extremely useful in problem-solving and adapt nicely to many common situations found in everyday life. For example, suppose that a child knew that candy bars were on sale at three bars for nineteen cents rather than the normal price of ten cents each. If this same price existed for larger volume purchases, a child could compute that the cost of candy bars purchased implies a proportional increase in price. Although perhaps most common, price comparisons are by no means the only proportional relationships which are used in everyday life. Some of these will be discussed in the pages that follow.

Teaching Ratio
Many teachers inadvertently cause children confusion by attempting to teach the notation for a ratio before the concept is well established. Initially the class may be divided into groups of three or four, and each group given a set of multicolored blocks and an activity card similar to the following:

Activity Card: Ratio and proportion   Level: Intermediate

1. Using your blocks, how can you show that 1 red block is worth 2 white blocks?

2. How can you write that 1 red block is worth 2 white blocks?

3. See if you can write the relationship expressed below:

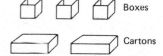
Boxes

Cartons

4. Are there any other one-to-many or many-to-one relationships you see in our classroom? Our school? List three of them.

After the class has gained the concept of ratio, you will want to introduce them to a standard system of notation. Before doing this, you may want to have groups discuss how they chose to express a ratio, and then have each group try to convince the others that their system of notation is best. This elicits conversation concerning the strengths and weaknesses of each notational form. When children can decide on a "best" notational form, it can further focus interest on ratio, as well as provide an intuitive notion of the arbitrariness within systems of notations.

Teaching Proportional Relationships Once children have gained a firm grasp of the idea of ratio, let them expand this understanding to include proportional relationships and their usefulness in solving problems. For example:

> If it costs $.50 for two rides on the ferris wheel, how many rides can you have for $1.50?

Give them tickets or other objects to use in solving the problem. They should quickly discover a means of solution (see Figure 9.30).

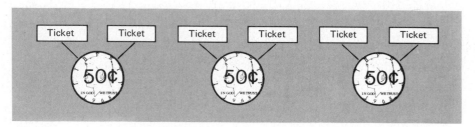

(9.30)

Here the group has solved the problem through the use of a one-to-two correspondence between sets. Once the relationship between rides and money is established as a ratio, the group need only duplicate this relationship until they run out of money. In this case the group correctly aligned two tickets (indicating rides) with $.50. This process was repeated two more times until the $1.50 was used. The solution, then, is represented by the tickets (rides), which have been matched to the money (price).

Exercises on ratio and proportion lend themselves to graphic representation. For example, after children have had a chance to work three or four problems, give them some graph paper, another problem, and the direction: "Record your answer to this problem on graph paper." Such an open-ended activity requires that children have prior experience with graphing. If not, the teacher may have to be somewhat more directive in showing how to graph. As they develop the graph of the original problem, have them predict other relationships by asking questions such as: "How many ferris-wheel rides can I get for $2.00?" (see Figure 9.31). Through discussion and observation, be sure the children discover that once the first relationship is graphed, they can predict any other proportional relationship by extending a straight line on the graph and reading the value where the lines intersect.

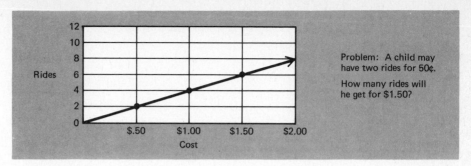

(9.31)

Algorithms for Determining Proportional Relationships

After children demonstrate an understanding of proportional relationships, they are able to use a more efficient procedure in determining quantities. These procedures utilize algorithms which rely on the fact that proportional relationships have the same properties as rational numbers. Their difference from rational numbers is determined through examination of context. For example, if a ball team wins one-half of the 100 games it plays, we know that the team won 50 games. We do not, however, know how many games the team had won by mid-season, or at any other given time; we know only that it won 50 games in all. The rational number 1/2 correctly describes this situation. A ratio, 1:2, though, gives more precise information. The ratio 1:2, read "1 per 2," indicates that the ball team wins one ball game for every two it plays. It does not immediately indicate that the team won 50 games in all, but we can determine at any given point how many games were won. For example, if the team played 8 games, and won one for every two it played, we could determine that the team won 4 games.

One of the algorithms employed is perhaps the least generalizable. However, because the algorithm does involve the notion of proportionality, many teachers elect to introduce it first. The sequence of steps necessary to solve the following problem is outlined in Figure 9.32.

Louise found a shop where hair ribbons were two for twenty-five cents. How many can she buy for seventy-five cents?

$2/25¢ = n/75¢$ (Read 2 ribbons for 25¢ is proportional to n ribbons for 75¢.)

$(3 \times 25¢ = 75¢)\ 2/25¢ = n/75¢$ (Note the relationships of the denominators: 75¢ is exactly three times as large as 25¢.)

$3/3 \times 2/25¢ = n/75¢$ (Multiplying by 1.)
$6/75¢ = n/75¢$

$75¢ \times 6/75¢ = n/75¢ \times 75¢$ (Multiplying by 75¢ to clear denominators.)

$6 = n$

(9.32)

An activity card, such as this one, is a very effective device for introducing children to the ratio and proportion algorithm.

Activity Card: Algorithm for ratio and proportion   Level: Intermediate

1. Solve the problem: Louise found a shop where hair ribbons were priced at 2 for 25¢. How many can she buy for 75¢?

2. The following number sentence describes the action in Question 1. Answer the questions which follow:

    $2/25 = x/75$

    a. What does the 2 represent?

    b. What does the 25 represent?

    c. What does the 75 represent?

    d. What does the x represent?

3. Try to discover how to make the quantities equal. What must you do to the denominator of the ratio 2:25? How will you need to change the numerator?

4. Now that the quantities are equal, what is the value of x?

5. Compute the following, using procedures similar to those you have just employed:

    $3/15 = x/45$ $4/7 = x/35$ $1/6 = x/12$

Although the previous algorithm is useful when the relationship between denominators is observable by inspection, a more generalizable algorithm is needed for problems when such relationships are not readily apparent. Children can be helped to perceive the need for a more efficient algorithm by providing them with such a problem (see Figure 9.33).

$$2/17 = n/102$$
$$\frac{102 \times 2}{17} = \frac{n \times 102}{102}$$
$$204/17 = n$$
$$12 = n$$
(9.33)

Patty's father is a painter who uses 17 gallons of paint every two days. How many days can he paint with the 102 gallons he has in the garage?

Help children discover the algorithm in Figure 9.33 by observing them as they work and by asking questions such as: "How can I clear n?" and "Since you have multiplied $n/102$ by 102, what must be done to the ratio 2:17?" Continue observing, discussing, and illustrating until the children are able to compute using the algorithm in Figure 9.33 and can explain each step in their computation.

DECIMAL FRACTIONS

Decimals are a logical extension of both the place value discussion and the discussion of ratios just concluded. Children have learned to describe whole numbers in terms of powers of 10. For example, they have learned that 100 could be renamed as 10^2, 1000 as 10^3, and so on. They have learned that certain numbers between 0 and 1 could be represented by using similar exponential notation with negative exponents; thus, 1/10 could be renamed as 10^{-1}, 1/100 as 10^{-2}, and so forth. Children have also learned that 1:10 is a ratio read "1 to 10." These background experiences have given them the knowledge they need to work with and understand decimal notation.

Begin teaching by using concrete models that provide children with a brief review of the meaning of a fraction. For example, ask the children to use the hundreds board to show 1/10. Many children will immediately think of 1/10 as a ratio and show it by placing a marker on one of each of tens pegs until all of the pegs have been accounted for (see A in Figure 9.34). Others will mentally divide the board into ten parts and place markers on the ten pegs contained in one of these parts (see B in Figure 9.34).

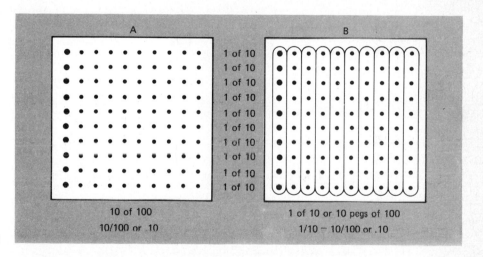

(9.34)

A		B
10 of 100		1 of 10 or 10 pegs of 100
10/100 or .10		1/10 = 10/100 or .10

Explain that the number of pegs may be represented in several different ways and write 1/10, 10/100, and .10 on the board. Encourage the children to discuss what they think .10 means before explaining that .10 is read as ten hundredths.

Continue instruction by asking the children to use their hundreds boards to show numerals which are written on the board. Write numerals such as .13 and .27 and provide enough time for the children to represent each correctly. Encourage them to find "shortcuts," such as circling ten pegs with a rubber band to show the .10 in the numeral .13. Finally, include numerals such as 1.24 and .073, and inform them that their boards may have to be changed or that more boards may be needed. Have the groups discuss what has just been done, and suggest that they make up two or three problems for each other.

Activity Card: Decimal fractions   Level: Intermediate

1. Use the stack of 100 cards on your desk to find the width of:

   (a) a drinking straw
   (b) a leaf
   (c) your arithmetic book
   (d) your pencil

   Record your findings as a portion of the total stack (decimal fraction and common fraction).

2. Use a ruler to measure your desk to the nearest tenth of an inch. Record your answer.

3. Count the first fifty children you see at recess. What fraction are boys and what fraction are girls? Record as both decimal and common fractions.

4. Make up three measurement problems which require the use of tenths and hundredths of an inch.

Addition and Subtraction of Decimals

The processes involved in the addition and subtraction of decimal fractions are similar to those used to add and subtract whole numbers.

Thus, when a child adds quantities such as .07 + .05, he must use his knowledge of place value to mentally rename one-tenth and two-hundredths as .12.

As is the case with common fractions, children respond well to an introduction to the addition and subtraction of decimal fractions through the aid of concrete models (see Figure 9.35).

Use felt cutouts to show that 1/2 + 1/4 = 3/4. Since children have had previous work in describing fractional parts with decimals, they can rename 1/2 as .50 and 1/4 as .25. What remains is for them to note that .50 + .25 = .75. When previous knowledge of the commutative and associative properties is adequate, the teacher may wish to show that .50 + .25 = (.50 + .20) + (.05) or .70 + .05 = .75. In some cases additional experience with the commutative and associative properties using whole numbers may have to be provided before making such a presentation.

1/2 or .50

1/4 or .25

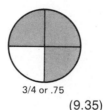

3/4 or .75

(9.35)

Once children understand that addition and subtraction of decimal fractions follow the same principles as these operations on whole numbers, illustrate how the vertical algorithm simplifies their work. Place-value pockets and the abacus are both effective devices in helping children utilize the vertical algorithm. For example, have children use the place-value pocket shown in Figure 9.36 to observe the patterns involved in adding ones, tenths, and hundreths, and to recognize that any required renaming follows the same rules as that for whole numbers.

A great deal of understanding can be obtained when children have a need to describe a problem situation shown concretely. They may write an appropriate addition sentence and then correctly alter it to algorithmic form for computation. For example, using an abacus, present activities like Figure 9.37. A child would be asked to write an addition sentence to describe the action in the illustration, and then to compute the sum correctly. His learning could then be extended by asking that he use the abacus to show a number sentence written on the board.

Up to this point, little specific attention has been given to the operation of subtraction. Because subtraction is the inverse of addition, similar teaching procedures to those already discussed can be used. However, because subtraction requires a renaming of the minuend, it occasionally

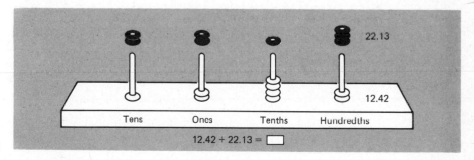

(9.36)

(9.37)

disturbs children for a brief time. They are familiar with renaming to form tens, regrouping tens to form hundreds, and so on; but they are often less confident of the inverse. They can be helped to attain confidence by discussion and use of the inverse each time a new addition concept is introduced. Figure 9.38 is an example.

$$
\begin{array}{cc}
2.17 & 3.56 \\
+1.39 & -1.39 \\
\hline
3.56 & 2.17
\end{array}
$$

(Renaming hundredths   (Renaming tenths to form
to form tenths.)   tenths and hundredths
respectively.)

(9.38)

Multiplication and Division with Decimals

Understanding multiplication and division of decimal fractions has frequently posed a problem for elementary school children. Many have learned simply to count the number of places to the right of the decimal in both the multiplier and the multiplicand in order to determine the number of places in the product.

When considering division, many pupils find it even more difficult to determine the placement of the decimal point in the quotient.

Look for a generalization regarding how the decimal places needed may be determined from a problem, and allow pupils time to generate an answer. It is amazing how logical the thought processes used by some children are as they attempt to answer this question. Some will proceed directly to the algorithm and simply state that the number of places in the multiplier plus the number of places in the multiplicand must equal the number of places in the product. Other responses may be much more divergent. For example, one small group of children made this generalization:

> There are two decimal places needed, because when you multiply 1/10 by 1/10 you multiply the 1×1 first, and then the 10×10 to find the denominator. When you multiply by 10, you can count the number of tens and add one zero for each ten so $10 \times 10 = 100$. Multiplying $.10 \times 0.1$ is the same, so the product should have two zeros in it, or .00. The numerator is 1×1 or 1, so the answer is 0.01.

Unless children are encouraged to make such discoveries, they probably will not observe, record, and generalize. Thus, they will lose the chance for depth of understanding.

When learning division involving decimal fractions, it is extremely important that children recall the meaning of division. They must know that $3 \div 0.4 = \square$ asks the question: "How many 4/10s equal 3?" A child may then use many different concrete mediums to solve the exercise. For example, he may be guided to use rectangular areas as in Figure 9.39.

When children perceive division of decimal fractions as merely an extension of division with whole numbers, they are ready to begin relating their understanding to the division algorithm. Simply ask: "How can I compute the following?" $0.4\overline{)3}$

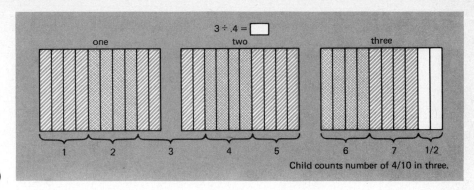

Child counts number of 4/10 in three.

(9.39)

At first, children may need help to relate what they have done so that they can determine the restatement of the problem as 4 tenths $\overline{)30\ \text{tenths}}$ (see Figure 9.40).

$$4 \text{ tenths} \overline{)\overset{7}{30 \text{ tenths}}} = 7 \text{ R2 or } 7\ 1/2 \ (7.5)$$
$$\underline{28}$$
$$2$$

(9.40)

Next the teacher can ask: "We changed the dividend to tenths to solve the problem in Figure 9.40. Is there a way that we could solve this exercise by changing the divisor to a whole number?" Let the groups determine that changing .4 to 4.0 involves multiplication by 10.

$10 \times .4 = 4$ (Changing .4 to whole number.)
$10 \times 3 = 30$ (Making proportional change in dividend.)

$$4\overline{)\overset{7}{30}}$$
$$\underline{28}$$
$$2 = 2/4$$

(9.41)

Once the children have a firm idea of the division of decimals with the algorithm described, they are ready to proceed with more advanced examples, such as $2.5\overline{)3.15}$. At this point, most children will quickly adopt the algorithm which changes the divisor to a whole number (see Figure 9.42). However, they must understand that the question asked now is, "How many 25s are there in 31.5?" This question provides guidance in assessing the reasonableness of a quotient and, consequently, the correct placement of the decimal point in the quotient.

$$2.5\overline{)3.15}$$

(9.42) $25\overline{)31.5}$ (Multiply divisor and dividend by 10.)

As children attempt to invent the mechanics of the algorithm, the teacher can help by recalling for them that they must divide 315 tenths into sets of 25 tenths (see Figure 9.43).

$$2.5\overline{)3.15}$$

$$25 \text{ tenths}\overline{)31.5 \text{ tenths}}$$

$$(3.15 \times 10) \div (2.5 \times 10) = 31.5 \div 25$$

$$
\begin{array}{r}
1.26 \\
25\overline{)31.5} \\
\underline{25} \\
65 \\
\underline{50} \\
150 \\
\underline{150}
\end{array}
$$

(9.43)

PERCENT   Teachers of upper elementary grades usually consider percent to be one of the more difficult topics to teach. Because of the precision of the language, and the abstract nature of percent, children are often frustrated and confused by percentage problems. On the other hand, percent is widely used to express relationships, and every child is likely to have some use for it. Therefore, percent is usually included in the fifth- or sixth-grade program, and most programs contain certain readiness exercises that occur earlier.

Readiness   Percents are actually just a special class of ratios. Whereas 5 per 100 can
for Percent   be expressed as a ratio, it can also be expressed as a percent. Thus the notation 5:100 reads "five per one hundred," and 5% reads "five percent"; both indicate the same quantity. This relationship may be shown using a chart or hundreds board (see Figure 9.44).

Many teachers prefer to use a guided discovery approach to the introduction of percent. Rather than simply using a chart or other device to show how percent relates to ratio, children can be presented with problem settings on an activity card.

The teacher can use activity cards of this type to let children discover the relationship of percent to ratio. They will find that the relationship is always indicated as some number per 100.

This concept of percent is still very restricted. What if the team played 110 games and won 73? This problem requires children to consider percent as a fractional part of a whole. They must know that the fraction 73/110 may also be described as percent. Again, the relationship of a

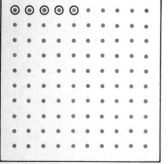

Hundreds board

(9.44)

Activity Card: Percent   Level: Intermediate

1. Using your hundreds board, show what you mean when you say that your team won 7 out of every 10 games. The team plays 100 games in all. Record how many games your team won during the year. Your team won 70% of its games. What does 70% mean?

2. Using your hundreds board, show what you mean when you say that 4 out of every 10 games were won by your team. Your team plays 100 games. Record how many games the team won during the year. You may also say that your team won 40%, read "forty percent," of their games.

3. Using your hundreds board, show what you mean when you say that 9 out of every 10 games were won by your team. Your team plays 100 games. Record how many games you think would correctly show the quantity of games won? _____ %.

fraction to the ratio is apparent. To solve the exercise, children must know $73/110 = n/100$.

Problems Involving Percent   Three problem situations involving percent are readily identified; they used to be identified as case 1, 2, or 3 problems, and each required that a particular formula be memorized for its solution. Case 1 problems were generally introduced in the late fifth grade, while case 3 problems were considered difficult even for eighth-grade students. Here, the three problem situations are identified and solved through both the formula and the ratio approaches. Although other approaches exist, these two give a variety of methods for solutions to percentage problems.

The Formula Approach Business people often make a great deal of use of the formula approach in dealing with percentage problems. There is basically one formula involved, rather than three discrete situations as in the decimal method. A child must learn to consider carefully what is given and what is asked before he attempts to solve each problem with the

Activity Card: Percent   Level: Intermediate

1. Color one square, then leave one uncolored

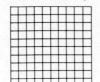

until you have used all squares in the box. What do you notice?

2. Color one square, then leave three white, until

you have used all the squares in the box. What did you notice?

3. What percent correctly describes the blackened surfaces?

4. Make up a percent illustration or drawing of your own.

formula approach. Illustrations of each case, and how the formula is applied, are given below:

Formula: Rate × base = percentage ($r \times b = p$)

Case 1: What is 30 percent of 80?

$p = r \times b$

$p = .30 \times 80$

$p = 24$ (24 is the percentage.)

Case 2: 30 is what percent of 80?

$p = r \times b$ (Basic formula.)

$30 = r \times 80$ (The rate is unknown in this problem.)

$30/80 = r$

$.375 = r$ or 37.5%

Case 3: 80 is 30 percent of what number?

$p = r \times b$ (Basic formula.)

$80 \div .30 \times b$

$80/.30 = b$

(9.45) $266.6 = b$

The formula approach is efficient for those who make frequent use of percent. However, children who make prolonged use of the formula method tend to consider percent as separate from other mathematics. Thus, if the objective is to integrate percent into the total mathematical structure, the ratio approach should probably be used.

The Ratio Approach The ratio approach does not rely on memorizing a formula or a series of computational situations. Rather, it is merely an extension of the problem-solving approach used with other problem situations:

Case 1: What is 30 percent of 80?

$$\frac{30}{100} = \frac{n}{80}$$

$$\frac{80 \times 30}{100} = \frac{n \times 80}{80}$$

$$24 = n$$

Case 2: 30 is what percent of 80?

$$\frac{n}{100} = \frac{30}{80}$$

$$\frac{100 \times n}{100} = \frac{30 \times 100}{80}$$

$$n = \frac{3000}{80}$$

$$n = 37.5$$

Case 3: 80 is 30 percent of what number?

$$\frac{30}{100} = \frac{80}{n}$$

$$\frac{30 \times n}{100} = \frac{80 \times n}{n}$$

$$\frac{30n}{100} = 80$$

$$30n = 80 \times 100$$

$$n = \frac{800}{30} \text{ or } 266.6$$

(9.46)

Note that only one algorithm was used in computing each of the percentage problems in the ratio approach. For case 3, a student with an understanding of the "cross-product" approach would find this a much more efficient method than the algorithm used. Further, the relationship of percent to other mathematics is apparent to children, not artificially separated. When considered in this context, then, percent becomes an extension of the mathematics previously learned.

SUMMARY   Because of the historic difficulty children and adults appear to have with fractions, meaning and understanding take on added importance when teaching the fundamental concepts necessary to understand and use rational numbers. Perhaps the use of two numerals for writing fractions as an expression of one number is at the base of the difficulty. Indeed, fractions are more than "a part of a number."

Since a fraction is already an indicated division, they can be difficult for children to rationalize. For this reason, careful instructional procedures resulting in pupil competence in determining equivalent fractions are crucial. It is essential that the teacher rename fractions in order to simplify the basic operations with them. Subsequently, that ability is the key to computations involving all four operations. And while it is true that there are few situations in which the average adult must solve verbal problems involving common fractions, quantitative settings described in words do offer children the best opportunity to develop problem-solving ability when using rational numbers.

Ratio and proportion are relation ideas that are quite useful in practical problem-solving settings. Most modern programs treat ratio and proportion as a means for setting up a relation that can be completed by seeking the missing term for sets of two equivalent fractions.

The computational techniques children have learned for whole numbers transfer directly to the algorithms of decimals. The only idea that is "new" involves location of the decimal point. However, since there are no changes in principles governing regrouping, placement of the decimal point is a relatively straightforward matter.

Percents are probably the most widely used ratios that effect our daily lives. They are basically ratios whose second term is 100. The principal advantage of percents is they permit a fast comparison. However, when percents are used to report information, they can be misleading unless the numbers upon which they are based accompany the percents.

ACTIVITIES,   **1.** Write a statement which describes the difference between a fraction or
PROJECTS, A   decimal and a rational number.
POINT OF VIEW   **2.** Compare two pupil texts for the same grade level. Identify the author(s) and publisher of each, and write a brief regarding the approach to division of common fractions.
3. From all your work examining pupils' texts and teachers' editions, have you found any containing the requirement that pupils write out the steps of a process they are to learn? Give an example. Write out the steps appropriate to the common denominator method. Have a friend read it for accuracy.
4. Ratios may be used to determine the most economical purchase. For example, consider twenty-two ounces of tomato juice for seventy-two cents against thirty ounces for ninety-four cents. Completion of the com-

putations 22 oz.$\overline{/72¢}$ and 30 oz.$\overline{/94¢}$ reveals the latter as the more economical purchase. Use local newspaper advertisements and set up three ratios that may be compared. Do the computation. What did you discover? What generalizations can you make about ratios and advertising?

5. Which notation, fraction or decimal, is easier to use for the computation below? Why? Do the computation. Now what do you think?

$$a. \frac{1}{4} + \frac{5}{8} \text{ or } \begin{array}{r} .250 \\ +.625 \\ \hline \end{array} \qquad b. \frac{4}{5} + \frac{1}{4} \text{ or } \begin{array}{r} .80 \\ +.25 \\ \hline \end{array}$$

$$c. \frac{2}{5} + \frac{7}{16} \text{ or } \begin{array}{r} .4000 \\ +.4375 \\ \hline \end{array} \qquad d. \frac{2}{3} + \frac{1}{3} \text{ or } \begin{array}{r} .666 \\ +.333 \\ \hline \end{array}$$

6. *The Arithmetic Teacher* abounds with articles and teaching ideas about fractions, decimals, and percents. Choose four concepts and prepare an activity card that could be used to teach each concept. Base each activity card on one article.

7. What is the basis of your agreement or disagreement with these statements?

a. It is a sound teaching procedure in elementary school mathematics to occasionally require fifth- and sixth-grade pupils to "write out" the steps of a process they need to learn.

b. If the price of gasoline were increased 18 percent and thirty days later reduced 18 percent, it would be selling at the original price.

c. A statement that the crime rate has been reduced 45 percent is virtually meaningless.

d. The next decade will bring new prominence to decimals as an element in the elementary school mathematics curriculum.

SELECTED READINGS

Ashlock, Robert B. "Introducing Decimal Fractions with the Meterstick." *Arithmetic Teacher*, Vol. 23, No. 3 (March 1976), pp. 201–206.

Coppel, Arlene Cohen. "Blueprint for Ratio and Scale." *Arithmetic Teacher*, Vol. 24, No. 2 (February 1977), pp. 125–126.

Dumas, E., and Schminke, C. W. *Math Activities for Child Involvement*, 2d ed. Boston: Allyn and Bacon, Inc., 1977, Chapter 6.

Firl, Donald H. "Fractions, Decimals, and Their Futures." *Arithmetic Teacher*, Vol. 24, No. 3 (March 1977), pp.238–240.

Green, G. F. *Elementary School Mathematics—Activities and Materials.* Lexington, Mass.: D. C. Heath and Company, 1974, Chapter 9.

Marks, J. L.; Purdy, C. R.; Kinney, L. B.; and Hiatt, Arthur. *Teaching Elementary School Mathematics for Understanding*, 4th ed. New York: McGraw-Hill Book Company, Inc., 1975, Chapters 7 and 8.

Prielipp, Robert W. "Decimals." *Arithmetic Teacher*, Vol. 23, No. 4 (April 1976), pp. 285–288.

Riedesel, C. Alan, and Burns, P. C. *Handbook for Exploratory and Systematic*

Teaching of Elementary School Mathematics. New York: Harper & Row, Publishers, 1977, Sections 13 and 14.

Robidoux, Dennis, and Montefusco, Nicholas. "An Easy Way to Change Repeating Decimals to Fractions—Nick's Way." *Arithmetic Teacher,* Vol. 24, No. 1 (January 1977), pp. 81–82.

Rosenberg, Herman. "The Distributive Law: A Powerful Aid in the Addition of Fractional Numbers." *School Science and Mathematics,* Vol. 76, No. 2 (February 1976), pp. 93–96.

CHAPTER 10

Geometry

PERSPECTIVE   The word "geometry" is derived from the Greek and means "measure of earth." Today, in most elementary schools, geometry encompasses any study of space. Just as mathematics is considered to be the study of quantitative relationships, geometry may be viewed as the study of spatial relationships. It is that branch of mathematics concerned with observation, construction, and description of shapes, and with location of points in one-, two-, or three-dimensional space.

The geometry with which most people are familiar is called Euclidean geometry after the Greek mathemetician Euclid (about 290 B.C.). Euclidean geometry is based on several postulates. Some of them are:

a. Through a single point there are infinitely many lines.

b. Through two different points, there is exactly one line.

c. Two different lines either intersect in exactly one point or never at all, in which case they are parallel.

In the past few years mathematics educators have become interested in geometries other than the Euclidean. All of these geometries serve to parallel a child's intellectual growth and to broaden his experiences with space. Those most clearly related to the child's needs and interests are topology and metric geometry.

Children approach Euclidean and metric geometries through a background of topology. They consider models of curves and develop beginning ideas of conservation, order, enclosure, and so forth. These topics are then extended to help children consider concepts such as point, line, segment and angle, and so on. At this time children become interested in one-, two-, and three-dimensional measurement, and their ability to describe their environment precisely is enhanced. Their geometric observations and descriptions are recorded on charts and graphs of many varieties; these observations are then generalized through formulas.

Numbers and geometry are related in many ways. Initially, numbers are used to describe geometric dimensions of real or simulated figures in a child's environment. Later, coordinate geometry is used to help her plot the curve of an equation, and even to solve formal simultaneous equations. Thus, the geometries of today's mathematics form an integral and important portion of the child's total mathematical development. As you study this chapter you will find no formal theorems; that is intentional. You will find some special ways of organizing ideas for teaching about shape in space.

As a result of studying Chapter 10 you should be able to:

1. Write a clear statement distinguishing formal and informal geometries.
2. Outline a preferred hierarchy for geometric concepts in elementary school mathematics.
3. Name and illustrate four topological relations.
4. Prepare an activity card designed to enable children to utilize the basic topological relations.
5. Identify three examples of the coordinate planes which exist in your classroom.
6. Prepare a flow chart lesson which would enable children to conceptualize a coordinate plane.
7. Plan a trip outside the classroom which would enable children to recognize environmental models for concepts such as point, line, symmetry, parallel, congruent, and so forth.
8. Prepare an activity card which would enable children to find a classroom model for each of four common geometric angles.
9. Design a flow-charted lesson utilizing environmental models to help children understand selected concepts related to solids.
10. Prepare a series of original activity cards that utilize the geoboard or dot paper in teaching geometric concepts.

A GEOMETRY HIERARCHY Any study of the teaching of geometry in the elementary school which is not tied solely to Euclidean geometry requires some careful thought relating to hierarchical organization. Such thought must take into account that before children enter school they know more about geometry than about reading, spelling, and the language arts combined. Even before they speak, they acquire an extensive geometric background. They know that curved objects will not hurt while hard-edged or pointed objects can hurt. They know that some shapes are hard and unyielding while others are soft and pliable. They learn to crawl in a straight line to reach a desired object. They know that flat-surfaced objects will stack, while round ones will not. The list of what has been learned from the environment is endless. That same educationally efficient environment is ready to be used at school and should be utilized informally and intuitively.

Figure 10.1 depicts concepts and principles that elementary school children can learn in a general order that proceeds from the early years in school through the intermediate grades. The order is by no means exact, but rather suggests a grouping of concepts for instruction. For example, children could study a unit on solids or topology, or polygons, or coordi-

Concepts and Principles in Geometry

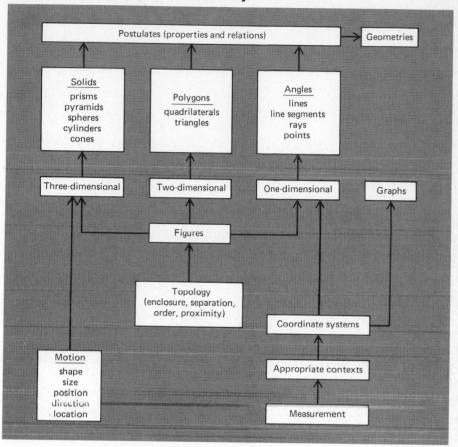

(10.1)

nate systems, and so forth. Measurement is related to geometry in many areas. As an example, angles are measured in degrees, whereas regions bounded by polygons constitute an area which can be measured in square millimeters, square centimeters, square meters, or hectares (about 2.47 acres). Topology appears at the bottom of the chart while properties and relations appear at the top; while very young children are ready to study topology, they require considerable background to study postulates. Thus, the purpose of the hierarchy is to help teachers identify concepts that children can study, as well as provide a general sequence for concepts they study.

TOPOLOGY Topology is a relatively new branch of mathematics, in which shapes are not considered to be rigid or fixed (see Figure 10.2). They may be stretched or squeezed so that they assume a different shape. Thus, a triangle and a circle, being simple closed curves, are equivalent topologically. This characteristic has led to the alternative name for topology, rubber-sheet geometry.

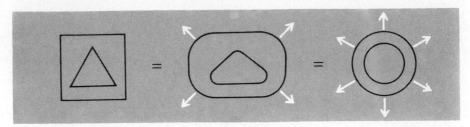

(10.2)

Geometry, as it is often taught in the elementary school, is structured on the assumption that a child's first conception of space is Euclidean. Piaget maintains that this assumption is incorrect. In *The Child's Conception of Space*,[1] Piaget supplies evidence to show that the child's first concepts of space are topological. For example, while a triangle is a unique figure in Euclidean geometry, it is not unique in topology. When young children are asked to make a copy of a triangle, they may draw a circle, an ellipse, or many other figures which are correct topologically. They do this because they cannot distinguish between a square and a triangle. Topologically speaking, both are merely simple closed curves.

The Basic Relations of Topology

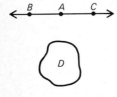

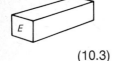

(10.3)

As they grow, children conceptualize four basic topologic relationships. These are proximity, separation, order, and enclosure. Proximity refers to *nearness* of objects. Children need experience to help them distinguish relative nearness among objects. Separation experiences enable children to differentiate one object from another or the parts of an object from each other. Experiences with order help them determine the sequence of objects or events. Experiences with the enclosure relation involve one-, two-, and/or three-dimensional space. For example, is point A between B and C on Figure 10.3? Is D enclosed by the simple closed curve? Is E enclosed by the prism?

The four relations—proximity, order, separation, and enclosure—are drawn together by another topologic relationship, continuity. Continuity implies that physical relationships continue in the same relative order, proximity, and so on. For example, if asked to draw several figures of decreasing size, children must be able to construct a total pattern mentally (see Figure 10.4). Contained within this pattern are the four relationships previously stated. Proximity—are the figures where they logically should be? Order—do they proceed from largest to smallest? Separation—are the figures separated by similar apparent distances? Enclosure—are all the figures closed?

[1]Jean Piaget and Bärbel Inhelder, *The Child's Conception of Space* (New York: W. W. Norton & Co., Inc., 1967), Part One.

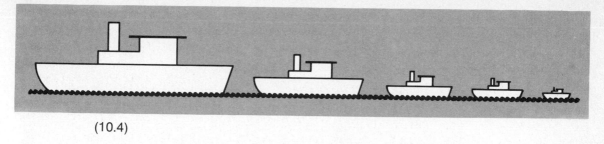

(10.4)

The relationship of continuity does not occur until children are able to grasp the concept of unlimited subdivision of space—at about age eleven or twelve, the formal operations stage. Until this time, children's reasoning is based on their perception of events or objects. When they reach the formal operations stage, children think in abstract terms and are no longer tied to perception. They become able to construct mental figures of decreasing size until they reach infinity.[2]

This presents a serious implication for teachers. If children have not attained the concept of continuity, then the current practice of teaching that geometric concepts—lines, squares, space—are infinite sets of points may be psychologically unsound. If this is true, primary teachers must reshape their programs. Rather than dealing with the abstract, they must provide experiences which encourage children to observe, classify, and manipulate concrete materials. Thus, primary children should work with models of lines, planes, and so on, rather than being asked to think in terms of infinite sets of points as making up a line, three nonlinear points as defining a plane, and so forth. The commitment of the authors on this point is reflected at all times in the pages of this text.

Topological Activities with Primary-Grade Children

Since children's first geometric concepts are topological, the initial geometric activities should be topological in nature.

Proximity The most elementary topological relationship that children normally learn is that of proximity. They explore space in terms of its nearness to them. Things that are "close at hand" are likely to receive far more attention than things distant from them.

The nursery school or kindergarten teacher may wish to have the children divide into groups to examine a set of objects. For example, arrange a series of physical objects so that some are close together and some are distant (see Figure 10.5). Ask each group to determine which object is closest to the tractor, which object is farthest from the tractor, and so on. Have the children move the car so that it is not the closest object to the tractor. Which object is now closest to the tractor?

[2]Richard Copeland, *How Children Learn Mathematics: Teaching Implications of Piaget's Research* (New York: The Macmillan Company, 1970), Chap. 8.

(10.5)

Questions of this nature help children begin to grasp the relationship of proximity. Later, this early understanding can be expanded by showing children tagboard models of a house with paper windows, doors, and a chimney. Children could be asked if these items are placed where they should be. If not, they could remove the items and place them into proper perspective. Other lessons might involve placing arms on a stick man, wheels on a car, and so on. In each case, the proximity of one object to another determines children's understanding and apparent readiness for the relationship of separation.

Separation As children grow older, they become better able to distinguish one object or part from another. Objects are considered by themselves with a certain amount of space between them. A tire on a car is thus drawn as separate from its fenders, or the swings on a playground as separate from the mechanism which supports them. A child with well-developed concepts of proximity and separation will draw a human figure with the eyes adjacent to the nose, yet distinctly separate from one another. Such a demonstration is in distinct contrast to the child who draws a picture with one profile blending into the other.

Children may be helped to grasp the concept of separation by giving them experiences where they must either construct separate but related configurations, or where they must distinguish how objects or drawings might be separated. The children might draw three circles which are distinct and are separated from one another by some degree of space. This can gradually be expanded until the child draws one circle inside another without touching the outer circle—a demonstration of knowledge of enclosure and separation.

An interesting beginning exercise for young primary children is to use the model of a face. The face has movable representations of a mouth, nose, ears, and eyes. Place two of the objects into contact with each other and ask the child to determine whether or not the figure needs improvement (see Figure 10.6).

(10.6)

(10.7)

Another interesting activity is to have children construct a horse from a felt cutout (see Figure 10.7). When they have completed their activity, have each group discuss why they felt it necessary to place the tail where they did, the mane where it was placed, and so on. The group involvement and their discussion serves to stress the importance of keeping the appropriate parts in proximity with parts of similar nature. It also helps stress the need of keeping individual parts separated. Initially, with young children, you may expect some to have the horse's mane overshadowing the eyes, or the tail appended to his legs, and so on. Do not attempt to correct this. Instead, exchange these models among other groups, asking each group to comment on and demonstrate changes which they feel should be made. Such interaction among groups serves to reinforce earlier learning about proximity and separation, and provides children with an opportunity to participate in their own construction as well as review the work of others.

Children who have attained proximity and separation relationships are able to progress to the order relationship, since they are now able to determine the relative closeness of objects while maintaining their distinct nature.

Order The order relationship is seemingly so apparent that adults tend to minimize the complexity of such an understanding. No matter how adults try, they cannot duplicate the perception and accommodation of children as they attempt to understand order. Teachers can give children many experiences to help them develop this relationship, and can observe reactions so that progress can be assured.

The following lesson, which has been given with a high degree of success, is normally used with late kindergarten children, but it seems equally appropriate for first-grade children without kindergarten background.

Arrange several blocks in patterned order by color (see Figure 10.8). Notice that the pattern repeats the color scheme of blue, red, yellow, and green for each of the three arrangements. Give children an opportunity to study the arrangement and ask a question similar to the following: "What do you notice about the blocks?" Expect a great divergence of responses,

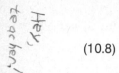

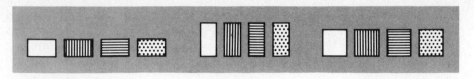

(10.8)

such as: "They are all colored." "There aren't any black ones." "They are all in a row." Although not dealing with order relations, these responses are indicative of a beginning awareness of classifications and should be encouraged. Children seem to respond well to instructional phrases such as: "That's right, but I'm thinking of something else." Or, preferably, "That's a reasonable answer, but let's see what else you can find." Generally it takes only a few minutes for pupils to state that the colors have a particular pattern to them. Ask the group to explain what this means.

Then expose them to another set of objects which is similar in every way but the order of the colors is altered. Say: "See if this set of objects is arranged in the same way as the other." Try this by inverting the arrangement so that blue is last. Again repeat the question. Be certain that pupils explain why the arrangements differ. They must understand that there is no change in the shape of the objects, only in the arrangement (order).

(10.9)

When children demonstrate competence with this task, expose them to an experience similar to the following. Present a model of a freight train (see Figure 10.9). Notice that the arrangement of the engine, the different types of cars, and the caboose is at random. Now ask them if they would operate a train that was arranged in this way. Have them rearrange the train so that it will operate better. Notice that this lesson involves all three of the relationships previously discussed: (1) it involves proximity, in that cars of a similar nature appear to belong together; (2) it involves separation, in that each car group is to be separated by its apparent function; and (3) it involves order, in that the engine must appear first and the caboose last, with the remaining cars in between.

These lessons are only representative of the order experiences which are appropriate for children at the early primary level. Other lessons include patterned stringing of beads, description of the pattern of floor tile in the music room, drawing of color or shape patterns which are to be reproduced, and so on. These experiences, many discovery-oriented, provide a firm foundation for later geometric understanding, and lead nicely to a unit designed to provide children with an opportunity to assimilate and accommodate the enclosure relation. All of these activities should be of a developmental character, and should occur in settings that emphasize interaction.

Enclosure Children's study of enclosure is generally limited to one- and two-dimensional figures considered on a plane surface. As pupils progress, they can assimilate and accommodate the concept of enclosure with three-dimensional objects. Once again, to an adult, the idea of enclosure appears absurdly simple—something is either enclosed or it is not. To children, the idea of enclosure is considerably more complex, and worthy of consideration.

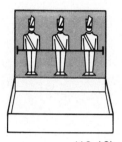

(10.10)

An interesting activity is to have children use their cigar box flannel-boards (see Chapter 2) to represent a line. On the line have them place three figures (see Figure 10.10). Now ask them to examine how far the middle figure can move without jumping over one of the other figures. After a moment, children will decide that the middle figure can only move inside the territory bounded by the other figures. Explain that the middle figure is enclosed by the other two figures. Continue with similar experiences, varying the number of geometric figures enclosed by a given two figures so that at times a child must say that the green, red, and yellow figures are enclosed by the two black figures or by the black figure and the white figures, and so on.

When a performance on this task indicates understanding of the one-dimensional enclosure relationship, change the task slightly. Give pupils a pile of five or six objects and tell them to arrange the objects on the line so that two serve as boundaries and all the remainder but the green and the purple are enclosed by two objects. Have selected children explain which objects are serving as the boundaries and which are enclosed by the boundaries (see Figure 10.11).

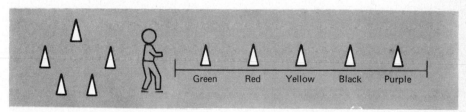

(10.11)

Because of their work with one-dimensional space, children have a concept of what it means to be enclosed. Given the rules forbidding jumping over the line, they now understand that an object is said to be enclosed if it cannot "escape" from a given space. It is free to roam within that space, but cannot free itself. Now, children are ready to begin work with two-dimensional space.

Once again, have children use their cigar box flannelboards. Give them a piece of colored yarn and ask them to tie a knot so that a loop is formed. Now have them place an object inside the loop and ask them if that object is enclosed if the object cannot jump over the yarn. Children will rapidly determine that this is true by stating that the object cannot escape from within the loop; therefore, it is enclosed.

Devise a series of activities to reinforce and extend this understanding. Provide settings where several objects are enclosed within a loop and ask the child to describe them, or provide several examples where the child is to determine which objects are enclosed by the loop and which are outside the loop (see Figure 10.12).

(10.12)

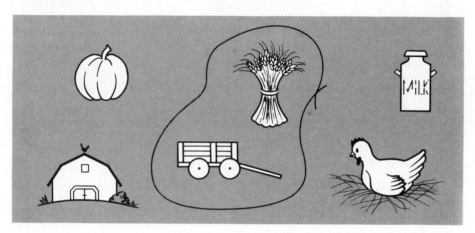

Extend children's understanding to include curves which are not closed. For example, ask the pupils to examine a farm set complete with fence. Leave one gate open so that the enclosure is not closed and ask, "Are the animals enclosed by the fence?" Allow discussion as to whether or not the animals are fenced in. Extend this idea by asking if the school is enclosed by a fence, whether or not their back yards are enclosed by a fence, and so on. A good culminating activity might be for children to make and exchange sketches representing closed and open curves. Have them determine which sketches show enclosed figures and which do not.

In time, children should be involved in activities that deal with enclosure of three-dimensional space. The farm set could be used for this. Set out some animals and enclose them by a fence. Ask which animals could escape. Children will quickly agree that the birds could easily fly over the fence. Enclosing them would require a "top" to be added. Related activities include opening a can and pouring out the contents, and puncturing an egg and sucking out the contents to show that once an enclosure is opened, the contents may escape.

Though it may not seem readily apparent, learning about topology is basic to conceptualizing space and benefiting from further study. You will recall that the geometry hierarchy in Figure 10.1 contained additional concepts such as location, direction, position, motion, size, and shape. These concepts are related to basic topological concepts and usually arise as a natural part of children's experiences with topology. In time, children will raise questions about the size and shape of enclosed points, regions, and spaces. They will inquire about the position of objects in relation to others as well as their locations, the directions in which they are pointing, and the ways in which they can move about. Several additional developmental activities can be used to exploit this curiosity.

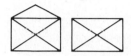

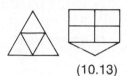

(10.13)

1. Provide each child with a blank sheet of paper and suggest they "take a crayon for a walk" by starting at one edge of their paper and make a continuous curve which ends at the opposite edge. Have them fill in any regions that may have been formed with a contrasting color.
2. Obtain a model of a simple maze, reproduce it, and let the children trace "the short way home."
3. Considerable motivation for the study of topology can be found in challenging pupils to find ways of tracing the lines in each of the designs shown in Figure 10.13 without lifting the pencil or retracing. (Designs 2 and 4 cannot be done.)

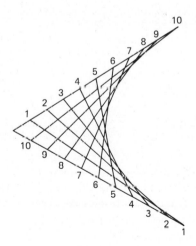

(10.14)

4. Designs containing only straight lines that give the impression of curves can interest children in the intermediate grades. The example in Figure 10.14 is made by marking dots equidistant from each other on each side of an angle, numbering in opposite order, and connecting similarly numbered dots with a straight edge.

(10.15)

5. Interesting to children is the Mobius strip, which is said to have only one side (see Figure 10.15). To make one, cut a 40 cm strip of tagboard about 5 cm wide and form it into a loop; but before gluing, give one end a half twist. One may now place his finger at any side on the surface and move it along to any other point without crossing an edge. Permit the pupils to check this unusual fact for themselves.

Ask the children what the result would be if they were to cut the Mobius strip in two by cutting along the center, making the strip only one-half as wide as it is now. After discussion, let someone cut to verify the conclusions reached. If the strip is wide enough, follow with a second cut to make the strip half again as wide. Also, try making the first cut one-third of the width.

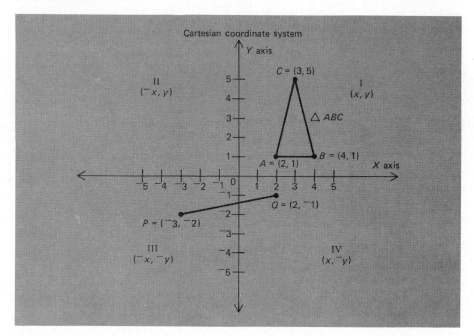

(10.16)

COORDINATE SYSTEMS Children of all ages enjoy experiences working with coordinate systems. The coordinate system that most people know about is called a Cartesian coordinate system after its creator, René Descartes, the French mathematician (1596–1650). The basic concept is shown in Figure 10.16. Notice point a in Figure 10.16. Its location is given by the ordered pair (2,1) where 2 corresponds with a line perpendicular to the X axis at point 2, and 1 corresponds with a line perpendicular to the Y axis at point 1. Thus, to locate point b, go right to 4 on the X axis and up to 1 on the Y axis. To locate point p, go left on the X axis to $^-$3 and down on the Y axis to $^-$2. The Roman numerals I, II, III, and IV represent the four quadrants of the coordinate system. In quadrant I both the x and y coordinates are positive. In quadrant II the x coordinate (called the abscissa) is negative, while the *y* coordinate (called the ordinate) is positive. In quadrant III, both coordinates are negative, while in quadrant IV the abscissa is positive and the ordinate is negative. Conceptually, a coordinate system relates numbers and space by permitting one to use numbers to locate points in space.

The Cartesian coordinate system is an excellent vehicle for active learning at all levels. Especially important is the ease with which coordinate activity can be geared to the children's stage of development. To show this, four activities are shown below in order from kindergarten to intermediate level.

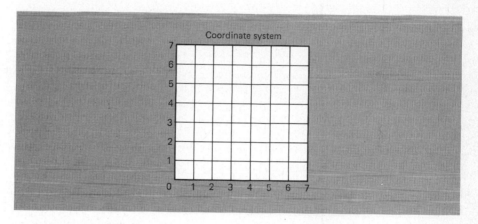

(10.17)

**Activity I
(Kindergarten
or First Grade)**

Obtain a piece of heavy duty clear plastic that is 3.5 meters on a side. Affix a grid of masking tape at 0.5 meter intervals. Put masking tape along the left and bottom sides and affix numerals as shown in Figure 10.17. Spread the coordinate system out on the floor and involve children in varied experiences which require them to begin at 0 and walk to various locations by moving first along the X axis and then parallel to the Y axis. Have children determine their coordinates when they form such configurations as horizontal lines, vertical lines, diagonals, triangles, squares, and so on. Have them identify who is close, who is far away, who is in between, and so on. Have pupils make the smallest square possible. Then have them make larger squares by locating pupils at (1,1), (2,1), (3,1), (1,2), (1,3), (2,3), (3,2) and (3,3). Ask them if they could enclose anyone. Pupils will quickly see that a child located at (2,2) is within the square and that pupils located at (1,2), (2,3), (3,2), and (2,1) are between the people at the "corners."

Activity I is significant because it incorporates many aspects of developing a concept of number in relation to space. The children have to deal with both cardinal and ordinal numbers. They do considerable counting as they walk along the grid. They focus on all the topological relations; proximity, separation, order, and enclosure, and they utilize direction, location, position, size, shape, and motion.

Activity II (First or Second Grade)

Give children geoboards and have them afix red and yellow rubber bands to represent the X and Y axes as shown in Figure 10.18. Then have children experiment with as many different shapes, sizes, and transformations with respect to the X and Y axes as they can. Some of the configurations they will make are shown in Figure 10.19. As the children work, encourage them to talk about their configurations. Have them do this as accurately as is developmentally sound, but do not insist on correct mathematical terms.

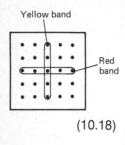

Yellow band

Red band

(10.18)

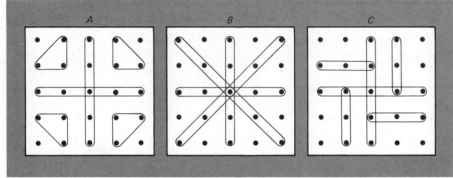

(10.19)

Activity II is important because it contributes to the ability to abstract shape at a time when most children are capable of concrete operations but nowhere near being capable of formal operations. The activity contributes to fine motor development while it facilitates concept and principle learning (for example, parallel, perpendicular, symmetric, and congruent). It also helps children make a transition from topological to Euclidean considerations of geometry.

Activity III (Third or Fourth Grade)

Give children a large piece of graph paper and have them label the X axis with the days of a week and the Y axis with a temperature range appropriate to conditions for the current season. Then have the children select four different cities. Decide on some colors to represent them. Next, have the children plot the daily high and low temperatures for a week. Plot highs with Xs and lows with Os using the color assigned each city. Finally, have the children connect corresponding Xs and Os in order for each city to complete the line graphs of their temperatures. Then lead a discussion of such things as: (1) the daily range of temperature of each city; (2) which city had the greatest range, the highest temperatures, the lowest temperatures, the least range, and so on; and (3) possible geographical and climatological factors that may have accounted for the temperatures.

Activity III shows the natural relationship between coordinate systems and graphs while focusing on basic inquiry. The activity requires children to collect and analyze data for the purpose of drawing conclusions while relating mathematics to other subjects in a setting that could occur in real life.

Activity IV (Fifth or Sixth Grade) Recall that methods for teaching and solving equations of the form $\square - 3 = 5$ were discussed in Chapter 7. The authors support Piaget, who recommends that children be given equations of the form $\square + \Delta = 6$ for solution as they learn addition combinations. This work relates nicely to coordinate systems. Give children centimeter graph paper and label the axes from -10 to 10. Then give children an equation such as $\square + \Delta = 10$. As children find solutions, have them list the pairs of numbers which make the sentence true (see Figure 10.20).

$\square$	Δ	$\square + \Delta = 10$
9	1	$9 + 1 = 10$
8	2	$8 + 2 = 10$
5	5	$5 + 5 = 10$
0	10	$0 + 10 = 10$
$^-3$	13	$^-3 + 13 = 10$

(10.20)

Next, have the pupils graph the pairs and draw a line through them. They will discover that the "graph" of the equation is a line. After this, try a variation of this work with equations such as $\square \times \square = \Delta + 2$, $2\,\square + 1 = \Delta$ and $\square + 3 = \Delta$. The results are shown in Figures 10.21 and 10.22. Have the pupils discuss the results and think of things in real life that look like their graphs (for instance, mountain slopes, roof lines, and flashlight reflectors).

The worth of Activity IV is perhaps deceptive because it does not seem related to the emphasis in the fifth and sixth grades on division and decimals. Actually it deals with graphs of functions. But teachers should be aware that upper intermediate children are nearing the end of the concrete operational period and entering the formal operational period. They can benefit from experiences which guide them to transform equations into graphs and speculate, hypothetically, about what certain equations might look like.

GEOMETRY IN THE ENVIRONMENT As a final note before moving to one-, two-, and three-dimensional aspects of geometry, teachers should not overlook children's natural surroundings as a vehicle for teaching. Often a teacher will struggle to reproduce a model for a geometric concept, only to discover a multitude of models in

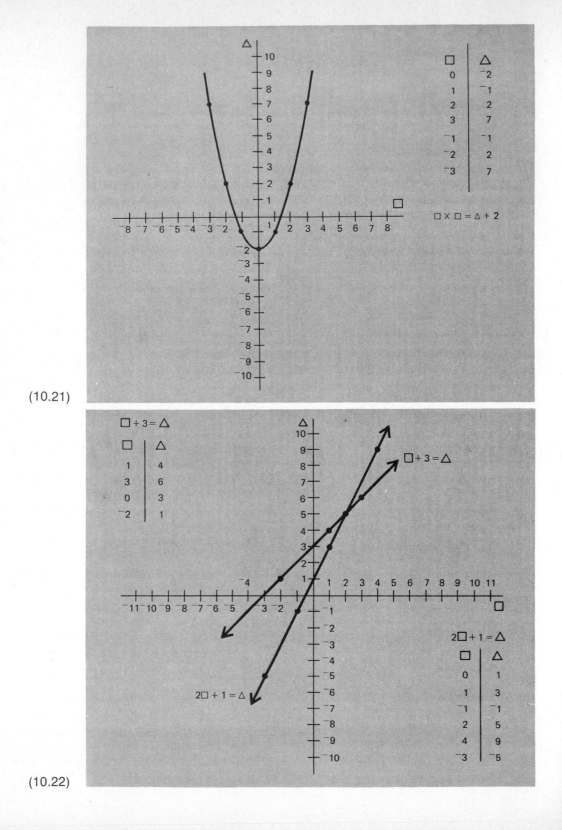

(10.21)

(10.22)

the environment. For example, examine a few models for the concept of parallel. Power poles and lines are parallel to each other, as are house windows, fence posts, wire on a fence, and so on. Other examples include rows of brick, curbing on streets, and pickets on a fence. Are there any spheres in Figure 10.23? Any rectangles? Parallelograms? What other figures are there?

(10.23)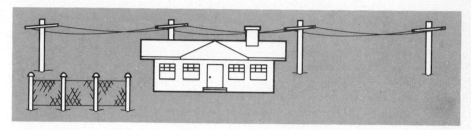

Children are excited by holidays and changes of season. Make use of these events to capture new excitement for mathematics. For example, the jack-o'-lantern makes a vivid model to show the interior, boundary, and exterior of a sphere. Bales of hay are rectangular solids, while the kernels of an ear of corn or the rows in a cornfield demonstrate the concept of parallel. During the Christmas season the stores abound with rectangles, triangles, circles, and other shapes. Now look about the classroom. There should easily be twenty-five more models. With a little direction the class could do the same thing—and enjoy it.

Make geometry fun by asking children to actually search for a model of the geometric figure they are studying. After some discussion of circles and triangles, divide children into groups of five and have them examine the playground closely for these models. Each group could record their findings and bring these into the classroom. Have each group show their models to determine who found the most. Disputed models with somewhat doubtful credentials as triangles or circles can form the basis for lively and informative discussions by the class.

ONE-, TWO-, AND THREE-DIMENSIONAL GEOMETRY

Some Basic Concepts of Geometry

Some concepts are subordinate to an understanding of almost all of geometry. These concepts are used to define basic figures and are essential to a description of these figures. Piaget has made it clear that formal postulates and theorems are unintelligible to most elementary school children. Therefore, the teacher must provide children with experiences which allow them to discover for themselves the meaning of basic concepts and their use in describing figures. The approach should be inductive and informal rather than deductive and formal. Some teaching suggestions for these concepts are given below.

Point Mathematically, a point may be considered as a nondimensional location. It has neither height nor width, and takes up no space. Adults know that a wall or floor contains an infinite number of points. This concept is foreign to children. Their thinking is tied to what they perceive. For example, if asked how many points there were on the teacher's desk, the child would almost certainly count those areas where the parts making up the desk come to a "point." An ice-cream cone would be considered as having only one point; the sharp end of a needle would be considered as the "pointed end."

To extend the concept of a point as more than just these perceptual configurations, children need a planned series of experiences. For example, a group's previous experience with graphing can be used to expand their ideas of point. Have them mark a point to show where two physical characteristics intersect on a line graph (see Figure 10.24). Next have them connect these points with a series of line segments. Questions might then be asked: "What would happen if three more boys took the test, receiving scores of 15, 20, and 30? Show how your graph would look now. Is there room to record the scores of more boys? How many different points do you think you could make on this graph?" and so on.

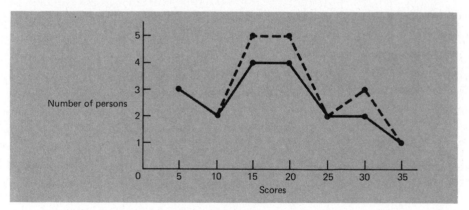

(10.24)

Children's eagerness to construct things can be utilized by seeking opportunities where knowledge of points can be helpful. For example, provide children with a large sheet of butcher paper and ask them to make an envelope to hold their mathematics papers. As they work, discuss the ways in which points and line segments are used as the children draw and construct their envelopes.

Through repeated experiences over an extended period of time, children develop understanding of point to include the intersection of two lines. Further, they view the surface of the graph as being made up of many points. They are no longer tied to the idea of a point as the "sharp end" of something. A teacher can expand the concept of point by providing other examples. Children can locate points on a map, for example, or points on a number line. Activity cards are easily prepared which help to reinforce concepts regarding points.

Activity Card: Point   Level: Intermediate

1. Find the color of the brick which is at a point halfway from the sidewalk to the parking lot and one meter up from the ground.

2. Using your meter stick and a ball of string, locate the following points:

    a. the center of the playground.

    b. the closest point at which you can stand and not be hit by the swing.

    c. the center point between the apple tree, the slide, and the school.

3. Use your string to stake out eight points which are exactly the same distance from the corner of the school.

4. What do you notice about points in all of this work?

Curves In the past, curves have been described as being made up of an infinite number of points. Unfortunately, this description is often meaningless to many students because it is based on two concepts that are not fully understood: point and infinity. Rather than being concerned with a definition, it is wise to provide children with experiences utilizing curves of many types. Later, after an intuitive concept for curve is established, children may wish to discuss the number of points in a curve, and so on. Encourage this, but do not become concerned by a child's failure to make the generalization, for many children will not fully grasp this concept until they are in secondary school.

Unlike their limited concept of point, children usually have an all-encompassing view of the concept of curve. Thus, when asked to describe a curve, they may think of the oblong shape of the wall of a bank building, or the shape of a barrel, and so on. The concept of a curve as a one-dimensional path is beyond them.

Begin teaching by asking children to construct a map of where they live in relation to the school. When this is done, ask that the route home be traced. Then discuss the map, and state that this path is called a curve. Ask the class to state why this is so (see Figure 10.25).

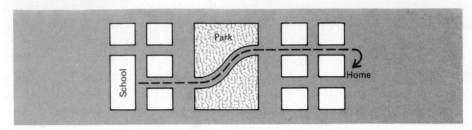

(10.25)

Most children usually indicate that a curve gets its name from the fact that one part of the path curves through the park. To have children understand that a curve includes straight lines, ask if only one part of the path home is a curve, or whether it should all be called a curve. Finally, after providing time for discussion, indicate that both straight and curved lines are representative of what we call curves. Because terms evolve from logic and common usage, tell the children that someone has "made up the term 'curve.'"

You have probably noticed that much discussion of familiar events is integrated with geometry activities. The reason is that children literally operate in space. From a readiness point of view, they have a good basis for intuition regarding what geometry ought to be. Only the formal language and drawings are foreign to them.

Lines, Rays, and Segments When mathematicians talk of a line, they infer a straight line (by definition). Once children have a grasp of the idea of a curve as a one-dimensional path, it is relatively easy to introduce the concept of line as a restricted form of a curve. Discussion of a line as the shortest distance between two points may be the most efficient way to begin discussing a line.

It is necessary that the teacher is aware that a line segment (piece of line) is actually being considered rather than the line itself. A line extends infinitely into space in two directions. Although it may seem inappropriate to use a restricted case of a line (segment) to develop a concept of line, teachers often find this the most effective method to use. Moreover, children do not usually differentiate the two ideas.

One way to introduce lines is to make use of a visual, concrete model. This allows children actually to see and feel a representation for a line and to extend their thinking as much as they are able. For example, give two children a piece of string and ask them to stretch it tightly. Ask the class what the taut string resembles. Among other comments, children will normally observe that the string resembles a line. Although the string is merely a line segment, do not discourage such responses. Instead, relate this response to their earlier work with curves and ask questions such as: "Could I call this path shown by a string a curve?" "Why did you call it a line?" "If I allowed the ends to drop, would it still be called a line?" Questions like these force comparisons, which help children clarify the concept of line. They learn to discriminate lines from curves, and soon reach the generalization that "lines are curves, but represent a special case involving the shortest distance between two points."

If a twinge of guilt is felt because these activities appear to be designed to help children attain a fallacious concept—the children have substituted the term "line" for the true term "line segment"—do not be concerned. Clarification of the concepts and extension of pupil understanding are accomplished when sufficient maturity and development have been attained. Ask two children (C and D) to hold the ends of a piece of string and two other children (A and B) to hold the string several feet along each side. Now ask: "Which is the line, that portion held by children A and B or by children C and D?" (see Figure 10.26) From this, the children will learn that many points can determine a line and that line segments are "pieces" of a line that have end points. When developed in this fashion, children's concept of line versus line segment is likely to be meaningful and thus be retained. Because the children have been involved, the evolution of the terms is logical. Although the label may differ from an adult's, the difference is one of semantics, not understanding. Such a situation should be comfortable for a conscientious teacher.

(10.26)

In contrast to earlier activities, helping children discover rays is simple. The following example can be posed: "We know that a line extends into space in both directions. We also know that a line segment goes from one labeled point to another. Is there any other possibility for a line that you could think of?" If the group does not offer the idea of a line with only one end point, with the other part extending into space, suggest it and ask for a descriptive name. Then introduce the term "ray." Be certain that they compare rays with line segments, lines, and so on. Children will use their concepts of curves, lines, rays, and segments to help them understand and describe more advanced concepts.

Working with Angles

Much of geometry concerns itself with the identification and measurement of angles, and with the use of angles to identify plane figures or to determine other relationships. For example, an essential characteristic of a rectangle is that its sides intersect to form right angles.

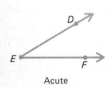

(10.27)

Types of Angles An angle is formed by two rays, both of which have the same end point (see Figure 10.27). Rays $\overrightarrow{BA}$ and $\overrightarrow{BC}$ form the angle. The point represented by B is common to both rays. This point is called the *vertex* of the angle. The notation for the angle shown in Figure 10.27 is $\angle ABC$ or $\angle CBA$. In either situation, the first symbol [$\angle$] tells the reader that an angle is being considered. The middle letter represents the vertex of the angle. The four common angles in geometry are illustrated in Figure 10.28. An acute angle is one whose rays form an angle greater than 0° but less than 90°. A right angle is one whose rays form an angle of exactly 90°. An obtuse angle is one whose rays form an angle greater than 90° but less than 180°. A straight angle is one whose rays form an angle of 180°.

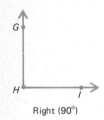

Acute

Notice that this classification of angles is dependent on another concept: the measure of an angle. In the intermediate grades, many interesting and worthwhile activities involving measurement of angles can be undertaken. Some involve developing the concept of measurement. Others involve skill using a protractor.

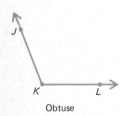

Right (90°)

Measurement of Angles Some teachers expect children to construct and measure angles long before they are ready to do so. Until children reach the age of about nine or more, they are usually not able to use a protractor to measure angles properly. To illustrate this, the results of an actual lesson conducted by a student teacher are described and shown below. The children, a heterogeneous group of beginning third graders, had been given extensive experience with one-dimensional measurement. The teacher felt they were "ready" for more advanced work, and decided to introduce them to geometric constructions involving angle measurement. Part of the activity called for the children to construct a figure which was congruent to a figure which the teacher provided. Each child worked independently. Constructing the figure involved drawing congruent angles. Examples of their work are shown in Figure 10.29.

Obtuse

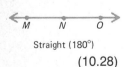

Straight (180°)

(10.28)

The great majority of the children correctly measured the length of segments $\overline{AB}$ and $\overline{AC}$. However, the diversity of the size of the angles was extreme. The children apparently paid little attention to angle measurement, except that all their angles were acute.

The children were then asked to compare their drawings with the original model, and with the drawings of each other. Despite the apparent divergence of shape, the children relied on their rulers to measure only

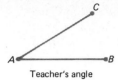

Teacher's angle

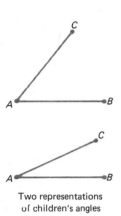

Two representations
of children's angles

(10.29)

the two segments. When they found that these segments were congruent to their own, they agreed that the figures were the same. A few of the children were somewhat confused as to why the figures did not look alike, but were willing to accept the measurements as proof of similarity. The children were simply not ready for this lesson. They needed exposure to other, more appropriate, intuitive experiences before attempting these constructions. For example, cardboard cutouts and tongue depressors could have been used effectively to compare angles or to make congruent angles (see Figure 10.30).

Other experiences might have involved comparing angles in the room—corners, desks, or geometry materials, for example—or using tongue depressors and recording the findings of each angle by tracing them on a sheet of paper.

Think for a moment about the problem of angle measurement from a child's viewpoint. A new idea must be integrated with what is already known. More precisely, the new idea must be assimilated and accommodated. This means that the child must make the new idea a part of an existing cognitive framework and be able to adjust her behavior to this new knowledge. Therefore, ask: "What is the measure of an angle?"

(10.30)

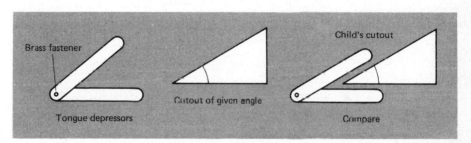

Parts of the angle

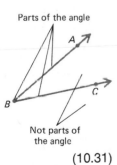

Not parts of
the angle

(10.31)

An angle seems to involve two rays that have a common end point. Thus, none of the space around an angle is part of the angle (see Figure 10.31). Stare at the angle long enough to realize that distance has absolutely nothing to do with angle measurement (see Figure 10.32). The measure of the angle is theta (θ). But the length of one curve that shows θ is clearly much longer than the other curve that shows θ. Instead, it seems as if the measure of an angle is affected by the position relationship of its rays!

Using a ruler, a pencil, and a piece of paper work through the directions below and observe this phenomena:

1. Draw a point. Label it B. B can be the end point of an infinite number of rays.
2. Use a ruler to draw a ray from point B. Label the ray $\overrightarrow{BA}$. Study the ray. Notice that it has direction, that is, depending on how the ray was drawn, it goes up, down, left, or right of the point B.

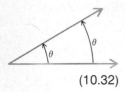

(10.32)

3. Now use the ruler to draw another ray from point B in almost, but not quite exactly, the same direction as ray $\vec{BA}$. Label the new ray $\vec{BC}$. Study $\angle CBA$. Notice that its measure is small, perhaps barely discernible.

4. Now use the ruler to draw another ray from point B in a direction much different from that of ray $\vec{BA}$. Label this ray $\vec{BD}$. Study $\angle DBA$. Notice that its measure is much larger than that of $\angle CBA$.

5. Repeat this procedure a number of times, changing the direction of the new ray from ray $\vec{BA}$ each time. Study the results.

This investigation shows that the measure of an angle is dependent on the relative direction of its two rays. As the rays of an angle tend toward one direction, the measure of the angle approaches 0°. As the rays tend toward opposite directions, the measure of the angle approaches 180° (see Figure 10.33).

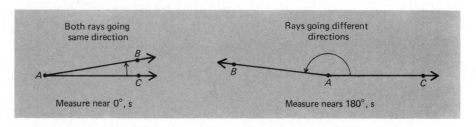

(10.33)

This is not the only way to consider angle measurement, but it does demonstrate the complexity of conceptualizing the unit employed to measure angles, the degree. A degree is one of the few measurement concepts which is in no way related to a position instead of a fixed distance. Other units—such as length, area, and volume—are closely related to some fixed distance.

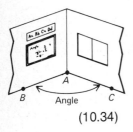

(10.34)

Units of Angle Measure By the age of nine, children have the necessary mental growth to deal with abstract angle measurements and to begin work on geometric constructions. Select an appropriate model for an angle—for example, the corner of the room. Tell the children that their assignment is to determine the correct size of the angle. This is best done in small groups of about three or four children. Allow each group enough time to measure the angle after selecting an appropriate instrument. Rulers and yardsticks are allowed (see Figure 10.34).

Expect a great deal of confusion and divergent activity. One group may measure the angle by means of arbitrarily determined pairs of segments for each side. Another may measure the distance from B to C on line segments $\overline{AB}$ and $\overline{AC}$. A variety of measurements are to be expected. Allow the groups to present their methods of measuring the angle, and let them try to defend their systems as "better" than others. Children will very likely make observations similar to the following (see Figure 10.35).

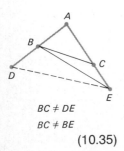

$BC \neq DE$

$BC \neq BE$

(10.35)

1. You can't just measure the two walls, because you don't know where to stop. Should you measure clear to the other wall, or what?

2. You've got to measure the space between the two walls.

3. You've got to decide on a certain point to measure, because if you don't, it changes.

4. You've got to go the same distance on each wall or the measurements change.

Children will almost certainly try several procedures in an effort to get an answer. The teacher can be of some help by asking whether or not they might need a new kind of measuring unit. This question is usually enough to get children to select a variety of new units. Lead them to discover that a unit called "degrees" is necessary. Sometimes the teacher will have to take a more direct approach and suggest that a unit angle must be used to measure angles.

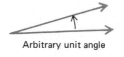

Arbitrary unit angle

To measure an angle, one must determine the number of nonoverlapping unit angles contained within the angle (see Figure 10.36). Thus, we may record the measure of △XYZ in Figure 10.36 as being three units.

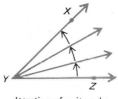

Iteration of unit angle

(10.36)

When beginning the study of angle measurement, let groups of children choose and draw their own unit angles. Advise them to make the unit relatively small. Have them cut out their unit angles so they may use them in measuring angles. By using activity cards or ditto activities containing drawings of angles, each child can gain experience measuring angles. Later, when the results of their measuring activities are discussed, the variety of measurements for the same angle will make it evident that a standard unit of measure must be adopted if results are to be communicated to other people.

The development of a standard unit angle from an historical perspective can then be introduced by explaining that a circle was arbitrarily divided into 360 unit angles. Each of these unit angles has the same size and is called a degree. Children can now enjoy constructing their own instruments, and later using them to measure angles, locate directions, measure inclines, and so on. Spend several days constructing and using protractors, circle protractors, and simple hypsometers (see Figure 10.37).

(10.37)

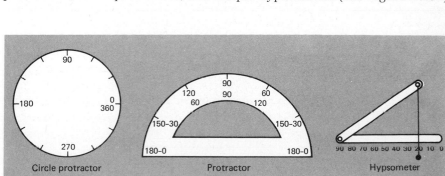

Circle protractor   Protractor   Hypsometer

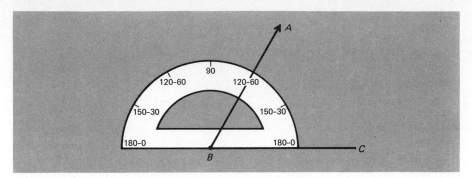

(10.38)

Children may need some help in using their new instruments, and the teacher should be prepared to give assistance. For example, protractors are manufactured in a variety of shapes and sizes. Most are semicircular; some are circular. One procedure common to the use of all protractors is that the center of the circular material from which the protractor was cut is to be placed on the vertex (point of origin of both rays) of the angle. After placing the center of the protractor on the vertex of the angle, be certain that the children also align the edges of their protractors with a ray of the angle. This must be done so that the other ray intersects the protractor at some point. The measure of the angle is determined by reading the degree mark where the second ray intersects the protractor (see Figure 10.38). Notice that $\overrightarrow{BC}$ intersects the protractor at 0° and $\overrightarrow{BA}$ intersects the protractor at what is either 60° or 120°. The measure is 60°. Thus m $\angle ABC$ = 60°. This notation is read as "the measure of angle ABC equals 60 degrees." Children often misread the scale on the protractor. Tell them always to begin reading at 0, not 180.

Polygons   When children have learned the concepts of point, line, line segment, ray, and angle, they are ready to study polygons and solids at the concept, principle, and problem-solving levels. As is the case with all of geometry, the activity features readiness, development, and enrichment. Informal geometry does not really lend itself to drill.

Properties of Polygons   In working with polygons, four principles that recur are perpendicular, parallel, similar, and congruent. By definition, a polygon is any closed figure bounded by line segments. Thus, triangles, quadrilaterals (squares, rectangles, parallelograms), pentagons, and hexagons are polygons. The most familiar polygons are triangles and quadrilaterals. What differentiates one quadrilateral from another relates to conditions of perpendicularity, parallelism, and so forth. Thus, a rectangle is different from a parallelogram because, although the opposite sides are parallel in both figures, all the angles of a rectangle measure 90°, a property not required for parallelograms.

Again, the environment abounds with objects which show perpendicularity and parallelism. Sides of roads, railroad tracks, and telephone lines seem parallel. Crossroads, the lines that meet to form corners of windows, and pavement cracks seem perpendicular. From discussion of these things, children can conceptualize and understand that two lines are perpendicular if they intersect so as to form 90° angles, and are parallel if they exist beside each other without ever intersecting. Again, do not strive for too formal a level. It is true that two different lines are parallel only if their intersection is an empty set, but such formality of definition is beyond young children.

The shape and size of polygons relates directly to similarity and congruence. Attribute blocks work well to show this. Give children several sets of attribute blocks. Pour them on the floor. Direct the pupils to sort blocks only according to shape. This situation is shown in Figure 10.39. From this experience, children will quickly see that figures are similar when they have the same shape. In another activity the teacher should require that children sort the blocks according to shape and size, ignoring any other attributes. From this they will understand that there are two conditions (shape and size) for congruence of polygons.

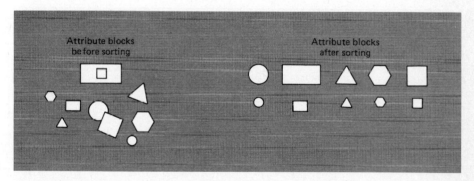

Attribute blocks
before sorting

Attribute blocks
after sorting

(10.39)

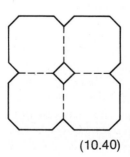

(10.40)

Beyond this, there are innumerable contexts within which children can investigate polygons. One involves paper folding, a type of activity which has unlimited variations. For example, give children square pieces of paper (about 20 cm on a side). Fold the paper in half (not diagonally). Rotate the paper 90° and fold in half again. Now use scissors to cut triangles off each corner and unfold the paper (see Figure 10.40). Point out that the children folded the paper twice. Then ask how many octagons were formed (four), how many notches were formed (four), how many corners were cut off (four), and how many squares appear "inside" (one). Repeat this activity but fold the paper four times (see Figure 10.41). Again, cut triangles off each corner and unfold the paper. This time sixteen octagons will appear, twelve notches will appear, four corners will be cut off, and nine squares will appear inside. Repeat this once more

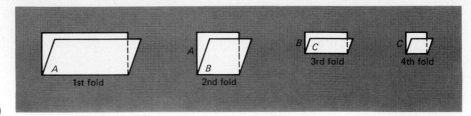

(10.41)

but fold the paper diagonally four times. The results will be similar but with interesting differences.

In another context classification of polygons is easier if children employ tables to record information. For example, have pupils prepare a table as shown in Figure 10.42. Then give the pupils paper cutouts of the figures listed. Have them perform the tasks indicated for each column. Then discuss the results. The pupils will discover the ways in which the figures are similar and different.

	Length of sides	Number of parallel sides	Measure of angles	Sum of measure of angles	Diagonals— are they equal?	Figure formed by folding on diagonal
Rectangle						
Square						
Parallelogram						
Rhombus						
Trapezoid						
Other quadrilaterals						

(10.42)

Solids   Three-dimensional figures abound in the child's environment. Take advantage of this by using objects from the environment as models. Thus, a cereal box is a prism, a monument may be a pyramid, a ball is a sphere, a can is a cylinder, and an ice cream cone, of course, a cone. These are familiar solids to children and require little more than labeling. Some work with familiar objects should enable children to understand the concepts related to solids. These are the interior, boundary, and exterior as shown in Figure 10.43, and the edge face and vertex as shown in Figure 10.44.

Regular Geometric Solids There are five regular geometric solids. They are called Platonic solids. Three have faces formed by equilateral triangles. One has faces formed by squares and one has faces formed by pentagons. Each Platonic solid can be made by cutting and folding paper. Each solid is named and shown in Figure 10.45.

To draw these solids so they may be cut from paper, remember that angles of equilateral triangles measure 60°, angles of squares measure 90°, and angles of pentagons measure 180°. Also, have the children leave convenient tabs for pasting edges together. These solids make exceptional Christmas decorations, especially if their faces are colored or painted.

SUMMARY

Through the study of informal geometry, children may begin to appreciate the role of geometry in their everyday lives. Early contacts with geometry should not require the learning or memorizing of precise, abstract definitions. Rather, these initial contacts should stress the observation of physical characteristics of certain figures; the description of what is observed; and finally, classification by properties.

Teachers at all levels should take advantage of the many learning experiences children can have handling and feeling differently shaped objects. Instructional activities should encourage children to be creative, to discover relationships and characteristics, and to make generalizations. Such activities will help make the classroom a conditioned environment for active learning. A few additional selected activities are listed below.

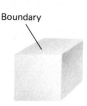

Boundary

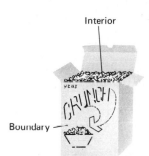

Interior

Boundary

Exterior

(10.43)

1. For children in first and second grade, label some boxes "squares," "triangles," "circles," and so forth. Invite children to find or make appropriately shaped objects to place in the boxes. Have a contest!
2. Have individual children take a common object—for example, a toy garage—and describe or list all the geometric figures they observe about the object.
3. Use old magazines and have children cut out examples of various geometric shapes. Sort them into piles according to characteristics. Place a random selection of them in a large paper bag and have children find and name, without looking, various geometric shapes.
4. The geoboard is an excellent tool to help develop children's perceptual sense about space. In initial work with geoboards, children may be given some rubber bands and experiment without directions. After five or ten minutes of free play, these kind of directions can be supplied:
   a. Make your favorite numeral.
   b. Make some road signs.
   c. Make your favorite toy.
   d. Make some letters.
   e. Make your name. Make your friend's name.
   f. Make a star.
   g. Make standard geometric figures. Count the pegs and line segments.
5. Children can record geoboard experiences on "dot paper." Provide dot paper by simply utilizing regular-sized sheets of paper covered with uniformly spaced dots from a spirit master. Fill other sheets with simulated 5 × 5 or 6 × 6 geoboards.

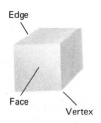

Edge

Face

Vertex

(10.44)

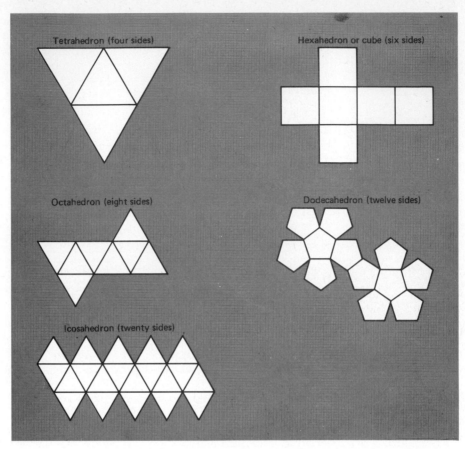

Tetrahedron (four sides)

Hexahedron or cube (six sides)

Octahedron (eight sides)

Dodecahedron (twelve sides)

Icosahedron (twenty sides)

(10.45)

a. Use line segments to make numerals.

b. Make all the letters of alphabet you can.

c. Use line segments to make some open figures. Count the dots and segments.

d. Use line segments to make some closed figures. Make some double closed figures. Count the dots and segments.

6. Tangram puzzles are available from numerous commercial sources, but they are easy for teachers and children to make. Have children divide a large square (10 cm × 10 cm) of oaktag like the model shown in Figure 10.46. The children can store their tangrams in manila envelopes. Initial exploration should be informal, using all seven pieces to form the original square. Later, depending upon the age and experience of the children, some teacher-directed activities like those below are appropriate.

a. Make a square from two pieces. Record the numerals which name the pieces used.

b. Make a letter of your name.

c. Write the name of all the pieces you have.

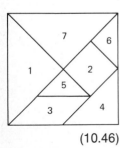

(10.46)

d. See how many standard geometric shapes you can make (other than the square) using all seven pieces.

e. Make a horse.

Children from kindergarten through grade two should experience measurement without reference to standard measures, in order that intuitive understandings of measurement take shape.

By the end of third grade nearly all children begin to conserve length and area. After nine- and ten-year-olds experience the need for standard measures, the meter stick can be used to provide actual measuring experience. Geoboards and graph paper can also be used to explore and discover perimeter formulas.

Area formulas, formula activities with volume, and application of formulas in indirect measurement are principally fifth- and sixth-grade topics. They require the formal operational thought characteristic of eleven- and twelve-year-olds.

ACTIVITIES, PROJECTS, A POINT OF VIEW

1. The following could occur at almost any grade level two through six. Answer the parent's note.

> Dear Teacher,
>
> I don't understand why you are wasting so much time in your math class on geometry when Gilbert doesn't even know his basic facts. I can't help him with that geometry stuff, but I sure can with basic facts if you will just tell me to—
>
> Mrs. Cowelly

2. Choose a grade level at which you would like to teach. Use Figure 10.1 as a guide. Analyze a pupil's text for your preferred grade. What is the relative emphasis given to geometry? What kind of geometry predominates? List topics and concepts emphasized. Make a brief oral report to the class.

3. Write three to five behavioral objectives for the topological concepts you think children in the primary grades ought to understand.

4. Design a game whose purpose is to help teach students to identify points on a coordinate plane, and to develop an understanding of the one-to-one correspondence between points of a plane and the set of ordered pairs of real numbers. For a content source, you may use an article by W. R. Bell, "Cartesian Coordinates and Battleships," *Arithmetic Teacher*, Vol. 21, No. 5 (May 1974), pp. 421–422.

5. Make a list of models from the natural environment that represent the concepts point, line, plane, segment, ray, and perpendicular and parallel lines.

6. Obtain a pencil and unruled paper.

a. Study the drawing. It shows intersections, segments, and regions. The entire configuration is a closed path (curve).

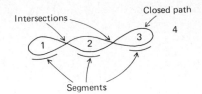

The numbers show regions. There is always one exterior region (4) and any number of interior regions (1, 2, 3).

b. Make a table like this.

Figure	Intersections	Segments	Regions
⌒	0	0	2

c. Draw a closed path that has no intersections. Your path can look like this ⌒ . It has no intersections, no segments, and two regions. Fill in the table.

d. Now draw a closed path that has one intersection. Fill in the table. Repeat for two intersections; three intersections.

e. Study the table and predict the segments and regions for a closed path that has four intersections. Draw it to verify. Why is this kind of activity important for elementary school children?

7. Dot paper with line drawings or geoboards and rubber bands are very useful in helping children develop visual images of geometric concepts. Acquaint yourself by obtaining one or the other of three concrete aids and try the following activities. Make up two additional ones.

a. Construct a square with a perimeter of twelve units and a square with an area of twenty-five square units.

b. Construct an equilateral triangle, an obtuse triangle, and a scalene triangle so they have the same area.

c. Construct a triangle and a square. They should have the same area. Which figure has the greater perimeter? Is this always true?

8. Construct paper models for some of the common polyhedrons suggested in the chapter.

9. Invest a concrete model for showing the area of a trapezoid as its height times the average of its bases.

10. Support or reject this statement: the abstract nature of geometry should preclude its formal introduction to children before seventh grade.

SELECTED READINGS

Bauer, G. R., and George, Linda. *Helping Children Learn Mathematics: A Competency Based Laboratory Approach.* Menlo Park, Calif.: Cummings Publishing Company, Inc., 1976, Chapter 11.

Bruni, James V. *Experiencing Geometry*. Belmont, Calif.: Wadsworth Publishing Company, Inc., 1977.

Dumas, E., and Schminke, C. W. *Math Activities for Child Involvement*, 2d ed. Boston: Allyn and Bacon, Inc., 1977, Chapter 5.

Grant, Nicholas, and Tokin, A. "Let Them Fold." *Arithmetic Teacher*, Vol. 19 (October 1972), pp. 420–425.

Green, G. F., Jr. *Elementary School Mathematics: Activities and Materials*. Lexington, Mass.: D. C. Heath & Company, 1974, pp. 294–369.

Kidder, R. F. "Euclidean Transformations: Elementary School Spaceometry." *Arithmetic Teacher*, Vol. 24 (March 1977), pp. 201–207.

Morris, Janet P. "Investigating Symmetry in the Primary Grades." *Arithmetic Teacher*, Vol. 24 (March 1977), pp. 181–186.

Niman, John, and Postman, R. D. "Probability on the Geoboard." *Arithmetic Teacher*, Vol. 20 (March 1973), pp. 167–170.

Readings in Geometry from the Arithmetic Teacher. Washington, D.C.: National Council of Teachers of Mathematics, 1970.

CHAPTER 11

Problem-Solving Activities for Selected Topics in Elementary School Mathematics

PERSPECTIVE   There are a variety of topics for which there is no apparent consistent educational rationale regarding whether or not they shall be a part of the elementary school mathematics curriculum. Such topics include the history of the development of number and early number systems, finite number systems, selected topics from number theory, and probability. This is an unfortunate state of affairs, for it is clear that elementary school children can gain a basic understanding of the mathematical notions involved in these topics. It is also true that informal presentation of these topics as an integral part of the basic instructional program can enrich the mathematical learning of children by providing opportunity for logical thinking, the base of problem-solving skill. Equally important, the study of such topics provides teachers with unique and interesting settings to utilize wherein children can gain satisfying practice and confidence in the fundamental computation of arithmetic.

As a result of studying Chapter 11 you will be able to:

1. Invent a number system that may be used to communicate quantitatively.
2. List the essential features of nondecimal and finite systems of numeration.
3. Discuss selected advantages of our Hindu-Arabic number system.

4. Construct a model of a Sieve of Eratosthenes.
5. Outline a teaching strategy to help children discover a prime factorization for any natural number less than 100.
6. Describe the substance of teaching a method for computing the sum of *N* consecutive odd numbers, natural numbers, and even numbers beginning with 1.
7. Name at least two elements from number theory that can be utilized in providing problem-solving drill for whole number operations.
8. Prepare a flow-charted teaching sequence to that which will help children understand probability and prediction.

HISTORICAL DEVELOPMENT OF MATHEMATICS

Perhaps the most interesting aspect of mathematics is that it is learned by children in about the same order as it was invented. Previous chapters have shown that children begin with numbering. Then they study operations and numeration. Measurement and fractions are introduced. In time, children study decimals and related operations. In learning these concepts, children move from concrete to symbolic representations.

Chronology

Just who invented mathematics is not known. It is known, however, that at first people worked at a concrete level. They did such things as: (1) bundle sticks in one-to-one correspondence with fingers; (2) make tallies on bones and sticks (often by fives); (3) arrange pebbles in rows, arrays, and piles; (4) tie knots in strings; and (5) create geometric patterns in baskets. These activities focus on numbering and date back to 30,000 B.C.

Thousands of years passed before people invented mathematical symbols. Preservation of records is always a problem and many early documents undoubtedly perished. Others have likely not yet been found. But documented evidence of work of mathematicians dates back to 2100 B.C. It also appears that the profession of mathematician is a very old one. To note the order of some major developments in mathematics, study the time line shown in Chart 11.1. The time line reveals several interesting things. Ancient people were concerned with geometry, but they concentrated more on numbers. The sequence of concepts invented (for example, sets of tallies, numbers, computation) is about the same as the order in which they are taught today. Most of the mathematics children learn was invented before the birth of Christ! Even by 1080 A.D., Omar Khayyam was advancing mathematics far beyond what most people learn today. The mathematics of our present-day elementary school curriculum is, indeed, old.

Between the mathematics created by Omar Khayyam and other early mathematicians is a period called the Dark Ages. During this time, few ideas in mathematics were advanced. Some monks worked to revise and update the calendar, but little else was done. Chart 11.2 presents a time

Chart 11.1   Historical Development of Mathematics (Early)

30,000 B.C.	Tallies on bones and sticks (sometimes in groups of five).
10,000 B.C.	Piled stones, arrays, geometric designs, possibility of "magical" number.
4000 B.C.	Intricate geometrical designs that contained many patterns in Neolithic societies.
3000 B.C.	Some advanced mathematics credited to pyramid builders.
2100 B.C.	Clay tablets in Sumer depicting computation.
1950 D.C.	Tablets from Babylon which contain arithmetic, algebra (linear and quadratic equations), and story or verbal problems. Symbols for numbers and conceptions of place value and operations.
1650 B.C.	Papyrus Rhind, a "book" found in Egypt which contained eighty-five problems that were of arithmetical nature and included fractions.
500 B.C.	Chinese and Hindu decimal systems of numeration and advanced computation.
290 B.C.	Euclid wrote thirteen books called *Elements*, which featured logical deduction of theorems from definitions, postulates, and axioms, some of which constituted a system of geometry. This work included use of variables.
270 B.C.	Aristarchus used inequalities to estimate errors which constituted a forerunner of the calculus.
230 B.C.	Archimedes calculated, in principle, the value of π by using fractions and inequalities.
215 B.C.	Apollonius developed ruler and compass constructions and worked with ellipses, parabolas, and hyperbolas.
250 A.D.	Diophantus wrote books on problems many of which involved theory of number and equations. Made the first use of variable symbols.
625 A.D.	Brahmagupta examined arithmetical and algebraic aspects of solving equations.
825 A.D.	Muhammad made real advances in development of the Hindu system of numeration which featured digits, place value, and zero.
1080 A.D.	Omar Khayyam contributed advancements of algebra, the calendar, and geometry.

line of some major developments since the Renaissance. Many of the concepts developed between 1200 and 1800 (algebra, logarithms, analytic geometry, and calculus) are those studied by secondary school students. Most of the concepts developed during the 1800s are studied by college mathematics majors. The one interesting exception is numeration. Systems of numeration evolved slowly, possibly because numeration is based on other basic concepts (number, multiplication and addition, zero, and exponentiation).

Chart 11.2   Historical Development of Mathematics (Recent)

1202 A.D.	Leonardo of Pisa (Fibonacci) wrote *Liber Abaci* which contained arithmetical and algebraic information. Most important, it introduced the Hindu-Arabic system of numeration to Western Europe.
1250 to 1500 A.D.	Mathematical advancement shaped by the merchant cities whose businessmen wanted mathematicians to study trade, navigation, astronomy, and surveying. Businessmen studied counting and computation. Johannes Müller, among others, produced texts, tables, instruments, and illustrations that related to applied mathematics.
1585 A.D.	Simon Stevin introduced decimal fractions to help measurement within the Hindu-Arabic system of numeration.
1614 A.D.	John Napier and Henry Briggs each invented logarithms to facilitate computation.
1637 A.D.	René Descartes wrote *Geometrie*, which unified algebra and geometry to form analytic geometry (coordinate geometry). His work featured more advanced notation.
1638 A.D.	Galileo studied motion in relation to distance, velocity, and acceleration, and helped restore some vigor in mathematics.
1654 A.D.	Pascal and Fermat created a theory of probability as a result of an interest noblemen had in playing cards.
1662 A.D.	Royal Society of London was founded, as were others, which sought to educate mathematicians, publish their work, and promote development of methods of mathematics.
1665 to 1676 A.D.	Newton and Leibniz, separately, invented the calculus.
1700s A.D.	Major and continuous advances in the calculus and mechanics were created by mathematicians such as Leibniz, Jakob and Johann Bernoulli, Euler, Lagrange, and Laplace. Collectively, these ideas helped produce the Industrial Revolution. In particular, Leonhard Euler was eventually credited with 886 manuscripts and may have been the most productive mathematician ever.
1800s A.D.	Mathematicians generally focused on pure and applied mathematics as each related to the Industrial Revolution. In particular Carl Gauss created many ideas that contributed to statistics. Mathematicians of the 1800s included Joseph Fourier, Nicolai Lobachevsky, Henri Poincaré, Augustin Cauchy, George Canton, Joseph Lagrange, and George Reimann. All men have famous theorems or views of mathematics named in their honor. Basically, they filled in gaps in existing systems, extended certain systems, and invented some new theories. The latter included development or extension of functions, algebra of complex numbers, non-Euclidean geometries, trigonometric series, group theory, and topology.

Perhaps more than anything else, the two time lines provide teachers with an opportunity to put recurring recommendations about mathematics curricula into perspective. Teachers are bombarded by requests to "update the curriculum," "get back to basics," and "meet children's needs in a complex society." Most recently, minicalculators which do most of the mathematics taught in elementary school are readily available and inexpensive. Amid these oftentimes conflicting demands, teachers should stay calm and realize that mathematics is a tool which some invent and all can use to enrich their lives.

Common Features of Numeration Systems

Because the problems that many early societies encountered were somewhat similar to each other, the numeration systems that were developed share common features:

1. Numeration systems were developed to enable man to communicate ideas about amounts. This means that mathematics has its genesis in a consideration of the physical world—numbers describe quantities.
2. Numeration systems are based on many concepts that exist in man's mind, irrespective of ways in which these concepts may be represented by language. What a child attempts to learn in school is the representation of amounts and not the ideas inherent in the fact that amounts exist.
3. Numeration systems consist of concepts and actions. For example, the procedure for identifying amounts is usually based on the concept of one-to-one matching. But the action used to do this may be counting.
4. Numeration systems are all based on certain fundamental ideas. There is always a finite set of symbols which are assembled in some way to represent an amount. The systems have an additive and sometimes a multiplicative property. They have a definite collection point or base, and some symbol that acts as a place holder. The systems are repetitive—that is, large numbers are represented by repeating the symbols in accordance with some fixed procedure.

Numeration Systems of Past Civilizations

As Egyptian society developed along the Nile River, two basic needs arose. One was to survey land so that farmers could redetermine the location of their property after each yearly flood. The second was to be able to account for such things as the distribution of goods and to record numerical aspects of events. The Egyptian numeration system was cumulative and represented amounts in tens and multiples of ten (see Table 11.1).

With this system, it is easy to represent amounts. Symbols are repeated until the sum of all the amounts represented by the symbols equals the desired amount. Thus, 75 would be written $\cap\cap\cap\cap\cap\cap\cap||||/$ or $\cap\cap||\cap\cap\cap||\cap\cap|$, or in some other configuration of the symbols in Table 11.1, as long as there were seven heelbones and five units (strokes). The order in which the symbols are written is irrelevant, since this is a nonpositional system.

TABLE 11.1

Egyptian	Representation	Amount in Hindu-Arabic
I	Unit (stroke)	1
⌒	Heelbone	10
℮	Scroll	100
⚘	Lotus flower	1,000
⟋	Pointed finger	10,000
⌔	Burbot (fish)	100,000
⚲	Astonished man	1,000,000

Probably because the Roman civilization was more advanced, their numeration system is a somewhat complex one with many interesting features. The symbols used are shown in Table 11.2.

TABLE 11.2

Roman	Amount in Hindu-Arabic
I	1
V	5
X	10
L	50
C	100
D	500
M	1,000

The Roman system does not suggest a single base; instead, multiples of five and ten are involved. Besides being an additive system, it has a subtraction property. For example, 1 is represented by I, 2 by II, and 3 by III, but 4 is not represented by IIII; it is represented by IV. Thus, order is of unique importance in the Roman system. I followed by V, which is written IV, means subtract 1 from 5, while V followed by I means add 1 to 5. The subtractive feature is also visible in other representations. Nine is represented by IX, 11 by XI, 95 by XCV, and 276 by CCLXXVI.

The Roman numeration system also had a multiplicative property that enabled representation of large amounts. A horizontal bar drawn over some part of a numeral indicates that part is to be multiplied by 1,000 and added to any part of the numeral not under the bar. Thus, 20,111 could be written $\overline{XX}$CXI.

Neither the Egyptians nor the Roman numeration system facilitate the operations of addition, subraction, multiplication, or division. This is most likely because man had not thought of these operations, and the commerce of the day required record-keeping in the form of determining quantities and keeping track of amounts rather than computation. With our present knowledge, we are aware that cumbersome computations can be made which involve substitution of single symbols for collections of symbols that represent the same amount. As an example, XXIII + LXXXII

= L(XXXXX) IIIII = LLV = CV, and

$$\overbrace{\cap\cap\cap}^{}\atop\cap\cap\cap /// + \overbrace{\cap\cap}^{}\atop\cap\cap // = @\cap /////.$$

Children can study early numeration systems as a natural introduction to nondecimal systems. This can create new interest in learning about mathematics and provide for broader insights into the structure of a place value system. Chart 11.3 suggests one way to begin a study of the Egyptian numeration system. As a result of such a lesson, children will develop some understanding of amounts associated with symbols and the nonpositional nature of the system. Direct instruction can be followed by an activity card like the following one.

Activity Card: Egyptian math fun   **Level:** Intermediate

1. ACROSS

1. 11	DOWN
1. 11	1. 10,211
3. 110	2. 12
5. 120	3. 100
8. 1	4. 11
9. 4	7. 1,011
13. 10,000	12. 100,101
14. 1,110	16. 20
17. 200	18. 100
19. 100,010	

1 ∩	2 /		3 @	4 ∩
5 @	6 ∩	7 ∩		8 /
9 /	10 /	11 /	12 /	
13 𝘱		14 𝔇	15 @	16 ∩
17 @	18 @		19 ∽	20 ∩

Use Egyptian symbols to fill in the cells.
(*Note to teacher:* The answers are shown. You would leave the cells empty.)

2. Make up your own crossword puzzle.

3. Find the sums:

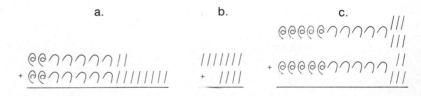

a.
@@∩∩∩∩∩ //
+ @@∩∩∩∩∩∩ /////////

b.
///////
+ ////

c.
@@@@@∩∩∩∩ ///⁄///
+ @@@@@∩∩∩∩ //⁄///

Chart 11.3.   Flow Chart Lesson Plan—The Egyptian Number System

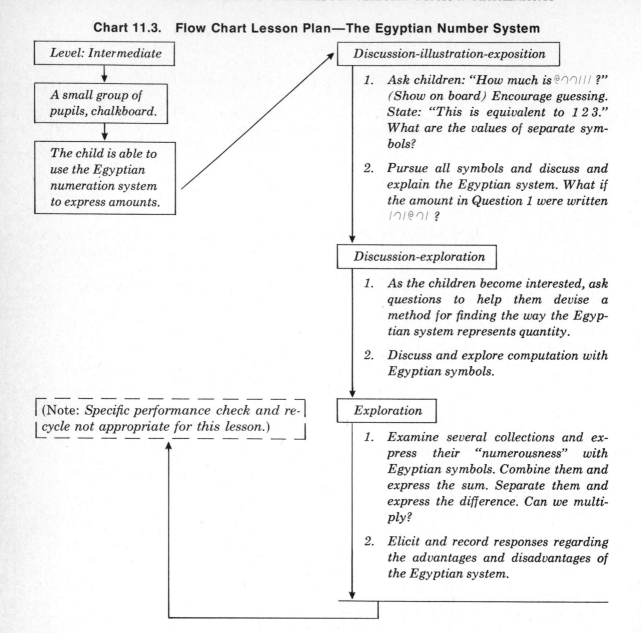

Level: Intermediate

A small group of pupils, chalkboard.

The child is able to use the Egyptian numeration system to express amounts.

(Note: *Specific performance check and re-cycle not appropriate for this lesson.*)

Discussion-illustration-exposition

1. *Ask children: "How much is ⌐⌐⌐|||?" (Show on board) Encourage guessing. State: "This is equivalent to 1 2 3." What are the values of separate symbols?*

2. *Pursue all symbols and discuss and explain the Egyptian system. What if the amount in Question 1 were written |⌐|⌐⌐| ?*

Discussion-exploration

1. *As the children become interested, ask questions to help them devise a method for finding the way the Egyptian system represents quantity.*

2. *Discuss and explore computation with Egyptian symbols.*

Exploration

1. *Examine several collections and express their "numerousness" with Egyptian symbols. Combine them and express the sum. Separate them and express the difference. Can we multiply?*

2. *Elicit and record responses regarding the advantages and disadvantages of the Egyptian system.*

Activities with Bases Other Than Ten

Many children have little desire to learn a nondecimal system of numeration. They see no relevance in operating with a base eight or a base twelve system, since their world is involved with decimal mathematics. For this reason, it is usually profitable to have children develop their own system of numeration. It can be both interesting and instructive for children to represent amounts by using bases (collection points) other than ten, and new symbols to represent number. In engaging children in such activities, it is important to emphasize that no matter what symbols are used, the numbers are the same; only the representations are different. Appropriate settings can be established through the use of activity cards, and the work of children may be done individually or in small groups. Two original activity cards for initiating purposes have been given here. During this initial period, teacher talk may be kept at a minimum. However, even though experiences on the cards are designed to be sequential, there should be extensive teacher–pupil and pupil–pupil consideration of the first activity card before the second one is undertaken.

Activity Card: Expressing amounts through grouping   Level: Intermediate

1. _____ groups of ten and _____;
   we write _____.

2. _____ groups of four and _____;
   we write _____ 4.

3. _____ groups of four and _____;
   we write _____ 4.

4. _____ groups of sevens and _____;
   we write _____ 7.

5. _____ groups of five and _____;
   we write _____ 5.

6. Write the decimal equivalent for each exercise 2-5.

7. What do you think the notation 413_5 means? Can you determine its decimal equivalent?

8. What is the least number of symbols needed to represent any set of objects in base 4? Base 5? Base 7?

Activity Card: My numeration system   **Level:**   Intermediate

1. Create a collection of symbols to count the objects below. Associate your symbols with each object in a systematic way.

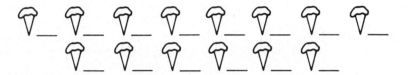

2. Make the number line drawing for your non-decimal symbol system. The number line should extend through base squared.

3. How would the number of students in our class be symbolized in your system? _____

4. Prepare one two-digit addition example and one two-digit subtraction example for which a classmate can do the computation by referring to Problems 1 and 2 above. (You will need to know how to symbolize the appropriate sum and difference.)

As a result of developing their own numeration system, the children in the class will gain an appreciation of the need for an orderly system, and of the problems involved in creating such a workable system. This will stimulate interest in how other civilizations or groups of people developed systems that worked for them.

After exploratory work, it is appropriate to directly investigate bases other than ten using some subset of the Hindu-Arabic digits 0, 1, 2, . . . 9. For example, suppose you decided to initiate an activity dealing with base four using the digits 0, 1, 2, and 3. Note that the number of digits required always equals the base and that one of the digits is usually 0 so that it functions as a place holder just as in our decimal system. An activity can be initiated with a discussion of how a person would count in this base. In so doing, actual objects should be counted and grouped. Careful guidance of the discussion will lead children to see that counting would involve saying 1 (one), 2 (two), 3 (three), 10 (one-zero), 11 (one-one), 12 (one-two), 13 (one-three), 20 (two-zero), 21, 22, 23, 30, 31, 32, 33, 100 (one-zero-zero), and so forth. Ask children why the decimal names ten, eleven, and so on are inappropriate. Next, children can group and count blocks in order to develop a table of addition facts (see Figure 11.1). Once children have an addition facts table, they can engage in a variety of different activities. By using the table, children can compute answers to the accompanying exercises shown in Figure 11.1. Besides solving exercises, children could use the table to identify number patterns and properties. This reveals the fact that the many patterns and properties one can discover are remarkably similar to those which characterize a base ten addition facts table. For example, children will quickly observe that the table is symmetric about its main diagonal as is a base ten addition facts table, thus verifying that addition in base four is commutative.

(11.1)

Base 4 Addition Facts							A	B	C
$\vert$	0	1	2	3	10		13_4	33_4	130_4
0	0	1	2	3	10		$+\ 21_4$	$-\ 12_4$	$+\ 221_4$
1	1	2	3	10	11		100_4	21_4	1011_4
2	2	3	10	11	12				
3	3	10	11	12	13				
10	10	11	12	13	20				

Consistent with prior recommendations, a teacher-made activity is exceedingly useful for promoting individual investigation. You can discover this as you study the activity card on page 304 and complete the sequential activities. What did you learn?

The purpose of nondecimal work is to help children discover the remarkable flawlessness and consistency of numeration systems and to enhance their appreciation for the beauty of mathematics. To achieve such an objective, realize that it is not the number base children work with that is important; nor is developing skill and accuracy in nondecimal computation or conversion procedures of primary importance. Instead, creating possibilities for attaining new insights and a positive attitude toward the study of mathematics is the primary consideration.

Activity Card: Number base, groups of four   Level: Intermediate

B × B× B× B	B × B × B	B × B	Base	Units
256s	64s	16s	4s	1s

1. Use a base four pocket chart to show the following number: 1201_4

2. How many units do each of the numerals represent?

3. Can you discover a way to show the value of 1201_4 base ten?

4. Convert the following base four numbers to base ten:
   a. 212_4 b. 10021_4 c. 22001_4

5. Make your own pocket chart for base five. How many units do each of the pockets represent?

6. Convert 4300_5 to an equivalent base ten number.

FINITE SYSTEMS   Modular arithmetic, more often called clock or circle arithmetic, comes from the Latin word *modulus,* meaning small measure. With careful guidance, the study of modular arithmetic by children provides an appropriate means for achieving some very worthwhile objectives in the study of elementary school mathematics. Initially, it can give upper-grade children a sense of exploring new territory, thereby motivating them to discover or rediscover ideas on their own. In short, it can be a refreshing counterbalance to the previous labors of regular mathematics study. Secondly, it provides a substantive vehicle of study which can stimulate imagination and intuition, two characteristics essential to the search for pattern and order in the study of mathematics. Finally, because it is a finite, miniature number system that may be thoroughly explored, it provides lucid illustrations and new insights for structural properties such as closure, commutativity, and associativity.

Modulo Seven   To help children develop a simple example of a modular arithmetic system, it is appropriate to utilize mod 7 because 7 is a prime number and because the teacher can relate mod 7 to the familiar notion of the days of the week and their systematic recurrence.

   To initiate this study, one teacher wrote the following problems on the board and told the children to get the answers the best way they could.

1. "Today is Tuesday. Imagine you have a birthday twelve days from today. On what day of the week will it occur?"
2. "Tomorrow is Wednesday. Six days later we get our report cards. On what day of the week will we get them?"
3. "What day of the week comes eight days after Thursday?"
4. "If it takes you twenty days to write your book report and you begin on Thursday, on what day of the week will you finish?"

The teacher gave the class an appropriate amount of time to devise and record their answers, and then procedures were discussed. The methods employed by children included counting on their fingers; beginning with naming the appropriate days and continuing until the days of the week which corresponded to the twelfth finger were reached; looking at a calendar in the room; adding 7 and subtracting 1; and so on. The teacher commented: "These are all good ways, and whether you know it or not you all used 'circle' or 'clock' arithmetic to solve the problem."

The teacher then placed a large chart on the chalk tray. On the chart was an illustration similar to that shown in Figure 11.2. She continued: "I would like to have each of you study this chart and use it to help you write a number sentence to obtain a sum for each of the previous problems."

(11.2)

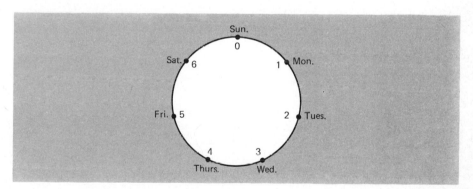

A short time later, the teacher placed the pupil-developed number sentences ($4 + 8 \equiv 5, 4 + 20 \equiv 3, 2 + 12 \equiv 0, 3 + 6 \equiv 2$) on the board. She then said: "You have just solved the four problems using modulo 7 arithmetic and obtained some very unusual answers. Can you tell me why?"

Since one of the purposes for engaging children in the exploration of modular arithmetic is to stimulate imagination and intuition in the search for pattern, a brief transition to addition in regular arithmetic should be made by reviewing patterns and examining structural properties. Begin by placing an ordinary addition matrix on the chalkboard as shown in Figure 11.3. Extend it as far as appropriate, recalling that the possibilities for addition are infinite.

+	0	1	2	3	4	5	6	7	8	9
0	0	1	2	3	4	·	·	·		
1	1	2	3	4	·	·	·	·		
2	2	3	4	·	·	·	·	·		
3	3	4	·	·	·	·	·			
4	4	·	·	7	8	·	·	11		
5	·	6	7	·	·	10	·	·		
6	·	·	·	·	·	·	12	·		
7										
8										

(11.3)

After the teacher has demonstrated how the numerals along the left and top margins represent addends, students can be directed to make their own individual addition matrices. As they complete the matrix, filling in all sums of pairs at the intersection of the appropriate horizontal row and vertical column, some children will observe recurring patterns and will probably finish the task more quickly than others.

Ask them why they were able to finish so quickly. Their answers provide a pointed illustration of the usefulness of pattern. Additional discussion may focus on how children can check the correctness of sums without comparisons to a model table, looking at a friend's work, or recomputation. The desired observation is that the pattern of sums which form a triangle on either side of a diagonal from the upper left-hand corner to the lower right-hand corner of the matrix is identical.

Such an introduction provides sufficient background so that children discover additional patterns independently. Working in pairs on small groups, have children write their observations and discoveries for later whole-group discussion. Among the characteristics and observations that they should note about addition in ordinary arithmetic are:

1. The counting sequence is maintained across any row and a subsequent turn down any column.
2. The sums in the top row are the same as the addends above the top margin.
3. The sums in the left-hand column are the same as the addends outside the left-hand margin.
4. No sum is repeated in any row.
5. Pairs of addends have the same sum irrespective of the order in which the addends were considered.
6. The sums are in a counting sequence in each row and in each column.
7. Geometric arrays of sums from the matrix reveal interesting characteristics—that is, the sums in the rectangle below equal fifteen.

Operations in   The transition to consideration of the operation of addition within a finite
Finite Systems   system can now easily be made. As an example, children can construct an
addition matrix for modulo 7, supply the appropriate sums through use of
a model modulo 7 "clock," and record corresponding discoveries relative
to the completed addition matrix for modulo 7. The recorded observations
regarding the patterns and characteristics of the operation of addition in
mod 7 may then be discussed and compared to the previous observations
the children have made about the operation of addition in regular
arithmetic.

An alternate or supporting teaching strategy would be to provide an
activity card to enhance individual discovery.

Activity Card: Exploring mod 7   Level: Intermediate

1. After you have completed the mod 7 matrix,
   check it carefully for patterns. Write down all
   the observations you can.

2. Check your work with the previous list of patterns in regular arithmetic. How do they compare?

3. Is the operation of addition closed in this set?
   Is addition commutative in this arithmetic? Is
   addition associative in this arithmetic? Provide
   an illustration for each of your answers.

4. Use the clock below to find the sum of 8 +
   7. Remember, in regular arithmetic 8 + 7 =
   15. Sum the digits of 15, that is, (1 + 5) = 6.
   How does this compare with the "clock answer?" Test this result with other sums.

As a result of the previous teaching sequence, many children will
probably develop a shortcut for addition in modular arithmetic. For

example, they will probably discover that two numbers in modular arithmetic can be added by finding the sum of the two numbers in traditional addition, dividing the traditional sum by the given modulo number, and utilizing the remainder as the modular sum. This is an essential understanding, and children should determine that it results in the same sum as "counting around the clock" (see Figure 11.4).

$$8 + 5 = \text{what number (mod 9)}$$
$$8 + 5 = 13; \ 13 \div 9 = 1r4$$

(11.4) $$8 + 5 \equiv (\text{read "is congruent to"}) \ 4 \ (\text{mod } 9)$$

Children may be encouraged to build other examples of circle or clock arithmetic which utilize more or fewer numbers than mod 7. This activity could be independent of the teacher's direct involvement in its early stages. With children in groups of three or four, provide each group with a ruler, a compass, a piece of paper, pencils, and an activity card such as the one shown below.

Activity Card: Mod 3 addition   **Level:**   Intermediate

1. Draw a circle which has a two-inch radius and draw an equilateral triangle in it (show on board).

2. Label the vertices of the triangle clockwise with 0, 1, and 2.

3. Set up an addition matrix by adding all combinations of values obtained by moving clockwise to 0, 1, and 2. Thus $0 + 1 = 1$, $1 + 2 = 0$, and so on.

4. Determine a largest sum and a smallest sum. Does the system have an identity element? Is addition still a commutative operation? What other observations can you make?

Through exploration and observation, children will find that the largest sum is 2, the smallest sum is 0, and the system has an identity element which is 0. They may also note that addition is commutative because the table is symmetric about its main diagonal. Other observations children may make include that of the nine possible sums: three are 0, three are 1, and three are 2. Another is that their location suggests that the additive inverse of 1 is 2; the additive inverse of 2 is 1; and the additive inverse of 0 is 0.

Subsequent to the study of modular addition, children can be guided to build a modular multiplication matrix. It would be well to help children recall that multiplication may be interpreted as repeated addition. This will enable them to use the matrix of addition facts in mod 7 to build a multiplication matrix in mod 7. Appropriate questions to guide students in this adventure include: "Is the set closed under multiplication?" "Does the distributive property hold in this arithmetic?" "Are fractions possible in this arithmetic?" "Does the division short cut work for obtaining products?"

Subtraction in modular systems provides an opportunity for further interesting observations by children. To perform a subtraction in "circle" or "clock" arithmetic, simply turn the hand backward or move it in a counterclockwise direction. Study the illustration in Figure 11.5.

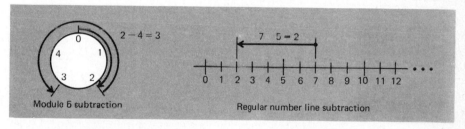

(11.5)

Modulo 5 subtraction Regular number line subtraction

Modulo 5 addition matrix   Modulo 5 subtraction matrix

(11.6)

+	0	1	2	3	4
0	0	1	2	3	4
1	1	2	3	4	0
2	2	3	4	0	1
3	3	4	0	1	2
4	4	0	1	2	3

Addend

−	0	1	2	3	4
0	0	1	2	3	4
1	4	0	1	2	3
2	3	4	0	1	2
3	2	3	4	0	1
4	1	2	3	4	0

Minuend

A setting which children might use for initial study would be the comparison of a mod 5 addition matrix with a mod 5 table of subtraction facts. An example of each appears in Figure 11.6.

During exploration and comparison, children will discover that all subtractions in mod 5 have an "answer"; the useful notion of the inverse relationship between addition and subtraction may be verified by children.

A study of the operation of division within a finite system—for example, mod 4—results in some startling discoveries. The first relates to the role of prime and composite numbers. If the modulus is a prime number, every non zero number has a multiplicative inverse and division is always possible (except by zero). However, when the modulus is a composite number, some numbers do not have multiplicative inverses, and therefore division is not always possible. As a consequence, a most instructive approach with children is to first construct with them a table of division facts in mod 5, utilizing the application of the inverse relationship between division and multiplication, their previously derived mod 5 multiplication matrix, and the repeated subtraction rationale. After this has been accomplished in a whole group setting, have small groups of children replicate the activity with each group of children utilizing a different composite number for the modulus (4, 6, and 8). An oral comparison of group work by the children will clearly indicate that the study of finite number systems affords an unusual opportunity to promote active learning.

NUMBER THEORY   Number theory deals with relationships that exist for natural numbers, 1, 2, 3, 4, . . . , and is independent of computation with these numbers. Procedures for computation utilize algorithms and are basically concerned with obtaining "correct" answers efficiently. For example, consider the exercises shown in Figure 11.7.

A	B	C
22	152	369
55	25 /3819	214
267	25	+ 875
× 48	131	1458
2136	125	
1068	69	
12816	50	
	19 r	

(11.7)

The procedures for doing these computations do not indicate why certain numbers are multiplied, added, borrowed, carried, and so on. To understand why the computations result in the correct answer, it is necessary for children to investigate the nature of the numbers themselves and how they are affected by operations.

**Odd and
Even Numbers**

Children can make elementary observations which promote a rudimentary understanding of the natural numbers. For example, they might consider the nature of odd and even natural numbers. This partition of natural numbers can be the basis for an active learning experience at a primary grade level, shown in the following example.

Give a group of children some chips or bottle caps. Through guided exploration and discussion, have the children count out sets of varying amounts, attempting to divide the objects into two equivalent subsets. Some of the configurations the children might develop from 5 and 8 are shown in Figure 11.8. As this is done, the teacher notes the results on a table drawn on the chalkboard, as is shown in Table 11.3.

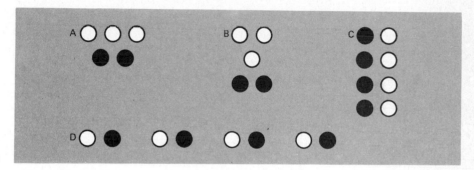

(11.8)

TABLE 11.3

Even numbers	Odd numbers
2 = 1 + 1	1 = 1
4 = 2 + 2	3 = (1 + 1) + 1
6 = 3 + 3	5 = (2 + 2) + 1
8 = 4 + 4	7 = (3 + 3) + 1
10 = 5 + 5	9 = (4 + 4) + 1

When children have finished manipulating and counting the sets of chips, discussion can help them note the similarities and differences between the numbers. From this discussion, they can discover why the numbers on the left are called even numbers and those on the right are called odd numbers. Further work can be done using other sets of materials. When they can correctly determine even and odd numbers and state the rationale for such a determination, the children have attained the principle level of learning.

**Prime and
Composite Numbers**

Another observation about the natural numbers is that they are either prime or composite. A group of pupils might examine the equations shown in Figure 11.9, and be asked to record their observations. They may notice that for some numbers it looks as if the equations involve only 1 and the number as factors. In Figure 11.9 this is true for 2, 7, 5, and 17. Such numbers are called prime numbers. Composite numbers have more than two factors. In Figure 11.9 this is true for the numbers 16, 12, 4, and 9. The number 1 is not considered to be either a prime or composite number. It is not a prime number, since these must have only two distinct factors and 1 times itself is considered as only a single distinct factor. It is not composite since it does not involve multiplications other than 1 and itself.

Number	Some multiplications that equal the number
2	$1 \times 2 = 2$, $2 \times 1 = 2$
16	$1 \times 16 = 16$, $4 \times 4 = 16$, $16 \times 1 = 16$, $2 \times 8 = 16$
7	$1 \times 7 = 7$, $7 \times 1 = 7$
12	$4 \times 3 = 12$, $6 \times 2 = 12$, $1 \times 12 = 12$
4	$1 \times 4 = 4$, $4 \times 1 = 4$, $2 \times 2 = 4$
5	$1 \times 5 = 5$, $5 \times 1 = 5$
9	$3 \times 3 = 9$, $1 \times 9 = 9$
(11.9) 17	$1 \times 17 = 17$, $17 \times 1 = 17$

There are several additional observations that the class might make about prime and composite numbers. For example, they may notice that the primes do not occur at regular intervals. The primes from 1 to 100 are: 2, 3, 5, 7, 11, 13, 17, 19, 23, 29, 31, 37, 41, 47, 53, 59, 67, 71, 73, 79, 83, 89, 97.

The fact that the primes are irregularly distributed affords an excellent opportunity for contrasting process and outcomes, and to appreciate the difference between telling children something and letting them discover it. Initiate a lesson by making a guided exploration move that directs the children to construct a ten-by-ten array of natural numbers beginning with 1. Pupils can be directed to circle the numeral 1 to indicate that it is neither prime nor composite (see Figure 11.10).

1	2	3	4	5	6	7	8	9	10
11	12	13	14	15	16	17	18	19	20
21	22	23	24	25	26	27	28	29	30
31	32	33	34	35	36	37	38	39	40
41	42	43	44	45	46	47	48	49	50
51	52	53	54	55	56	57	58	59	60
61	62	63	64	65	66	67	68	69	70
71	72	73	74	75	76	77	78	79	80
81	82	83	84	85	86	87	88	89	90
91	92	93	94	95	96	97	98	99	100

(11.10)

When the array is complete, ask children to erase all composite numbers. They may begin by erasing every second number after two because each of the latter will have two as a factor. Continue in the same fashion for the numbers 3, 5, 7, 11, and 13. When this is finished, there will remain the prime numbers less than 100. This configuration of primes is known as the Sieve of Eratosthenes. As children complete such a configuration, they can obtain a great deal of practice in both multiplication and division as they mentally examine factors or test for divisibility. They may also note that relatively few primes have only one counting number between them, as for example, 11 and 13 or 41 and 43. Prime numbers with such a relationship are called twin primes.

Goldbach's Conjecture The teacher can help children discover another relationship by asking how many even numbers greater than 2 can be found by adding only two primes. For example, $2 + 2 = 4$, $3 + 3 = 6$, $5 + 3 = 8$, $7 + 11 = 18$, and so forth. Given enough time, groups may discover that apparently every even number greater than 4 can be formed by adding two primes. This discovery was made by a Russian mathematician, Christian Goldbach, in 1742. An exception has never been found, but neither has a formal proof been made; therefore, the discovery is known as the Goldbach conjecture. There are many unsolved problems of a like nature in mathematics, and recognition of this is another legitimate objective for teaching number theory in elementary school mathematics.

Prime numbers are most often utilized in established elementary school programs in connection with the computation of rational numbers. Consider this example:

Multiply and reduce to lower terms:

$$\frac{8}{9} \times \frac{7}{12} = \frac{56}{108}$$

Here, 56 and 108 can be expressed as a product of primes. A factor tree is useful for showing this:

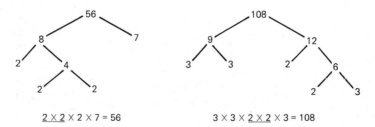

$\underline{2 \times 2} \times 2 \times 7 = 56$ $3 \times 3 \times \underline{2 \times 2} \times 3 = 108$

The greatest common divisor is the product of the common primes. In this case, the greatest common divisor is $2 \times 2 = 4$. Consequently, $56/108 \div 4/4 = 14/27$ and the product is reduced to lowest terms.

Fundamental Theorem of Arithmetic

Activities which emphasize divergent and convergent thinking in a complimentary manner are likely to be productive as well as interesting. As one example, children can explore together all of the possibilities for solving a particular problem, and then examine what they did in order to arrive at a generalization. Another example is found in guided exploration, which results in the discovery of a theorem. A theorem is a general mathematical statement which either has been proved or can be proved on the basis of certain stated assumptions, undefined terms, and definitions. Upper-level elementary school children could quite easily discover the fundamental theorem of arithmetic (also called the unique factorization theorem) as a natural consequence of investigating all of the ways in which to express selected composite numbers as prime factorizations.

The basic task is to have the child consider ways of expressing several numbers such as 12, 24, and 36 as multiplications involving factors less than 12, 24, or 36 respectively (see Figure 11.11).

$$12 = \quad 3 \times 4 = \boxed{3 \times 2 \times 2}$$
$$12 = \quad 6 \times 2 = \boxed{2 \times 3 \times 2}$$

Same factors for each numeral, but different orders. According to the commutative property, order does not affect the product, so the prime factorizations are the same.

$$24 = 12 \times 2 = 6 \times 2 \times 2 = \boxed{3 \times 2 \times 2 \times 2}$$
$$24 = \quad 6 \times 4 = \boxed{3 \times 2 \times 2 \times 2}$$
$$24 = \quad 8 \times 3 = 4 \times 2 \times 3 = \boxed{2 \times 2 \times 2 \times 3}$$

$$36 = \quad 6 \times 6 = \boxed{3 \times 2 \times 3 \times 2}$$
$$36 = 12 \times 3 = 4 \times 3 \times 3 = \boxed{2 \times 2 \times 3 \times 3}$$
$$36 = 18 \times 2 = 9 \times 2 \times 2 = \boxed{3 \times 3 \times 2 \times 2}$$
$$(11.11) \quad 36 = \quad 9 \times 4 = \boxed{3 \times 3 \times 2 \times 2}$$

When all the possibilities for expressing 12, 24, and 36 have been explored, the teacher can ask the children to examine the factors for each prime number. A little speculation, perhaps together with some verification from the teacher, can lead the children to indicate that there is a unique factorization for each composite number. If the children successfully do all of this, the teacher can tell them that these results for composite numbers constitute what is called the fundamental theorem of arithmetic. The fundamental theorem of arithmetic may be stated: "If the order of the factors is disregarded, every composite number in the set of counting numbers can be expressed as the product of prime numbers in just one way." This discovery further emphasizes the importance of primes in the set of natural numbers. Remember, children discovered that any composite number may be expressed as the sum of only two primes. Now they see that every composite in the set of natural numbers may be formed as the product of primes.

Relatively Prime Numbers Once children can effectively factor a number and recognize the distinction between prime and composite numbers, there is yet another theoretical relationship related to prime numbers that is useful to them. Numbers which have no factors in common are called relatively prime. Thus, a fraction whose numerator and denominator are relatively prime is in its lowest terms. Examine the pair of rational numbers in Figure 11.12. When children are engaged in the four fundamental operations with fractions, the usefulness of this notion is quickly appreciated.

Basic Fractions

$$
\frac{9}{14} = \frac{3 \times 3}{7 \times 2}
$$
$$
\frac{8}{15} = \frac{2 \times 2 \times 2}{5 \times 3}
$$

(11.12)

{ No factors common to both numerator and denominator.

Perfect Numbers A number that represents the sum of all its factors except the number itself is said to be a perfect number. As an example, 28 is perfect because it is the sum of $1 + 2 + 4 + 7 + 14$. Perfect numbers are very rare numbers. Only 23 have been discovered so far. Perhaps your students will enjoy searching for some. They could do it by trial and error. However, another procedure for doing so is to add the numbers that represent the place values of the binary numeration system (1, 2, 4, 8, 16, and so on). Whenever the sum is a prime number, multiply it by the largest number added. For example, $1 + 2 + 4 = 7$; then $7 \times 4 = 28$. Other perfect numbers are 496 and 8128.

Although there are many observations to be made about prime and composite numbers, not all of them can be appropriately investigated by elementary school children. Introduce pupils to ideas at a level appropriate to them. This can be done by varying such things as the magnitude of the numbers involved, the examples and illustrations utilized, the scope of the activities, and the extent to which the idea is presented in a concrete manner through particular examples or materials.

Square and Triangular Numbers The early Greeks perceived a relationship between number and geometric concepts. They classified a number as a square if one of its arrays formed a square (see Figure 11.13).

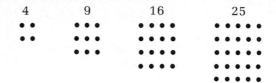

(11.13)

Begin a lesson by asking the children to lay one chip on their desks, and remind them that the numeral which represents this set of chips is 1. Assuming extensive experience with arrays, ask the children to lay out the next larger set of chips which forms a square array. They will decide that this takes four chips. Then ask the children to write a number sentence to describe these actions. They should decide that the correct expression is 1 + 3. Similar procedures can be pursued during the remainder of the lesson for sets of chips that form other square arrays. The numerals that represent these square arrays are 9, 16, 25, . . . , and the expressions are (1 + 3 + 5), (1 + 3 + 5 + 7), (1 + 3 + 5 + 7 + 9), . . . respectively. As they work to make these observations, children will compute, argue, guess, make false starts, verify, and perhaps discover in some fashion the fact that the sum of N consecutive odd numbers equals N^2 (see Figure 11.14)

$$1 + 3 = 4 \qquad\qquad 1 + 3 + 5 = 9 \qquad\qquad 1 + 3 + 5 + 7 = 16$$

(11.14) $N = 2 \quad 2^2 = 4 \qquad\qquad N = 3 \quad 3^2 = 9 \qquad\qquad N = 4 \quad 4^2 = 16$

The activity just described was developed and taught by a preservice teacher to a group of ten second-grade pupils. Teacher and pupils alike enjoyed the activity, and two boys verbalized the generalization. The flow chart lesson plan the teacher utilized is presented for careful scrutiny.

Children can explore triangular configurations like those shown in Figure 11.15 in several ways. If children need to use manipulative objects, have them use chips to help them identify expressions which equal 1, 3, 6, 10, 15, 21. . . . On the other hand, to focus attention on addition and the process of noting ways to partition the configurations in order to identify the numbers, one should add that the configurations could be drawn on a worksheet before the lesson begins. Another possibility is to have individual children draw the sets of dots on the chalkboard as they are needed.

Chart 11.4.   Flow Chart Lesson Plan—Square Arrays

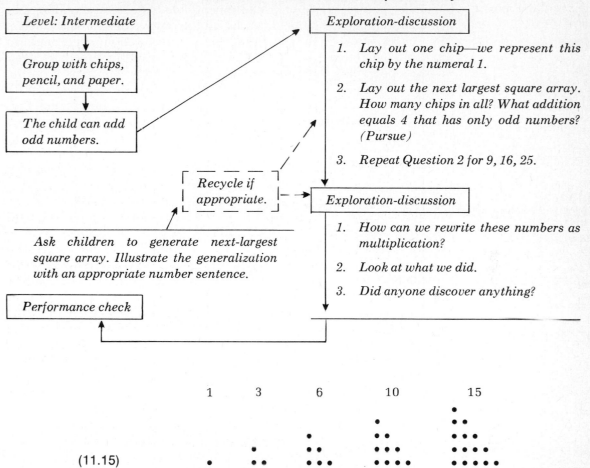

(11.15)

Regardless of how the children work with triangular configurations, they should eventually realize that the number associated with the Nth configuration is obtained by adding the first N consecutive natural numbers. For example, the number associated with the fourth set of dots shown in Figure 11.15 is obtained by adding 1, 2, 3, and 4 $(1 + 2 + 3 + 4 = 10)$. The formula for determining the sum of N triangular numbers is $[N(N + 1)] \div 2$, where N is allowed to represent the number of configurations involved. This formula was developed by Karl Gauss in response to the need (which, according to some historians, was imposed by his teacher) to discover a way to add the first N consecutive natural numbers, because he did not appreciate the labor associated with actually doing it.

Summing Consecutive Even Numbers We have established that triangular numbers are obtained by adding consecutive natural numbers, and that square numbers are obtained by adding consecutive odd numbers. This suggests the notion that adding consecutive even numbers ought to produce something. Use a pencil and paper to add consecutive even numbers beginning with 2. If this is done correctly, the sums form the sequence: 2, 6, 12, 20, 30, 42. . . . Now see if these numbers can be associated with arrays which are arranged in some regular manner. Can you discover a formula that would give the nth element of the sequence?

(11.16)

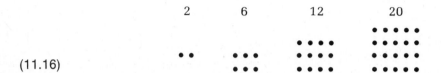

Study Figure 11.16, where sums of the sequence are represented by arrays. Observe that the first number in the sequence is 2. This suggests that the first array could look like •• . Some speculation about how to produce an array which contains six dots suggests that we should expand the initial array in each direction. This makes the second array look like ••• . In fact, this procedure works. The first four arrays are shown in Figure 11.16. Recall that the formula for the sum of N consecutive odd numbers beginning with 1 was N^2. For even numbers the sum seems to be $N^2 + N$ or $N(N + 1)$. To check this formula, add the first six consecutive even numbers. According to the formula, this is $6(6 + 1) = 6 \times 7 = 42$, which is the correct answer. Trying this for three even numbers, we get $3(3 + 1) = 3 \times 4 = 12 = 2 + 4 + 6$, which is the correct answer. In fact, the formula will always work. Or will it? Actually, it is probably better to say that a case where it will not work has not yet been found.

The Fibonacci Series A Fibonacci series is a series of numbers such that each number after the first two is the sum of the two preceding numbers. For example, 3, 2, 5, 7, 12, 19, 31, 50, 81, 131, . . . form a Fibonacci series. Such a pattern does form an exceedingly interesting process for gaining practice in addition. In a small group setting, ask a pupil to place on the chalkboard, while your back is turned, such a series of ten numbers, choosing any two numbers with which to begin. When the student has finished, turn around, glance at the numbers, and write the sum of the series. You can do this quickly because the sum of the Fibonacci numbers in a series of 10 is 11 times the seventh number. In the series above, the seventh number is 31 ($11 \times 31 = 341$). An easy way to compute this is by beginning with $10 \times 31 = 310$; then $310 + 31 = 341$.

To provide individual practice in addition, ask each pupil to prepare a Fibonacci series. As they are doing so, move about the group giving the sum of each series. Pupils should check your answer and attempt to discover how you are arriving at the sum so quickly.

The progression for the series above is portrayed in Figure 11.17. Note that the sum is (55 × the first number) + (88 × the second number) or 11 [(5 × the first number) + (8 × the second number)].

$$
\begin{aligned}
3 &= a \\
2 &= b \\
5 &= a + b \text{ or } 3 + 2 \\
7 &= a + 2b \text{ or } 3 + 4 \\
12 &= 2a + 3b \text{ or } 6 + 6 \\
19 &= 3a + 5b \text{ or } 9 + 10 \\
31 &= 5a + 8b \text{ or } 15 + 16 \\
50 &= 8a + 13b \text{ or } 24 + 26 \\
81 &= 13a + 21b \text{ or } 39 + 42 \\
\underline{131} &= \underline{21a + 34b \text{ or } 63 + 68} \\
341 &= 55a + 88b \text{ or } 165 + 176
\end{aligned}
$$

(11.17)

Palindromes and Palimages A palindrome is a natural number of two or more digits that is the same read either forward or backward, for example, 33, 44, 3443, and so forth. Palimages are pairs of natural numbers that have the same number of digits but are in reverse order—for example, 358 and 853, 2345 and 5432, and so forth.

Palimages and palindromes have some surprising characteristics when it comes to adding and subtracting, and children can gain skill in obtaining sums and differences as they discover these characteristics. For addition, if two palimages are consecutively summed, one soon finds a palindromic number as the sum. The question then arises: Can every natural number be made a palindromic number? Add its palimage (reverse) to the integer; if the sum is not palindromic, add the sum and its palimage, and so forth. Eventually this will produce a palindrome. Have children write down any multidigit number. Reverse the digits and add. Repeat until a palindromic number occurs. In Figure 11.18, the starting number was 453.

$$
\begin{array}{rl}
453 & \text{palimage } 1 \\
\underline{+354} & \\
807 & \text{palimage } 2 \\
\underline{+708} & \\
1515 & \text{palimage } 3 \\
\underline{+5151} & \\
6666 & \text{palindrome}
\end{array}
$$

(11.18)

If the palimages are subtracted consecutively, one often finds a palindrome difference like 99 or 999 or 909. Occasionally, a repeating pattern will occur in the palimage subtraction which prevents a palindromic difference. As the children work with palindromes and palimages, they can record the number of steps needed and classify the work as one-step, two-step, three-step, and so forth.

ELEMENTARY PROBABILITY THEORY

Elementary probability can be demonstrated in many interesting ways in the classroom. Children at all grade levels can investigate probability concepts. Intermediate-grade level children are especially able and eager to explore these.

Given a certain set of circumstances, what is the chance for a particular event to occur? Questions such as this are questions of probability, and they are a part of every child's life. The question, "Do you think you have a chance to beat John in the race?" infers an elementary concept of probability. The answer to the question is predicted on past performance and could be derived mathematically through observation and record-keeping of race events. When the mathematics involved at the elementary school level is kept relatively simple, children find that probability problems are quite enjoyable. They like to predict the unknown. In fact, they do so much of the time.

A First Lesson in Probability

Fill a bag with a certain number of marbles in two colors and tell the children that there are ten marbles of two different colors in the bag. (This particular lesson utilizes seven black and three white marbles.) Ask them to say how many black marbles and how many white ones are in the bag. They will quickly determine that any estimate of this type is purely guesswork. Each child writes his guess on a piece of paper so he can check back later.

When each child has made a guess, the teacher checks the bag to see just who is right, but no one else is allowed to look. As the children watch, the teacher draws a marble from the bag and shows it to them. The color is recorded on a chart at the front of the room and the marble is replaced in the bag. The process is continued until the marbles have been drawn ten times. Then have the class examine the entries on the chart to determine how many of the ten marbles they think are white (see Figure 11.19).

	Black marbles	*White marbles*
(11.19)	/ / / / / / / / /	/

Most pupils will agree that there are probably nine black marbles and one white marble in the bag. This is the logical answer, and students should be given an opportunity to explain why they made such an observation.

Next, empty the marbles on the desk and ask the class to explain why the chart showed only one white marble in ten drawings, while there actually are three white marbles. Children's observations will include:

1. You rigged the experiment (teacher commented that this was untrue).
2. The black marbles are larger (examination showed the marbles to be of equal size).
3. You didn't put it back when you drew (teacher commented each would not have an equal chance of being drawn).
4. You were just lucky (that only 1 white marble was drawn).
5. I don't know —do it again.

(11.20)

Trial	Black	White
1	111111111	1
2	111111	1111
3	11111111	11
4	1111	111111
Total	27	13

Repeat the experiment three more times, each time recording results of the ten draws. Sum the results of the four trials on a chart like Figure 11.20 and discuss with the children how the chart information could be useful. Someone will usually suggest finding the "average" number of times each color was "selected" over all four trials. Of course, from the computation children will immediately observe that the cumulative results are close to the actual number of black and white marbles in the bag: $27 \div 4 = 6\ 3/4$ and $13 \div 4 = 3\ 1/4$.

There are additional effective ways that children can learn of the meaning of probability as "the likelihood that an event will occur." Since some foundation probability activities can be exceedingly time-consuming when utilizing whole-group instruction, teacher-made cards may be utilized to advantage.

Coin Flipping and Pascal's Triangle

An interesting investigation may be initiated by discussing how many outcomes can occur with a given event. As an example, ask children the possible outcomes of one flip of one coin. They will respond clearly heads or tails, with no other outcomes possible. Next, ask the children to determine the possible outcome for one flip of two coins. The possible outcomes can be determined as two heads, one head and one tail, one tail and one head, and two tails, and may be represented as hh, ht, th, and tt.

Activity Card: Probability   **Level:** Early intermediate

Material: One red and one green die.

1. Roll each die and sum the dots. Record your findings below.

2. Roll again and record. Was the sum the same? The number of dots on each die?

3. Roll the dice fifteen times and record the results of each roll. How many different combinations formed 4? 7? 2?

4. Continue to roll the dice until you think you have all the possible ways of forming each number 8 through 12. Make a graph to show the number of rolls it took to determine all the possible combinations for each number. What did you find? How can you be sure you have all possible combinations?

Dots on red die	Dots on green die	Sum	Number of rolls	Possible combinations

Subsequently, the results may be recorded in chart form and attention called to the pattern (see Figure 11.21). This pattern, called Pascal's triangle, permits prediction of each coin flip with a successively larger number of coins. See if you can discover the pattern for yourself in Figure 11.21.

Possible outcomes from one flip:

1	1 coin—either head or tail
1 2 1	2 coins—hh, ht, th, or tt . . .
1 3 3 1	. . .
1 4 6 4 1	. . .
1 5 10 10 5 1	5 coins

(11.21)

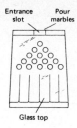

Entrance slot   Pour marbles

Glass top

(11.22)

A demonstration of the probability of an occurrence is provided through the use of a simply constructed model following the configuration of Pascal's triangle. Figure 11.22 uses five variables.

As children drop marbles through the entrance slot, they observe that the probability of a marble landing in the center slots is greater than the probability of it coming to rest in one of the end slots. Actually, the distribution of the marbles closely approximates the probability noted in Pascal's triangle. Other models for more than five variables can be made by simply following the configuration suggested by Pascal's triangle.

THE HAND-HELD CALCULATOR

The hand-held calculator, popularly known as the minicalculator, has a relatively short history. Originally produced in the middle 1960s and priced at $1,500, current standard models are inexpensive and virtually identical among major distributors. They are designed to perform the four basic operations on whole numbers and decimals. Most have separate keys which extract square root and determine a percent. The most common output display is an eight-digit LED (light emitting diode). The calculators are durable, adults and children may easily learn to operate them, and they are currently priced from six to twelve dollars. Industry surveys conducted in late 1977 estimate that one out of every eight Americans has one.

In spite of their prevalence in life outside school, there appears to be a real reluctance to accept calculators in elementary school classrooms. In fact, it is not difficult to find teachers, parents, and "experts" who take widely differing positions. The positions, if placed on a value-to-learning continuum, would range from "the minicalculator can make a rich contribution to concept development and problem-solving skills" through "its chief value is as an answer checker" to "it is a sinister technological crutch which assures further deterioration of basic fact knowledge and disappearance of paper-and-pencil skills." Such disagreement about a potentially valuable learning aid is puzzling when there is such apparent unanimity among these same people regarding the need to improve the mathematics learning levels of all children. The latter would appear to be the most compelling reason the calculator should become a natural part of the mathematics curriculum as a functional aid to learning.

It is, of course, too early to tell what the complete impact of calculators will be upon elementary school mathematics, but research reported to date does not support proclaimed fears. While the research is difficult to characterize in a conclusive manner, early indications are that calculators which are appropriately employed in elementary classrooms (1) do improve the amount of work children complete; (2) do not negatively affect attitude, interest, or confidence; (3) do not lead to deterioration of paper-and-pencil skills; (4) do lead to overall improved achievement as well as improved achievement in selected dimension such as estimation and problem solving; and (5) do lead to the transfer of general skill and achievement gains to subsequent activities not using a calculator.

Principles of Classroom Use

When experiences provided are built around the use of calculators, the chief focus can be on ideas. It seems evident that in such a context, the calculator can be an important aid to learning. As with all aids to learning, we ought to observe some cautions when employing calculators. Initially, the teacher can emphasize there are some things we "do better in our heads." As an example, the calculator ought not replace a student's knowledge of basic facts. When a child sees 9×6, there is a need to automatically recognize it as another name for 54. In fact, children readily discover it is more efficient to "just know it" than to have to obtain a product by first turning on a switch and then depressing four keys. Second, it is not realistic to use the calculator early and solely as a check on complex paper-and-pencil calculations. When eleven-year-old children have spent six or seven minutes completing a division with a three-digit divisor and a five-or-six digit dividend and it is instantaneously determined to be "right" or "wrong," they may reasonably conclude school is truly unreal.

An important aspect of the development of desirable pupil attitudes toward the calculator rests in their observation of its positive use by teachers. Children need to see the teacher utilizing a calculator in a natural manner that makes teaching more interesting and challenging while helping them learn. There are at least two basic settings through which teachers may provide the appropriate model.

The first setting occurs within periods of supervised work when the teacher is freely moving about the room providing help, observing the work of pupils, asking questions, and providing checks. During these times, the calculator can be a useful aid in diagnosing and correcting specific pupil weaknesses, and it is more than a portable answer key. In column addition, as well as in multiple-digit addition and subtraction requiring regrouping, children often fail to account for the regrouped or "unseen" digit. Such oversight can be quickly diagnosed and remedied. In multiplication, obtained partial products can be readily reviewed as a source of error. With division, initial or other selected quotient figures may be quickly analyzed. The separate computations necessary to complete the algorithms of both operations may also be accessed.

The other basic setting occurs within the discussion and recitation period of class time. One or two students may serve as resource persons to check student conjectures, provide models, try out ideas, or calculate answers quickly as the need arises. Beyond providing checks for general calculations, students in the role of resource can quickly determine percents, locate decimal points, and change common fractions to their decimal equivalents. In this way, discussion and recitation can more readily focus on ideas and there is more effective use of instructional time.

**Calculator
Activities**

Although the calculator may be of some benefit as a learning aid in the early primary grades, it seems most reasonable at this time to focus on the later elementary grades. Consequently, the recommendations here are most appropriate for children in grades 3–6. Further, all of the suggestions which follow may be implemented whether you have only five or six calculators per classroom or whether you have a complete classroom set.

Getting Acquainted Since rigorous training to learn to operate the calculator is not required nor even desirable, try some of the following "get acquainted" activities with children.

1. What is the largest number you can show on the calculator?
2. Make all "twos" appear on the display.
3. Add 12 and 48 on the calculator.
4. Depress the "C" key. What does it do?
5. Add 1 + 1 on the calculator. What sum do you have? Depress the "equals" key five times; now what sum do you have? Can you count with your calculator? By fives? By nines? Do it.
6. Use your calculator to count to 100 by ones. Count to 1,000 by tens. Count to 100,000 by hundreds. Time yourself. How long did it take? Try 1,000,000.
7. How many times must you subtract 14 from 154 to obtain a zero on the display? (Enter 154, subtract 14, now continue to depress the "equals" key.) Is this like division?

Basic Skills and Problem Solving The calculations involved in sloving practical problems and even recreational problems can often be so burdensome that we simply avoid them. With calculators truly in the role of aid, it is possible to bring a positive influence to this persistent problem.

1. Solving problems related to physical measurements from the real world provides a superior setting for the natural use of calculators. Teams of students may take dimensions of ordinary areas or shapes. Each team will have one student with a calculator who provides answers by performing the necessary operations with the calculator.
2. Estimation skills may be improved by students working in pairs or small groups. Provide examples like 24 × 62, 128 ÷ 6, and so forth. Have one student provide the true calculation while others provide an oral or written estimate. Compare the estimates with "true" answers and commend all reasonable estimates.
3. Multiplying a number by itself is called squaring a number. As an example, 8 squared is 8 × 8, or 64. Find a number which when squared yields 196.
4. Individually or in pairs, children may substitute calculator drill activities for flash card games. Enter a number, depress the operation sign, and enter another number. One child then gives an oral or written response. The "equals" key is depressed to check.
5. Activity cards may be designed to contain interesting exercises with successive operations. Children may work one on one or in pairs, and the task is self-checking.

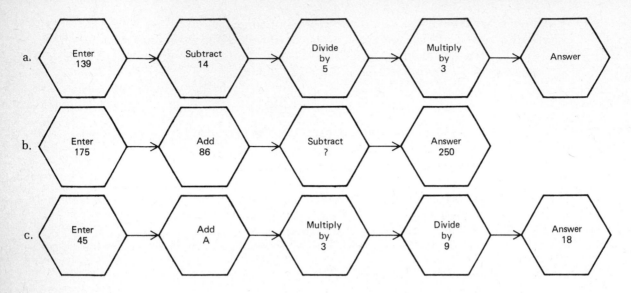

Occasionally, it may be preferable to have the children set up some problems like these for each other and verify their solutions.

6. Suppose your family car travels 15.5 miles on one gallon of gas. If you could drive your car around the world, how much gas would it use?

7. Do the following multiplications and record the products:

$$1089 \times 1 = \underline{\hspace{2cm}}$$
$$1089 \times 2 = \underline{\hspace{2cm}}$$
$$1089 \times 3 = \underline{\hspace{2cm}}$$

Can you predict the product for 1089×4? Continue with 4, 5, 6 . . . as factors. Record what happens.

8. Each time we multiply a number by itself, we raise the number one power. For example, 6×6 is six to the second power and is written 6^2. Further, $6 \times 6 \times 6$ would represent six to the third power and is written 6^3. Use your calculator to find a number which when raised to the fourth power yields 4096.

Calculator Games and Recreations It is sometimes useful to take advantage of calculator games and activities that are simply fun. Several of the examples which follow involve open-ended, trial-and-error processes. Some provide practice in following a step-by-step set of directions in basic mathematical operations. All contribute to the development of logical thinking skills.

1. *Twenty-one.* Find a partner to play "21." To play, clear the calculator display to zero and take turns adding 1, 2, or 3 to the display. The player forced to produce the sum 21 loses. Play five times, rotating who goes first. Do you win best of six? How? Variation: Start with 21 on the display. Subtract 1, 2, or 3.

2. *Goalie.* Pick an arbitrary number—for instance, 18. Determine a finite set of keys that must be used for the game. With 18 as the goal, the permissible keys

could be "4," "plus," "minus," "multiply," "divide," or "equals." The winner is the one who is able to make 18 appear on the display with the least key depressions. One solution would be $4 \times 4 + 4 + 4 \div 4 + 4 + 4 + 4 = 18$. This solution requires fifteen key depressions. Can a shorter one be found? Make up an original "Goalie" problem.

3. *Disappear.* The object of this activity is to make one digit disappear from a given display number without changing any of the other digits. In a small group of children, one is the number supplier and each of the others operates a calculator. The supplier provides a number for all players to enter on the display, then tells which digit is to disappear.

Example: "Enter 4321." "Three disappear!"

The final display would read 4021. Would 421 also be correct?

4. For most calculators, it is a happy coincidence that when the LED is turned upside down, most of the digits look like letters.

Digit	Reverse Look-alike
0	O
1	I
2	Z
3	E
4	h
5	s
6	g
7	L
8	B

One way you can take advantage of this number–letter relationship is through utilization of numerical activities which need an appropriate word answer.

a. To fail to win is to _____ (lose) (Find 5×7; multiply by 100; add 10; subtract 3)

b. An effective stroke in tennis is a _____ (lob). (Square 20; double the product; add seven.)

c. Make a list of three-letter words you can spell with the calculator.

d. Display a four-digit number that describes the bottom of your shoe.

e. The capitol of Idaho is _____ (Boise).

f. What is the longest single word you can make with calculator letters?

g. Choose a calculator word and devise a mathematics problem for it like (a) or (b) above.

SUMMARY Learning mathematics today parallels the history of its development. Documented evidence of formal mathematics dates back to 2100 B.C., and there is informal evidence of the utilization of quantitative notions much earlier in history.

Numeration systems facilitate communication about amounts. They are abstract, and all useful systems exhibit several fundamental characteristics. A finite set of symbols is basic, including one for placeholder, additive and multiplicative features, and a predetermined collection point or base. In most early systems one or more of these features was absent.

Children in today's elementary schools can appreciate our decimal system more fully through study using collection points and multiples other than ten. Equally useful insights can evolve when children study and compare finite systems with our infinite decimal system. Finite systems called modular arithmetic provide lucid illustrations of such structural properties as commutativity, associativity, and closure.

Number theory may be studied independently of the utilization of a numeration system. Direct study of odd and even numbers, prime and composite numbers, number patterns, conjectures, and probability can aid children in understanding and appreciating mathematics as a useful system of line and related ideas. The hand-held calculator finds appropriate applications here.

The most important consideration in the study of early number systems, number theory, and probability is not whether the children produce correct answers at all times, but whether these activities benefit the children by engaging them in meaningful and productive thinking. Some guidelines to practice are listed below.

1. Use the history of number to enhance appreciation for the study of mathematics.
2. Number theory can serve as the motivation and foundation for problem-solving drill.
3. Probability theory appropriately utilized will promote discovery and active learning in both group and individual activities.
4. Instructional strategies can be developed in a manner that promotes an emphasis on divergent thinking rather than always on "right" answers.
5. The hand-held calculator can be promulgated as a genuine aid to learning.

ACTIVITIES, PROJECTS, A POINT OF VIEW

1. Make a collection of not less than five activity cards patterned after some topics or concepts suggested in the chapter. The activity cards should be sufficiently self-explanatory so as to be used independently by children.

2. Obtain a school supply catalog. Make a list of (three) concrete models you could use for teaching three different concepts referred to in the chapter. Obtain one of the models, describe it briefly to a peer, and tell how you would use it to teach the selected concept.

3. Do the activity card entitled "Number Base, Groups of Four." It is located in the chapter.

4. List some advantages of using a finite system as a model when illustrating the common principles of numeration systems.

5. Write factor trees and concomitant factorization for any two of 27, 42, 63, or 84.

6. Use a hand-held calculator on the palimages 89 + 98 to obtain a palindromic sum. How many additions were necessary? Try some other palimages. Can you find a pair that takes more than five additions? Six? What do you conclude about the hand-held calculator and number theory?

7. Take a spinner with six congruent sections labeled 1 through 6. Spin the arrow sixty times. Record. What is the observed frequency of each outcome, 1 through 6? How did it compare with the expected frequency? Have several classmates spin the arrow sixty times and find the average frequency for each outcome. How does it compare to yours? What did you do when the arrow stopped on a line?

8. As a content source, use either the bibliographic entry Billstein or Niemann. Prepare a flow chart lesson plan for use with children. Teach it to a small group of peers.

9. Write a letter to the parents of the children in your classroom. Explain that you would like each child to have a hand-held calculator for the entire year in the mathematics class. Be on your toes here!

10. Design an activity card containing the instructions that would enable children to work independently in pairs on drill activities for the basic facts.

11. Obtain a hand-held calculator, get a friend, and play *Twenty-one*. Record your method of winning.

SELECTED READINGS

Billstein, Rick. "A Fun Way To Introduce Probability." *Arithmetic Teacher*, Vol. 24 (January 1977), pp. 39–42.

Dumas, E., and Schminke, C. W. *Math Activities for Child Involvement*, 2d ed. Boston: Allyn & Bacon, Inc., 1977, pp. 285–336.

Frame, Maxine R. "Hamann's Conjecture." *Arithmetic Teacher*, Vol. 23 (January 1976), pp. 34–35.

Green, G. F. *Elementary School Mathematics: Activities and Materials*. Lexington, Mass.: D. C. Heath and Company, 1974, pp. 440–471.

Heddens, James W. *Today's Mathematics*. Chicago: Science Research Associates, Inc., 1974, Units 4, 9, and 22.

Higgins, James E. "Probability with Marbles and Juice Container." *Arithmetic Teacher*, Vol. 20 (March 1973), pp. 165–166.

Marks, J. L.; Purdy, C. R.; Kinney, Lucien; and Hiatt, Arthur. *Teaching Elementary School Mathematics for Understanding*, 4th ed. New York: McGraw-Hill Book Company, 1975, Chapter 10.

Niemann, C. E. "Let's Play Mod 7." *Arithmetic Teacher*, Vol. 23 (May 1976), pp. 348–351.

Omejic, E. "A Different Approach to the Sieve of Eratosthenes." *Arithmetic Teacher*, Vol. 19 (March 1972), pp. 192–196.

CHAPTER 12

Teaching Mathematics to Special Children

PERSPECTIVE It is the child for whom instruction is intended. No matter how well we organize, plan, and execute instruction, it is the child who must learn. Unfortunately, progress in learning is uneven. Individual students of the same chronological age learn different things from the same instruction. Many children are able to learn the same things, but they do so at varying rates. Further, all children are the products of their total environment as well as prior teaching. Both can have a profound effect upon their progress in mathematics. All of these are conditions the teacher must orchestrate to assure reasonable and responsible pupil growth in mathematics.

In today's elementary school classrooms, the need for teachers to be skilled at meeting the needs of all children is probably greater than at any time in the history of our schools. Legally as well as morally, local educational agencies have always been responsible for the education of all children, but recent federal and state mandates have created some imperatives. The focus on individual needs of children is receiving new attention through a national movement termed "mainstreaming." Mainstreaming encompasses a reaffirmation of the ideal that all children have the right of equal access to educational opportunity. In the past, many exceptional children were isolated for great portions of their educational experience through rather rigid labeling and classification systems. One result was a disquieting alienation from the educational system for many, adults and children alike. Another has been "undereducation" for large numbers of children.

Mainstreaming as a process is generally described as enrolling and teaching exceptional children in a regular classroom for a majority of the school day. Functionally, it may be thought of as anything we can do in teaching all children which will help them find satisfaction in their daily lives and an appropriate place in the world at large. Clearly, mainstreaming places heavy demands on the teacher for the individualization of instruction and, equally important, demands a change in attitude for all persons engaged in educational activities related to teaching children.

After study of Chapter 12 you should be able to:

1. Write a brief statement of the impact of mainstreaming on teachers in the regular classroom.
2. Design a useful instrument for accessing pupil status in the affective domain.
3. Distinguish norm-referenced and criterion-referenced tests.
4. Utilize pupil error patterns to design an instructional sequence for reteaching selected concepts to low achievers.
5. Describe the educational value of low stress algorithms for low achievers.
6. Write an activity game card consistent with principles for teaching low achieving children.
7. State the classroom teacher's responsibility for fulfilling needs of more able children.

ANALYZING PUPIL GROWTH

Strategies and techniques for evaluating children's strengths and weaknesses are crucial to effective teaching. It is only through intentional activity in assessment that teachers gain specific information about each child's relationship to quantitative ideas. It is necessary to obtain information in both the affective and cognitive domains. The former refers to the child's feelings, attitudes, and self-confidence, while the latter refers to the child's concepts, knowledge, and skills.

The Affective Domain

Like adults, children's emotions about mathematics have a marked effect on their achievement in mathematics. In the case of children, the way they feel about mathematics is directly related to the efficacy with which they acquire mathematical concepts. There are numerous ways of obtaining important data relating to the affective domain. The three discussed here include pupil preference surveys, systematic teacher observation of pupil behavior, and more formal pupil attitude inventories.

Pupil Preference Surveys It is a rather simple and inexpensive matter to gain a general impression of a group of pupils' relative likes and dislikes regarding the subjects they study in school. Specifically, you gain information about the individual attitudes that children have toward mathematics. Figure 12.1 portrays an example of a teacher-made subject preference instrument that is easy to administer and score. The subject areas are listed alphabetically, and the instructions are self-contained as well as self-explanatory.

My Favorite Subjects

Instructions: From this list of all your school subjects, choose the one you like best. Write the number 1 in the space provided. Next, choose the subject you like second best. Write a 2 beside its name. Do the same for your third, fourth, and fifth choices. Now choose the subject you like least and place a 9 by it. Place an 8 by your next least favorite subject. Do the same with 7 and 6, and you will be through.

____ Art (drawing, painting, ceramics, and so forth)
____ Health
____ Language Arts (spelling, grammar, writing)
____ Mathematics
____ Music
____ Reading
____ Science
____ Social Studies
____ Physical Education

(12.1)

Teacher Observation Systematic teacher observation of individual student behavior related to mathematics and formal instruction can also be revealing. The value of observation has long been recognized, though frequently overlooked. This is unfortunate when we consider the fact that alert teachers, after having worked with pupils for relatively short periods of time, can predict with great accuracy which students will score well and which pupils will do poorly on an examination before it is given. The illustrative teacher-made observation form shown in Figure 12.2 can be completed inconspicuously for individual children in a relatively short period of time. The instructions are self-explanatory and a composite score is obtained by summing the values to the left of each statement. Of course, a higher composite score indicates more positive pupil behavior toward mathematics.

A Formal Attitude Inventory A third technique for developing individual student profiles in the affective domain is the semantic differential scale. The technique was originally developed by Charles Osgood[1] for determining a generalized attitude toward a concept, an idea, or an event.

[1]Charles E. Osgood, G. Suci, and P. Tannenbaum, *The Measurement of Meaning* (Urbana, Ill.: University of Illinois Press, 1957).

Math Observation Form

Key: 1—never; 2—seldom; 3—sometimes; 4—often; 5—always

____ Listens carefully during instruction.
____ Asks questions and makes observations during class.
____ Completes math work on time.
____ Talks about math outside of classtime.
____ Likes to "play" with math-related ideas.
____ Works ahead in math books.
____ Enjoys math class.
____ Brings math "things" from outside school.
____ Chooses math "things" from library.
____ Likes to help classmates with math.

(12.2) _____

The design employs bipolar descriptive adjectives weighted on a seven-point scale. Seven short lines between each pair of adjectives accommodate the subject's response and represent a scale weighted in the following manner:

$$^-3 \quad ^-2 \quad ^-1 \quad 0 \quad ^+1 \quad ^+2 \quad ^+3$$

Mathematics is

fun	___	___	___	___	___	___	___ pits
useful	___	___	___	___	___	___	___ worthless
unimportant	___	___	___	___	___	___	___ important
boring	___	___	___	___	___	___	___ exciting
easy	___	___	___	___	___	___	___ hard
sad	___	___	___	___	___	___	___ happy
pleasant	___	___	___	___	___	___	___ painful
awful	___	___	___	___	___	___	___ great
necessary	___	___	___	___	___	___	___ unnecessary
smart	___	___	___	___	___	___	___ dumb

(12.3) _____

The illustrative adaptation shown in Figure 12.3 utilizes the general concept "mathematics." Other, more specific concepts or terms, such as "subtraction," "fractions," "the metric system," and so forth, might just as well serve. Children simply place an X on the line nearest to the adjective that best represents how they feel about themselves in relation to the concept. The plus scores are summed and the sum of the minus scores is subtracted. In general, a plus composite score indicates a positive attitude, while a minus composite suggest a negative attitude.

Notice that in constructing the scale in Figure 12.3 the direction (positive-negative) of adjective pairs three, four, six, and eight was switched. This is to guard against response by mental set and must be taken into account in the scoring process. In the case of the illustration, the $^+3$ composite suggests a positive attitude towards mathematics.

Once pupils' attitudes and anxieties have been assessed, it is important for the teacher to create an environment which will aid in the development and maintenance of positive attitudes. Negative pupil attitudes toward mathematics generally cluster around the following:

1. Insufficient time to complete assigned work.
2. Impatient and uninteresting teachers.
3. Genuine lack of understanding of mathematical principles.
4. Too many boring daily computation assignments.
5. Lack of application or required mathematics to real life situations.
6. Failure to experience success.

It is interesting to note that each of the above conditions constitutes a variable that the teacher can control. In addition to the four dominant theoretical features for a personal philosophy of teaching mathematics that were presented in Chapter 1, each period of instruction in elementary school mathematics should be structured such that all pupils experience some success. Beyond this, there must be variety in assigned tasks, sufficient time to complete tasks, appropriate understanding of the mathematics involved, and reasonable applicability of the mathematics studies to real life situations.

The Cognitive Domain

Assessment of pupil growth in the cognitive domain is a continuous process. It is irrevocably an integral portion of the total teaching act. Since we are never able to really "see" how learning occurs, we must rely upon exhibited behavioral activity.

A general teaching model that incorporates continual diagnosis and assessment in the cognitive domain was presented in Chapter 2. The model consists of developing a content hierarchy of concepts and skills for a mathematical topic—for example, addition—from which objectives may be determined. Subsequently, it is necessary to state the desired outcomes in terms of observable pupil behaviors. Throughout the design for cognitive assessment, requisite subordinate learnings and the child's developmental stage must be considered. Judgments are also necessary regarding the level of cognition in relation to the complexity of the task. Thus, the steps in a continuous cycle of diagnosing cognitive development are:

1. Selection of appropriate content.
2. Specification of desired behaviors.
3. Identification of subordinate prerequisites.
4. Consideration of the child's developmental stage.
5. Designing the content–behavior test items.
6. Administering the test or implementing the instruction.

Thoughtful consideration of these steps will reveal they serve equally well as 1) a preassessment process for determining cognitive needs, 2) a guide to the development of instructional sequences, and 3) a postassessment process to determine how well children have learned what we set out to teach. You will recall that the flow chart lesson plan serves as a vehicle that easily accommodates the assessment model during daily and weekly instructional planning.

Criterion-Referenced Tests The tests to be designed for use in the previous assessment model are generally referred to as criterion-referenced tests. Criterion-referenced tests are those designed to insure that the behavioral objectives of a curriculum, a sequence of instruction, or an entire course of study have been assessed. The items (content–behavior activity requirements) for such tests are keyed to predetermined, specifically stated behaviors. For teachers, this is perhaps the great advantage of criterion-referenced tests. The levels of assessment described in Chapter 2 contain examples of criterion-referenced tests.

Norm-Referenced Tests Often in the process of assessment in the cognitive domain, teachers must administer to students tests that do not directly assess the teacher's objectives. This is most often the case when employing norm-referenced tests. Most norm-referenced tests are commercially prepared (as are increasing numbers of criterion-referenced tests), and designed such that an individual score or its percentile may be interpreted as performance at a given grade level. As an example, when a raw score indicates performance at grade level 4.6 (fourth grade, sixth month), this means that the test authors found that specific raw score associated with the mean performance of students at grade level 4.6 who participated in the norming of the examination.

One of the much publicized shortcomings of norm-referenced tests is their apparent heavy reliance on computation and their inability to accommodate items related to concepts and problem solving. Nonetheless, norm-referenced tests have a significant advantage in that they are short and do provide a good general rating of individual (as well as class and school) performance in relation to the performance of the sample population upon whom the norms are based. Assuming a nationally representative sample population, the results of norm-referenced tests can provide realistic evaluation information to classroom teachers and other school officials.

There is a wide variety of commercially prepared elementary school mathematics tests and test batteries available. In selecting a commercially prepared test, the potential user should examine specimen sets which are available through publishers. The literature that accompanies a specimen set is informative, and the *Mental Measurements Yearbook*[2] provides detailed information regarding most published tests. The several tests listed below are representative of tests available, and each brief annotation may be useful in choosing a test review.

1. *California Achievement Tests, 1970 Edition.* Monterey, California: California Test Bureau/McGraw-Hill, 1970. In this battery, tests are available at five levels scaled as grades 1.5–2, 2–4, 4–6, 6–9, and 9–12. Tests at each level yield scores for computation, concepts, and problems. These are norm-referenced tests with good reliability.

2. *Comprehensive Tests of Basic Skills: Arithmetic.* Monterey, California: California Test Bureau/McGraw-Hill, 1968. In this battery, there are three tests for each of three levels. The levels are grades 2–4, 4–6, and 6–8. The three tests for each level examine computation, concepts, and application. All tests are norm-referenced and have a high reliability.

3. *Metropolitan Achievement Tests.* New York: Harcourt Brace Jovanovich, Inc., 1971. The mathematics portion is part of a battery of tests which examines a broad range of elementary school instructional areas. Tests are available for six levels from kindergarten through ninth grade. Beyond the first level of K.6–2.5, the tests yield subscores for computation, concepts, and problem solving. The tests are norm-referenced and reliable.

4. *Modern Mathematics Supplement to the Four Tests of Basic Skills.* Boston: Houghton Mifflin Company, 1968. These tests are norm-referenced, reliable, and contain a good breadth of content. Tests are available for grades 3–9.

5. *Prescriptive Mathematics Inventory.* Monterey, California: California Test Bureau/McGraw-Hill, 1972. These four tests yield diagnostic and prescriptive information for groups and individuals in relation to 351 behavioral objectives. The objectives were developed from the most frequently used textbooks for grades four through eight. The publisher provides elaborate scoring procedures for these criterion-referenced tests.

6. *Stanford Early School Achievement Test.* New York: Harcourt Brace Jovanovich, Inc., 1970. This is a test battery at only two levels, K–1 and 1.0–1.5. It is norm-referenced and appropriate for young children. The publishers report moderate reliability, but only one of several scores produced by the battery is for mathematics.

[2]Buros, O. K., ed., *The Seventh Mental Measurements Yearbook* (Highland Park, N.J.: The Gryphon Press, 1972).

Employment of systematic procedures of assessment in the affectives and cognitive domains will only provide more detailed information about that which we already know—namely, that children are unique, that they have special strengths as well as weaknesses, that they learn by varying embodiments, and that some learn more quickly than others.

MEETING THE CHALLENGE OF INDIVIDUAL NEEDS

Individualization of instruction continues to be an important goal in modern programs of instruction. Yet the ever-present range of unique abilities, achievement levels, social factors, and emotional maturity of children necessitates modification and accommodation within teaching models and styles. It is a perplexing challenge for even the most able and experienced teachers.

In all instructional settings, children are grouped on some basis. Ordinarily, that basis is consistent with the effort to meet special learner needs. Age is the traditional basis by which children are grouped in school, but many other criteria are frequently employed for grouping children within classrooms. In mathematics, these include standardized achievement test scores, intelligence test scores, informally determined rates of learning, and social–emotional adjustment indicators.

Most thoughtfully designed and carefully executed instructional plans can effectively accommodate that large group of children in the middle, usually about 60 or 65 percent of the average sized class. Often, however, normal teaching procedures must be consciously supplemented to effectively meet the needs of children who lie outside the middle range. One group may be thought of as hard to teach, and usually comprise approximately twenty percent of an average class. The other group can be termed "fast learners," and their number does not usually exceed 15 percent of a normal-sized class. Parenthetically, the challenge of teaching able children should cause us no less concern than the challenges involved with hard-to-teach children.

Providing for the Hard-To-Teach

Regardless of what label may be attached, all hard-to-teach children have one thing in common. They are low achievers. Their low achievement may be due to low ability, less than adequate motivation and interest, physical or psychological handicaps, or even poor teaching. The result is precisely the same. They meet little success in school and very likely none in mathematics. In turn, they develop a lack of confidence, negative attitudes, and the habit of poor performance. Of course, the cycle repeats itself because poor performance results in little success.

There are some general principles to be observed when teaching all children. These principles are magnified when meeting the needs of special children. Many of the principles are familiar and have been enunciated throughout this text. Yet the assumptions underlying them take on added perspective from the point of view of hard-to-teach children.

1. Success is important, and immediate success is crucial. The opportunity for success is maximized when subject matter is presented through smaller increments and frequent fresh starts involving a single idea.
2. Entry levels must be carefully and patiently determined to assure that children will be involved with tasks at which they can succeed.
3. Practice is important to success because it facilitates memory. Further, practice is most effective when it immediately follows instruction, since the larger increments of forgetting occur soon after instruction.
4. The notion of immediate feedback (that is, constant knowledge of results) is an important element of improved performance. This is because frequent feelings of success have a positive cumulative effect.
5. Habitual low achievers progress more slowly and generally perform at a less abstract level than average and bright children. As a consequence, more time and exposure are necessary at concrete levels of concept development.

The important ideas embedded in the previous statements may be executed through daily instruction in a variety of ways. The three discussed here include analysis of pupil errors, utilization of low-stress algorithms, and recreational activities or games that have mathematical concepts embedded in them.

Analysis of Pupil Errors We teach children to look for patterns in dealing with numbers. This enriches the study of our system of numeration. Similarly, teachers should look for patterns of error in the work of children who are experiencing difficulty with concepts and computational skills. Practice has shown that systematic errors are remediable and that without intentional intervention, children continue to repeat common errors over long periods of time. This amounts to instruction in error practice.

All teachers are fully aware of children who appear to have been instructed in the rote application of an algorithm but who are generally not successful with it. They are the ones who always seem to have messy papers with wrong answers. While these children may be low achievers, a goodly number of them are neither slow learners nor of low ability.

There are several sources from which data may be collected regarding individual pupil error patterns. Of course, there is observation of pupils at work as well as the written record from daily work. There are results from norm-referenced and criterion-referenced tests. Finally, as a supplement to both of the previous sources, there are individual personal interviews for the purpose of determining the thinking associated with a written record. In fact, with a little practice, teachers are likely to find individual questioning the most effective diagnostic device of all. Surprisingly, children can often articulate their computational strategy. For example, it is not appropriate to assume that additional drill on the basic facts is needed by the child who has performed a two-digit addition in this manner: $\begin{array}{r} 75 \\ +47 \\ \hline 1112 \end{array}$. The problem may be something so simple as recording separate sums as units. It may be more fundamental relating to place value and regrouping or the "number action." The point is that one cannot tell until he talks to the child.

Following are some typical error patterns related to general concepts and computational skills. Each is accompanied with one or more suggestions for reteaching. All are representative of sound teaching procedures for all children, but they make a special contribution to fulfilling the principles of teaching special children.

In working with addition, children often develop error patterns related to the algorithmic form used for computation. These are significant because they impede concept development and cause children to experience continuous failure. Five kinds of easily discernable error patterns are represented by the examples in Figure 12.4.

$$
\begin{array}{lllll}
\begin{array}{r} 10 \\ A. \quad 27 \\ +89 \\ \hline 206 \end{array}
&
\begin{array}{r} B. \quad 16 \\ +27 \\ \hline 33 \end{array}
&
\begin{array}{r} 3 \\ C. \quad 16 \\ +27 \\ \hline 61 \end{array}
&
\begin{array}{r} D. \quad 89 \\ +97 \\ \hline 172 \end{array}
&
\begin{array}{r} E. \quad 218 \\ 1621 \\ 109 \\ \hline 14 \end{array}
\end{array}
$$

(12.4)

In the first example, the regrouped 10 is improperly placed. In the next, no regrouping was carried out. In the third example, the digits involved in regrouping were transposed. The fourth example is one in which the smaller number in the bottom addend was subtracted instead of added. The last example simply represents poor alignment of digits in the column arrangement.

Following are recommendations for reteaching once error patterns like those above have been discovered. Of course, the recommendations are not equally applicable to all of the error patterns. Individual remedies can only be assigned with confidence after interviewing a child who has made a particular kind of error.

1. Additional practice in regrouping with multibase blocks, abacuses, tens frames, and counting discs.
2. Short, regular practice sessions in recording numbers from dictation.
3. Practice in recording numbers in expanded notation form.
4. Utilizing lined paper sideways so the lines form a guide to vertical columns.

5. Labeling columns.
6. Emphasizing patterns in higher decade addition using a horizontal format such as 8 + 4, 18 + 4, 28 + 4, and so forth.
7. Employing a variety of algorithmic formats for checking.

In the original teaching of subtraction, more time usually needs to be spent because it seems to be more difficult for children. The same is true for reteaching after individual error patterns have been diagnosed. Figure 12.5 portrays common error patterns for children who have difficulty with subtraction.

(12.5)

	A.	B.	C.	D.	E.
			61		5
	46	464	276	72	605
	−42	−238	−53	−36	−347
	88	234	2113	46	268

In order, the illustrative pupil errors in Figure 12.5 include: A) disregard for the operation sign; B) subtracting the smaller digit from the larger regardless of whether it appears in minuend or subtrahand; C) regrouping a minuend as though necessary; D) failure to account for regrouping where necessary; and E) difficulty with multiple regrouping.

Some of the reteaching procedures recommended for the error patterns of addition are also appropriate for subtraction. Several additional activities can also be useful.

1. Provide short oral practice periods in decomposing numbers in a variety of ways. As an example, 554 is five hundreds, five tens, and four ones, but it is also fifty-five tens and four ones. It can also be four hundreds, fifteen tens, and four ones, as well as five hundreds, four tens, and fourteen ones.
2. Supply short practice sheets where children supply missing operation signs such as 6 4 3 = 7, 125 30 = 95, and so forth.
3. Practice estimating differences before actually computing them.
4. Have children verbalize the steps involved in multiple regrouping.
5. Have children write the steps involved in multiple regrouping.
6. Employ both additive and subtractive checks.

The previous examples of error patterns for addition and subtraction are not unlike those that will be found in multiplication, division, and the operations on rational numbers. Further, the nature of reteaching is essentially the same. Admittedly, the examples in Figure 12.4 and 12.5 do not represent all possible errors that will occur in children's work. Rather, common errors representative of those made by low achievers have been highlighted to clarify the kind of procedures that are needed in order to remedy the difficulties experienced by hard-to-teach children.

Low-Stress Algorithms A promising practice for meeting the individual needs of low-achieving children has received renewed attention of late—the employment of low-stress algorithms. The idea can be considered an implicit part of reteaching activities associated with error analysis. The distinguishing feature of low-stress algorithms is a clear, easily discernable notation that permits a distinct kind of recording for each intermediate step in the computational process. In so doing, the identification of specific errors and error patterns is facilitated for the learner as well as for the teacher. Also, the introduction of a new algorithmic format during reteaching provides children with a setting that is not associated with failure.

Figure 12.6 shows the notation of basic addition facts in conventional and low-stress form. Comparison reveals that sums in the new notation are recorded differently, and both the operation sign and usual line are dropped. The facts would be read, "Seven, four (slight pause) eleven," and "nine, eight (slight pause) seventeen."

(12.6)

(12.7)

Column addition utilizes an extension of the low-stress basic fact notation. Examine Figure 12.7 by following the steps in it. Can you tell before reading further how the algorithm operates? Initially, the digits 5 and 7 are summed and recorded as in basic fact notation. Next, the units digit of the previous sum and the next digit in the column are added (in this case, 2 + 8) and the sum is recorded as before. The process is repeated for steps three and four. When complete, the final units digit will be the units digit for the entire sum, and one need only count the number of tens on the left to obtain the tens digit of the total.

Advantages of this procedure include the necessity of recording every basic fact included in the algorithm, and elimination of the continuous mental regrouping that is required in the conventional algorithm. The process can be conveniently extended to column addition involving more than one column. The only adjustment required is a bit more spacing between the digits of each addend that form the columns.

Conventional   *Low-stress*

$$
\begin{array}{r}
5\ \textcircled{1\,1} \\
\cancel{6}\ \cancel{2}\,{}^1 3 \\
-\ 2\ 7\ 5 \\
\hline
3\ 4\ 8
\end{array}
\qquad
\begin{array}{r}
6\ \ 2\ \ 3 \\
5\ \ {}^1{}1\ \ {}^1 3 \\
-\ 2\ \ 7\ \ 5 \\
\hline
3\ \ 4\ \ 8
\end{array}
$$

(12.8)

$$
\begin{array}{r}
6\,2\,3 \\
3 \\
-\,2\,7\,5 \\
\hline
\end{array}
\quad
\begin{array}{r}
6\ 2\,3 \\
1\,{}^1 3 \\
-2\,7\,5 \\
\hline
\end{array}
\quad
\begin{array}{r}
6\,2\,3 \\
5\,{}^1 1\,{}^1 3 \\
-\,2\ 7\ 5 \\
\hline
\end{array}
\quad
\begin{array}{r}
6\,2\,3 \\
5\,{}^1 1\,{}^1 3 \\
-\,2\,7\,5 \\
\hline
3\,4\,8
\end{array}
$$

The "regrouping in reverse" which is a part of the operation of subtraction has always been troublesome for many children. The conventional algorithm has not helped much. Study the differences between the completed examples shown in Figure 12.8. The first obvious difference is that the necessary regrouping of the minuend is recorded between the minuend and subtrahend. Secondly, a left side superscript number is a required convention for renaming column values of the minuend. For example, the 23 in the illustration is two tens and three ones, but it may also be expressed as $1^1 3$—that is, one ten and thirteen ones. Finally, in utilizing the format, all renaming of place values is completed before any subtraction takes place. The principle advantages of this algorithm lie in its contribution to reteaching about grouping numbers and the elimination of the need to "borrow across" any numbers.

Returning for a moment to the low-stress recommendations relating to addition, it is easy to see how that format can be used for reteaching the basic multiplication and division facts to low achievers. The only change in the format from the column addition one is that all addends are equal. Consider the example of 7×8 provided in Figure 12.9. The procedure for generating a basic multiplication fact is precisely the same as for producing the sum of a column addition. Furthermore, in the example a child merely needs to slide an oaktag marker down the column to produce an eights multiplication fact at any point. What procedure could you invent to use this algorithmic form for producing and reteaching the basic division facts?

(12.9)

(12.10)

Low-stress algorithms may also be used beyond the basic facts in multiplication and division. Notation for the vertical form of basic multiplication facts was shown in Figure 12.9. The notation for multiplication involving facts of more than one digit is shown in Figure 12.10. The case of two multidigit factors is not unlike multiplication with Napier's bones (Chapter 8). The multiplication may be accomplished by moving either direction within the algorithm. Initial research suggests that left-to-right multiplication may have some advantages. The only convention to be observed is that partial products generated by the second digit of the multiplier (in vertical form, the bottom factor) are always begun with placement directly beneath the left digit of the lower previous row.

A low-stress algorithm for division has also been examined. However, it does not seem to provide much comparative advantage over the conventional algorithm. This is because the importance of initial quotient estimation cannot be escaped or simplified to any great degree. Further, application of low-stress subtraction and multiplication procedures to the division cycle appears to unnecessarily complicate the "number action" as well as the notation. Reteaching the long division process employing multibase arithmetic blocks in the context of serial subtraction is probably superior. Anyone wishing to explore low-stress division algorithms should consult the *1976 Yearbook of the National Council of Teachers of Mathematics.*[3]

Low-stress algorithms are not a panacea. Yet they can help some children find success in mathematics, and low-stress algorithms contribute to sound principles of teaching low achieving children by: 1) breaking learning into smaller components; 2) providing a written record of each step; 3) eliminating the abstractness of working with "unseen" digits; 4) facilitating the analysis of individual pupil errors; and 5) offering the advantage of immediate feedback and the reinforcement of quick success after brief exposure.

Recreational Games and Activities Mathematical games, activities, and recreations are often associated with rewards for good work. Good work and rewards do not usually accrue to low achievers; this is unfortunate because games can be used to good advantage with low achievers. When appropriately designed and employed, games can contribute greatly to children with special types of learning problems. They fit well into the general philosophy of active learning, and they can provide teachers with diagnostic information that can be used to reteach fundamental concepts during formal instruction.

In designing recreational activities which have mathematical concepts embedded in them, several guidelines are useful. First, the desired outcome ought to be clear, and the rules, procedures, and materials that are necessary to participate should be simple. Second, the nature of the activity ought to be such as to provide immediate feedback to the children. Third, it should not always be necessary that someone "win." Finally, the game or activity should be so designed that children will be able to participate in an assessment of its worth unless its worth is self-evident.

To start a collection of games, an adjustment in the activity card format can be utilized. Two examples are shown below.

---

[3]Barton Hutchings, "Low Stress Algorithms," *1976 Yearbook* (Reston, Va.: National Council of Teachers of Mathematics, 1976), pp. 218–239.

Topic: Cardinality

Objective: Students must demonstrate the matching of numerals with sets of objects

Game: Hot Dog

Procedure: Dog-shaped pieces of paper containing one of the numerals 1–9 are placed about the room. Collections of objects on a table, collections shown on an overhead projector, or poster-sized pictures of collections are shown to the children. They must identify the cardinality of the collection, then run to the numeral that names it. Each child stands on the numeral that he identified until every child has a hot dog. Children may continue to play from their hot dogs. In the event they correctly identify a second collection, they may take their first hot dog with them as they stand on a second. A winner could be declared.

Topic: Addition

Objective: Intensive oral practice of addition facts

Game: Tag-Add

Procedure: Each child is given an oaktag reproduction of one of the numerals from 1 through 9. The teacher designates a tagger and the game begins. The tagger may go to any child, tag him, then orally give the sum of his number and the number of the child he flagged. When he does so correctly, the child that has been tagged becomes the tagger and the game is continuous. There are no penalties for mistakes and no one has to drop out of the game. The game can also be limited to children who have difficulty and need additional practice.

There are many sources for ideas. One of the most fruitful is *The Arithmetic Teacher*. In addition, the following are representative of available collections and anthologies that are exceedingly useful as teacher resources. Selected games from these sources can be easily translated to activity game cards.

Ashlock, R. B., and Humphrey, J. H. *Teaching Elementary School Mathematics Through Motor Learning*. Springfield, Ill.: Charles C. Thomas, Publisher, 1976, 159 pp.

Dumas, E., and Schminke, C. W. *Math Activities for Child Involvement*, 2d ed. Boston: Allyn and Bacon, Inc., 1977, 341 pp.

Kelley, Jeanne S. *Learning Mathematics Through Activities—A Resource Book for Elementary Teachers*. Cupertino, Calif.: James E. Creeland Associates, Inc., 1973, 121 pp.

Malehorn, Hal. *Encyclopedia of Activities for Teaching Grades K–3*. West Nyack, N.Y.: Parker Publishing Company, Inc. 1975, 244 pp.

Moore, Carolyn C. *Why Don't We Do Something Different? Mathematical Activities for the Elementary Grades*. Boston: Prindle, Weber and Schmidt, Inc., 1973, 188 pp.

Polon, Linda, and Pollitt, Wendy. *Creative Teaching Games*. Minneapolis: T. S. Denison & Company, Publishers, 1976, 71 pp.

Providing for the More Able   Meeting the individual needs of special children in teaching mathematics has many dimensions. Just as efforts to meet the special needs of low achievers through segregated instruction have been reevaluated, so have teaching techniques designed for high achievers. A decade or two ago, it was relatively common practice to isolate the more able children for specific periods of instruction, especially in mathematics. Testimony to the change in that practice may be found by perusing copies of *The Arithmetic Teacher* for the years 1975 through 1977. Not a single article has appeared during those years that is devoted exclusively to the gifted in mathematics. Thus, in current practice, the responsibility for providing for the more able rests primarily with the regular classroom teacher.

Characteristics of More Able Children in Mathematics The more able child in mathematics is usually not difficult for the classroom teacher to identify. This is especially true when the child is also highly motivated. In general, he is enthusiastic and verbal. His work is generally done on time or ahead of time, and often he requests additional work. Although they are as diverse in character as low achievers, the children who are high achievers in elementary school mathematics share with is perhaps the most crucial aspect of the teaching—learning process—the experience of success. As a consequence, they are self-motivated and welcome additional challenge. They maintain a consistent interest in mathematics and are intrigued by logic. Very often they will present the teacher with a "brain teaser," an example involving mathematical awareness that they have experienced outside school. Their perceptiveness includes other personal injections of mathematical ideas and models they have observed in the environment. Finally, they generally do not need the same amount and kind of concrete representation of concepts during instruction, and they often exhibit an implicit understanding of the functional value of mathematics in daily life activities. In short, they embrace the exploration of mathematical ideas.

Meeting Needs in the Regular Classroom Experience and good judgment suggest that the needs of able learners can be met with efficacy within the regular classroom. When the basic organization for instruction is the self-contained classroom, the strategy is often referred to as horizontal enrichment. It embodies the idea of special preparation and execution of those activities (during the regular mathematics period) which will extend the high achievers' breadth and depth of understanding, constantly enrich mathematical background, stimulate natural curiosity, and maintain a high level of motivation.

Easy accessibility to functional materials for high achievers can be a problem for teachers. The best idea is to collect and design a series of activities from existing available resources. As was the case with low achievers, translating ideas to the acitivity card format is expeditious. In this instance, the activity cards may be designed to take advantage of the able child's independence—that is, utilization of the cards requires considerably less teacher direction. At the same time, it is well to sound a note of caution. Activity cards designed in this context must be truly enriching and not merely an extension of previous paper-and-pencil practice to keep active children busy.

Within the resources previously listed in this chapter are many ideas that can be used to challenge the most able child. The same thing may be said regarding the content, material, and activities presented in Chapter 11. In addition, monthly suggestions from sections of *The Arithmetic Teacher* entitled "Ideas, Let's Do It" and "From the File" are particularly appropriate. The half-dozen resources cited below are by no means exhaustive but merely illustrative of the many sources available to alert and caring teachers. Obtaining access or purchasing selected personal copies can be especially helpful and rewarding in meeting the needs of able learners.

Berloquin, Pierre. *100 Geometric Games*. New York: Charles Scribner's Sons, 1976, 47 pp.

Buckeye, Donald. *Experiments in Probability and Statistics*. Troy, Mich.: Midwest Publication Company, Inc., 1970, 28 pp.

Dumas, E., and Schminke, C. W. *Math Activities for Child Involvement,* 2d ed. Boston: Allyn and Bacon, Inc., 1977, Chapter 8, "Problem Solving," pp. 285–335.

Fostering Creativity Through Mathematics. Tampa, Fla: Florida Council of Teachers of Mathematics, 1974, University of South Florida, Tampa, Florida, 33620.

Holt, Michael. *Maps, Tracks and the Bridges of Konigsberg: A Book About Networks.* New York: Thomas Y. Crowell Company, 1976, 33 pp.

Smith, S. E., and Backman, C. A., eds. *Games and Puzzles for Elementary and Middle School Mathematics: Readings from the Arithmetic Teacher 1956–1974.* Reston, Va.: National Council of Teachers of Mathematics, 1975, 280 pp.

SUMMARY   The growing practice of keeping children together for most of the day in the regular classroom has enlarged responsibilities for regular classroom teachers. The range of differences which must be met are as broad as they can possibly be. Careful analysis of affective and cognitive needs is crucial. Subsequent individualization of instruction, regardless of the techniques employed for assessment, must involve the child actively in his or her learning or relearning. Further, the affective and cognitive interests of all children must be nurtured in an unthreatened, enlightened, and secure learning environment. It is well to remember that children are keenly aware of what teachers do, as well as what they say. Deliberate attempts to make mathematics instruction a happy event will not go unnoticed by children. For children, success is the dominant feature of a happy event. Further, both experience and research consistently reveal that children acquire attitudes through imitative and adaptive behavior. Consequently, your own attitude toward mathematics and your feelings of success regarding teaching children mathematics will be significant factors in the attitudes that children will ultimately hold.

ACTIVITIES,   **1.** Obtain a printed copy of the goals for special education in your state. Is
PROJECTS, A   "mainstreaming" mentioned? Is "least restrictive environment" men-
POINT OF VIEW   tioned? What is the latest official position taken in your state? Speak with a practicing teacher. Determine firsthand, if possible, the effect "mainstreaming" has had on the regular classroom. Give a brief report to the class.

2. Design an original instrument that will assess a pupil's attitude toward mathematics. Use as a guide one of the models in Chapter 12. Try it on a classmate. What did you find out about your classmate's attitude? Revise as appropriate, and try it with several children. The class should report as time permits.

3. Use the *Mental Measurements Yearbook* from your reference library. Assume you wish to find a "good" norm-referenced test to give a regular class. Choose one and write a brief report citing its strengths. Include a rationale for choosing that particular test.

4. If possible, obtain a specimen set of a criterion-referenced test from a file in a curriculum materials center. Review the literature provided by the publisher concerning the examination. Check those assertions against the analysis provided by the *Mental Measurements Yearbook*. Are there discrepancies?

5. Obtain a set of papers from a small group of children who have completed some computation exercises in any basic operation. Analyze them for error patterns. What did you find out? Was this activity instructive for you?

6. Set up the addition of 85, 35, 61, 72, and 94 in vertical column form. Complete the addition using the low-stress format. Make up a subtraction or mulitplication example. Complete it utilizing the low-stress process. What advantages do you find? Are there any disadvantages?

7. Take the name of a year—for example, 1827. See how many of the counting numbers you can write using only the four digits 1, 8, 2, 7 in combination with the four basic operations. All four digits must be utilized, and they may be utilized only so often as they appear in the original number. Study the example. Now write:

$$1 = (7 + 2) - (8 \times 1)$$
$$2 = (8 + 2) - (7 + 1)$$
$$3 = (8 + 7) - 12$$
$$4 = (8 + 2) - (7 - 1)$$
$$5 = \frac{8 + 7}{1 + 2}$$

Compute the remaining numbers 6–10 in the same fashion. Write a statement on why this would or would not be a good enrichment activity for a high-achieving elementary school child.

8. The game of Tri appeared in *The Arithmetic Teacher*, Vol. 24 (April 1977), p. 318. Use that as a resource and design a single or a series of enrichment activity cards around it. Try it on a small group of able children. How did it work?

9. What is the basis of your agreement or disagreement with each of the following statements?

a. There are no justifiable educational reasons for placing special children in the regular classroom.

b. Most children who hate mathematics and do poorly in it at school acquire those characteristics outside school.

c. Recreational games and activities as part of the regular mathematics program in a classroom serve less well as a teaching strategy for low achievers than for high achievers.

SELECTED READINGS

Ashlock, Robert B. *Error Patterns in Computation,* 2d ed. Columbus, O.: Charles E. Merrill Publishing Co., 1976.

Bloom, Benjamin S. "Affective Outcomes of School Learning." *Phi Delta Kappan,* November 1977, pp. 193–198.

Cox, L. S. "Diagnosing and Remediating Systematic Errors in Addition and Subtraction Computation." *Arithmetic Teacher,* Vol. 22 (February 1975), pp. 151–157.

Hutchings, Barton. "Low-Stress Subtraction." *Arithmetic Teacher,* Vol. 22 (March 1975), pp. 226–232.

Jordan, June B., ed. *Teacher, Please Don't Close the Door—The Exceptional Child in the Mainstream.* Reston, Va.: Council for Exceptional Children, 1976.

Lankford, Francis K., Jr. "What Can a Teacher Learn About a Pupil's Thinking Through Oral Interviews?" *Arithmetic Teacher,* Vol. 21 (January 1974), pp. 26–32.

Pincus, Morris, et al. "If You Don't Know How Children Think, How Can You Help Them?" *Arithmetic Teacher,* Vol. 22 (November 1975), pp. 550–585.

Reisman, Fredricka K. *Diagnostic Teaching of Elementary School Mathematics.* Chicago: Rand McNally College Publishing Company, 1977, pp. 49–63.

Reidesel, C. A., and Burns, P. C. *Handbook for Exploratory and Systematic Teaching of Elementary School Mathematics.* New York: Harper & Row, Publishers, 1977, pp. 25–34.

Underhill, R. G. *Teaching Elementary School Mathematics,* 2d ed. Columbus, O.: Charles E. Merrill Publishing Company, 1977, pp. 27–50.

Appendix
Materials Sources

Recommendations throughout this book have focused on active learning. This requires extensive use of concrete material. Much of what is needed may be collected or made by the teacher and the students. Consequently, the costs for materials may be kept modest. Frequently, however, it is useful to refer to a publisher's or supplier's catalog, for some obvious reasons. First, they often suggest additional ideas of instructional aids that can be fashioned by teacher and children. Second, the catalogs are generally free of charge. Third, they provide a ready location of crucial supplies that may be too cumbersome or complex to construct. Finally, commercial firms are aggressive and their promotion publications provide constant, current information regarding the never-static market of mathematics teaching and learning aids.

In general, commercially prepared material may be thought of as "software" and "hardware." Software would include textbooks, enrichment books, curriculum guides, task cards, and so forth. Hardware includes such things as multibase blocks, color rods, bead counters, and the hand-held calculator. In fact, it seems that any list of supplies and suppliers of commercially prepared mathematics materials might approach infinity.

The sources that follow are not exhaustive, but they are representative of contemporary sources, publishers, and materials. Initially, this appendix provides a specific list of thirty instructional aids. The list is keyed by number to nineteen sources. Second, the nineteen selected sources (keyed to the previous list of materials) is accompanied by additional examples of the wide range of material available through each one. A modest supplemental list of sources constitutes the final portion of the appendix.

A CROSS
REFERENCE

Instructional Aid	Supplier Number*
1. Abacus	3, 11, 16
2. Activity cards	3, 5, 8, 10, 14, 15
3. Attribute blocks	3, 8, 12, 16, 18
4. Centimeter rods	7, 10, 11
5. Counting discs, beads, etc.	8, 9, 11, 12
6. Cuisenaire rods	5
7. Dice	3, 12
8. Dominoes	10, 12, 15
9. Dienes blocks	3, 12
10. Enrichment books	1, 3, 5, 9, 14, 16, 19
11. Games	1, 3, 4, 5, 19
12. Geoboards	3, 4, 5, 14, 15, 17
13. Geometric solids	3, 5, 6, 8, 15, 19
14. Geostrips	8, 15
15. Hand-held calculator	8, 15
16. Mathematical balance	2, 3, 4, 12, 15, 16
17. Measurement tools	2, 3, 8, 12
18. Metric materials	3, 7, 11, 19
19. Mirror cards	12, 18
20. Napier's bones	19
21. Number line	3, 11, 12
22. Number spinners	3, 10
23. Place-value pocket	9
24. Poleidoblocks	15
25. Prenumber, number materials	2, 3, 5, 8, 10, 11
26. Soma cubes	3, 5, 6
27. Stern materials	10
28. Tangrams	1, 3, 4, 8, 14, 16, 18
29. Tens frame	9, 11
30. Trundle wheel	8, 12

SOURCES:
MATERIALS
AND SUPPLIES

Sources	Supplies
1. Activity Resources Company 24827 Calaroga Avenue Hayward, California 94545	Games, enrichment books, multi-base blocks, tangrams.
2. Childcraft Education Corporation 964 Third Avenue New York, New York 10022	Prenumber, number materials; mathematical balance; measurement tools.

*Numbers refer to list of 19 sources below.

3. Creative Publications
   P. O. Box 10328
   Palo Alto, California 94303

   Tangrams, enrichment books, Dienes blocks, Unifix materials, attribute games, mathematical balance, measurement tools, geoboards, activity cards, metric materials, games, geometric solids, abacus, dice, beads, discs, number spinners.

4. Creative Teaching Associates
   P. O. Box 293
   Fresno, California 93708

   Games, tangrams, geoboards, mathematical balance.

5. Cuisenaire Company of America
   12 Church Street
   New Rochelle, New York 10805

   Cuisenaire rods, geoboards, geometric solids, activity cards, games, Soma cubes, enrichment books.

6. Edmund Scientific Company
   EDSCORP Building
   Barrington, New Jersey 08007

   Geometric solids, Soma cubes, probability kit, graph set.

7. Enrich, Inc.
   760 Kifer Road
   Sunnyvale, California 94086

   Metric materials.

8. General Learning Corporation
   3 East 54th Street
   New York, New York 10022

   Attribute blocks, counting chips, prenumber materials, activity cards, geocards, balance cards, trundle wheel, metric materials, tangrams.

9. Holt, Rinehart and Winston
   Box 2334 Grand Central Station
   New York, New York 10017

   Counting discs, number frame, place-value pockets.

10. Houghton Mifflin Company
    53 W. 43rd Street
    New York, New York 10036

    Stern materials, centimeter rods, activity cards, number spinners.

11. Ideal School Supply Company
    11000 South Lavergne Avenue
    Oak Lawn, Illinois 60453

    Place-value board, tens frame, flash cards, abacus, beads, felt board, cross-number puzzles, number line.

12. Moyer-Vico Ltd.
    1935 First Avenue, North
    Saskatoon, Saskatchewan
    Canada

    Flannelboards, dominoes, dice, mirror cards, games, integer cards, fraction set, cross-number puzzles, pattern boards, wipe-off

number line, counting discs, scales, weights, trundle wheel, Dienes blocks.
Hand-held calculator.

13. National Semiconductor Consumer Products Division, Novus
1177 Kern Avenue
Sunnyvale, California 94086

14. Scott Resources, Inc.
P. O. Box 2121
Fort Collins, Colorado 80521

Tangrams, geoboards, enrichment books, activity cards.

15. Selective Educational Equipment, Inc. (SEE)
3 Bridge Street
Newton, Massachusetts 02195

Poleidoblocks, geometric solids, mathematical balance, activity cards, geoboards.

16. Silver Burdett
Box 362
Morristown, New Jersey 07960

Enrichment books, attribute blocks, tangrams, abacus, mathematical balance.

17. Walker Educational Book Corp.
720 Fifth Avenue
New York, New York 10019

Geoboards.

18. Webster/McGraw-Hill
Manchester Road
Manchester, Missouri 63011

Elementary Science Study Units (attribute games and problems, mirror cards, geoblocks, tangrams).

19. Western Educational Activities Ltd.
10577 97th Street
Edmonton 17, Ontario
Canada

Wiff'n'Proof games, Napier's bones, digital computer, geometric models, math lab experiments, enrichment books.

ADDITIONAL SOURCES

Allyn and Bacon, Inc.
470 Atlantic Avenue
Boston, Massachusetts 02210

American Book Co.
450 W. 33rd St.
New York, NY 10019

Beckley-Cardy Company
1900 North Harragansett Avenue
Chicago, Illinois 60639

D. C. Heath and Company
125 Spring Street
Lexington, Massachusetts 02173

Fearon Publishers
2165 Park Boulevard
Palo Alto, California 94306

Gel-Sten Supply Company, Inc.
911–913 South Hill Street
Los Angeles, California 90015

Gerard Publishing Company
123 West Park Avenue
Champaign, Illinois 61820

The Judy Company
310 North 2nd Street
Minneapolis, Minnesota 55401

Kenworthy Educational Service
45 North Division Street
Buffalo, New York 14205

Mainco School Supply Company
Canton, Massachusetts 02021

Charles E. Merrill Publishing Co.
1300 Alum Creek Drive
Columbus, Ohio 43216

Midwest Publications Co., Inc.
P. O. Box 307
Birmingham, Michigan 48012

Miles Kimball Company
41 West 8th Avenue
Oshkosh, Wisconsin 54901

Milton Bradley Company
Springfield, Massachusetts 01101

Minneapolis Mining and Manufacturing Co. (3M)
2501 Hudson Road
St. Paul, Minnesota 55119

Motivational Research, Inc.
4216 Howard Avenue
Kensington, Maryland

National Council of Teachers of Mathematics (NCTM)
1201 Sixteenth Street N.W.
Washington, D.C. 20036

Playskool Manufacturing Company
3720 North Kedzie Avenue
Chicago, Illinois 60618

Products of the Behavioral Sciences
1140 Dell Avenue
Campbell, California 95008

Responsive Environmental Corp. (REC)
Learning Materials Division
Englewood Cliffs, New Jersey 07632

G. W. School Supply
5626 East Belmont Avenue
P. O. Box 14
Fresno, California 93708

Schoolhouse Visuals, Inc.
816 Thayer Avenue
Silver Springs, Maryland 20910

Science Research Associates, Inc.
259 East Erie Street
Chicago, Illinois 60611

Scott, Foresman and Company
Glenview, Illinois 60025

Stanley Bowman Company, Inc.
4 Broadway
Valhalla, New York 10595

Teachers' Exchange of San Francisco
600 35th Avenue
San Francisco, California 94121

Glossary

Abscissa The directed measure of a line segment parallel to the horizontal axis with one end point common to the vertical axis; the horizontal coordinate of a point in a plane rectangular coordinate system.

Acute angle An angle whose measure is greater than 0° but less than 90°.

Addend A number from a set of numbers on which the addition operation is to be performed.

Addition An operation with a pair or more of numbers called addends which results in a third number called the sum.

Affective domain The psychological factors which determine emotional behavior.

Algorithm A rule or procedure for finding a solution to some particular problem or exercise.

Angle The union of two rays with a common end point.

Area The measure of the region inside a closed plane figure.

Array An arrangement of elements into rows and columns, where each row has the same number of elements and each column has the same number of elements.

Associative property of addition When more than two numbers are added, the order of adding the numbers does not affect the sum. For example, in finding the sum for $3 + 5 + 6$ either the 3 and 5, the 5 and the 6 or the 3 and the 6 may be added first. In general $(a + b) + c = a + (b + c)$.

Associative property for multiplication When the product for more than 2 factors is found the product is not affected by the order of multiplying. For example, in finding the product $3 \times 4 \times 5$, the first multiplication may be either 3×4, 4×5, or 3×5. In general $(a \times b) \times c = a \times (b \times c)$.

Base 1. A side or face of a geometric configuration; 2. the reference number in the construction of a numeration system.

Binary operation An operation defined on a set which assigns each pair of elements in the set to a unique element in the set.

Cardinal number A number which designates how many elements there are in a set.

Cartesian product For two sets, A and B, the cartesian product ($A \times B$),

359

read A cross B is the set of all ordered pairs (a, b) such that a is an element of A and b is an element of B.

Circle The set of points in a plane which are equidistant from a point in the plane called the center of the circle.

Circumference The perimeter of a circle; the distance around a circle.

Closure property A set S is closed with respect to the operation defined on S if the domain of the operation is the Cartesian product $S \times S$ and the range of the operation is a subset of S, that is, the set S is closed with respect to the operation, when x is an element of S and y is an element of S, and $x * y$ is also an element of S.

Cognitive domain The psychological factors which determine intellectual behavior.

Collinear points The set of all points which lie on the same line.

Common denominator A quantity which is divisible by all the denominators in question; fractions which are expressed with the same denominator are said to have a common denominator.

Common Multiple k is a common multiple of m and n if $k = a(m)$ and $k = b(n)$ for some counting number(s) a and b. Example: 24 is a common multiple of 3 and 4 because $24 = 8(3)$ and $24 = 6(4)$.

Commutative property A binary operation defined on a set S is commutative if the results of the operation are not affected by the order in which the members are taken, that is, the operation defined on the set S is commutative if and only if $a * b = b * a$ for all a and b in S.

Complex fraction A fraction which has a fraction for its denominator or numerator or both.

Composite numbers The set of natural numbers greater than one which are not prime; the natural numbers which have more than two factors.

Congruent angles Angles which have the same measure.

Congruent figures Figures which have the same shape and size.

Counting numbers The set of numbers $\{1, 2, 3, 4, 5, \ldots\}$; the positive integers.

Criterion-referenced test A test in which an individual's performance is interpreted relative to arbitrary standards.

Curve The set of points (which may not be on a straight line) connecting and including two given points.

Decimal fraction A fraction whose denominator is a power of 10. This power is indicated by the number of digits to the right of the decimal point.

Decimal point A point in a numeral which is between the ones place and the tens place.

Denominator The part of a fraction below the dividing line; the quantity that divides the numerator (b is the denominator of a/b).

Note: * is a symbol for "operation."

Diameter of a circle A line segment which has both end points on the circle and a point in common with the center of the circle.

Difference The results obtained when one quantity is subtracted from another quantity; the remainder (c is the difference in $a - b = c$).

Digit Denotes any of the integers 0, 1, 2, 3, 4, 5, 6, 7, 8, and 9.

Disjoint sets Two sets are disjoint if they do not contain an element in common.

Distributive property An operation * is distributive with respect to an operation o, if by performing the operation * on a set of elements where the operation o has been defined gives the same results as performing the operation * on the set and then performing the operation o, that is, $a * (b \ o \ c) = (a * b) \ o \ (a * c)$.

Dividend The quantity which is to be divided by some other quantity (a is the dividend in $a \div b = c$).

Divisor The quantity which is to be divided into some other quantity (b is the divisor in $a \div b = c$).

Edge The intersection of two faces of the same solid.

Element of a set A member of a set; an object of quantity belonging to a set.

Empty set A set which has no elements; the null set.

Equal sets Sets A and B are equal if and only if each element of A is also an element of B, and each element of B is also an element of A; containing exactly the same elements.

Equation A statement which designates the equality of two expressions.

Equivalence of sets Sets A and B are said to be equivalent if there exists a one-to-one correspondence between the elements of A and the elements of B.

Equivalent fractions Fractions which represent the same number.

Expanded notation A numeral is expressed as the sum of the place value components: $267 = 200 + 60 + 7$ or $267 = 2 \times 100 + 6 \times 10 + 7 \times 1$.

Exponent A number which is usually placed to the right and above a quantity called the base. If the exponent is a positive integer it indicates how many times the given quantity is taken as a factor. When the exponent is 0 and the base is not 0 the value of the expression is defined to be equal to 1. When the exponent is a negative integer it indicates that the quantity is to be reciprocated either before or after the exponential operations are performed.

Exterior of a figure The set of points which lie outside the boundary of the figure.

Face One of the plane surfaces of a polyhedron.

Factor Any quantity which is to be multiplied to obtain a product (a and b are both factors in $a \cdot b = c$).

Finite set A set is finite if a one-to-one correspondence between it and any of its proper subsets does not exist; not infinite.

Formula A formula is a general rule which is expressed in symbols; a principle expressed in mathematical terms.

Fraction. The indicated quotient of two quantities.

Function A function from a set A to a set B is a rule which assigns to each element of A a unique element in B; a mapping.

Graph A drawing or representation which pictures a relationship between sets of numbers.

Greatest common divisor The largest quantity which will divide all the quantities being considered.

Hexagon A polygon which has six sides.

Hindu-Arabic numeration system The numeration system which we commonly use. The numerals 0, 1, 2, 3, 4, 5, 6, 7, 8, and 9 are from the Hindu-Arabic numeration system.

Identity element e is an identity element relative to the operation on the set S if and only if $a * e = e * a = a$ for all a in S.

Individualized instruction A system of instruction which attempts to meet the unique needs of individuals including rate of learning, social needs, emotional needs, and cognitive needs.

Infinite set A set is infinite if there exists a one-to-one correspondence between it and a proper subset of itself.

Integers The set of counting numbers together with their additive inverses.

Interior of a figure The set of points which lie within the boundary of the figure.

Intersection of sets The set of elements which are common to all the sets being considered.

Inverse element a' is the inverse element of a in the set S with respect to the operation defined on S if and only if $a' * a = a * a' = e$, where e is the identity element for the operation $*$ in S.

Inverse operation An operation that does the opposite of another operation, for example, addition is the inverse operation of subtraction and vice-versa.

Least common denominator (L.C.D.) The least common multiple of the denominators under consideration.

Line The set of points which extends infinitely in two opposite directions.

Line segment The set of points on a straight line between and including two given points which are called the end points.

Mainstreaming A process whereby all children are placed in the least restrictive environment for purpose of acquiring full benefits from formal education.

Mapping If for each element a in the set A there exists a unique element b in the set B, then there is a mapping of the set A in the set B, and b is the image of a; a function.

Matrix A rectangular array of elements.

Minuend The quantity from which some other quantity is to be subtracted (a is the minuend in $a - b = c$).

Mixed number A number which is the sum of an integer and a fraction.

Modular arithmetic An arithmetic which is defined on a finite set of numbers.

Multiple of a number A product of a given number with some other whole number.

Multiplicand The quantity which is to be multiplied by another quantity.

Multiplier A quantity which is to multiply another quantity.

Natural numbers The counting numbers; the set of numbers {1, 2, 3, 4, 5, 6, . . . }.

Negative numbers The set of real numbers which are less than 0.

Nondecimal numeration system A numeration system which uses a base other than ten.

Norm-referenced test A test in which an individual's performance is interpreted in relation to the performance of others on the same test.

Number sentence A statement expressing some fact about some numbers, usually expressed symbolically.

Numeral A symbol used to represent a number.

Numeration The process of expressing numbers in order of their magnitude.

Numeration system A system for counting and naming numbers.

Numerator The part of a fraction which is above the dividing line of a fraction; the quantity which is divided by the denominator (a is the numerator of a/b).

Obtuse angle An angle whose measure is greater than 90° but less than 180°.

One-to-one correspondence There is a one-to-one correspondence between sets A and B if there exists a pairing of the elements of A with the elements of B such that each element of A is paired with one and only one element of B, and each element of B is paired with one and only one element of A.

Operation An operation is the process of executing an algorithm; or rules of procedure like addition, subtraction, multiplication, division, finding square roots, integration, and so on.

Ordered pair Two elements with the property that the elements can be distinguished as a first element and a second element.

Ordinal number A number which designates an ordered relation among the elements of a set.

Ordinate The directed measure of a line segment parallel to the vertical axis with one end point common to the horizontal axis; the vertical coordinate of a point in a plane rectangular coordinate system.

Parallel lines Lines in a plane which do not intersect.

Parallelogram A quadrilateral whose opposite sides are parallel.

Partial product Part of the product. In the product 24×7, 28 is part of the product, 168, and 140 is part of the product, 168. Hence, 28 and 140 are called partial products.

Partial sum Part of the sum. In the sum 36 + 27, 13 is part of the sum, 63, and 50 is part of the sum, 63. Hence, 13 and 50 are called partial sums.

Pentagon A polygon which has five sides.

Percent Hundredths; per hundred; the number obtained when some non-negative number is divided by 100 (percent is denoted by the symbol %).

Perimeter The length of the boundary of a closed plane figure.

Place value Place value is the value assigned to a digit with respect to the place it occupies relative to the units place (in 524.3, 5 represents 500 units, 2 represents 20 units, 4 represents 4 units, and 3 represents 3/10 units).

Plane A surface such that a straight line having two points in common with the surface will lie completely in the surface.

Polygon A closed plane figure with line segments as sides.

Polyhedron A solid banded by plane polygons.

Positive numbers The set of real numbers which are greater than 0.

Prime number Any number greater than 1 which is only divisible by itself and 1.

Prism A polyhedron with two faces that are congruent and parallel and whose other faces are parallelograms.

Probability The chance or likelihood of an event occurring.

Product The quantity obtained when two or more quantities are multiplied (c is the product in $a \cdot b = c$).

Proof A logical argument which shows the validity of a statement.

Proportion A statement of equality between two ratios.

Pyramid A polyhedron with a polygon as one of its faces (the base) and triangles with a common vertex as the other faces.

Quadrilateral A polygon which has four sides.

Quotient The quantity obtained when one quantity is divided by another quantity (c is the quotient in $a \div b = c$).

Radius of a circle The length of the line segment from the center to the circumference of the circle.

Ratio The relationship between two quantities; the implied quotient of two numbers (a/b where b does not equal 0).

Rational number Any number which can be expressed as the quotient of two integers where the divisor does not equal 0.

Ray The set of points including a point referred to as the origin and all points of a straight line extending in one direction from the origin.

Reciprocal of a number The number whose product with the given number is the multiplicative identity.

Rectangle A polygon with four sides and four angles where each angle is a right angle and the sides opposite each other are parallel and equal in length.

Relatively prime numbers Numbers which only have 1 as a common factor; numbers which have a greatest common divisor equal to 1.

Rhombus A parallelogram which has equal adjacent sides and equal opposite angles.

Right angle An angle whose measure is 90°.

Set A term used in mathematics to apply to any assemblage of things where identification of membership or nonmembership is clear cut. A special qualification of the assemblage or collection idea should be noted, namely, that a set may have only 1 or 0 members, and therefore is not an assemblage of things in the usual sense of that term.

Space The set which contains all points.

Sphere The set of points in space which are equidistant from a point called the center.

Square 1. The result attained when a quantity is multiplied by itself; 2. a quadrilateral with all sides equal and each angle a right angle.

Square numbers The set of numbers $\{1, 4, 9, 16, 25, 36, \ldots\}$.

Straight angle An angle whose measure is 180°.

Subset Set A is a subset of set B if and only if every element in A is also in B.

Subset (proper) Set A is a proper subset of set B if A is a subset of B and B is not a subset of A.

Subtrahend The quantity to be subtracted from some other quantity (b is the subtrahend in $a - b = c$).

Sum The results obtained when two or more quantities are combined.

Trapezoid A quadrilateral with two parallel noncongruent sides, called the bases.

Triangle A polygon which has three sides.

Triangular numbers The set of numbers $\{1, 3, 6, 10, 15, 21, \ldots\}$.

Union of sets The union of set A and set B is the set which has all the elements of both A and B and no other elements, denoted by $A \cup B$.

Unique One and only one.

Variable A symbol used to represent a numeral.

Vertex The common point of two rays which determines an angle.

Volume The measure of the region within a closed space figure.

Whole numbers The set of non-negative integers; the set of natural numbers together with 0; the set $\{0, 1, 2, 3, 4, 5, 6, 7, \ldots\}$.

Index